REFRAMED

A Self-Reg Revolution, Revised Edition

Stuart Shanker's *Reframed* presents a comprehensive exploration of self-regulation, grounded in cutting-edge neuroscience, to help individuals thrive and society flourish. Aimed at parents, educators, and all adults invested in individual well-being, this revised and expanded edition is presented in a reader-friendly format, with engaging vignettes that appeal to a wider audience.

Employing the same proven techniques from his earlier volumes, *Calm, Alert, and Learning* and *Self-Reg*, Shanker delves into the science and principles behind the Shanker Self-Reg method, emphasizing that understanding our own brains is the key to understanding one another and rethinking black-and-white labels such as "bad," "lazy," and "stupid." He argues that everyone has the capacity to self-regulate in ways that foster growth and that life trajectories can shift at any point with the right tools. For Shanker, the foundation of a just and free society begins with how we understand and nurture ourselves as well as our children.

In an era marked by social challenges, *Reframed* not only illuminates the complexities of the modern world but also inspires hope for a better future. This essential work equips readers with the knowledge and tools to help build a more compassionate society, one mind at a time.

STUART SHANKER is a distinguished research professor emeritus of psychology and philosophy at York University.

Other Books by Stuart Shanker

Self-Reg Schools: A Handbook for Educators, co-authored by Susan Hopkins (2019)

Self-Reg: How to Help Your Child (and You) Break the Stress Cycle and Successfully Engage with Life, with Teresa Barker (2016)

Calm, Alert, and Learning: Classroom Strategies for Self-Regulation (2012)

Human Development in the Twenty-First Century: Visionary Ideas from Systems Scientists, co-edited by Alan Fogel and Barbara J. King (2008)

The First Idea: How Symbols, Language, and Intelligence Evolved from Our Primate Ancestors to Modern Humans, co-authored by Stanley I. Greenspan (2004)

Apes, Language, and the Human Mind, co-authored by Sue Savage-Rumbaugh and Talbot J. Taylor (1998)

Wittgenstein's Remarks on the Foundations of AI (1998)

Reframed

A Self-Reg Revolution, Revised Edition

STUART SHANKER

UNIVERSITY OF TORONTO PRESS

Toronto Buffalo London

ISBN 978-1-4875-6093-5 (paper)   ISBN 978-1-4875-6095-9 (EPUB)
                                  ISBN 978-1-4875-6094-2 (PDF)

Library and Archives Canada Cataloguing in Publication

Title: Reframed : a self-reg revolution / Stuart Shanker.
Names: Shanker, Stuart, author
Description: Revised edition. | Includes bibliographical references and index.
Identifiers: Canadiana (print) 20250124319 | Canadiana (ebook)
  20250124327 | ISBN 9781487560935 (paper) | ISBN 9781487560959 (EPUB) |
  ISBN 9781487560942 (PDF)
Subjects: LCSH: Self-control. | LCSH: Self-control – Social aspects. |
  LCSH: Stress management. | LCSH: Child psychology. |
  LCSH: Self-management (Psychology) | LCSH: Stress (Psychology) |
  LCSH: Stress (Physiology) | LCGFT: Self-help publications.
Classification: LCC BF632 .S49 2025 | DDC 158.1–dc23

Cover design: Sebastian Frye
Cover image: Sebastian Frye

We wish to acknowledge the land on which the University of Toronto
Press operates. This land is the traditional territory of the Wendat, the
Anishnaabeg, the Haudenosaunee, the Métis, and the Mississaugas of the
Credit First Nation.

University of Toronto Press acknowledges the financial support of the
Government of Canada, the Canada Council for the Arts, and the Ontario
Arts Council, an agency of the Government of Ontario, for its publishing
activities.

Canada Council   Conseil des Arts   ONTARIO ARTS COUNCIL
for the Arts   du Canada   CONSEIL DES ARTS DE L'ONTARIO
                                            an Ontario government agency
                                            un organisme du gouvernement de l'Ontario

Funded by the   Financé par le
Government   gouvernement
of Canada   du Canada

MIX
Paper | Supporting
responsible forestry
FSC® C016245

To Ginny, my besherta

Contents

Acknowledgments

Shortly after I came to York University, I was invited to give a public lecture to the university professoriate. After the lecture a number of my new colleagues took me out to lunch, and all said very nice things about the lecture. But then one, a political philosopher, piped up that he had thoroughly enjoyed hearing all of Pierre Trudeau's old ideas once again.

I confess that I was taken aback but also curious why he should have levelled such a charge. When I got home, I dug out my copy of *Towards a Just Society*.[1]

Sure enough, the book was heavily highlighted, and I was shocked to see how many of the things I had said in my lecture were taken almost verbatim from Trudeau's writings. I hadn't just been reading; I had been absorbing Trudeau's thinking, incorporating it into my own to the point where I couldn't have distinguished between who had said what. And I realized that it does not matter, but it makes writing an Acknowledgments section fiendishly difficult.

We are living in a period that constitutes a new Renaissance. The profusion of articles and books flowering every week is mind-boggling. But what makes it even more overwhelming is the quality of the research involved. As I write this, I am looking at my library shelves, and I hesitate to open up any of the books to see how much highlighting is in each. In truth, I know what I will find and know also that I cannot even begin to acknowledge all the wonderful ideas that I have absorbed.

So, this must be only a partial list of acknowledgments. To all those who have contributed to this paradigm revolution but are not cited, I offer both my gratitude and my regrets. There are a number of individuals, however, who cannot be overlooked.

It is almost pointless to mention Stanley Greenspan's impact on Self-Reg; it is obvious on every single page. Nor can I do justice to the influence that Paul MacLean, Jaak Panksepp, Stephen Porges, Allan Schore, and Robert Thayer have had on me.

Over the years a number of people have been especially influential on my thinking: Teresa Barker, Beatrice Beebe, Jerome Bruner, Jeremy Burman, Jeff Coulter, Roger Downer, Alan Fogel, Norah Fryer, Ross Greene, Peter Hacker, Louise Lamont, Marc Lewis, Andrew Meltzoff, Fraser Mustard, Darcia Narvaez, Sue Savage-Rumbaugh, Brenda Smith-Chant, Digby Tantam, Talbot Taylor, Michael Thompson, Ed Tronick, and, of course, Pierre Elliott Trudeau.

It is those who have not just helped but, in truth, pushed me to do this work that I especially want to acknowledge. But here too must go unmentioned a large number of people: all those teachers, professors, students, and colleagues who are the backbone of this book and, I suspect, of every book.

There are simply too many people involved with The MEHRIT Centre for me to mention them all by name, but I do need to single out Jamie Barker, Frederica Black, Maria Botero, Stephanie Cudmore, Dylan Doyle, Aviva Dunsiger, Travis Francis, John Hoffman, Paula Jurczak, Cathy Lethbridge, Ashley Marcoux, Tania Moher, Stephanie Pellett, Stephen Retallick, Liz Shepherd, and Taylor Wilson. For a full list of our presenters and other staff members, see https://self-reg.ca/about-us/.

Louise Beard has had a profound effect on my thinking. The school that she runs, Venture Academy, inspired the very last line of the last chapter: the motto that I hope will be placed over the doorway of every single school.

Barbara King has been with me from the start. We have long been working on the same issues from opposite ends of the spectrum. It is exciting for me to see how, after all these years, our work has met up in the middle.

Last – or perhaps first – there is Susan Hopkins. She has single-handedly created in The MEHRIT Centre the organization that Milt Harris and I dreamed about. She has created the army of Self-Reggers for whom I have written this book and to whom I am indebted for so much of the content. She has taught me far more than she has ever learned from me.

I would never have been able to develop Self-Reg had it not been for the support that I received from Milt and Ethel Harris; David, John, Judith, and Naomi Harris; Kenneth Rotenberg and Doris Sommer-Rotenberg; and York University. My experience at MEHRI was life changing. To this day my thinking continues to evolve as a result of the work of the DIR community, the therapists at MEHRI, the families involved in the study, and, above all, Devin Casenhiser.

All I can say about Colleen Dickinson and Heather Wesley is that my wish for everyone involved in this kind of demanding intellectual work is that they have a Colleen or Heather by their side.

My editor at the University of Toronto Press, Meg Patterson, is the kind of editor that every author dreams of having.

I worship the memory of my parents, while my sister gets my never-ending gratitude and love; she has always been and will always be my doppelganger.

Finally, there are my wife and children. Everything I do is because of and for them.

Preface to the Second Edition

My new editor at University of Toronto Press, Jodi Litvin, made a simple (ʕ) request for this new edition: Could I make the book more accessible for readers who are new to Self-Reg, and even, readers who are not familiar with some of the ideas and even fields that are anything but familiar? I knew right away that she was right, and not just for publishing reasons. You write a book for the reader, not for yourself; or in this case, not for those who are already experienced Self-Reggers. What's more, Self-Reg has become an international phenomenon. I needed to think about those coming to Self-Reg with backgrounds and perspectives that are entirely different from what I'm familiar with. But readers who are deeply concerned with the problems that this book addresses.

I've tried to meet this challenge, and then some. So much of this new edition has changed. Pretty much every sentence. Plus, I've added around 25 per cent new material, which is the result of work I've done since the original *Reframed* was published. In truth, this new version could be titled *Reframed 2.0*.

On top of the need to make the book more reader-friendly – or at least, friendlier – there is what has been happening on the societal front. How could I ignore the ominous political threat posed by the gathering forces of authoritarianism? How could I ignore the ominous psychological threat posed by the gathering forces of anomie, the crippling state in which society's moral norms break down?

But my goal in this new edition is not descriptive. The subtitle of my 2016 book *Self-Reg* was "How to help you and your child successfully break the stress cycle and successfully engage with life." Perhaps the subtitle (or the sub-subtitle) of this new edition should be "How to break the societal stress cycle and help democracy survive."

The central thesis of *Reframed, Revised Edition* is easily stated (without the inverted question mark used to signify irony). If we are to break the perennial societal stress cycle, we need to understand the nature of *non-rational conviction*. In what follows I will unpack what this bold statement means so as to highlight *the Self-Reg path to restoring homeostatic balance*. Only then can we restore rationality, and thus, the psychological as well as political freedom that is the defining feature of a Just Society.

Introduction

Reframed: Self-Reg for a Just Society completes the trilogy that I started working on twenty years ago. I wrote the first book, *Calm, Alert, and Learning*, for educators.[1] The second, *Self-Reg*, was written for parents.[2] This one is for Self-Reggers: the science they have been asking for and the thinking behind the conceptual distinctions that are the very lifeblood of Self-Reg.

Siena Hopkins-Prest came up with the name "Self-Reggers" when she was eight years old and explaining Self-Reg to her class. At the time I thought that it was just a cute way of describing someone who had enrolled in one of the Foundations courses offered at The MEHRIT Centre (TMC).[3] But no one should never underestimate the musings of an eight-year-old, especially one whose middle name is Xaeli.

Xaeli is the name of the place where Susan and her husband had stopped to make an offering to the "rock of safe passage" on their way from Behchoko to Whati, a few hours northwest of Yellowknife.[4] The Tlicho elders in the community where Siena was born approved of the name, but they warned Susan that it meant that she must watch Siena for her gifts, because she had been gifted from the rock. Gifts could take many forms, so she had to listen very carefully, or she might miss them. Listen not just with her ears, but with her spirit and her heart. This piece of ancient wisdom applies to every child.

Listening to what a child is telling us isn't something we do solely in the moment. It can take time to absorb what we've heard.

Ultimately, I grasped that what Siena had intuited is that a Self-Regger is someone who is driven to create a Just Society, who can't abide seeing any child or youth suffer because of inherited biases that colour our thinking, and who believes that *helping children to realize their full potential* is a way of life and not a platitude. These are the traits that absolutely define me.

I first started thinking about this issue when I was sixteen years old. I had attended a political rally in which Pierre Elliott Trudeau talked about a Just Society: one in which "equality of opportunity is ensured, and individuals are permitted to fulfil themselves in the fashion they judge best."[5] Like everyone who had gathered at Nathan Phillips Square, I came away energized. I stayed up late that night writing a manifesto that I titled *"HOW Does a Society Become Just?"* It is a question that has consumed me ever since.

From the beginning, I was convinced that the answer lies in more than establishing liberal-democratic institutions and laws. Creating a Just Society isn't simply a matter of "permitting" individuals to fulfil themselves. Having a purpose in life has to be *psychologically* and not just politically possible. And it all starts with how a society sees and nurtures its children.

A few years later I had the opportunity to meet the prime minister privately before I left for Oxford. I poured out how much I had been moved by his speech and my qualms about how many kids we were failing. His response instantly became my lodestar: "The secret," he said, "lies in their education. So, make the most of the one you are about to receive. And then bring it back here." And that is just what I have tried to do.

The problem is, universal education demands so much more than *equality of opportunity*. Children need to be capable of seizing that opportunity. The one constant is that all children will respond positively to the challenge of education, provided they are in a neurobiological and emotional state that supports not just learning but also character development.

Wanting to live in a Just Society is perhaps the most profound – and demanding – of all the prosocial drives that we have inherited from our distant past. But the reality is that many children can only manage their stress in a way that actually blocks this prosocial drive. The demand for justice and equality ends up adding more stress to a stress load that is already crushing.

A second person was to say the same thing to me as the prime minister did, using almost the same words. This was no coincidence, as Milt Harris had been closely involved with the Liberal Party, and he too had "absorbed" a lot of Trudeau's thinking. Milt approached me with the idea of setting up a research centre at York University whose purpose would be to help turn the dream of a Just Society into a reality.

The one thing on which Milt was very clear was that he didn't want to see us doing research for the sake of research. He wanted a rigorous study that would spark a revolution in parenting and education across the country. Yet on more than one occasion (i.e., every time we met for lunch at Coppi's) he told me: For this to happen, you need to take the next step in your own thinking! The result of the wonderful team that we assembled at the Milton and Ethel Harris Research Initiative (MEHRI) was Self-Reg.

Self-Reg is a five-step method for managing stress:

1. **Reframe** behaviour by learning the difference between *misbehaviour* and *stress-behaviour* and the signs of each.
2. **Recognize** stressors, looking always at the totality of physical, emotional, cognitive, social, and prosocial stress and how they interact.
3. **Reduce** stress and the stress response, addressing all five of the stress domains and not just one that may stand out.
4. **Reflect** on what it feels like to be calm and what it feels like to be overstressed, and when the latter, reflect on what the stressors were that led to this state.
5. **Restore**, not just physiologically, but psychologically, socially, and spiritually.[6]

These five steps must not be seen as *a program for managing a child's behaviour*. Rather, these are five steps to promote *understanding a child's behaviour* so as to enable restoration. The former approach is intent on eliciting compliance; the latter is intent on learning how to listen.

Programs are like recipes. Implicit in every recipe is a story. The cookbook writer is telling us: *This is how I have learned to bake an angel food cake, and if you want yours to look like mine in the picture, you need to follow the steps exactly as I've written them. Don't substitute ingredients and don't be sloppy in how you measure.*

The behaviourist tells us the same thing: *This is the recipe you must follow if you want your child to be a little angel.* But raising a child isn't like baking a cake. There is no recipe. And it's not just because every child is different, or because the individual they will grow up to be is perfectly unique, or because the world around them is constantly changing; it is also because the stresses they must learn to cope with are constantly shifting.

If not as a *behaviour recipe*, how should we see Self-Reg? The metaphor that has guided my own thinking is that of Jacob's ladder (Genesis 28:12). Jacob's dream is about constant change. Just as with a ladder, you are going either up or down; so, too, in life you can grow spiritually or regress. ("And behold, angels of God were ascending and descending upon it.")

But what if we are dealing with a child who is afraid of heights? Such a child can easily get stuck, afraid to go either up or down, clinging to a rung and desperately waiting for someone to come to the rescue. God reassured Jacob that every day would offer an opportunity for growth, or the opposite. It would all depend on how he responded. But he would never be alone. God would always be there as a constant presence, providing the inner strength needed to climb the ladder. We must do the same for a child. For (to borrow from Donne's great "Meditation XVII") "no child is an island entire of itself; every child is a piece of the human continent, a part of the main; if a clod be washed away by the sea, we are all the less."

In other words, the goal of Self-Reg isn't simply to help children self-regulate, it is to do so in a manner that helps them climb the ladder. So often, children and youth adopt modes of self-regulating that block empathy and social relationship, or, for that matter, education. The child who self-regulates by avoidance, escape, withdrawal, or what is most common today, escapism or self-sedation, is in no state to learn, let alone to develop the attitudes and emotions that fuel a Just Society.

But there is an even bigger lesson here. This is a book about *homeostasis*, and a central theme is that this concept applies as much to groups as it does to individuals. The key to a Just Society lies in the manner in which it self-regulates. Does it deal with stress in a way that enables it to climb up or leads it to slide down the ladder of social growth? Is it a society that confronts its deep-rooted problems – and all societies have them – or one that splinters into factionalism, with rival groups blaming each other for their troubles? Is it a society that knows what *harmony* feels like, or one that is constantly flirting with cacostasis, a state of disharmony?

When a society is dysregulated, it finds itself at the mercy of ancient non-rational urges that pose the greatest of all threats to democracy: demagoguery and/or tonic immobility. A Just Society is constantly aware of this danger and takes the necessary steps to prevent it: in its politics, in its cultural activities, in the manner in which it cares for those in need of help, in its attitudes towards equity and towards its knowledge-bearers, and, most important of all, in the education it gives to its children. And it responds to a crisis, if and when this does happen, by first reframing the behaviour of those who have become dysregulated.

The distinction between *misbehaviour* and *stress-behaviour* applies as much to the voting class as to an elementary class. We can start searching for the societal stresses that have put us into this perilous state and the ways in which these can be mitigated. Above all, the society needs a respite. Calmness doesn't just precede, it potentiates potential. And finally – or rather, initially – we attend to the needs of our children and youth. Only in this way can a prosocial drive be awakened – or reawakened.

Psychologists, I was once told, write papers while philosophers write books. I guess this book confirms that I am indeed a philosopher: one who seeks to understand, from the inside as it were, what psychologists and neuroscientists are thinking and discovering. What they have already accomplished amounts to a paradigm revolution in our understanding of children and ourselves, and how the two intersect. It will take philosophers and scientists, parents and educators, all working together to understand the full dimensions of this paradigm revolution. My intention in what follows is to provide signposts indicating some of the paths that I feel we should be following.

This book feels like coming home. I started out at Victoria College in the University of Toronto in 1972. The college had its own bookstore that was stocked with University of Toronto Press publications. I slowly made my way through the shelves, starting with Marshall McLuhan, through Harold Innis and Robertson Davies, and ending up with Northrop Frye. Looking back at that experience, I am truly humbled by the giants who taught and befriended us. I didn't realize it at the time, but they were all Self-Reggers, and they inspired in me the longing to be the same.

The opening chapter sets the scientific stage. Self-Reg is grounded in the paradigm revolution that has taken place in the human sciences that sees *relationships* at both the neurobiological and the psychological level as "the hidden heart of the human cosmos."[7] The twin pillars of this new framework are the Triune Brain and the Interbrain. These two hypotheses are tailor-made for each other. Together, they point us back to the original, psychophysiological definition of *self-regulation*, and forward to the differences drawn in Self-Reg between *maladaptive* and *growth-promoting* modes of self-regulation; *self-control* and *self-regulation*; *misbehaviour* and *stress-behaviour*. This foundation will not only enable but indeed drive us in the remainder of the book to reframe several fundamental concepts, such as *temperament* and *personality*; *rationality, irrationality,* and *non-rationality*; *intelligence* and *perseverance*; *freedom* and *virtue*.

Building on the ideas presented in the opening chapter, the second chapter introduces the basic distinction drawn in Self-Reg between *Blue Brain* and *Red Brain*. The point here is not that the neocortex sits atop and rules over subcortical processes but rather that there is a dynamic interplay between *higher* and *lower* neural systems. With this distinction in place, we can begin to unpack one of the most significant of all the reframings presented in the book: that of *human nature*. The starting point is to see that the Red Brain is so much more than just a sentinel or home of powerful urges and emotions. The Red Brain provides a suite of functions that are critical to our existence as social creatures. A holistic understanding of human behaviour begins with a holistic understanding of the human brain.

Self-Reg is fundamentally an anti-determinist way of thinking about development, beginning with the very concept of *development*. The goal of chapter 3 is not to *refute*, however, but rather to *reframe* determinist views of *temperament* and *personality*. Reframing involves an entirely new way of thinking about these concepts in terms of an infant's stress-reactivity and vagal tone. Just as Self-Reg insists that there is no such thing as a "bad child," so too it holds that there is no such thing as a "difficult baby." Accordingly, caregivers need to understand and to respond effectively to the stress overload that leads to a baby being classified as "difficult," before maladaptive modes of self-regulation become entrenched in the child's developing personality.

In chapter 4 I return to my philosophical roots with a discussion of Descartes's Cogito, not as an exercise in the History of Ideas, but as an attempt to understand the rise of irrationalism that we are witnessing today. I fully embrace the standard reading of Descartes as the father of rationalism, but only after having reframed the concepts of *rationality* and *non-rationality* in the manner in which Descartes himself intended. *Rationality* is grounded in doubt; *non-rationality*, in unwavering conviction. But how do we encourage the former and forestall the latter when so many forces are now bent on doing the exact opposite? The answer, I will argue, lies in practising Self-Reg as a method for nourishing rationality in every child – and ourselves!

In Self-Reg we are forever asking *why*. Chapter 5 looks at two particularly salient examples of this practice: Why does this child appear to be not trying? Why is this child having so much trouble with truthfulness? The first step is to recognize how much our attitudes are shaped by ancient views of *effort* and *honesty*, both of which are reframed in terms of the Blue Brain/Red Brain distinction. Here I draw on Kahneman's remarkable discovery that when we fail to solve a challenging problem there is an inverted-V curve, and after the peak we suddenly stop. The lesson here is that there are "interlocking brakes." Through Blue Brain cognitive competencies (e.g., reappraisal, self-soothing) we can reduce and even halt Red Brain hyperarousal; but the hypothalamus can also stop us from working on a problem by triggering "limbic brakes." The Blue Brain/Red Brain distinction thus enables us to reframe such critical concepts as *motivation, social stratification,* or, indeed, *lying.*

The concept of *limbic braking* needs to be both unpacked and applied. Both of these demands are addressed in chapter 6, in the context of intelligence testing. This chapter shows how the purpose of *reframing* is to capitalize on, rather than dismiss, work that's been done in the past. The Triune model opens up an entirely new way of thinking about this research. The crux of the model is that intelligence is a *whole-brain* phenomenon, that is, a function of limbic braking *and* prefrontal (cognitive) processes. If a child's limbic brakes should become sticky, they will have a more attenuated inverted-V curve than peers. The whole point of an IQ test, *qua* stress test, is exactly that: to determine a child's stopping point vis-à-vis a representative sample. This argument does not diminish the value of such tests, provided they are seen as a guide to "releasing a child's limbic brakes."

In chapter 7 we delve deeper into the realm of the applied: in this case, maths. This is a pressing issue for many reasons, not just because maths skills are so important for success in the modern world, but also because maths has become a metric for measuring educational success. Yet the harder we try to reverse the downward trend, the worse the situation becomes. What is most worrying is the steady increase in the number of young students with High Math Anxiety, which leads to avoidance and disruptive behaviour. Neuroscientists have discovered that maths is sending these students into a fight-or-flight response. But how could maths have become a threat? The answer lies in the fact that maths is a *cognitive stress.* It makes significant demands on working memory and induces a level of tension/energy depletion that easily triggers limbic braking. We can always push children to override their limbic brakes. But the limbic system keeps a careful record of such events, and the brakes are triggered at the first cue that the experience is about to be repeated. Through Self-Reg, we can learn to read the signs of impending "output failure" and work on underlying cognitive problems so that learning maths becomes a joy and not a penance.

Chapter 8 explores the idea that, of all the stresses a child must contend with, none is greater than the fear of being left behind. This idea runs contrary to the Victorian mindset, which insists that it is up to every child to decide whether or not to keep up. As the great nineteenth-century guru of self-help Samuel Smiles put it: "With Will anything is possible." The heart of his message, which Smiles sought to demonstrate with several case studies, is that the greater the liability, the greater the effort required. If a child should fail to keep up with peers, it is because that child *chooses* to give up. Such a child *deserves* to be left behind, since they aren't prepared to make the effort required to succeed. According to the dictates of social Darwinism, this is the attitude that makes a society great. But recent findings in paleoanthropology and primatology suggest that it is helping those who need assistance, especially children, that makes a group strong. Self-Reg thus sets out to counter *Victorian misattribution*: the automatic perception that a child who straggles is lacking character when there are neural, emotional, cognitive, social, or psychological causes. Self-Reg teaches us to recognize when a child's problem isn't that they aren't working hard enough, but rather that they are working too hard. Instead of pushing them to override their limbic brakes, we set out to reduce the stress load that is holding them back. And by potentiating that child's potential, the whole group benefits.

Chapter 9 explores a major problem for the youth of today: children may be born with the capacity to *become* free, but teens everywhere are in chains. It is a generation enslaved not just by trivial pursuits but by meaningless ones that sap their will, their drive to challenge themselves, find purpose in life, have a dream. They did not *choose* for this to happen; we allowed it to be done to them, by exposing them to products and activities designed to hijack dopamine. Yet the problem is not one that can be solved by introducing regulatory controls. The real heart of the issue lies in our understanding of *freedom*. Accordingly, the chapter sets out to reframe Isaiah Berlin's classic distinction between positive and negative freedom. For there is a hidden tension in Berlin's dichotomy that comes from the self-control framework in which the argument is couched. According to the dictates of Self-Reg, it is not self-control but calmness, produced by Blue Brain/Red Brain balance, that enables us to *choose*. To be free means that we are not compelled to act a certain way, neither psychologically nor politically. It is not self-control but self-regulation that enables teens to choose, and explain their choices by reference to their ideas and purposes, precisely because they are forming ideas and having purposes. Hence the upshot of chapter 9's reframing is that we replace Berlin's disjunction with a conjunction: *freedom to AND freedom from.*

I wanted to write a book that was relevant to the troubled times in which we are living. And nothing is more troubling than the decline of virtue, to the point where the very term sounds quaint. But as is indicated by the title of chapter 10, the argument will once again be grounded in reframing: this time, the view that *virtue* is something that needs to be imposed on a nature that is not naturally so inclined. The key, yet again, lies in the distinction between self-control and self-regulation. For the ancient Greeks, reason was not enough. Reason tells us that greed is harmful to self and society, but reason alone can't protect us from greed. We need a further factor to save us from greed, and that is self-control. In theory, *irrational* may have meant "without reason," but in practice it meant "without *thumos.*" But another tradition, dating back to Maimonides, sees virtue as the result not of inhibiting base impulses but of having positive ones. It is balance that produces the latter, and the lack of balance that results in the former. In the first chapter, I argue that the Interbrain is the substrate for the development of empathy; in chapter 10, that the same is true for the development of virtue. How we respond to a child's stress-behaviour is critical for experiencing the calmness that virtue demands. But then, we have to contend with the issue looked at in chapter 9: the ubiquitous presence of dopamine-hijacking products and activities. If we are to cultivate virtue in the youth of today, we need to help them become aware of when and why they are overstressed, know what to avoid, and know how to restore. And to have adults in their lives who will never give up on them, no matter what the setbacks.

Chapters 1 through 10 are all intended to lead, via their different pathways, to the fundamental question raised in this book: How do we create a Just Society? Chapter 11 tries to answer this question by raising further ones. So, it is more of a prolegomenon than a denouement. Why is it that reason doesn't hold up very well in the face of excessive stress? What exactly are we supposed to learn from history so that we don't repeat it? Why do we see *cognitive lability* when individuals are overstressed, and why is this so serious? What drives an individual to join a group in Red Brain and abandon their autonomy? Why are so many today seeking to flee from self-awareness and personal responsibility?

The crux of Self-Reg is that we cannot begin to build a Just Society until we have grappled with these issues. Where denial spawns despair, awareness breeds hope – and the psychological and social balance on which the future of a Just Society depends.

Chapter 1

The Science of Self-Reg

Reframing the Triune Brain

Paradigm revolutions aren't visited on us like a bolt out of the blue. There is always a slow build-up leading to an explosive work that, seen with the 20/20 vision of historical hindsight, stands out as "pivotal." The Copernican Revolution is the classic (dare one say, paradigmatic) illustration of this point.[1]

The mounting pressures on the ancient view that the earth stands at the centre of the universe trace back to the thirteenth century, with Averroes' criticisms of Ptolemaic theory, and then, following in his footsteps, the work of fourteenth-century Persian astronomers. Copernicus didn't only extend and transcend their thinking. *De Revolutionibus* changed the world.

It wasn't just the position of the earth but that of humanity in the universe that was forever transformed. *Common sense* was supplanted by scientific observation. Humanity could no longer see itself as the centre of the universe (although some benighted individuals still have trouble absorbing this point).

The same can be said for what has taken place in the life sciences. There was a build-up of pressures leading to a transformation in the biological view of human functioning. We are only just beginning to realize the full extent of this transformation. Every week sees exciting advances in neuroscience, physiology, biology, psychology, psychiatry, anthropology, all gravitating around the discovery of the "the hidden heart of the human cosmos" in processes occurring in the hidden heart of the human brain.[2]

Self-Reg is firmly grounded in this neo-Copernican paradigm-revolution, which traces back to the early twentieth-century work of Walter Bradford Cannon, and mid-century, that of Hans Selye. Also, to the work of Alan Turing, Warren McCulloch, Norbert Wiener, Stafford Beer, and the first generation of AI scientists.[3] All of them were engaged in the analysis of self-regulation: biological, psychological, neural, social, and of course, computational.

There have been major breakthroughs over the past half-century, which we'll touch on over the course of this book. But two in particular stand out as pivotal. The first was the publication, in 1990, of Paul MacLean's *The Triune Brain in Evolution*.[4] We'll get to the second shortly, the Interbrain metaphor.

The essence of MacLean's thesis is that three different brains – reptilian, paleo-mammalian, and neocortex – evolved in different epochs, each serving different needs. The reptilian brain evolved to meet the needs of solitary organisms. The paleo-mammalian brain evolved for the more complex social-emotional needs of mammals. And then the neocortex evolved to serve the increasingly complex cognitive and interpersonal demands of hominins. The neocortex is said to be layered on top of these two "earlier" brains, which were retained because of their survival value.

No contemporary neuroscientist worth their salt believes that brain systems were added on top of earlier systems over the course of evolution. Instead, neuroscience now thinks in terms of homologous structures that were modified in different ways in different lineages. No longer are mammals thought to lack a neocortex comprising six cortical layers (although, to be sure, smaller mammals don't have the sulci and gyri that we see in the primate neocortex). Nor do any neuroscientists assume that the same group of nuclei perform the same function in different species. That includes our own species (e.g., the assumption that the amygdala in *H. sapiens* operates in the same way as it did in *H. erectus*). Not to mention the changes in the prefrontal cortex that have taken place over the past forty thousand years.

Scientists think instead in terms of a *neuroaxis*, proceeding from the least plastic parts of the brain (the midbrain and brain stem) to the most plastic structures in the prefrontal cortex. "Plastic" means that these parts of the brain are "experience dependent": i.e., shaped early in life.[5] Signals pass up and down the neuroaxis, down and up, not to mention down to the "enteric brain" and the "little brain" in the heart. The model of causality is circular rather than linear, involving multiple kinds of internal and external information.[6] Pictures of the brain's connectivity look like a traffic articulation map gone crazy, and not the cartoon model of a monkey sitting on top of a gopher on top of a dinosaur.

But to view a text as paradigm-revolutionary is not to treat it as sacrosanct, as is more than clear in the case of De Revolutionibus. For example, Copernicus adhered to the classical view of planetary orbits as circular and thought that the sun was the centre of the universe (rather than of our planetary system). It would be another sixty-six years before Kepler proved that planetary orbits are elliptical, and not until 1 January 1925 that Edwin Hubble proved the vastness of the universe. Yet it was De Revolutionibus that set off shockwaves, and much the same can be said about The Triune Brain.

The events that led up to The Triune Brain had been going on for some time in physiology, in the theory of homeostasis: that is, the theory of self-regulating systems that maintain internal stability in the face of changing external conditions. The origins of the idea of homeostasis go back to Hippocrates, but the modern version begins with the mechanist/vitalist debates at the start of the nineteenth century, and Claude Bernard's writings on the "milieu intérieur" (1865). This idea was significantly advanced – indeed, baptized as "self-regulation" – by Walter Cannon.

What the theory of homeostasis most desperately needed was a brain overseeing these multiple and interlocking self-regulating systems. This was precisely what MacLean offered, and what his followers seized on and developed. But before we can get to their advances, we first need to consider the flaws in the Triune Brain model, starting with MacLean's view of reptiles. Not, I hasten to add, because we need to expose the shortcomings in MacLean's thinking, but rather, to clarify the significance of his core insight that the human brain houses the residue of pre-human elements.

Therein lies the point of reframing. We are not interested in identifying errors that may have been made, solely for its own sake.

Scientists will do that for us, and they don't need our help. Rather, the point of *reframing* is to think through the hidden riches or broader implications of a work – in this case, MacLean's deep dive into the depths of the brain.

It is our reaction and our efforts that render a text paradigm-revolutionary.

Not Quite the Solitary Creatures That MacLean Assumed

MacLean's view of reptiles was as much of a caricature as his "onion" model of the brain. But like the drawings of the great Al Hirschfeld, it is a caricature that serves as a jumping-off point, an inspiration for subsequent efforts to understand how *ancient survival systems influence what we think and how we act, what we feel and what we say.*

MacLean saw dinosaurs as singletons that had to defend themselves from the moment of birth. They needed a brain suited for a perilous existence in which every animal was either predator or prey. Chief amongst these survival mechanisms – and pretty much the only one that ever gets talked about – is fight-or-flight, which, according to classical Triune dogma, turned out to be so effective that it was absorbed into the mammalian brain and now sits at the bottom (in MacLean's model) of the human brain. But were dinosaurs the solitary creatures that MacLean assumed? Recent research suggests otherwise.

Conservation biologists have established that reptilian behaviour is far more complex than hitherto thought. Studies show that snakes hang out in "communities" that are organized and led by females. There is even evidence of pair bonding – to the extent that reptiles demonstrate a primitive form of mammalian affection and grief.

Could the same be said of dinosaurs? The recent discovery of the *Mussaurus Patagonicus* site in southern Argentina provides us with a glimpse of dinosaurs living in herds, sitting on nests, and jointly caring for their young. There is also growing evidence that dinosaurs communicated with each other vocally.

This latest finding rests on the understanding that ears aren't needed to process sound. Sound waves cause vibrations that are felt by an inner ear connected to the jawbone. This is one of the ways that snakes communicate with each other. And paleontologists have discovered that the same anatomical feature was present in dinosaurs.

Take the recent research done on turtles, which have long been regarded as mute. It turns out that they make all sorts of sounds. More research will need to be done looking at how these sounds relate to turtles' social behaviour before we can say they are used to communicate. But one thing is clear: as Ed Yong shows in *An Immense World*, we are a long way from understanding the reptilian *Umwelt*. And a long way from understanding the social dimension of *ancient survival mechanisms*.

From a neuroscientific perspective, the main criticism of MacLean's argument is that his model of neuro-evolution is far too simplistic. The study of brain evolution, like everything else in neuroscience, has exploded over the past two decades.[7] For example, the structures in the limbic system are now known to be far older than MacLean envisaged. The hypothalamus may be 450 million years old – which touches on the further question as to whether it should be situated in the limbic system or atop the "reptilian brain." And there are few who would assign the same prominence to the hippocampus as did MacLean.

LIFE ON MY ISLAND
I have thought quite a lot about MacLean's view of reptiles while turtle-watching. Sometime in May, the females lay their eggs and then disappear. In the middle of September, the eggs hatch and the hatchlings trundle down to the water. A few years later the survivors will return to the spot and lay their own eggs.

> This phenomenon speaks to the singleton view. But then, I often see several turtles basking together in the sun on a log. At the slightest hint of danger – say, a gull flying overhead – they instantly disappear into the water. Once the gull is past they all simultaneously climb back onto the log. It could, of course, just be a case of "follow the leader." Or they could be communicating with each other via some sub-aquatic signal.

A More Nuanced (Biological) View of the Triassic Period (252–201 mya)

There is a big problem talking about *THE mammalian brain*. Over six thousand mammals exist today, and there have been countless extinctions. The conservative guess is that over the last fifty million years, there have been hundreds of thousands of mammals. All warm-blooded, all with mammary glands, and all with fur or hair (even cetaceans have hair at some point). And they all have a six-layered neocortex, although this varies considerably in size and organization. (Even dinosaurs had a neocortex, although only three-layered.)

Let's start with the most basic question that the Triune Brain hypothesis raises: How do mammals differ from reptiles? We all learned in grade school that reptiles are cold-blooded, mammals are warm-blooded. Lizards, snakes, and turtles bask in the sun in order to absorb heat. They don't have to expend too much energy on thermoregulation. They have short bursts of activity and long periods of inactivity.

We don't see mammals basking in the sun all that often. Instead, they move around a lot, which is a way of generating their own heat. The squirrels in my backyard seem to be forever climbing, leaping, running, fighting, chasing, barking, chattering. That means that they are burning tons of energy. Which means that I am forever trying to figure out ways to squirrel-proof my bird feeders.

We now know that there were warm- as well as cold-blooded dinosaurs: dinosaurs with feathers and fluffy coats, who thermoregulated by panting and basking in the sun. We also know that dinosaurs had receptors to signal energy deficiency, neurons to activate the search for food, providing the energy needed for fight-or-flight.

In other words, dinosaurs had an energy-SEEKING system that was homologous with the mammalian SEEKING system, which in turn is homologous with the human system, viz., the mesolimbic pathway that transports dopamine from the Ventral Tegmental Area (VTA) in the midbrain to the nucleus accumbens (NAcc) and amygdala (AM) in the limbic system.

> Jaak Panksepp identified seven core survival circuits that originate in the midbrain and ascend to the limbic system: SEEKING, RAGE, FEAR, LUST, CARE, PLAY, PANIC/GRIEF. He used capital letters to indicate that these are nonconscious survival circuits that trigger sensations, both pleasant and unpleasant. Pleasant sensations are tied to actions that promote homeostasis; aversive sensations to actions that drain energy and thus exacerbate homeostatic imbalance (such as having too little or too much glucose in the bloodstream).

The most glaring problem with the Triune Brain is that it proposes sharp discontinuities: three of them. One that occurred roughly 250 million years ago, another around 201 million years ago, and a third that occurred at some time in the Pleistocene (although MacLean was vague on when the human neocortex evolved). Discontinuity theories are always a sign of when someone is stymied. To make up for their knowledge gap, the scientist may postulate a genetic mutation, which is essentially a way of confessing that there's not enough information to give a decent explanation. But that information has been forthcoming in recent years, in a way that runs directly counter to discontinuity thinking.

We now know that mammals appeared the same time as dinosaurs, and they certainly did not evolve from dinosaurs. For that matter, even reptiles didn't evolve from dinosaurs. Rather, they evolved from squamates.

Mammals evolved from therapsids, which evolved from synapsids around 280 mya. Synapsids split off from sauropsids around 312 mya. So maybe MacLean's "reptilian brain" is really an "amniote brain" that evolved around 340 mya. In the cartoon model of the Triune Brain, maybe the bottom level should be depicted as a really big lizard.

Mammals inhabited small ecological niches that dinosaurs couldn't access. They co-existed throughout the Triassic period. Around sixty-six million years ago, the dinosaurs died out while only mammals managed to survive. The big question for paleontologists is: How did mammals manage to survive the "great asteroid apocalypse"? In the past two decades paleontologists have discovered that *they very nearly didn't*.

Only around 7 per cent of mammals survived the mass extinction. The larger mammals died out alongside the dinosaurs. It was the smaller *generalists* who survived, simply because they were able to adapt to the post-apocalypse environment. Bear in mind that dinosaurs and mammals had similar survival systems, whatever these might have been. But in the case of the dinosaurs and the large mammals, these survival systems couldn't deal with the energy scarcity that occurred after the great asteroid impact (rather like those electric cars that stopped working in the brutal winter conditions caused by the polar vortex).

But that still leaves the third of MacLean's discontinuities: viz., between animals and humans. Or rather, between two different kinds of mammal: "altricial" and "secondarily altricial." We'll get to what this distinction involves below. But for the moment, we can see how it was this third discontinuity argument that led to the fiercest battles of all: *within* the ranks of MacLean's followers!

The Gloves Are Off

What is invariably true of paradigm-revolutionary texts is that they trigger a colossal fight. In the case of *De Revolutionibus*, it was a fierce battle between theologians who held fast to the Bible's view of the earth standing at the centre of the universe and a new breed of astronomers who looked to the stars rather than the Book of Genesis to settle the issue.

In the case of *The Triune Brain*, it was a battle between those who held fast to the Great Chain of Being, the view that there is a rupture between animals and humans – although not, I hasten to add, for theological reasons – and those who, following in Darwin's footsteps, argued for continuity between animals and humans. The former will be horrified by what I said above about how reptiles demonstrate a primitive form of mammalian affection and grief. The latter will respond, tell us more!

The big reason why MacLean's thesis was so contentious is because it served as a flashpoint for the long-standing conflict between those who, like Descartes, saw animals as automata and those who saw animals as both conscious and emotional creatures, albeit lacking the "higher" emotions that only language speakers can experience.

We are dealing here with a clash between *neurobehaviourists*, led by Joseph LeDoux, and *affective neuroscientists*, led by Jaak Panksepp. But to describe their disagreement as a "clash" is an understatement. At times it has been more reminiscent of a pub brawl than a scientific dispute.

Panksepp picked up on Darwin's continuity thesis that animals display rudimentary emotions that are similar to – and precursors of – basic human emotions, such as fear, sadness, happiness, anger, and surprise and show similar facial expressions, gestures, body movements, and neurochemical events. Hence, we learn about the neurobiology of basic human emotions by studying the brains of animals.

LeDoux's response to the continuity argument is that only humans are aware of what they are feeling, and thus, only humans experience emotions. My computer is not "afraid" that it is running out of battery when it starts to beep, and neither is an animal that bleats when it's threatened. Accordingly, he insisted on a categorial distinction between *nonconscious survival mechanisms*, which are present in both humans and animals, and *emotions*, which are unique to humans. The latter only occur when we are *aware* that we are angry, afraid, happy, lonely.

> *"I am, like most people, drawn to the idea that animals feel pleasure and pain when they act as if they do have such feelings. But as a scientist, I am compelled to ask: How can we distinguish behaviour due to presumed consciously felt hedonic states in animals from behaviour due to nonconscious processes?"* (Joseph LeDoux, *Anxious: Using the Brain to Understand and Treat Fear and Anxiety*)

Not surprisingly, LeDoux was unhappy with MacLean's idea that the limbic system is a "proto-emotional brain" sitting beneath the neocortex. One of LeDoux's main arguments stems from research establishing a direct circuit for threat detection, which runs from the thalamus to the amygdala. His studies, using subliminal images, have shown that a threat response can be activated, as registered by changes in the autonomic nervous system, with no awareness on the subject's part that this is happening.[8] Hence, according to LeDoux, no fear.

The Philosophical Ramifications of Paradigm-Revolutionary Texts

The continuity/discontinuity clash raises a number of complex issues, some of which we will look at throughout the course of this book. Questions about how we make decisions. How we measure intelligence. (Why we measure intelligence!) Why maths causes not just anxiety but distress – and not just in students! Why we punish children when we could be helping them manage their stress. Why virtue is in peril. Why society is so dysregulated. But most important of all, why we insist on privileging a Blue Brain response to the psychological and social problems that we are wrestling with today.

This last point touches on the work that's been done in psychology of reasoning on the biases we use when making decisions. And from there, the neurobehaviourist attack on the concept of *autonomy.* Psychologists have documented how decision making is often the result, not of deliberation, but shortcuts that we unconsciously employ, "heuristics" that are a function of the properties and limitations of our information-processing system. But the neurobehaviourist goes a step (a massive leap) further, arguing that "decisions" are *always* the result of subcortical programs.[9]

Suddenly, our foray into the technical – and definitely overheated – controversy over the significance of the Triune Brain has turned into a debate over *free will*! Never fear, Self-Reg will come to the rescue. (Well, sort of.) Our mandate is to save our *ability to choose*, not abandon it to the exigencies of the distant past. But that distant past plays a major role in how we deal with the exigencies of the present. Demands that each and every one of us is struggling with.

That is where the real significance of *The Triune Brain* lies: in a new way of thinking about how the "lower" levels of the brain influence the "higher." MacLean's "three separate brains" can be reframed as three distinctive neural states, what in Self-Reg we refer to metaphorically as *Blue Brain, Red Brain,* and *Gray Brain*. In Blue Brain, those prefrontal systems that subserve cognitive processes are dominant. In Red Brain, it is limbic processes that subserve emotions and motivational states that are dominant. In Gray Brain, ancient survival circuits designed to maintain homeostasis operate as the caboose that pushes the train.

To say that one part of the brain is *dominant* does not mean that the other parts of the brain are dormant. The connections between the different levels of the neuroaxis are bi-directional and co-actional. When the Gray Brain is in the ascendant, we can still think and talk – well, talk. Gray Brain dominance plays a critical role in *what we think and how we act, what we feel and what we say*.

MacLean adhered to a self-control model of neuroevolution, in which the prefrontal cortex sits atop and rules over subcortical impulses (e.g., through reappraisal). But *"inhibition" is bi-directional*. Red Brain systems inhibit Blue Brain processes through *limbic braking*, and ancient survival systems in the Gray Brain inhibit Blue Brain processes (e.g., cause dysteroception, a lack of interoception), ancient survival systems that involve not just fight-or-flight, freeze, and fawn but how we self-regulate, mate, nurture our young, care for each other, cooperate with each other, avoid separation from the group.

It may not be obvious on first reading, but this argument is forcing us to reframe *rationality* in the manner proposed by Descartes (see chapter 4). Since biblical times, Reason has been construed as the ability to choose how we act, and then to justify our actions, when pressed, by explaining our reasons. But we are now confronted with the argument that our actions are often caused by ancient survival systems, and what we *say* is nothing more than an attempt to *appear* rational – to convince ourselves as well as others that we are in control of our actions.

It is as if we are locked inside a brain that struggles to make sense of reality – including our own subjective reality and actions. In other words, we remain singletons at heart! Modern neuroimaging conforms to this outlook. We lock a subject inside a chamber, inject some dye, present them with stimuli or a problem, and then watch to see which sets of neurons light up. MacLean's greatest insight is that, regardless of what may or may not have been true of dinosaurs, we are not singletons. But it took another great pioneer to clarify this point.

The Interbrain

Interest in the Triune Brain might have remained confined to neuroscience circles were it not for the work of an obscure Dutch zoologist. Or rather, Stephen Jay Gould's discovery of a paper that Adolf Portmann published in 1941, which introduces the concept of *secondary altriciality*: the second of our two "Self-Reg pivotal events."

Secondary altriciality refers to the idea that humans share some traits of precocial animals (e.g., we have small litters) and some traits of altricial animals (e.g., the helplessness of our newborns). What makes our species biologically unique is the long period of time in which our infants remain dependent: in some cases (many cases these days) a *very* long time.[10]

Thanks to Gould, *secondary altriciality* has transformed our view of the evolutionary history of the modern birth mechanism.[11] And it established that the *Dyad* – the infant/caregiver pair – and not the isolated child is *the fundamental unit of development*.[12] We are not singletons and were not meant to become singletons.

Babies learn the meaning of words, facial expressions, gestures, eye gaze, and posture and develop their emotions and empathy not by having Pleistocene-fashioned genes unlocked or "potentiated" by a stimulus,[13] but from endless back-and-forth interactions with their primary caregivers.[14] But a baby who is hyper- or hypoaroused is in no position to learn anything. They have to be able to attend to their caregiver for any sort of learning to occur.

Before we can study the role of the caregiver in communicative, emotional, social, and cognitive development, we must first consider the role of the caregiver in modulating the baby's arousal.[15] As we will see below, a baby is bathed in stress from the moment they "see the light." All kinds of stresses: light, sound, temperature, textures, gravity. All of them requiring the newborn to expend the limited amounts of energy they possess. Some babies release too much catecholamines – dopamine, epinephrine, norepinephrine – to deal with all this stress, which is what causes them to become hyperaroused: their brain and body working too hard, their sensations overwhelming. And some babies respond to this stress overload by "shutting down": i.e., blocking the stimuli that are flooding their delicate nervous system.

Nature's plan was to have a "higher-order" brain regulate a developing organism that is years from being able to manage this feat on its own. A baby cannot down-regulate or up-regulate themself, i.e., cannot soothe or rouse themself. It is up to the caregiver to perform this role, which they do by triggering the release of neurochemicals that stop the stress response at its source or by triggering the release of neurochemicals when it is time to feed.

The gist of describing "human babies as embryos" is that the newborn *remains a foetus* for the early months of life.[16] This foetus is transitioning from one type of womb to another: an "external womb," as it were, that allows for synaptogenesis: a burst of synaptic growth, when the "plasticity" that I mentioned above can start to take effect. And then, beginning at around eight months, synaptic sculpting, or pruning, begins to adapt the baby's brain to the environment. But if a newborn remains an embryo in some sense, this raises the question of what takes over the role of the umbilical cord.

The answer to this question has been dubbed "the Interbrain."[17] Digby Tantam coined this term to posit a brain-to-brain hookup that yokes a baby to their caregiver: a wireless version of the cord that keeps an astronaut tethered to a spaceship, and that enables the mother-craft to read and regulate their baby's arousal states.[18] But not just any old brain hookup: a *paleo-mammalian brain* hookup.

It turns out that the concepts of *Interbrain* and *Triune Brain* were tailor-made for each other. The Interbrain rests on *limbic communication*. There is a sub-cortical connection linking one brain to the other, a conduit that is maintained by touch, vocalization, eye gaze, facial expressions, smell, taste, and gestures. It is the Interbrain, not language, that makes the Dyad a dyad – barring some environmental disaster, neurogenetic challenge, or the intrusion of illness or excessive stress. Language will only start to emerge around the first birthday, piggybacking on the Interbrain.

In one sense this point is obvious enough. Caregivers don't *explain* to their newborn why they should calm down or *teach* them to be patient. And babies certainly don't *inform* their caregiver that they are hungry or *complain* about the service. But the danger here is that of assuming what we are supposed to be explaining, and then concealing this rhetorical sleight-of-hand with the strategic use of quotation marks. A baby doesn't tell their caregiver what they are feeling, but neither do they "tell" her.

The fact is, the Interbrain needs the Triune Brain if it is to constitute a non-question-begging explanation of neurobiological and communicative synchrony; and the Triune Brain needs the Interbrain if it is to avoid relapsing into self-controllism. Tantam likens communication between mother and baby to a Bluetooth connection. The image is that of the two brains "paired" via radio waves. Recent findings suggest that this idea should be taken literally. Heart rate and neurochemical secretions synchronize during bouts of shared gaze, and we now know that the same is true for brainwaves.[19]

According to the Interbrain, when a baby *feels* what their caregiver is feeling[20] and vice versa, the two are resonating. This concept of *resonance* comes from auditory science. It refers to the sound that is produced when an object vibrates at the same rate as that which produced those sound waves. If two tuning forks are placed at opposite ends of a room and one of them is pinged, the other vibrates. Musicians have long been familiar with this phenomenon. When a violinist plays the D-string, everyone's D-string begins to vibrate. Not just the violins but also the violas, cellos, basses: all the string instruments (which makes one think about how the vibrations between a teacher and student instantly spread throughout a classroom).

The transmission of vibration through soundwaves applies to all the sensory modalities and not just auditory. Through the various nonverbal modes of communication, a group of neurons vibrating in the caregiver's limbic system causes a similar vibration in the baby's limbic neurons. It is in this way that a hyperaroused amygdala in the one causes the same thing to happen in the other: a mechanism that brings, not just mother and baby, but the members of a group instantly into the same emotional/physiological state.

The importance of resonance began to be explored as a result of von Economo's discovery of spindle neurons.[21] The pivotal event occurred when Rizzolatti accidentally discovered mirror neurons.[22] His lab was studying the firing pattern of neurons in the premotor cortex of rhesus macaques when reaching for a peanut. A beep would fire if a neuron was activated. One day a graduate student walked into the lab eating an ice cream and beeps suddenly started sounding all over the place. The same neurons were vibrating as would have happened had the monkeys been eating the ice cream themselves.[23]

But MacLean made a further point, which takes this argument out of the mechanist realm of "monkey see neuron do." It is not just resonating vibrations, but shared emotions – negative or positive – that forge the limbic-to-limbic connection.[24] Neurons in the same limbic systems begin to vibrate. A connection serves as the substrate for all aspects of development.

Scientists have discovered that a trapped rat's distress vocalizations activate neuronal vibrations in the OFC-ACC-Insula-NAcc pathway in the observer rat. Amplify these distress vocalizations and they sound like shrieks, screams, or whimpers. These frequencies trigger aversive sensations in the observer rat, which causes them to free the trapped rat. The same thing happens in a Dyad. Nor are we just dealing with vocalizations. When observers watch someone put their hand in a bowl of ice water, their own body temperature drops. A neuroceptive mechanism is operating here that causes neuronal resonance.

A Child's Future Lies in Our Species' Past

A "master" and "slave" device (yes, these are the terms used to describe a piconet, which uses Bluetooth to link devices) that "know" nothing about one another run a "discovery" process, with one sending out an "invitation" to "pair" and the other "listening" for this. This invitation contains the master device's name, address, and profile. The slave "reciprocates" and once an "exchange" has been executed the two devices "bond," and will henceforth do so whenever they are in close range. "Bonding" is made possible by sharing a common PIN or six-digit numeric code. Once paired, the two devices engage in a "conversation" in which signals are transmitted and received for as long as the two remain on the same radio frequency (2.4 GHz)

The metaphor of an *Interbrain* appeals to a mechanist metaphor that was itself based on the metaphor of the caregiver-infant Dyad, which was itself based on binding one object to another: just the sort of dizzying metaphor-dance that is so common in AI writings.[25] But there is one very big difference between electronic and human attachment (other than the roles played by Erics-son Mobile and Mother Nature). Whereas a shared alphanu-meric code maintains a Bluetooth connection, in the case of the Interbrain it is shared emotions that perform this role. A slave device cannot be described as "needing" a Bluetooth connection (although a frustrated user may wish that it did). But the heart of the Interbrain is that both members of the Dyad are driven by just such a need.

There are far too many scientists that have done ground-breaking work on attachment to be surveyed here.[26] Only a comprehensive history of developmental psychology over the past half-century could do justice to the contribution that so many have made to our understanding of the *primacy of relationships*. But in terms of this chapter's focus on self-regulation, two in particular stand out: Stanley Greenspan and Stephen Porges.

The fundamental question looked at by both is: What makes shared emotion possible? Their answer (which goes back to Bowlby) is: The child's *need to feel secure*. At the start of their careers, DeGangi, DiPietro, Greenspan, and Porges studied this phenom-enon in an NICU.[27] They looked at the implications of Cannon's theory of stress as *any stimulus that requires us to burn energy* by trig-gering bodily reactions that serve to maintain homeostasis (e.g., shivering to maintain an internal body temperature of 37 degrees). What happens if the stress load is too great? What happens if you then reduce that stress load?

If a baby's stress load is too great, too much energy is expended "fighting" to stay in homeostasis. We can speak of "fighting" here because the survival instinct kicks in early. Muscles are tensed, which causes heart rate and breathing to go up. This drains energy reserves, compromising the tropotro-phic (parasympathetic nervous system) processes needed for the immune system, cellular repair, digestion, and growth.[28] If the stress load can be reduced, this should boost metabolic restor-ative processes.

The NICU was the perfect place to test this theory. Premature babies have heightened stress-reactivity because of their immature sensory system. They are burning enormous amounts of energy trying to protect themselves from the stimulus onslaught. Hence, if it were possible to reduce their stress load significantly, this should result in marked improvements in their immune system, digestion, growth, and overall health.

DeGangi et al. reduced the stress load by regulating ambient temperature, reducing noise and light levels, substituting haptic for sound alarms, modulating staff behaviour, and introducing restorative caregiver practices (such as kangaroo care). They then looked at the impact of these changes on measurable health indices: heart rate, blood oxygenation, weight gain, growth, and length of stay in hospital.

So positive were the results that Greenspan went on to develop his *affect diathesis* model: the role of reciprocal chains of affective interaction in development.[29] Porges went on to develop his theory of *social engagement*: i.e., the social behaviours and neurophysiological mechanisms that regulate arousal and in so doing lay the foundation for attachment.[30]

Greenspan and Porges were both interested in the plasticity of the limbic system, but each with a different focus. Greenspan was interested in how a child's limbic system is "wired" to share the emotions of their caregiver and the impact of excess stress on the baby's ability to process nonverbal affect cues.[31] For Porges it was sympathetic/parasympathetic balance and the impact of excessive stress on recovery and growth (vagal tone).[32] Both were interested in how the limbic system shapes and is shaped by dyadic interactions.

This is the stuff of which paradigm revolutions are made. Greenspan and Porges present a biopsychosocial approach to dyadic interaction that integrates continuity and discontinuity thinking. A limbic-to-limbic connection makes the growth of emotions possible, which then shape a child's communicative, social, and cognitive development. They both ground their argument in an evolutionary framework: in Greenspan's case, social; in Porges's case, psychophysiological. Combined, they bring into sharp relief the heart of MacLean's vision: *our proto- and paleo-mammalian past provides the substrate for our prefrontal future.*

When Pairing Breaks Down

If our species has been biologically pre-programmed to pair, so to speak, why are there ever attachment disorders? Is it a case of "faulty wiring"? Do some dyads lack a "common PIN or six-digit numeric code"? No. The answer lies in excessive stress, which causes hyperarousal – typically in both members of the Dyad.

Excessive stress is the great enemy of attachment. Both the Triune Brain and the Interbrain make this point, each in its own way. In fight-flight-freeze, the neuroaxis is flooded with CRH (corticotropin releasing hormone), which triggers the stress-response chain, leading to the release of cortisol. After all, if stress causes us to burn energy, and too much stress causes us to burn too much energy, then we need to tap into all our reserves.

This applies to babies as much as to us. The baby goes into a precursor of Red Brain. In an infant, this manifests in their becoming irritable and inconsolable. Should the excessive stress persist, the result will be a state of learned helplessness (which is a bit like torpor: i.e., a way of conserving energy). When this happens, attachment is blocked before it can even get started.

The Interbrain hypothesis rests on a similar point. If we ping one tuning fork but hold the other tight, the latter will not vibrate. Hyperarousal has the same effect on limbic resonance: it hampers the transmission and/or reception of vibrations between limbic systems. When a caregiver is hyperaroused, their ability to feel what the baby is feeling is significantly impaired. The reason why the caregiver fails to respond to the baby's signals is not because of a *lack of interest*, but because this limbic channel has been blocked. This last point needs to be amplified.

It is quite remarkable how self-controllism has infused our thinking. We talk about "good" babies and "bad" babies, as if the infant was somehow responsible for being cranky or having sleep problems. We talk about "attentive" and "inattentive" caregivers, as if the caregivers are negligent if they "fail to attend" to their babies' needs.

The Triune Brain ushers in a desperately needed aspect shift, which is one of the more important consequences of the paradigm revolution. Excessive stress in either member of the Dyad is a huge obstacle to co-regulation. It can cause a baby to shut out a world that is aversive – including the stimuli emanating from their caregiver's eyes or voice.

Conversely, excessive stress can cause dysteroception in the caregiver. The problem here is not that the caregiver ignores the baby's signals: it is that the caregiver doesn't experience the aversive sensations that the Interbrain transmits. In standard situations, a caregiver doesn't just *see*, they *feel* when their baby is in distress.

The effect of a non-responsive caregiver on a baby is powerful, as Ed Tronick demonstrated with the Still Face paradigm. This was one of the first of the stress tests that developmental psychologists have been running and modifying ever since.[33] Tronick showed how stressful it is for a baby when the caregiver does not respond in any way. Not a smile or a frown or even a flicker of recognition. Some babies become listless while others become aggressive. When the Interbrain is restored, they return quickly to a regulated state. If they don't, this can be a sign that the baby is in allostatic overload (excessive wear and tear on the body due to stress), or of a deeper biological problem.

This effect does not simply apply to an eight- to ten-month-old infant (the age when we typically assess attachment). There is never a point in our lives when a Still Face doesn't cause us distress: a fact that the steely negotiator, poker player, stern boss, and sociopath all exploit. The Interbrain is as essential at the end of life as the beginning.

Reframing 101: Misbehaviour versus Stress-Behaviour

Nonverbal communication was seen by generative linguists as a paraverbal accompaniment to language. But the Triune Brain challenges the privileged status assigned to speech. It sees two equally vital channels of communication: limbic-to-limbic and perisylvian region of the brain-to-perisylvian. The question of which channel we "attend to" at any given moment depends on the arousal of the other. But in the language-centric universe that we inhabit, there is a tendency to stop attending to "limbic utterances" once children start to speak.

We saw this all the time at MEHRI. Parents would privilege language over limbic communication when their children turned three. They all recognized stress-behaviours as such in their infants. (In the original Latin, "infant" meant "unable to speak.") But once their child started speaking in sentences, they started to treat as *misbehaviour* what they would hitherto have seen as *stress-behaviour*.

For Self-Reg, this distinction between *misbehaviour* and *stress-behaviour* is one of the more important consequences of the Triune Brain. Misbehaviour is intentional; stress-behaviour is caused by systems deep in the midbrain. The concept of *misbehaviour* is inextricably bound to the concepts of *intentionality* and *choice* – and hence *responsibility*. Stress-behaviour is non-rational (see chapter 4).

When a child has gone Red Brain, their behaviour is reactive. If their SEEKING system in the midbrain (originating in the Ventral Tegmental Area) is blocked (e.g., the desire for a treat), their RAGE system (originating in the Periaqueductal Gray) is activated to overcome the obstacle. If left on their own to "let the tantrum play out" – which is a version of the Still Face paradigm – the child is flooded with stress hormones. Eventually they will stop, but only from exhaustion, not because they have *learnt* that throwing a tantrum gets them nowhere. If we soothe the child with our voice or touch while saying "no," they will continue to feel secure, albeit disappointed. And that is indeed an invaluable lesson.

That is hardly to say that children never misbehave! Rather, it entails that we need to learn the different nonverbal cues of misbehaviour versus stress-behaviour. For example, in misbehaviour, children have trouble looking you in the eyes; or they adopt a masklike visage to conceal any leakage. They speak too much or not enough. They repeat the question, change the topic, or go into too much detail. There is a noticeable lag between our questions and their responses. There are changes in proximity (e.g., they draw away); or they try to create a physical barrier (e.g., they cross their arms or hold something to their chest). Their affect cues indicate awareness of the truth, bearing in mind that children are very good at constructing the "truth" according to their wishes. (And not just children!)

As we will see in the next section, once we learn what they are, the signs of stress-behaviour are glaring. But we need to learn how to listen, not just with our ears, but with our eyes, our touch, and sometimes (literally) our gut.

Help: I Don't Speak Limbic!

One of the major continuity implications of the Triune Brain is that we can learn about limbic modes of communication by studying mammalian behaviour. Take vocalization: Rats make distress vocalizations in the 22-kHz range (which, when amplified, sound like shrieks, screams, and whimpers) and pleasure vocalizations in the 50-kHz range (which, when amplified, sound like giggles). This frequency change is evident in small children: e.g., when they scream in pain or frustration or gurgle in the bath or whilst being tickled. If our goal is to prevent a meltdown, it is essential that we listen for changes in pitch.

Where the distinction is pivotal is when we treat a *limbic utterance* – i.e., vocalization – as if it were intentional. The teenager's all-too-familiar "I don't care" response to being chastised for something that they've done or said only infuriates us more. But listen carefully and you'll pick up when their voice is high-pitched and strained, speech rhythms harsh and jarring.

There are so many things going on when a teen insists "I don't care." They may well be trying to convince themself that this is the case. Their utterance may be a burst of anger or a discharged fight response. It could be a cry for help. It could be denial, avoidance, escape, anxiety, panic. Odds are it's a mélange of all of the above.

Put it all together and what you have is the adolescent version of the 22-kHz distress cry. Far from being an act of defiance, it is more likely the result of feeling paralysed because of being constrained, not necessarily physically, but by the situation or by an authority figure. This is a feeling that, if consistently ignored, or still worse, punished harshly, can lead to an externalizing or internalizing disorder.

All too often, we misinterpret what a teen is communicating because we fail to note what arousal state they are in. We cease to hear the stress in limbic utterances, fail to note the paleness of their face or hands, their slouched or defensive posture, or their nervous tics. We undergo a form of *mindlessness*: i.e., commit the category error of misapplying concepts that apply to intentional acts.

Self-Reg teaches us how to "speak limbic": how to interpret the significance of affect cues and how to respond; to reframe what sounds *aggressive* as what may, in fact, be *defensive*. Whether or not the teen's limbic utterances are "requests" for assistance, they most certainly indicate the need for assistance. That is, for an Interbrain to provide the regulating influence that the teen cannot manage on their own.

The teen eventually needs to learn all this for themself: needs to know when they are in or on the verge of going into Red Brain. As we will see in the next chapter, there are times when we want to coax a child into Red Brain. But Red Brain in the wrong circumstances can be costly in so many ways: not just in terms of the amount of energy burned and the impact on mood and perception, but for learning and social relationships, personal insight, and moral growth. But you can't simply *tell* a teen – or for that matter, anyone – that they are in Red Brain, using the sort of language that you'd use when speaking Blue Brain to Blue Brain.

A teen's comprehension in Red Brain undergoes the same sort of transformation as their speech. They become attuned to *your* affect cues. What they're processing isn't the semantic content of what you're saying but, rather, your tone of voice, eye gaze, facial expression, gestures, body language. Even if this is not at all your intention, should you be inadvertently sending "threatening" messages, you can be sure that that is what they will pick up. And because of the impact of Red Brain on cognition, that may be all that they pick up, regardless of what you're saying!

The point is that, in Red Brain, a teen may have as little idea of what *you're really saying* as they have of what *they're conveying.* To help them transition back to language proper, we first have to help them restore homeostatic balance. We do this by softening our eyes, lowering our tone of voice, slowing our speech rhythm, relaxing our facial expression, gestures, posture. Nothing beats a gentle touch if they will permit it.

Provided we allow them the time it takes for safety messages to sink in – and every teen is different in this regard – they will eventually signal, in their own idiosyncratic way, that they do indeed care. And what's more, that they have absorbed at least some of the lesson that you so badly wanted to impart.

A teen doesn't know when they've gone Red Brain, and they may not know how to get out of it on their own. What's more, it's much easier to slip into Red Brain than out. We continue to guide these transitions until such time as the teen can do so on their own, rather like the way that an instructor helps teens in Driver's Ed.

The Triune Brain drives home why it is so important to recognize which part of the brain is dominant and know how to respond accordingly. It is next to impossible to have a mindful response to a teen's hyperarousal if we ourselves are hyperaroused – which happens if we don't recognize stress-behaviour as such. There is no greater stress than not understanding how your teen could do or say the things they are doing or saying. But before you lose your own temper, first ask yourself whether they truly *intend* what they are saying or doing.

When we ignore or misread a teen's limbic utterances and respond in a punitive manner, we easily end up triggering their RAGE + FEAR. That is why arguments with teens so quickly descend into insane shouting matches. Similarly, the teen's capacity to pause and reflect hinges on our own ability to pause and reflect. *But this is no more a matter of self-control in us than it is in them.* It is a case of being aware of the stress we are both under and knowing how to manage it. This is the reason why in Self-Reg we like to say: Calm begets calm begets calm. And hyperarousal begets hyperarousal begets chaos.

If you are looking for a really useful Self-Reg idea, look no further than *Red Brain*. This idea refers, in neurobiological terms, to the dominance of limbic over prefrontal processes. In emotional terms, to the blast of negative emotions. In neurochemical terms, to the surge in catecholamines and stress hormones. In social terms, to the decline in empathy or compassion. And in psychological terms, to a state of dysteroception, where one is unaware of sensations signalling homeostatic imbalance.

There is something even more worrying about Red Brain. With the subduing of the prefrontal cortex (PFC), we become more susceptible to dopamine hijacking and the power of suggestion, and vulnerable to being swept up in group emotions (limbic contagion) and the loss of the sense of self.

The Jewell

In 1906, Mark Honeywell brought the "Jewell" to market: a programmable thermostat with a built-in clock, enabling users to turn down the heat at night and have it automatically adjust to a pre-set temperature in the morning. Honeywell went on to dominate the plumbing and heating industry. And, inadvertently, physiology.

Walter Cannon seized on the metaphor of the thermostat to explain how biological "self-regulating mechanisms" maintain a stable environment in the human body: i.e., the theory of homeostasis. It wasn't long before neuroscientists were looking for the control switches in a "self-regulating brain."[34] Self-regulating systems are found at each level of the neuroaxis: brainstem, midbrain, diencephalon, limbic system, and neocortex.

In neurophysiological terms, self-regulation begins with an ancient breathing mechanism. In historical terms, the scientific study began with Cannon's study of thermoregulation.

In extreme cold, heat shifts from the extremities to internal organs, heart, and brain, rendering us vulnerable to physical problems such as chilblains, frostbite, and urticaria. The greatest risk is hypothermia, which causes extreme fatigue, poor coordination, and disorientation. In the ultimate stage of hypothermia, terminal burrowing occurs.[35] Interestingly, children display this behaviour when they are overstressed (by building forts, nestling under blankets, or hiding in the closet or under furniture). Even babies demonstrate the burrowing instinct by trying to bury their face in your shoulder or chest when they are overstressed.

According to Cannon's definition, a *stress* is any stimulus that causes us to expend energy (e.g., heart rate and breathing go up) so as to keep a homeostatic system operating within its functional range.[36] Cold causes us to burn energy to maintain a core body temperature of 37°C. Thermosensitive neurons in the hypothalamus trigger the release of thyroid hormones when body temperature drops below a set point. This causes blood vessels in the skin to constrict so that blood is diverted to internal organs that need heat. It causes shivering, which produces heat as a by-product. (Teeth-chattering is a form of shivering.) But shivering consumes a considerable amount of energy: approximately seven calories a minute.[37] Which brings us to where humans, and not their brains, excel.

Or rather, where the Interbrain excels. It is not an internal mechanism but the Interbrain that keeps the child in homeostasis. The child is exposed to myriad and constantly changing stresses. It requires an Interbrain to help the child remain stable and their energy reserves topped up. The child does have a thermoregulating mechanism, but not one designed for long-term use.

Newborns, infants, and young children cannot yet shiver. They rely on a different mechanism to thermoregulate: norepinephrine is released, which reacts with brown fat to produce heat. But this is an energy-expensive process – and very short term. It is therefore up to the Interbrain to regulate the child's body temperature.

The caregiver has to learn – typically from other caregivers – to recognize when their child is cold by monitoring changes in skin colour, feeling if their hands, feet, and torso are cold to the touch, recognizing when their child is too still or fussy because of cold, knowing when to put on an extra blanket – and equally important, when to take it off.

Our species has an extraordinary ability to adapt to hostile environments that would overstrain our thermoregulatory mechanism. We do so with learned self-regulating behaviours, like using clothing and shelters, which reduce the need for energy-depleting self-regulating mechanisms. We learn a different way of moving. We consume energy-rich foods, like *muktuk*, which provides for a slow, steady release of glucose into the blood stream. Or we can do something quite stupid, like drink alcohol.

Alcohol provides momentary relief from the cold (acetate is a source of rapid energy). But it is dehydrating; it causes vasodilation (which results in body cooling); and to make matters far worse, it impairs judgment. The result is that we can soon find ourselves in greater danger. Consuming alcohol to cope with the cold is an exemplar of a maladaptive response to stress, and not just cold stress![38]

Maladaptive versus Healthy Self-Regulation

The difference between *maladaptive* and *healthy* modes of self-regulation is critical. There has been a notable tendency in the recent literature to treat self-regulation as a normative skill: a milestone that children need to master, akin to walking or talking. On this way of thinking, self-regulation rests on self-monitoring, self-management, and self-control.[39] If a child has trouble inhibiting their impulses, paying attention, or regulating emotions, this is taken to mean that they have not yet mastered self-regulation.

The fact is, we learn to manage stress in all sorts of ways, some of them healthy (relaxing, exercising, listening to music, walking in nature) and some that provide short-term relief but exacerbate homeostatic imbalance and thus lead to greater stress down the road. For example, we may turn to a food that has been engineered to maximize the *bliss point*, which has a deleterious effect on health when carried to excess.[40] Or we resort to mind-numbing smartphone games to self-distract. Children these days are at an especially high risk of acquiring maladaptive modes of self-regulation unless the Interbrains in their lives recognize when this is happening and guide them into healthy modes of self-regulation.

Gaze aversion is an example of a potentially maladaptive mode of self-regulation. Our older son, who has autism, would avoid eye contact with us because he found the stress of shared gaze aversive.[41] The problem is that shared gaze is critical for learning the meaning of facial expressions, nonverbal behaviours, mind reading, and language. So, while gaze aversion may reduce stress in the moment, it can do so at the cost of increasing the stress the child will subsequently experience in social interactions.

One of the lessons that we learned from the MEHRI study is that, rather than trying to induce – let alone force! – these children to share gaze, the therapists had to figure out what the child's stressors were and how these could be reduced. As we hoped would be the case, the results were seen in the children's pleasure in and desire to initiate social interactions, their ability to stay engaged, and the development of the communicative skills that are needed to be so engaged.[42] This certainly proved to be the case with our own son.

Maladaptive modes of self-regulation ultimately impair our ability to cope with stress, and we lose the possibilities of growth that might otherwise have been afforded. Avoidance is the classic example. Forcing compliance in these situations is a sure way to make a bad situation worse. But healthy self-regulation is not at all the same thing as a coping strategy. We are not seeking to strengthen the child's ability to endure stress (although there may be cases where that is what is needed) but, rather, to transform what had hitherto been aversive – even extreme cold – into a positive catalyst for development.

As we will see in chapter 7, the perfect example of this point occurs when a child is struggling with maths. The solution is neither to force the child to persevere nor to shield them from the challenge. Both strategies have been tried; both have failed. Rather, we need to understand the reasons why the child finds maths aversive and what can be done to alleviate the cognitive stress load and thereby render maths a positive learning experience. This can only happen, however, if we understand the difference between *self-regulation* and *self-control*.

Self-Regulation versus Self-Control

I first started thinking about the difference between self-regulation and self-control when I looked at the longitudinal data on Mischel's original Marshmallow Task findings:[43] that is, the follow-up research comparing outcomes in those children who could wait for the experimenter to return and those who could not.

The message was clear: young children who were able to wait several minutes in a room without eating the marshmallow in front of them turned into young adults who did better in just about every metric you can imagine. Here is a case where the issue is not whether the data can be trusted[44] but, rather, why we are seeing these correlations. Was it a self-regulation or a self-control issue, and what exactly is the difference?

The Marshmallow Task is as close as you're going to get to a version of the isolation chamber that astronauts must undergo – a stress test designed for four- to six-year-olds. The child is exposed to all kinds of stresses in addition to that of the treat. They are left alone in a windowless bare room with nothing to distract themselves and no way of knowing how much time has elapsed and when the experimenter will return. They have to remain seated at a table with the marshmallow directly in their line of sight. And then they have to wait.

We mistakenly assume that the stress of waiting is the same for all children (an independent variable). But there are many factors that can make waiting a far greater stress for some children than for others. For example, anxiety; their state of hunger, fatigue, or tension; their internal biological clock; what for them are hidden stressors in the environment (e.g., the colour of the walls, an odour, extraneous sounds).

What is important is how we interpret their behaviour. On the standard self-control paradigm, the experiment is viewed as a *delay of gratification* task: how well the child can hold back from giving in to a temptation. A study of willpower! But once we recognize that this is a *stress test*, we realize that many – if not most – of the "non-delayers" may have eaten the marshmallow simply *to make the stress stop*. In other words, they self-regulate by eating the marshmallow! They may not even like marshmallows; it's just that, having been primed to fixate on the stress, they have no other means of inhibiting it.

In reality, the task was a study in different modes of self-regulation: namely, Mischel's "cognitive competencies" (e.g., reappraisal, self-distraction, self-soothing) versus eating the marshmallow. As such, the study may have much to teach us about the cascading effect of maladaptive modes of self-regulation. Indeed, it may have implications for addiction research.[45] Lacking healthy modes of self-regulation to break free from the stress cycle in which they are caught,[46] the addict is driven to surrender to the impulse, however strong their desire to resist. The stress becomes unbearable, and the addict can find no other means of relief. It is not *weakness* that they suffer from, but ongoing excessive stress created by the withdrawal, which tips them into Red Brain where there is no choosing.

Character Calisthenics

Many were tempted to see the Triune Brain as the neural vindication of the ancient self-control paradigm. On this outlook, the prefrontal cortex is seen as a strongman, sitting atop unruly forces surging up from beneath.[47] If a child has trouble resisting temptation, it means that we need to strengthen their medial-prefrontal cortex (mPFC): the structure in the prefrontal cortex that lies adjacent to the anterior cingulate cortex, which has been shown to be involved in decision making, social cognition, and modulating activity of the hypothalamic-pituitary-adrenal (HPA) axis.[48]

This idea that the "control" systems in the brain need to be strengthened is first encountered in von Sömmerring's *Vom Baue des menschlichen Körpers*:

> Does use change the structure of the brain? Does use and exertion of mental power gradually change the material structure of the brain, just as we see, for example, that much used muscles become stronger and that hard labor thickens the epidermis considerably? It is not improbable, although the scalpel cannot easily demonstrate this.[49]

The analogy here is to the development of a muscle: if the brain is vigorously exercised, this will force neurofibrils to grow. If children are to have control over their limbic system – that is, impulses and negative emotions – they need a robust mPFC, which they have to strengthen with brain exercises. Yet again we return to the ancient pedagogical question of what might constitute an effective "gymnasium for the mind."[50]

The Triune Brain + Interbrain represents a very different way of thinking: Archimedes rather than Plato, the metaphor of hydraulics in place of wild horses. Image the brain of a hyperaroused child and you see a limbic system lit up in red, with only a few splashes of blue in the adjoining prefrontal systems. The child is poised to trip into fight or flight. But reduce their stress and calm the child down and the flow pattern is reversed, with a largely blue prefrontal cortex (PFC) and just a sparse scattering of red in the limbic system.

The key here lies in the words *calm the child down*. The paradigm revolution that inspires Self-Reg involves the shift from a model of neural functioning suitable for singletons to the paramount role of the Interbrain. The concept of self-control is the offspring of the "singleton" outlook, which is that if you are plagued by maddening impulses and wild emotions, it is up to you, on your own, to acquire the internal strength needed to quell those disruptors.

The concept of *self-regulation* is tied to *social engagement*.[51] In the early months of life, when stressors are constant and overwhelming, the baby's limbic system registers how the soothing presence of their caregiver consistently brings neurochemical relief (in the form of oxytocin and endogenous opioids). The limbic system "records" how tension was reduced and energy restored. But *social engagement* – which serves as a first line of defence in dealing with stress – is not an automatic reflex (as Maier and Seligman showed in their early research on learned helplessness; see chapter 7). Whether or not a child's first response to stress is to seek help from others hinges on the quality of their early dyadic experiences.

What the child needs to learn is *that it is possible to be soothed*. Only on the basis of this embodied knowledge can they begin to learn how to manage their stress load in a manner that enhances, rather than constrains, restoration. It is not a matter of inhibiting strong impulses but, rather, reducing their frequency and intensity by managing stress load and recovery. Mindful self-regulation is what makes self-control possible – and in many cases, unnecessary. By calming the child down, you promote a state of homeostatic balance that facilitates the child's ability to learn, exercise cognitive competencies, and regulate themselves.

The limbic alarm in that teen who kept insisting "I don't care" was kindled – that is, triggered by the slightest provocation, sending them into repeated bouts of fight, flight, and freeze. Each time this happened, it set off a physiological/psychological wave:

- Activity in the subgenual PFC and dorsolateral PFC (dlPFC) was significantly reduced (a pattern that has been tied to mood disorders)
- They focused on threats, real or imaginary
- Fear-based thoughts ran rampant
- Sleep was affected
- Anhedonia (the reduced ability to experience pleasure) set in, deterring them from healthy modes of self-regulation (e.g., exercise)
- The diurnal cortisol pattern (where cortisol levels are highest early in the morning and lowest around midnight) was disrupted, resulting in early morning fatigue and heightened stress-reactivity.

What they needed was not greater self-control; it was to learn Self-Reg. To recognize:

1) When they were overstressed
2) How maladaptive modes of self-regulation were compounding the problem
3) That they suffered from a profound restoration-deficit.

I wrote this chapter six years ago. At the time I was deeply worried about the explosion of mental health problems that we were seeing in children, teens, and young adults: a generation running on empty, with more and more crying out "I don't care." And I was worried about the signs of the same thing happening to society at large: a society in deep Red Brain. It never occurred to me how much worse the situation would get. How I would begin to worry about the self-inflicted harm that now threatens the well-being of us all.

We desperately need a paradigm revolution. *A change in what we think and how we act, what we feel and what we say.*

Chapter 2

Reframing Human Nature

From Hierarchy to Heterarchy

Metaphors can have a powerful impact on how we see the world, how we see ourselves and each other.[1] How we see a child, a teen, or a young adult. No more striking example of this point could be found than the Triune Brain: MacLean's idea that we have not one but three distinct brains, each selected at a different point in our evolutionary history and preserved to perform unique functions.

As we saw in the opening chapter, MacLean's three brains are as follows:

- Neocortex, which subserves rational and linguistic functions
- Paleo-mammalian, which evolved to meet the needs of social species
- Reptilian, which oversees core metabolic functions and basic survival mechanisms

Self-Reg looks at the Triune Brain, not as a theory about neuro-evolution, but as affording a dramatic shift in the metaphors that we employ to understand behaviour.

According to this way of thinking, we have three distinctive mental states, each a function of the neural system that is dominant, what Self-Reg refers to as being in *Blue Brain*, *Red Brain*, or *Gray Brain*. You can see the origins of this colour scheme on any weather map, where clear weather is depicted in blue, stormy

Figure 2.1 The Triune Brain

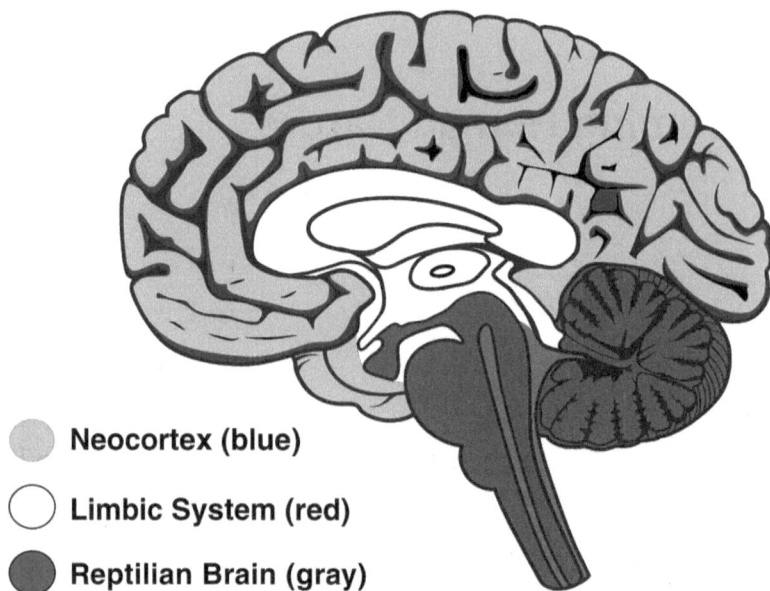

● **Neocortex (blue)**

○ **Limbic System (red)**

● **Reptilian Brain (gray)**

Source: Adapted from Stuart Shanker and Susan Hopkins,
Self-Reg Schools: A Handbook for Educators (Toronto: Pearson, 2019), 6.

weather in red, and all-hell-breaks-out (earthquakes, flash floods) in dark gray. These colour associations are so familiar that EEG designers naturally employed them for their visual representation of brain topologies (Figure 2.1).

I began using the language of *Blue Brain/Red Brain* to describe children's behaviour because of what we were seeing in the neurolab at MEHRI. When children were in a high arousal state and difficult to engage, their EEG waveforms were almost entirely red, and most vividly so in the structures in or closely connected to their limbic system. There was only a scattering of blue in the prefrontal areas of their brains. When they were calm and relaxed, the pattern was reversed: now the images were overwhelmingly blue throughout the PFC, with just a few scattered spots of red in limbic and paralimbic areas.

It was natural, then, to speak of *Blue Brain* to signify when pre-frontal systems are dominant and the child capable of sustained back-and-forth exchanges; *Red Brain* when limbic systems are dominant and interaction difficult; and *Gray Brain* when the child was having a meltdown or had shut down and the best that could be done was to soothe. It is tempting to see these three states as roughly corresponding to the distinctions drawn between *rational*, *irrational*, and *non-rational*, although, like everything else that we look at in this book, these concepts will also get reframed once we start down the path of Triune thinking.

At first, I was drawn to the metaphor of a Triune Brain because it added an extra dimension to how I already thought about children's behaviour. If a child is in Blue Brain, that means they are capable of pausing and reflecting before acting; sequencing thoughts; seeing the connection between causes and effects; inhibiting impulses; ignoring distractions; balancing short- against long-term goals; assessing the consequences of an action; explaining the reasons for an action. All this because the prefrontal systems that subserve these functions are dominant.

In Red Brain the processing dynamic has shifted, and limbic structures are running the show, especially the amygdala. The child is not choosing how they act – is not acting for reasons – and is perhaps not fully aware of what they are doing. In this state the child is often on high alert, constantly scanning for possible threats and, if arousal is great enough, seeing threats anywhere and everywhere. So much processing capacity is being shunted to the limbic system that there is not enough bandwidth left over to pause and deliberate.

If a child had slipped into Gray Brain, this was because we hadn't picked up the Red Brain warning signs. RAGE and FEAR, usually together, were dominant. That was the end of therapy for that session. The child could no longer attend to the therapist, let alone process anything said to them. Were their RAGE + FEAR circuits to be triggered during an EEG session, there would be a sharp spike in cortical and behavioural arousal, which marked the end of any neuroimaging for that day.

My original thinking was that, insofar as the primary goal of MEHRIT (**MEHRI** Therapy) was to enhance language-based social interactions, the child needed to be calm.[2] The first step was to turn off a child's limbic "alarm" if it had been triggered. In this way, Blue Brain systems could regain dominance. But I gradually came to see that far more was going on here than just reducing arousal so as to restore prefrontal hegemony. It wasn't simply a matter of soothing hyperarousal so as to bring the child back into Blue Brain; Red Brain functions were every bit as vital for successful therapy sessions.

In other words, my initial thinking was still tied to the old hierarchical metaphor that stretches from the ancient Greeks right up to the present. I had thought that "to regulate a child" meant to calm down their Red Brain so that (1) they didn't slide down into Gray Brain, and (2) the Blue Brain could regain control. If you think about it, there is nothing paradigm revolutionary about this way of thinking; it is more of a paradigm shift, a way of dividing subcortical impulses into separate categories.

On this interpretation, all MacLean had done was split the deep subterranean parts of the brain into two distinct levels: a subcortical version of the Asphodel Meadows, where benign limbic impulses reside, sitting on top of Tartarus, where ancient demons are housed. With, of course, the neocortex ruling over all like Zeus from Olympus on high. That is, the role of the neocortex is to inhibit emotional impulses; should these become overpowering, the survival functions seize control and send the neocortex fleeing from the field of battle, much like Achilles after the death of Patroclus.

What brings us into paradigm revolutionary territory is when we abandon the hierarchical mode of thinking altogether. Not a disjunction, but a conjunction. Not Blue Brain OR Red Brain but Blue Brain AND Red Brain. Not a *neural hierarchy* but a *neural heterarchy*.[3]

Reframing Human Nature

As far as the ancient Greeks were concerned, there were only three possible explanations as to why we ever act against our self-interest: either reason was deficient, the impulses too strong, or the will (*thumos,* a precursor of *will*) too weak to carry out the actions dictated by reason. But the Triune metaphor suggests a different way of looking at the matter. I highlighted in chapter 1 how, according to the Triune model, *inhibition is bidirectional.* That applies to reason as well as self-regulation. In Red Brain, the individual doesn't *choose* to self-harm. They are *caused* to act against their self-interest.

The problem is that we persist in looking at human behaviour through Greek eyes. If someone is being irrational, we seek to enlighten them. To restore their rationality. Only, the harder we try to convince them that they are being irrational, the more intransigent they become. In the end, we throw up our arms in despair: "They are beyond reason," or "They have been brainwashed." Both of which may be perfectly true, but then, that only means *we can't use reason to restore reason.* We need a different approach, just as, when a child went Red Brain in the MEHRI Clinic, we needed to self-regulate before we could engage.

The problem is that, despite everything, we still privilege rationality. When we press an agent to explain how on earth they could believe such-and-such, they never say, "I have no idea." Instead, they pretty much always have a ready answer – more often than not, parroting someone else's talking-point. Yet we treat their response as a – deeply misguided – reason, which as such we need to correct.

What's needed as we think through this issue is a clearer understanding of the self-regulating heterarchy, so as to prepare us for a reframing of *rationality* in chapter 4.

It's time to put the *problem of akrasia* (the question of why anyone would ever choose to act in a manner harmful to their well-being if they knew that this was the case) to bed. Time to reframe our view *of human nature.* To see the human being as:

A rational, an irrational, and on some (many? most?) occasions, a non-rational animal.

A Neuroscientific Revolution

The archetypal metaphor in Western culture was the Great Chain of Being.[4] According to this venerable doctrine, there is a continuum descending from God down through angels, humans, animals, plants, to inanimate matter (with all sorts of intermediary divisions in each grouping). Each link down the chain has a little less consciousness, intelligence, and intentionality than the previous; all the way down to rocks, whose only attribute is that of existence.

The position of humans was seen as unique. Situated between angels and animals, humans have a soul, self-awareness, language, reason, will. But they are locked inside a physical body and so must share animal impulses and drives. If humans are to ascend to heaven, they must co-opt their "spiritual" side to control the animal instincts within them.

In this metaphor, there are two sides to human nature: rational and irrational, higher and lower. Nothing could be more natural than to read the Triune Brain in these terms: that is, the neocortex sits atop the ancient paleo-mammalian brain with the reptilian brain lurking in the nether regions. The subcortex is the source of impulses, appetites, and urges. But for beings living in complex social organizations, these impulses, appetites, and urges need to be curbed. The neocortex must acquire self-control so as to keep the animal side of our nature in check.

Forget about Haeckel's view that *ontogeny recapitulates phylogeny* (the idea that an embryo goes through the same stages of development as in the evolution of its ancestors): this would amount to ontogeny recapitulating cosmology. On this hierarchical outlook, we end up, as the eighteenth-century physico-theologians argued, with the white European brain going through the same neurodevelopmental stages as earlier species and races but ending up with a sovereign organ ruling over its primitive forbears.[5]

But this is not at all how MacLean, or at least not his followers, viewed the issue. Like ideological revolutionaries, they set out to overthrow the old paradigm. They did not see the Triune Brain as an autocracy, but more like the US constitution: a system of co-equal branches of government, each with its own unique role and responsibilities. On this covenantal outlook, Blue, Red, and Gray Brains are conjoined, with different attributes, checks, and balances. Neural stability can occur only if Blue, Red, and Gray Brain work together in a state of neural homeostasis.

Homeostatic imbalance triggers aversive sensations: e.g., the ingestion of too many calories causes stomach discomfort, feeling tired, hot, sweaty, dizzy. Normally, these sensations stop us from eating more. It is no coincidence that we overeat when we are overstressed. The excessive stress blocks our awareness of aversive sensations (while sharpening the aversiveness of hunger). That is, it causes a state of *dysteroception*.

Dysteroception is also a mammalian survival function, so that we are not paralysed when in allostatic overload. The compulsive overeater does not overeat because they *lack willpower*. Does not *choose* to ignore these aversive sensations. This is not a failure on the part of the Blue Brain to control appetites and impulses. Rather, the compulsive eater is not conscious of these aversive sensations. Heightened stress load has caused dysteroception. When the stress load is too great, those ancient systems not only keep us going, they seize control.

Herein lies a key reason why the Triune Brain had such a powerful impact on the science of human behaviour. MacLean was read as arguing that we need to adopt a bottom-up as well as top-down approach to human functioning. Ancient survival systems evolved to deal with the myriad stresses that proto-mammals encountered. We may have added considerably to what they had to deal with, but the basics have remained the same.

The survival behaviours that have received the most attention are those that cluster around fight-or-flight: being hypervigilant for signs of danger (auditory, visual, olfactory); responding to a threat by triggering the release of catecholamines; mobilizing energy reserves to prepare the body for intense exertion. But a much broader range of ancient systems is essential to our survival.

These behaviours fall under the rubric of *neuroception*: a form of apprehension in which the limbic system picks up signs of safety or danger in the environment.[6] In the case of the former, it triggers affiliative behaviours (approach, shared gaze, smiling, low-frequency vocalizations, the release of oxytocin and vasopressin). In the case of the latter, defensive behaviours (withdrawal, eye contact avoidance, high-frequency vocalizations, the release of corticosterones).[7]

But neuroception is about so much more than threat detection. Or rather, our understanding of *threat* needs to be broadened. Neuroception refers to *internal* as well as *external threats*. Threats to survival, full stop.

The Self-Regulating Brain

Human survival is the result of a self-regulating heterarchy with remarkably ancient roots, bound together in a complex neurobiological network. Survival systems originate in the midbrain and have ascending pathways to the diencephalon, limbic system, and even directly from the VTA to the prefrontal and visual cortex.

These mammalian systems evolved from proto-mammalian survival mechanisms. Their first role is to ensure that there is enough energy to fuel survival. Aggression is triggered when energy seeking is blocked. Flight when there are dangers, which includes the threat of being alone. How we respond to being held and stroked and how we respond to a helpless infant who needs to be held and stroked. How we respond to another's fear and how we respond to our own anxiety.

Above the midbrain sits the hypothalamus in the diencephalon, located in the very centre of the brain. It serves as the homeostatic "master control," regulating body temperature, hunger, thirst, mood, sex drive, blood pressure, sleep. The hypothalamus has downward connections to the midbrain Periaqueductal Gray (PAG), Dorsal Raphe Nucleus (DRN), Ventral Tegmental Area (VTA) and brainstem. It has upward connections to the amygdala and hippocampus, and further, to the cerebral cortex and retina. In addition, the Periventricular Nucleus (PVN) in the hypothalamus is dedicated to regulating the stress-response system (Coritocotropin Releasing Hormone⇄ Oxytocin).

Immediately above and connected to the hypothalamus are four major structures in the limbic system: striatum (nucleus accumbens), cingulate cortex, amygdala, and hippocampus. They serve as the brain's switching control, relaying messages from below and above. They play a critical role in self-regulating the "Five F's": feeding, forgetting, fighting, family, and fornicating.

Inhibitory mechanisms in the mPFC are connected to the limbic system and in some cases directly to the midbrain. Systems in the fronto-parietal regions of the brain (where the frontal and parietal lobes meet) automatically disengage and redirect attention from a frightening stimulus. But homeostatic imbalance at lower levels of the neuroaxis overloads these regions, rendering us unable to disengage or self-distract.

These are just a few of the brain's self-regulating mechanisms. And overlying them all are learned modes of self-regulation. None of these mechanisms or behaviours operate in isolation from the others. The influences are bi-directional and constant, which is a big reason why we are drawn into maladaptive modes of self-regulation – behaviours that provide short-term relief but do nothing to ameliorate and may even exacerbate homeostatic imbalances deep in the Gray Brain.

The Gray Brain

Panksepp identified seven ancient survival systems in the Periaqueductal Gray (PAG), Ventral Tegmental Area (VTA), and the Dorsal Raphe Nucleus (DRN). Six of the Primitive Emotion Circuits (PECs) originate in PAG: RAGE, FEAR, CARE, PANIC/GRIEF, PLAY, and LUST. We are talking about a small system in the midbrain, about the same width as the average ring finger (fourteen millimetres). But what a powerhouse.

PAG contains enkephalin cells that modulate PAIN by suppressing the activity of ascending nociceptive (PAIN) pathways. In fact, it is the target site for brain-stimulating implants in the treatment of chronic pain. It contains a high density of vasopressin and oxytocin receptors, telling us that it serves an important role not only in the modulation of PAIN but also in maternal caregiving behaviour. Furthermore, it plays a critical role in defensive behaviour. Stimulate one part of PAG and it triggers freezing, immobility, running, jumping, locomotor activity. Stimulate another and this produces quiescence.

The PECs evolved to serve different aspects of survival. Each is tied to the pleasant and unpleasant sensations noted above, whose function is to stimulate behaviours that maintain or restore homeostasis. For example, we become thirsty if the body's electrolyte-water balance falls below a predetermined osmotic threshold. Thirst is an aversive sensation that impels us to drink; drinking is a pleasant sensation as a result of the endorphins that are released.

In general terms, negative sensations are triggered by internal states or stimuli that threaten homeostasis. They are produced by a drop in opioids, the activation of nociceptive neurons, the suppression of dopamine, and the release of corticotropin releasing hormone (CRH). Positive sensations are triggered by stimuli that promote homeostasis. They are produced by endogenous opioids, oxytocin, prolactin, and dopamine.

The more we study PAG, the less surprising it becomes that basic emotions like fear and anger – let alone secondary emotions like frustration or feeling rejected – are the sorts of mixtures noted by psychologists of emotion. Multiple PECs are activated by homeostatic imbalances, the neurons in one circuit causing referred activation in another. And what is even more significant, causing nociceptive activation (PAIN). Nociceptors run through all these pathways, rather like the "rogue's yarn" that the British navy wove into all their cordage.

The implication of this last point for understanding the aversiveness of internalizing and externalizing problems is profound.

Limbicity

The paleo-mammalian brain evolved to meet the needs of social creatures, and it is so effective that it has performed this role for two hundred million years – if not more. Hence, we need to study mammals closely if we are to understand our Red Brain: how they communicate and interact; how they raise their young and care for their infirm; how they play and how they grieve; what they think and what they feel; how they cooperate and coexist in harmony.[8] We need to study their "evolved developmental niche," as Darcia Narvaez describes it, to understand our own.[9]

Because of our engrained tendency to *privilege rationality*, we have treated the limbic system as a supporting actor and not one of the leads. We need a new concept, *limbicity*, to stand alongside that of *rationality*. The former needs to be unpacked every bit as much as the latter needs to be reframed. Limbicity is not to be seen in solely negative terms: a sub-human domain that needs to be suppressed. It has its own survival functions and distinct set of characteristics.

When we are in Blue Brain, we can be remarkably skilled at ignoring stress and discovering maladaptive ways of dealing with it. The limbic system is much more attuned to the needs of the neuroaxis, basically because it oversees energy expenditures – and stress tops the list in terms of cost overruns. Long before we become aware that something is a stress, neuroception has picked up on this fact and done its best to send this information to the PFC or the Interbrain. It is when neither listens that trouble ensues.

This last point is pivotal. In addition to its own mode of perception, the limbic system has its own array of communicative behaviours. As I write this, a study by a group of neuroscientists at NYU has just reported on the brain mechanism that enables Alston's singing mice to challenge competitors by singing in turns. Here is a case where the mammalian brain orchestrates rapid-fire duets.[10] We see a similar phenomenon in birds, as well as nonhuman primates.[11]

The ability of animals to engage in high-speed back-and-forth communication serves as yet another reminder of the complexity involved in what I described in chapter 1 as the "limbic-to-limbic" channel of communication. Pitch, rhythm, intonation, pauses, and stress are all involved, not to mention all the other aspects of nonverbal communication that our perisylvian top-heavy Blue Brains may overlook but our limbic systems do not (e.g., gaze, posture, movement, facial expression, gestures).[12]

Maybe it's because we regard the limbic system as a "paraverbal" distraction that we aren't inclined to learn how to speak – let alone see, hear, and feel – limbic. The most important part of all this is that limbic communication doesn't just accompany but actually shapes what we say or see. In fact, a phenomenon that we witnessed repeatedly in our work with children and teens is that, when they go Red Brain, pretty much *all* that they process are the messages that your limbic system is sending – generally, without you even knowing that you are doing so.

Or their limbic system completely distorts what you're saying – which, again, is something that is totally familiar to any parent of a teen.

Neuroceptive Overdrive

"The capacity to become anxious is part of the evolved emotional toolbox of the brain."[13] I'm pretty sure we can all agree to that. But the point that Panksepp and Biven were making is that our brain is equipped with a highly sensitive alarm that serves to distinguish between safety and threat, between homeostatic balance and imbalance. When this system is overused, which seems to be pretty much the norm amongst teens these days, the alarm goes off at the slightest whiff of smoke. Neuroceptive discrimination is skewed. Everything, and in some cases nothing, triggers the alarm.

Here is a prime example of why it is so important for Blue Brain and Red Brain to be working together. If the processing dynamic shifts too far towards Red Brain, Blue Brain reappraisal is impaired. Reappraisal is rightly seen as a fundamental mode of self-regulation. The stress response is instantly turned off. ("Trump's assault on the constitution has proved a wonderful tonic for the flagging democratic spirit.") So, when reappraisal is blocked, the stress response stays active. The result is a slide into *neuroceptive overdrive*. When that happens, the teen is incessantly scanning for danger and constantly (mis-)perceiving it.

Hyperarousal in multiple domains – physiological, neural, psychological, emotional – leads to heightened threat detection, reduced working memory, and kindled stress-reactivity. As we will see in the remainder of this book, getting caught in this kind of stress cycle impairs well-being across multiple domains. A major reason is because, in this case, it's not just reappraisal, it's the Interbrain that gets blocked.

We saw in chapter 1 how limbic-to-limbic resonance serves as the affective substrate for all aspects of development. Limbic communication is a direct channel between right brains that is governed by affect signals.[14] *Limbic resonance* is crucial not just for the synchrony between parent and child that makes secure attachment possible, but also for the shared emotions – both positive and negative – that sweep through and bind people together in a crowd. And it keeps us moving although longing for nothing more than to lie down and rest. From the dawn of time teens hunted and gathered together; now they go to the mall.

But what happens to the individual when they are separated from the group? There is a reason why social media has become so pervasive amongst the young. The technology serves as a mode of self-regulation: of keeping PANIC/GRIEF (separation anxiety) at bay. But if that technology should become a source of heightened stress rather than relief, such as happens when the teen is subjected to online bullying or false ideals that heighten insecurities, the result isn't just anxiety and depression.

Getting stuck in Red Brain leads to dysteroception, which involves more than just a lack of emotional awareness (such as is seen in alexithymia, which is also known as "emotional blindness"): it is a more generalized state of diminished interoception.[15] In dysteroception, awareness of homeostatic signals – such as pain, fatigue, hunger, thirst, body temperature – is blunted. Perhaps even shut down altogether.

Dysteroception would have been beneficial in all sorts of conditions, including war, migration, and famine. To this day we celebrate individuals who excel in this aspect of limbicity. Great athletes tap into their capacity to ignore pain, fatigue, thirst, and overheating, while scanning for threats (think of how runners look about to see where their competitors are). Champions are those who are able to push themselves beyond their limits – or at least, past the limits of others.

But what is pushing us is not just our Blue Brain visions of fame and fortune. Often it is a limbic system unbridled. A paleo-mammalian brain is driven to SEEK; apparently, it matters not what (see chapter 8).

Homo zetetes (The Human Seeker)

Social animals do not survive by threat detection alone. They survive by knowing when to rest and digest. Self-Reg is a pathway to restoration. One reason why Self-Reg has become so popular is because ours is a generation that finds it hard to restore, not so much because of an innate need for instant gratification as because of the constant manipulation of one of our core neurobiological mechanisms that creates the impulse for instant gratification.

Before perseverance, which is a Blue Brain phenomenon, comes perseveration, which is Red Brain. Psychologists tend to think of perseveration in a clinical sense; for example, the child on the spectrum who cannot stop repeating a word or a movement. Yet perseveration is much more common than that: just think of the student or co-worker who finds it hard to change focus, the baker or artist constantly striving for perfection. This may be one reason why athletes enjoy practising the same movements over and over, or why factory workers report enjoying working on the assembly line. Or why a teen can spend endless hours on TikTok.

No doubt perseveration was the paleo-mammalian trait that enabled *H. habilis* to spend a million years making the same tools. Perseveration is the result of what Panksepp dubbed the SEEKING system, which extends from the VTA to the NAcc and then on to the mPFC. The SEEKING system drives animals to "search for the things they need, crave, and desire."[16] In other words, SEEKING is one of the limbic secrets to survival. Remove it by bilateral lesions and the animal becomes listless and passive. In humans, illness and severe stress can have a similar effect, while overstimulation of the system (e.g., via dopamine hijacking: see chapter 9) leads to excessive compulsivity, anxiety, and depression.

The SEEKING system runs on dopamine, which produces the pleasant sensation known as *psychic energy*. "Mankind's great and unique achievements, the products of our prodigious neocortices, are firmly rooted in the psychic energy provided by [the SEEK-ING] system."[17] But the build-up of cortisol blocks the activation of dopamine neurons.[18] The greater the stress, the less positive sensations (psychic energy) and the more negative sensations (cortisolemia). And nothing triggers cortisol like *SEEKING without consummation* (just think of the game that has one more level and then one more level and then …).

What drives perseveration are the dopaminergic sensations produced, not the rewards (if any). But there is more involved in SEEKING than midbrain onanism. (Or at least, that was the case before the modern world.) The function of the SEEKING system was to drive animals to search for food, shelter, sex, and care for their offspring; companionship, assistance, empathy; being part of a harmonious group and not being isolated from one's group.

These lessons were learned from the close study of animals, despite the outraged howls of anthropomorphism. In fact, the question of what animals are capable of feeling or thinking turns out to be essential for the unpacking of *limbicity*. It is a question that can only be answered by physiologists in their labs and biologists studying animals in their natural conditions. Ethologists have made some truly astonishing and, for that matter, profoundly moving discoveries.[19]

Do animals grieve? The question may make us uncomfortable, but the research is unequivocal. Barbara King has shown, in meticulous and often painful detail, how dogs, cats, apes, elephants, goats, whales, dolphins, giraffes, even birds, grieve the death of a loved companion.[20] It appears that you can't SEEK a mate or be part of a group without paying an emotional price.

What applies to animal emotion also applies to animal cognition. The research on dogs' natural intelligence – the problems they can solve, their understanding of language and body language, their memory, even their theory of mind skills – utterly shatters the discontinuity myth.[21] Frustrated SEEKING is the great goad for creativity: and not just in humans! But overly frustrated SEEKING is the great killer of effort – and not just in humans.

None of this is to say that we are slaves of our mesolimbic pathway. The Blue Brain also has a say in how we act. In humans, the SEEKING system becomes closely bound up with goals and purposes. We seek knowledge, truth, enlightenment, or maybe just a promotion. Children and teens have a deep limbic *need to seek*, they know not what. We as parents and educators hope to have an influence on *what* they will seek – and these days, on *whether* they will seek.

The problem is that there are two different senses of the term "seeking" operating here, and if we aren't clear on which is which, they could end up SEEKING at the expense of seeking.

The Problem with Homonyms

The question of why goals are so important for purposive human behaviour takes us deep into the realm of *motivation*. This is the meat and potatoes of great novelists and playwrights. This is the issue that led Bandura to study self-efficacy and Tony Robbins to build an empire.[22]

Motivation is the quintessential Blue Brain phenomenon. The concept is internally tied to the concept of *intentionality*: you can't describe someone as motivated unless you can also describe them as *trying* to attain a goal. But, when neuroscientists study motivation, they are interested in something vastly different. What they understand by "motivation" is "generally conceptualized as energy for behaviors related to obtaining rewarding stimuli or situations."[23]

"Motivation" in this energic sense is a function of three major factors: the benefits associated with a stimulus (e.g., a burst of energy, feeling soothed, sedated); incentive salience (i.e., the anticipated payoff); and the pleasurable sensations generated by SEEKING (i.e., by dopamine). When the limbic system is "energized," it keeps us fixated on the reward. Reflective thinking is powerless to thwart its commands.

Hunger and thirst are examples of how SEEKING keeps survival systems in homeostasis. The processes driving us to obtain the reward (slake our thirst) are regulated by the hypothalamus. Someone crawling in the desert in search of water will keep going until they collapse. A reward in this sense is not something that we *earn* by our efforts but rather something that *causes* us to keep going. There is thus a huge difference between the operations of the mesolimbic dopamine pathway and the way we reward ourselves at the end of a hard week with a bottle of Chardonnay.

Motivation as it is ordinarily understood is anchored to *intentionality*. An agent can be described as "motivated to obtain a reward" only if it makes sense to say (i.e., their behaviour satisfies the criteria for saying) that they *wanted* to obtain that reward. Caterpillars have a heliotropic mechanism that draws them to the top of the tree, where food awaits. But they don't *want* the food at the top of the canopy – although we can explain the reason why they climb the tree.

To keep clear on what we are dealing with, we might distinguish between *motivation* and *motivation*$_{NS}$ (the neuroscience meaning of "motivation"). For example, between what Bandura is studying and what neuroscientists like Mogenson, Jones, and Yim are looking at in their research on the "influence of dopamine on the limbic inputs to the nucleus accumbens."[24] But there are complications here regarding the relationship between the two and, especially, how *motivation*$_{NS}$ impinges on *motivation*, and the reverse. The issue involves more than just a semantic distinction.

The Thayer Matrix

Robert Thayer discovered that *motivation* naturally varies according to mood, which he defined in terms of an energy/tension matrix (Figure 2.2). A subject is most motivated to obtain a goal when energy and tension are high, and least motivated when energy and tension are low, or when energy is low and tension is high. What this means, in the psychological sense of motivation, is that we try harder for longer and feel more positive in high energy/high tension (HE/HT).

Figure 2.2 Thayer Motivation Model

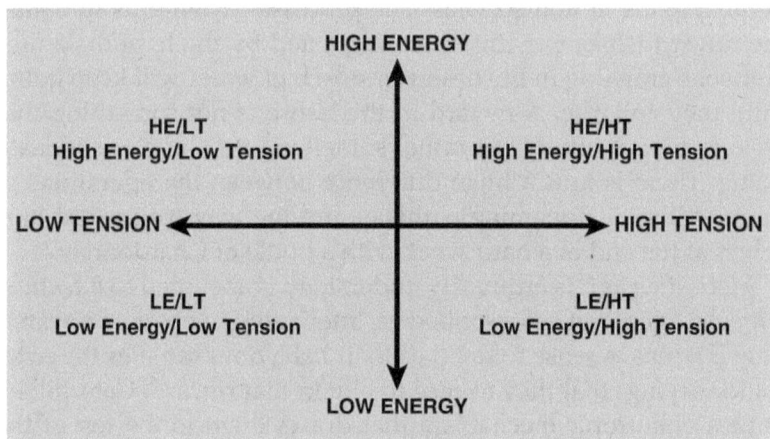

```
                        HIGH ENERGY
                             ▲
                             │
        HE/LT                │                HE/HT
   High Energy/Low Tension   │         High Energy/High Tension
                             │
LOW TENSION ◄────────────────┼────────────────► HIGH TENSION
                             │
        LE/LT                │                LE/HT
   Low Energy/Low Tension    │          Low Energy/High Tension
                             │
                             ▼
                        LOW ENERGY
```

Source: Adapted from Robert E. Thayer, *The Origin of Everyday Moods: Managing Energy, Tension, and Stress* (New York: Oxford University Press, 1996).

Consequently, a key to working on children's and teens' motivation is for us to recognize, and to help them recognize, when they are in or are going into a state of low energy. Then, what they need to do to restore energy. Only then will they experience positive sensations, physiological as much as emotional.

At a deeper level, what Thayer discovered is that *motivation* varies according to *motivation*$_{NS}$ (see above). One reason motivation drops sharply in LE/HT is because, in this state, dopamine decreases precipitously, and cortisol rises. Yet current interest in *motivation* centres on precisely how a child acts when in a low-dopamine/high-cortisol state. How to keep them going when the going gets tough (see chapter 9). This brings us to another critical function performed by the limbic system.

Limbic Brakes

The deeper we go into LE/HT, the stronger is the signal sent by the limbic system to cease our efforts; that is, the *limbic brakes* kick in.

This ancient mechanism was designed to prevent us from dipping into energy reserves unless we absolutely have to; these reserves are there for true emergencies. And schoolwork isn't one of those.

The limbic system has its own way of checking the operations of the Blue Brain, just as the Blue Brain can inhibit limbic operations with reappraisal. To be sure, we can *override* our limbic brakes: we can force ourselves to tap into the energy reserves stored in our fat cells if we push ourselves hard enough (hence the rise in cortisol). And so, we think that it is important for kids to learn this behaviour as early as possible if they are to achieve the sort of success that we desire (for them?). As we will see in chapter 6, we do this to kids all the time. Short-term we might get compliance; long-term we get avoidance, if not fight-or-flight.

The effect of overriding limbic brakes is comparable to driving a car when the engine has gone into the red zone. The occasional redlining doesn't harm a motor. But do this too much, or go well past the rev limiter, and this causes excessive wear and tear. The same is true if the limbic brakes are overridden too often, only in this case it is the parasympathetic system that is worn down.

Runners know that interval training is essential to improve their times, but if done too often, recovery is impaired and injury unavoidable. The stories shared these days of the serious mental and physical health problems seen in athletes, students, musicians, office workers, corporate executives, physicians, and educators is a sobering warning of the cost of overriding limbic brakes on a regular basis, relying on psychostimulants, steroids, opioids, cannabinoids, alcohol, nicotine, caffeine, junk food, or motivational posters to keep going.

The problem is that we can easily impair our recovery system without knowing it, especially when we have put ourselves into a trancelike state. We see this phenomenon in any activity that demands endless practice to excel (the "10,000-hour rule"). The repetitive actions induce an alpha/theta state similar to hypnosis, in which self-awareness is quelled and the limbic system is *primed for priming* by parent, peers, teacher, coach, boss, advertiser, or more malign influencers. The hardest part is generally getting started, but get past that and then the limbic system will keep you on task.

Back in the 1980s, Kenneth Cullen conducted a study on how long-distance running involves a form of auto-hypnosis brought on by rhythmic deep breathing and movement. Runners report that they are more creative during these trancelike states and blissfully unaware of what their body is doing. What is happening is that they are now driven by the physiological reward$_{NS}$ of the activity itself. [A. Eason, *Hypnosis for Running* (San Diego, CA: Awake Media Productions, 2013), 201. See also J. Ratey on the neurochemicals released, such as dopamine, BDNF, adrenaline: *Spark: The Revolutionary New Science of Exercise and the Brain* (New York: Little, Brown and Company, 2008)]

Do distance runners run for their health (*motivation*) or because it feels good (*motivation$_{NS}$*)? Yes. The problem is that the latter can overrule and undermine the former, for the limbic system will have a person running too hard or too long, just to keep the reward$_{NS}$ coming. The part of the time that one is in flow – "runner's high" – is wonderful. But good runners learn that they have to consciously intervene if they are going to benefit over the long term from a run; for example, by checking their heart rate monitor at various points to prevent going too deep into an anaerobic zone that affects sleep and recovery. In other words, self-regulation applies every bit as much to healthy as to unhealthy activities.

I speak here from personal experience, learnt the hard way.

We see the "overrunning phenomenon" in all kinds of *motivation$_{NS}$* behaviour. Rewarding yourself with chips or chocolate can be psychologically beneficial, but disengage your attention completely from what your limbic system is doing (as happens, for example, when you're watching TV, which has also been shown to induce an alpha/theta state) and, before you know it, you've eaten an entire family-size bag of chips or the whole box of chocolates. (It's interesting to set a timer that forces you to attend to what your limbic system has been up to while your attention has been elsewhere.)

To be sure, we could try to avoid potential confusion by refusing to allow scientists to resort to these sorts of technical homonyms, but they engage in this practice for a reason. As I said at the outset, we are looking to replace disjunctions with conjunctions. Motivation + motivation$_{NS}$. If you were hoping that this "reframing of *human nature*" might simplify matters, it is clearly time to disappoint that hope. If anything, behaviour becomes even more complicated.

True Grit

A disconcerting discussion appeared in the journal *Pediatrics* recently on the question of whether football should be banned from high schools in the US.[25] The debate centred on the alarming concussion rate – 60 per cent higher than the next highest sport, which is lacrosse – and how serious mild traumatic brain injury is for the teen's long-term mental and physical health. But most worrisome of all was that, despite their understanding of the gravity of the issue, droves of parents have continued to sign waivers for their sons to participate.

The question we are always asking in Self-Reg is Why, and it is especially important here. Why would anyone ignore the epidemic of Chronic Traumatic Encephalopathy in professional football players?[26] Maybe the answer can be found in all those television shows glamorizing high school football and the deep-seated conviction that football develops "grit."[27] No other character trait is quite so celebrated in US culture, and no other attribute do parents so long to cultivate in their children.[28]

But how could something so highly prized turn into something so potentially harmful? That is precisely the question that lies behind the problem of *akrasia*, not because there is some inherent danger in grit per se, but rather because of what grit can so easily turn into. In other words, we are back to drawing a fundamental conceptual distinction.

We are forever exploring such distinctions in Self-Reg: between self-control and self-regulation; misbehaviour and stress-behaviour;

oppositional defiance and Angstbeisser (just corner an angry and frightened dog and you'll know what it means); compliance and freeze; lying and confabulation; laziness and limbic braking; inattentive and "offline"; irrational and non-rational; impulsivity and heightened threat detection. And now, between *grit* and *compulsion*. In every case, reframing leads to a new way of seeing a child – or more importantly, ourselves – and as a result, is a powerful impetus to nurture rather than *desnutrir* a child (Spanish is richer than English in this, as in so many other regards).

Each of these aspect shifts is a consequence of the fundamental distinction between Blue and Red Brain. But when it comes to behaviour, things are rarely as straightforward as an either/or dichotomy. The danger here is thinking that, for example, *either* we have reasons for our actions (Blue Brain) *or* our behaviour is caused (Red Brain). The *reasons versus causes* distinction was the major issue in the philosophy of action when I was in graduate school. The problem is that the distinction seemed so much more straightforward in the classroom than it is in real life.

Certainly, in some cases it is easy to see which is which. But on countless occasions the apposite operator is *and*, not *or*. Occasions when both "brains" are influencing each other, and the pertinent question is which is the more dominant. Cases where it really is not at all clear where to draw the line between *nurturing and desnutrían*.

An All Too Relevant Example of "Abnormal" Behaviour

Compare the difference between "John clucked like a chicken to make everyone laugh" (Blue Brain) and "John clucked like a chicken because he'd been hypnotized to do so at the sound of a bell" (Red Brain). In the former, we can ask John all sorts of questions, beginning with "Why on earth are you clucking?" John can answer our questions, justify his action, and most important of all, stop himself if he wants.

In the hypnosis case, John clearly cannot be described as *choosing* how he acts. He does not know why he is clucking and cannot stop himself. John's limbic system has been entrained with a suggestion planted in him by the hypnotist: a prime that we find entertaining only because it is so absurd.[29] Yet at the same time we find such displays mildly disturbing. What is troubling is to see how easily a limbic system can be manipulated: possibly in beneficial, often in detrimental, and sometimes in insidious ways (see chapter 11).

Stage hypnosis is not, in fact, as bizarre a phenomenon as it might appear. It is only possible because we are constantly slipping into a theta state, such as when we daydream, meditate, begin nocturnal dreaming, are in flow, or lapse into autopilot.[30] It is fascinating how we have been able to tap into an ancient mechanism – designed for a lifetime spent walking, hunting, gathering, chewing, knapping – to cope with the daily commute. In this quasi-hypnotic state, the limbic system remains in control of our actions while the Blue Brain is free to roam – or do nothing at all.

Hypnosis is essentially a technique for inducing a theta state. During hypnosis, brain waves slow measurably (four to seven cycles/second), while the dlPFC and dACC are quiescent.[31] In other words, prefrontal systems that subserve our ability to *choose* how we act and be *aware* of what we are doing are suppressed. When one is in a theta state, the limbic system is *primed for priming*.

It is commonly said that only those who have heightened suggestibility are "hypnotizable": that is, those who do not resist having their self-awareness muted and limbic system hijacked. We will see in chapter 11 that there is a much more serious dimension involved to this hijacking of the Blue Brain. Indeed, it lies at the very heart of the threat to democracy that we must contend with today.

There are important lessons to be learned from the hypnosis example. The difference between mischievous John and hypnotized John is essentially that the latter needs to have his inhibitions lulled to act on his secret desire to clown around (similar to the effect of alcohol). The stage hypnotist capitalizes on this fact by recognizing and recruiting closet exhibitionists to serve as his volunteers.

Where things get confusing is that hypnotized John can still answer questions and, what's more, explain his actions. Asked why he is clucking, he can come up with a convincing answer. But although he apparently gives a reason for his action, his Blue Brain in this case is clearly consigned to the subservient role of confabulating. What's more, hypnotized John will struggle to continue clucking should we try to stop him; when it's in charge, the limbic system can be implacable in its demand to persist.

The case of hypnotized John is a potent reminder of just how difficult it can be to distinguish between rational and non-rational behaviour: to determine what best describes the behaviour we are observing. This is not just because confabulation is much more common than we may like to admit, but also because situations abound where self-awareness is lulled, the limbic system primed.

In these situations, we may see ourselves as acting for a reason. But it is really the limbic system that is dictating behaviour. We believe that we have freely – wholeheartedly – chosen our goal, when it is really a limbic prime that has been planted in our mind.

And in some situations, quite deliberately, we do this to ourselves.

The Willing Suspension of Rationality

"The mind," as Cicero put it, "is stronger than the body" – although he then went on to warn that "the ills contracted by the mind are more severe than those contracted by the body." Or at least, the mind – as Plato put it – can be trained to be stronger than the body. Famously, Plato referred to impulses and urges as "wild horses" that need to be restrained: the stronger the animal, the stronger the hands wielding the reins need to be. Parents have been searching for the self-control handgrips ever since.

As far as *grit* is concerned, the point is that the Blue Brain needs to ignore the Red Brain's pleas to quit. But when children are *forced* to override their limbic brakes, the Red Brain takes over and sends a message down to the Gray Brain to be ready to provide backup. Once the PECs are activated, the Blue Brain is cast in the subservient role of rationalizing and reinforcing. It is because of this neural shift that there can be such a high cost to mental and physical health.

The limbic brakes kick in when blood glucose drops below a set point. The only way to override limbic brakes is with a sudden spurt of energy. This is the reason why, in popular advertising, the exhausted athlete is shown instantly reviving with a glucose-laden drink. But sans drink in hand, the child's energy kick has to come from their reserves.

Parents certainly have a marked tendency to exhort or cheer their child on, and when that fails, to rely on fear or anger. (I've seen this more often than I care to remember at minor hockey league games; I've even succumbed to it myself.) The reason why these "parenting" behaviours are so effective is that RAGE or FEAR is activated, and, more often than not, both. Going into fight-or-flight provides the burst of energy (adrenaline) needed to override the limbic brakes, while at the same time muting the PFC systems that subserve inhibition and self-awareness.

Regularly tapping into a child's energy reserves can have a cascade of adverse effects. Restoration and cellular repair functions are compromised; digestion and the immune system are impacted; perception is altered; concentration and language are impaired; a negative emotional bias is induced; impulsivity and emotional lability are heightened; self-awareness is shuttered. But what is worst of all is when the child is conditioned to do this to themself.

We come back to the point that, in Red Brain, the limbic system is primed for priming. This is what is happening when a child is incessantly exhorted or pressured to go past their limits. A parent has to be careful that they are not doing this for their own needs (projection) or under the mistaken belief that they are building character. What they may really be doing is training their child to resort to fear or anger on their own to override their limbic brakes. Conditioning them to be the willing agent of suspending their rationality. In this way is a prized character trait like grit turned into something harmful.

To enter into a state in which we are harming ourselves, not just in some indefinable future (as in the case of smoking) but in the moment, demands a phenomenological shift. We are going into autopilot, consumed by the prime, oblivious of the costs. If you incessantly push a child to override their limbic brakes, you are sending them into a completely different mental space. You have shifted them from *perseverance* (a Blue Brain phenomenon) into the realm of *compulsion* (Red Brain).

Looked at through a Self-Reg lens, autobiographical accounts about the fruits of perseverance tell a very different story from what the self-control paradigm would suggest. What started out as grit has turned into out-and-out compulsion. Grit may be the secret to success, but compulsion comes with a heavy cost.

Límbico á límbico

In *Open: An Autobiography*, Andre Agassi presents an extraordinary account of how he recruited anger – against himself as much as his opponent – to become a tennis great, and the price he paid for this mentally, as well as physically. The story that he tells at the beginning of the book about his battle with Marcos Baghdatis in the semi-finals of the US Open is chilling.[32]

Agassi starts off describing himself as being in a dissociative state – he wakes up in a hotel room not knowing where he is, not even knowing who he is – and how this relates to the pain he is in: "After three decades of sprinting, stopping on a dime, jumping high and landing hard, my body no longer feels like my body … My mind doesn't feel like my mind."

As he stands in the shower, his self-awareness slowly returns, and with it comes a powerful emotion: *hope*. Hope that he might win another US Open: what a way to end his career. He begins to psych himself up, recalling the exhilaration of past wins and the devastation of losses. As becomes clear later in the book, he is replaying scripts drilled into him at an incredibly early age by his father.

He goes through rituals, part of which is his continuing reliance on the Interbrain. His trainer comes to fire him up: "When Gil says,

'It's on,' I feel my booster rockets for my adrenalin glands pump like geysers. I feel as if I can lift a car over my head."[33] A series of Interbrain partners in his career have performed this role of adrenaline cup bearers (his father; his coach, Nick Bollettieri; his brother Philip).

Then Agassi reveals something shocking: "I play tennis for a living, even though I hate tennis, hate it with a dark and sacred passion, and always have. As this last piece of identity falls into place, I slide to my knees and in a whisper I say: 'Please let this be over.'" This is his Blue Brain praying. But then he immediately thinks: "I'm not ready for it to be over."[34] This thought triggers a new emotion: hatred. And hatred – an intense combination of anger and hostility – is one of the most potent sources of energy that there is.

He is exhausted and suffering intensely from a congenital back problem. The image he presents is of an individual at war with his own body. He has been putting off retirement well past his due date and has relied on cortisone shots to keep himself going. The feeling of hatred he has summoned up is enough to override his limbic brakes so that he can go out and play the match.

He cruises through the first two sets, but Baghdatis begins to claw his way back in the third: "Suddenly, Baghdatis's despair has turned to hope. Or anger. He doesn't admire me anymore. He hates me, and I hate him, and now we're sneering and snarling and trying to wrest this thing from each other. The crowd feeds on our anger, shrieking, pounding their feet after every point."[35] What happens next is painful to read:

> We play a game that seems to last a week, one of the most taxing and unreal games of my career. We grunt like animals, hit like gladiators ... I've wrenched my spine. The spinal column is locked up and the nerves inside are keening ... I look across the net to see if Baghdatis has noticed my pain, but he's hobbling. Hobbling? He's cramping. He falls to the ground, grabbing his legs. He's in more pain than I ... I abandon all thought of subtlety and strategy. I say to myself, *Fundamentals*. When you play someone wounded, it's about instinct and reaction. This will no longer be tennis, but a raw test of wills.[36]

At this point Agassi is playing on full autopilot: the strokes, strategy, mantra, positioning – all a product of the endless hours spent in practice and games. Improbable as it seems, Agassi wins the match. And then: "I meet Baghdatis at the net, take his hand, which is trembling, and hurry off the court. I don't dare stop. Must keep moving. I stagger through the tunnel … my whole body is twisted. By the time I reach the locker room I'm unable to walk. I'm unable to stand. I'm sinking to the floor … I can't breathe."

This is a powerful example of how a primed Red Brain, with the support of the Gray Brain, will take charge and relentlessly pursue a reward, while the Blue Brain is consigned to the role of serving its commands, summoning up thoughts and emotions that will keep adrenaline flowing. The systems subserving self-awareness have shut down, his field of vision has narrowed to tracking what the "enemy" is doing.

It is not surprising that Agassi should describe this as a "test of wills." In reality, this wasn't so much *mano a mano* as *límbico a límbico*. It was Agassi's gruelling physical training, his previous experiences, and his psychological conditioning that enabled him to outlast Baghdatis. And the second the battle is over, and the adrenaline has stopped pumping, the Blue Brain comes back online and brings everything to a screeching halt. He suddenly reconnects with his body, and with this return to self-awareness comes agony.

The ending to this story is the most poignant part of all. Agassi and Baghdatis are lying side by side on tables in the trainer's room. The TV is on, replaying highlights from the match. "In my peripheral vision I detect a slight movement. I turn to see Baghdatis extending his hand. His face says, 'We did that.' I reach out, take his hand, and we remain this way, holding hands, as the TV flickers with scenes of our savage battle." Blue Brains restored, their Interbrain reconnects.

How do we describe Agassi's motivation? Certainly, he had a reason to push himself like this: to retire on a high, cement his place in the pantheon of tennis legends. And yet his actions seem not just irrational, given the harm he was doing to himself, but non-rational. He was not *ignoring* his pain but unable to register it. He was not *trying* to play out the match but *compelled* to do so.

He had stopped feeling and had stopped thinking about the consequences of his actions. This was not a hard choice that Agassi made in the heat of the moment, but the result of a prime that had been consistently reinforced over the span of a career – which started when he was in the crib! Not just self-awareness but also empathy completely shut down (and as we know from his subsequent actions, Agassi is a remarkably caring and generous human being). Coleridge talked about the willing suspension of disbelief; what we see here can best be described as the willing suspension of rationality: first by his father, and then, eventually, by Agassi himself.

The Power and the Perils of Limbic Priming

There is an unsettling similarity between what Agassi recounts and Larry Greenemeier's description of the assassination attempt on Gabby Giffords:

> The cognitive control capacities of the subject get somewhat redirected – we don't quite understand how – toward goals and activities that are violent in a very specific way. Not the violent outburst of somebody who has "lost it" in a bar, punching people right and left. The violence is channelled in a very specific plan, with a very specific target – generally fed by the media through some sort of rhetoric, political or otherwise – with very specific tools, in the Giffords case, a 9-millimeter Glock.[37]

Needless to say, there are socially acclaimed and socially abhorrent forms of limbic priming. But despite the fact that there is all the difference in the world between the kinds of goals with which limbic systems are primed, the result is that, if an individual goes full Red Brain, they can find themselves blindly following the urging of a prime. In which case, we have to be especially concerned about the deviant modes of limbic priming that have proliferated (e.g., on social media and major "news" outlets).

Far too much emphasis is placed on extrinsic rewards and far too little on intrinsic. That is, on experiencing what Maslow, before Csíkszentmihály, described as "moments of highest happiness and fulfilment."[38] Moments of *flow*. You don't strive for flow in order to obtain a prize. Flow is its own reward.

Where grit is exhausting, flow is energizing. The former is dogged, the latter, creative. The former leaves you in LE/HT, shattered and disillusioned; the latter in LE/LT, calm and inspired. The concept of *flow* is tied to the concepts of *absorption, euphoria,* and most important of all, *effortlessness* (one of the effects of theta waves). What flow is not tied to, however, is *success*.

Both *grit* and *flow* involve a loss of any sense of space and time; both are tied to detachment. But the former is detachment from distress, the latter, detachment from the ego. The motivation in flow comes not from the lure of status or prestige, but from the joy of the flow experience itself.

The lesson to be learned from an autobiography like *Surely You're Joking, Mr. Feynman* is very different from that of *Open*. Far from being irreverent, Feynman's title captures the essence of how he viewed physics and the attitude he sought to cultivate in his students.[39] Feynman's legacy is a testament to the achievements afforded by flow, but public recognition was never Feynman's goal. Whatever honours he garnered for his work, these paled in significance next to the pleasure he experienced in playing with ideas.

I think back to the teachers who inspired me the most and, without exception, they were just the same: motivating us by their own joy in what we were studying. I once went to see Northrop Frye about a problem I was struggling with, and with a twinkle in his eyes he said to me: "What you have to remember is that, at the end of the day, what they are saying is total bullshit!" What he was really telling me is that our work, no matter how serious it might be, should also be fun.

Children may indeed need to learn how to persevere, but it is so that they can experience flow in whatever sparks their interest and imagination. Agassi seems to have been in flow those first two sets. But then, as his energy dwindled and Bagdhatis had a surge of adrenaline brought on by anger, a momentum swing occurred, not just in the match but in Agassi's mind, from rationality to non-rationality. Not just his actions, but even his perception changed (he talks about how small the service box became). Consumed by an overpowering urge to be victorious, he was driven mercilessly to keep going by his limbic prime. And what he was left with, besides yet another "win," was not just physical and mental suffering, but extraordinary hostility to the one thing that was supposed to bring him satisfaction and fulfilment.

Of all things, Agassi's autobiography reminded me of the poem that Michelangelo wrote about painting the Sistine Chapel. He describes his work as "torture," his spine "knotted from folding over itself." But more punishing than the physical torture of painting a ceiling is the mental anguish: "My thoughts / are crazy, perfidious tripe." He ends the poem with the bold, and to our eyes unbelievable, statement "I am not in the right place – I am not a painter."

Painting was the Renaissance version of the ATP tour (Association of Tennis Professionals). Michelangelo excelled at it (although he himself didn't think so) and rose to the top of the rankings. And he hated painting with a passion.

It's hard not to compare this second stanza with what Agassi says about his spine.[40] Hard not to be struck by the bitterness each felt towards what had made them famous. And hard not to absorb from all this the importance of distinguishing between *what we want for children* and *what we are prepared to inflict on them* – or worse still, what we seek to train children to inflict on themselves.

Reframing *human nature* isn't just about how we see children; it is about how we nurture them so that they too can experience flow in their lives, whether it is doing philosophy, building cabinets, or, in the case of my own children, fixing cars and large machines. The starting point is to recognize the role we play – for better or for worse – in how a child's nature develops. This begins at the moment that is so evocatively referred to in Spanish as *alumbramiento*.

In more than one sense, reframing *human nature* is about seeing what the light affords. Which is what the power of metaphors is all about.

Chapter 3

Reframing Development

A New Way of Seeing

I look at *development* as someone trained in analytic philosophy at the height of its heyday. The pivotal event for the field occurred in 1953, when Wittgenstein's *Philosophical Investigations* was published. My work on the later Wittgenstein has shaped my approach to the topics covered in this book, beginning with how I read *The Triune Brain*. Were it not for Wittgenstein, I might have read MacLean's argument as an accretive model of neurodevelopment. Instead, I see it as presenting a new way of thinking about the impact of ancient survival mechanisms on human functioning.

For me personally, to be a Wittgensteinian means I reframe. My thinking about *reframing* was inspired by what Wittgenstein says about *aspect shifts*. See a philosophical question differently, he argues, and you arrive at a whole new type of answer.

Wittgenstein told Con Drury that he was thinking of using a quotation from *King Lear* – "I'll teach you differences" – as the motto for *Philosophical Investigations*. This line captures the essence of Wittgenstein's approach: the careful distinctions that he draws between, for example, *science* and *philosophy*; *grammatical* and *empirical* propositions; *first-person* and *third-person* psychological utterances;

> *reasons* and *causes*. The philosopher, as my supervisor
> Peter Hacker liked to put it, is like a labourer in the gar-
> den of metaphysics, pruning the tangled roots of concep-
> tual confusion. But the philosopher is also, I would add,
> someone who wants to see the garden flourish.

We could easily use the same quotation from *King Lear* as a motto for Self-Reg. I remarked in the preceding chapter how, in Self-Reg, we are forever concerned with important conceptual differences. Only in this case, what's at stake isn't metaphysical confusion; it's the well-being of children, youth, and young adults. For that matter, our own well-being and that of our society. I would not go so far as to say that the future is at stake; but I would say that the nature of that future is at stake.

Reframing Behaviour

What looks like misbehaviour when viewed through a Blue Brain lens jumps out at you as stress-behaviour when seen as Red Brain. But reframing is not an exercise in philosophical optometry: the result of changing from the blue-tinted glasses of self-control to the rose-tinted glasses of self-regulation. The perceptual shift operating here involves a fundamental re-categorization.[1]

This idea goes all the way back to Plato: namely, that we see the world through concepts that are acquired – implicitly – when we learn how to speak.[2] We *see* what our parents have guided us to see. They see what their culture has imbued.

Each of these ways of seeing is embedded in a network of concepts.[3] When we reframe, we are consciously shifting from one concept map to another.[4] The essence of reframing involves learning our way around the new terrain. For example, *misbehaviour* is internally related to the cluster of concepts that apply to purposeful actions, such as *intention, choice, justification,* and *responsibility.* It is because of these conceptual links that we respond to what is perceived as misbehaviour by chastising or punishing; or by paying attention to the expert counselling us to let our babies cry themselves to sleep.

Stress-behaviour belongs to the category of non-purposeful behaviour caused by subcortical processes. A baby doesn't *choose* to cry and obviously can't *decide* to stop. *Stress-behaviour* is tied to *arousal, tension, neuropeptides, activated PECs*. Our automatic reaction to stress-behaviour – at least until the child gets a bit older and parental mindblindness sets in – is to soothe.

When we reframe, we are not simply looking at the same thing through a different lens. The phenomenon *that we see* is a function of how we see it. But whereas for philosophy reframing is an intellectual exercise (what Kuhn referred to as "theory-ladenness"), for Self-Reg it involves an experiential shift every bit as powerful as the cognitive. It isn't just what we *see* that is so different, but also, and essential to this, what we *feel*.

These two aspects of reframing, the experiential and the cognitive, are bound up with each other. The more we can tease apart the conceptual links of a new framework, the more attuned we become to what our child is undergoing. Our automatic reactions undergo a radical readjustment. One of the things that changes most are the questions that we start to ask. For reframing not only involves a new way of looking at old and familiar biases but raises entirely new questions and leads us in directions that were not, and indeed could not have been, discerned in the old framework.

Reframing Determinism

Reframing sparks creative new ways of thinking about children, teens, and ourselves; about the concepts and theories that underpin psychology; about the manner in which experiments are designed and interpreted. In some cases, reframing operates like a "closure impossibility proof" in mathematics:[5] i.e., it closes off one line of thinking – e.g., Cartesian discontinuity theories – while opening up a completely new one, namely, continuity. This is why Gödel's theorem was so important for mathematicians and why reframing is so important for psychologists. The one led us to see the unlimited possibilities of the human mind,[6] the other, the unlimited possibilities of child development.

It was this anti-determinist *Weltanschauung* that drew me to Self-Reg in the first place: the idea that nothing is fixed in stone. Not even Excalibur. What's needed to free a mind that seems locked in place is not magic but science – together, of course, with nurturing Interbrains. And yet, the trend when I was in grad school was the opposite; biology, psychology, and linguistics were all dominated by thinkers who looked to science to validate rather than abrogate determinist thinking.

The determinist view of development goes all the way back to the classical doctrine that we are born with a set temperament: *sanguine* (brave, cheerful), *melancholic* (serious, despondent), *choleric* (quick-tempered, ambitious), or *phlegmatic* (subdued, thoughtful). The audience at a Greek drama knew the ending of a play from the moment that they saw the actors' masks, which, as I'll describe below, symbolized which of the four characters they possessed.

The most influential determinist way of thinking was the Hippocratic doctrine of the four humours: four elemental types of bodily fluid.[7] There are vestiges in this doctrine of the ancient view of the four elements of astrology (fire, air, earth, and water), which were paired with four qualities (hot, dry, cold, moist). There are four seasons, four cardinal points, four winds, four phases of the moon, and of course, the four-leaf clover (whose leaves represent hope, faith, love, and luck). What made Hippocrates' thinking so revolutionary is that he introduced an empirical dimension, likely by observing the four different layers of sedimentation that form when blood is left sitting in a glass container.

The physicians who followed in Hippocrates' footsteps were close observers of the human condition, and their scrutiny (which involved dissection) told them that illness, whether mental or physical (a distinction that Plato was the first to draw), results from *humoral imbalance* (what today we might see as an imbalance in the microbiome).[8] Walter Cannon may have been the one who coined the term *homeostasis*, but the idea is classical. It was central to the Aristotelian view of medicine and ethics: the idea that illness of any sort – physical, mental, or moral – is the result of a humoral imbalance.

The challenge for Hippocratic doctors was how to restore homeostasis when it is temperament that is the root of the problem. For example, if someone is born with too much black bile, they are at a heightened risk of melancholia. To treat depression, you had to resort to bloodletting, emetics, diuretics, diet, medicines, an exercise and relaxation regimen, soothing music, and incantations, all meant to counteract the effects of temperament by promoting humoral balance.

Today we might turn to SSRIs, probiotics, and a meditation app, and our explanation of the imbalance draws on the concept of gene methylation or poor attachment. But the determinist way of thinking remains present. Even the emphasis we place on the interaction between biological and environmental factors harks back to the Greek view that different climates have a profound effect on innate temperament.

For as long as I can remember, I've struggled with determinist thinking. Not, I hasten to add, because I harboured Behaviourist dreams of turning any child into a doctor, lawyer, artist, or merchant-chief. My thinking went in the opposite direction: namely, that any child can be made unhappy, anxious, susceptible to chronic health problems and unhealthy lifestyle behaviours. To be sure, scientists have firmly established that adverse life experiences can alter a child's stress-reactivity, which in turn can have a dramatic impact on the child's development.[9] But the better we understand the causes of a child's stress-behaviours, the better we can respond and help that child develop healthy modes of self-regulation.

Herein lies a key reason why Self-Reg is so effective, not just in helping the child or teen, but in lowering our own stress level. Not understanding a child's behaviour is incredibly stressful. Why does my baby refuse to eat or seem unable to settle? Why is my toddler so aggressive or withdrawn? Why is it so hard for my child to have friends or pay attention? Why is my teen having so much trouble at school or at home? And we don't just have these anxious feelings towards our own kids or students. It is highly distressing to read about how Indigenous teens compose only 8 per cent of the youth population yet account for 46 per cent of correctional admissions. Or how hard it is to close the achievement gap for black students.

Determinism appears to provide an answer, but in truth it is a form of avoidance. It takes the blame off our shoulders – and parents are always quick to put it there in the first place. But more than that, determinism provides a sort of quietus. You can't change the behaviour because it's caused by factors outside your control. Determinism reconciles us to the irreconcilable; it gives us permission to stop trying.

In other words, determinism is a mode of self-regulating: and a highly maladaptive one at that. It stops us from asking Why. It blinds us to our own role in the trajectories that get set and that, once set, strike us as having been predetermined. Like all maladaptive modes of self-regulation, it provides temporary relief but adds greatly to the stress down the road. It creates a problem for which self-control is the only apparent solution.

Self-Control Follows in Determinism's Wake

There is a compelling reason why the concept of *temperament* needs to be reframed: a reason that dates back to the ancient Greeks. Plato insisted that medicine needs "to proceed beyond Hippocrates." He was not questioning humoral theory when he said this; on the contrary, he formally subscribed to Hippocratic doctrine. What he meant is made clear in the *Laches*, which was the most influential of all Plato's writings in the Middle Ages.

In this Dialogue, Socrates speaks to the young Charmides, who has come to him seeking help for treating a headache:

> One should not attempt to cure the body apart from the *psuchē* [mind, soul]. And this is the very reason why most diseases are beyond the Greek doctors, that they do not pay attention to the whole as they ought to do, since if the whole is not in good condition, it is impossible that the part should be. The *psuchē* is the source both of bodily health and bodily disease for the whole man, and these flow from the *psuchē*. (Char 156de)

In addition to physic, the individual needs the philosopher's *epôdai*, which "consist of beautiful words. It is a result of such words that *sōphrosunē* [moderation or temperance] arises in the *psuchē*, and when the *psuchē* acquires and possesses *sōphrosunē*, it is easy to provide health" (Char 157a). In other words, any treatment to restore humoral balance has to incorporate the form of psychotherapy practised by philosophers. And yes, the origin of psychotherapy dates back to the ancient Greeks, as Pedro Laín Entralgo explained.[10] The goal of philosophy wasn't just to educate but to actually heal the mind.

You might be tempted, reading this, to see Plato as the first Self-Regger. But the reason Plato felt it was so critical to study philosophy was *to acquire the mental discipline needed to control the impulses resulting from a constitutional imbalance.* As far as well-being is concerned, there are "good" temperaments, in which humours are balanced, and "bad" ones, in which one or more of the disruptive humours predominates. It is far easier for someone born with a good temperament to control their impulses simply because they are fewer and less severe.

According to Plato, everyone will benefit from studying philosophy, but especially those born with a bad temperament. They need to acquire the "strength" to control their unruly inner nature. Their impulses cannot be changed – they are determined, after all, by humours – so instead they must be tamed.

The problem, Plato thought, is that reason alone is not enough to win these battles. He refers to a "war" that is waged between reason and bodily appetites. On its own, reason is doomed to fail. Reason understands *why* it is important to control impulses, but it is up to a third faculty, *thumos*, to see that reason's dictates are carried out. *Thumos* is "spiritedness," and unlike temperament, a child's *thumos* is not fixed at birth. It is shaped by experience and can be strengthened or weakened depending on how the child is raised.

How *thumos* is strengthened needs to be tailored to the child's biological temperament. Plato distinguished between the effects of too much flute music on a child born with an anemic *thumos* and the effects of flute music on one born with too much *thumos*.

The former "will become weak and dissolute," the latter will end up "quick-tempered, prone to anger and filled with discontent, rather than spirited." We're still having this particular debate today, albeit in terms of the effects of rap.

This idea that *thumos* needs to be strengthened ultimately inspired the early Christian attitude towards *willpower*.[11] According to the allegory of the Fall, Adam and Eve enjoyed perfect humoral balance in the Garden of Eden. But as a result of original sin, human impulses were strengthened, reason weakened. The only way for fallen mankind to resist impulses was by fortifying willpower, and this process has to start early with the young child.[12]

This mindset leads to the view that, because of the temperament with which they are born, some children are destined to suffer unless their parents intervene firmly and consistently. Even when they are babies – especially when they are babies – they have to have strict limits imposed and mustn't be overindulged. Parents are still being told that they must be careful not to spoil an infant, that if they resist the urge to give in when their baby is crying, even the most difficult of babies is capable of acquiring self-control.

But far from fostering resilience, the lack of nurturing breeds maladaptive self-regulation. As far as Self-Reg is concerned, the critical issue here is not simply what happens to the child's arousal if the Interbrain is removed from the picture. It is what happens to the concept of *self-control* if determinism should be removed from the picture.

Reframing Temperament

Every movement needs a motto, and for Self-Reg it is: *There is no such thing as a bad kid.* I don't think I've ever met anyone who challenged this tenet. But the one question that does regularly come up is: Aren't there some children who are at a much higher risk of *becoming a bad kid*? Children who are a handful from the moment they pop out of the womb: fearful or irritable, hard to soothe or regulate? Children born with a temperament that even the most attentive of parents finds challenging?[13]

The idea that the temperament a child is born with sets them on the path in life that they end up following willy-nilly – that is, regardless of what their parents might want or will – has been with us forever. And that just might be the problem. We are so used to thinking of temperament in determinist terms that we jump straight to the question of how to mould it. But Self-Reg is forever asking Why, beginning with: "Why do we still think about temperament in the same way as the ancient Greeks?" Pavlov, Steiner, and Kagan were all still grappling with humoral theory – in humoral terms! And any one of today's comic-book movies is little more than what in the Renaissance were known as "humoral dramas," dressed up with CGI.

This very persistence is a big reason why *temperament* needs to be reframed. To paraphrase what Wittgenstein once remarked about the source of metaphysical problems, if we are asking the same questions as the ancient Greeks, and are obsessed with the same problems, we need to look at the language that lies behind this fixation.[14] But *reframing* is not at all the same thing as *refuting*. The challenge is not to deny or dismiss all the research that supports a determinist view of temperament but rather to look at these findings in a new light.

As always, it is exciting to see what comes into view when we remove a cognitive blinder. But this particular cognitive blinder is a little different from your average conceptual bias. The big reason humoral theory persisted so long was because of the questions that it raised, not the answers that it provided. In fact, it was because the proffered remedies remained so ineffectual that the questions remained so captivating. Why do some newborns pop out of the womb eager to engage while others are nascent Greta Garbos who just want to be left alone? Why does temperament so strongly influence the development of personality and well-being?

One reason the determinist view continues to influence research interests is because we can classify temperament at a very early age, using one of the infant scales. What's more, certain behaviours cluster together, and we can make surprisingly good predictions about children's emotional, social, and prosocial development based on these groupings. Then there's the fact that we see similar temperaments in identical twins regardless of their upbringing. Or that we see the same temperament in families over extended generations.

Self-Reg asks whether we need to reframe *temperament*, not in spite of but precisely because of these factors! We have to remember that when we classify an infant's behaviour, that is all we are doing. We are not explaining why we see a disposition. We have to be careful about how we interpret correlations. An infant who scores high on certain temperament traits is likely to have more trouble on a delay of gratification task.[15] That is simply what the data tells us. What we cannot say is that the reason they have more trouble with the task is *because* of those traits. What the data really tells us is that we need to look for a deeper explanation, for both sides of this equation.

That is where the Self-Reg reframing of *temperament* comes in. The questions that Self-Reg raises are: Why can we identify a child's "temperament" in early infancy? Why can we make long-range prediction based on our reading of a child's temperament? Why is it so difficult to change this temperament?

The big problem with determinist thinking is that it closes the door on such questions. If a child is born irritable and fussy, parents must adapt to these problems as best they can. If a child turns out oppositional or aggressive, it's because the parents failed to deal effectively with their "difficult" baby. But Self-Reg worries just as much about describing a baby as "difficult" as about describing a child as "oppositional."

A baby's heightened reactivity needs to be reframed every bit as much as what is mistakenly labelled as misbehaviour in a child or teen. What "difficult" really refers to is the stress that *we* experience when trying to soothe a baby who is hard to soothe. We once had a parent ask us if his baby, who was suffering from colic, was going to grow up to have poor self-control. What his question really told us was just how stressful he found his daughter's colic.

We need to look at a baby's behaviour through the lens of secondary altriciality, that is, see how the "foetus outside the womb" is dealing with the onslaught of powerful stressors, internal and external. The baby's reactions show how a still-embryonic nervous system is dealing with this assault and, in some cases, what sort of stresses the baby had to deal with inside the womb. And then something important happens, we see a pattern start to develop.

The origins of this pattern may, in fact, have started well before the moment of parturition, as the womb is not stress-free: it is a stress-reduced environment. For some foetuses, the stress (e.g., drugs or tobacco, alcohol, pollution) is too high and impinges on the wiring of the baby's stress-reactivity system. The newborn who is highly reactive to stress may have been reacting to stress for quite a long time already. But our own stress is so high at the moment of birth that we may fail to register just what a shock being born is to such a delicate nervous system.

When I lecture on this point, I show a video made by Sonia Rochel of twins hugging each other in a "Thalasso Bain" (a basin filled with warm water in which the babies are supported).[16] The bath is supposed to replicate what it was like inside the womb for the "embryo outside the womb." The video shows twins nestling into each other's arms, at total peace as the warm water washes gently over their heads. But it's what Rochel says that I find even more arresting. She makes the point that we seriously underestimate how much tension a baby can be under. The bath helps the baby's muscles slacken, but first Rochel has to help the parents relax. She is working on the Interbrain, helping parents to be calm so that they can "hear" what their baby is "telling" them.

In other words, babies need to feel safe and secure in order for their tension to dissipate, and the same is true for parents. All of them will sleep better at night. The baby cannot be spoiled by being soothed when they're crying, and parents can never be remiss by soothing them when they're crying.

The newborn who is able to withstand the sensory assault – such as temperature; sounds; odours; tactile, visual, and social stimuli; afferent signals from internal organs – settles into rhythmic cycles (eating, sleeping, digesting, eliminating, thermoregulating), which further enhances her capacity to deal with, and indeed thrive on, new stresses. But the overloaded baby must work hard to stay organized: these babies demonstrate poor rhythmicity. These are babies that, as Porges showed, have lower vagal tone.[17]

Porges's theory isn't just a physiological breakthrough; it challenges the very foundations of the determinist view of *temperament*.

Vagal Tone and Temperament

The vagus nerve serves a number of parasympathetic functions: e.g., digestion, vasodilation, constriction of blood vessels, and, most important for the purpose of reframing *temperament*, heart rate variability. Where sympathetic nerve fibres increase heart rate to provide the blood glucose needed to deal with stress, parasympathetic fibres slow heart rate to promote recovery, cellular repair, and growth. But the more stress a child is under, the narrower the range between maximum and resting heart rate. The parasympathetic reflex is said to lose some of its elasticity, as reflected in reduced heart rate variability (low vagal tone).

We might compare what is happening here to the durability of a spring, a measure of how well the spring snaps back to its previous shape after having been subjected to a stress. If a spring is repeatedly subjected to too great a load, it loses its tensile strength over time. Similarly, if the parasympathetic reflex has been overused because the stress load has been too great, heart rate remains somewhat elevated, similar to what happens to a long-distance runner who has been overtraining.

Low vagal tone is a valuable tool for identifying when a baby has too high a stress load. Porges has developed a sophisticated statistical procedure for measuring vagal tone.[18] But parents have a much simpler tool to tell them when their baby's vagal tone is low: a "difficult" temperament. The strain on an overloaded parasympathetic reflex shows up in the baby's irritability or slow adaptability.

What Porges found is that the higher the baby's vagal tone, the healthier the baby, with better growth and rhythmicity. Babies with high vagal tone require less soothing, orient more, laugh and smile more, look longer at novel visual stimuli, demonstrate more approach behaviours, and are better at self-soothing. Babies with low vagal tone have problems with their motor control, expression of emotion, approach and withdrawal, communication, and sustained attention. The latter are more prone to problems in digestion, sleep, and social interaction. And these patterns become entrenched remarkably quickly, not because they are determined but rather *because they are constrained*.

Porges's argument amounts to much more than just another correlation; in this case, the theory is explanatory. An *attractor* forms, that is, an entrenched stress-response pattern. The limbic system is forming "expectations" and adopting defensive behaviours. A baby isn't avoidant because of an innate aversion to novel stimuli: they react in that way because the limbic system "anticipates" that an experience will be aversive. Certain experiences are overly stressful because of a complex mix of biological and environmental factors.[19]

From a Self-Reg perspective, what matters is how temperament shows us when a baby is overstressed. What we see here is *embodied stress awareness*, governed by the limbic system. The fourth step of Self-Reg is "developing stress awareness": becoming aware of when we find something overly stressful. But long before we develop this sort of mindfulness, we are aware subliminally that a stimulus is overly stressful. This limbic awareness is what is referred to as *neuroception*: an awareness that sets in incredibly early, long before we become consciously aware that we are overstressed.[20]

Neuroception

We saw in the previous chapter how neuroception is about much more than threat detection. Or rather, that our understanding of *threat* needs to be broadened; i.e., neuroception refers to our awareness of *internal* as well as *external threats*. Now we need to consider in what sense neuroception is about threat *detection* or threat *awareness*.

Detection and *awareness* are both terms of perception. Yet a brain – let alone a part of the brain – doesn't perceive things (e.g., safety and danger). Only persons have sense organs with which they can look or listen, detect a rustle in the bushes or a smile on someone's face. What the limbic system does have are self-regulating mechanisms that are tied to ancient survival systems.

Arturo was a seven-month-old baby who would begin to howl the moment he saw his grandmother approaching. Nona told Stanley: "Something must be wrong with this boy because all my other grandchildren adore me." But Arturo had sensory sensitivities unlike the other grandkids. Visual, tactile, and I suspect, olfactory. On their very first encounter, Nona had smothered Arturo in kisses. But while Nona was exhilarated, Arturo went into fight-or-flight.

The problem is that the tension involved in fight-or-flight uses an enormous amount of energy, so nature designed us with a simple mechanism to prevent its over-use: nociceptors are also activated. Arturo would howl when he saw her approaching because his limbic system was "anticipating" aversive sensations. Here was a case where reframing was the key to the incredibly warm relationship that soon developed: distinguishing between *rejection* and *stress-behaviour.*

The first thing to consider in the above example is Arturo's age. He wasn't saying to himself, "Oh-oh, here comes that old lady who scared me." Nor was his limbic system "thinking" this. His actions were reflexive. And what we want to know is, what was causing this reaction?

The answer lay deep in his midbrain: in the activation of FEAR + PAIN. This reaction can be triggered by *evolutionary memories*: e.g., the way the smell of a cat causes rats to flee to a dark corner of the cage. The sound of a branch breaking. Or the sudden lack of sound as the birds go silent. The sight of something slithering on the ground. Or something red in the branches.

There are direct pathways, bi-directional pathways, from the Periaqueductal Gray to structures in the limbic system. "Neuroception" refers to the operation of these pathways; e.g., in the case of fear, from FEAR in the midbrain to the amygdala. We are not *aware* of danger per se, but of the sensations triggered by FEAR. Or, in the case of safety, of the sensations triggered by CARE in PAG to the hypothalamus and the Bed Nucleus of the Stria Terminalis (BNST).

It is not just evolutionary memories that activate these neurons, but also acquired associations. In Arturo's case, the stress over-load he had experienced on their first encounter was so aversive that the mere sight of Nona was enough to trigger a defensive reaction (scrunching up the eyes). And, interestingly, an ancient communicative reflex summoning caregiver protection (PANIC/GRIEF).

Avoidance/approach behaviours triggered by the various PECS show up as temperament. Infants with hypersensitivities avoid stimuli associated with aversive sensations. Those with hyposensitivities approach stimuli associated with pleasant sensations. Withdrawal is a sign not of a child who is innately antisocial but of a limbic system that "expects" an interaction to be aversive. Approach is the result of a limbic system that "expects" the pleasant sensations of a novel stimulus.

The wiring of neuroception is an important factor in the centrifugal and centripetal forces constraining an attractor. These forces are not simply genetic. Recall how the basic principle of secondary altriciality is that the fundamental unit of development is the dyad, not the isolated infant. What a case like that of Arturo shows is that just as important as the reasons why the baby is reactive is how the caregiver responds to these signs of heightened stress-reactivity: for example, whether the caregiver is calm or anxious, stays present or flees (emotionally, if not physically), tailors their responses to the baby's sensory profile or is overly intrusive, feels resourceful or helpless, is patient and questioning or flustered and bewildered.

A baby's behavioural pattern is one of those gauges that I talked about in *Calm, Alert, and Learning* and *Self-Reg*, showing us not just how much stress the baby is contending with but, equally, how much stress the dyad is under, how well the dyad responds to and recovers from moments of intense shared stress. This is what all the work that Beatrice Beebe has done over the years is telling us:

that dyadic patterns form early and one of the results is the development of what we describe as the baby's "temperament."[21]

In other words, whereas on the determinist outlook temperament is an internal property of a solitary organism, on that of the Triune Brain/Interbrain model temperament *is relational*. How a caregiver responds to a baby's stress-behaviours is critical in the formation of an attractor. So much is involved in being a sensitive caregiver and adjusting parenting style to suit the baby's developing "temperament."[22] We need to recognize the signs of when a baby is overstressed, identify the stressors and figure out how to mitigate them, discover what a chronically distressed baby finds soothing, and how to stay calm ourselves. In other words, we need to do Self-Reg.

The very persistence of the Greek determinist view of temperament reflects how hard it is to dislodge an attractor – in this case, a bias. Porous biological thresholds tend to stay that way, as do interactive patterns. But it is important to reframe the concept of *temperament* because, in so doing, we transform it from *descriptor* into *heuristic*. Classifying a baby's temperament is a bit like a treasure map with "X marks that spot," telling us to "dig here." That is what happens when we reframe *temperament*: incredible self-regulation riches are waiting to be unearthed after we remove the determinist blinders that send us careening into the arms of the ancient Greek view of self-control.

Attachment Theory[23]

As far as the study of child development is concerned, one of the major events in its recent history was the publication in 1951 of John Bowlby's report for the WHO, *Maternal Care and Mental Health*. To understand why Bowlby had such a profound impact on the field, we first have to recognize John Watson's influence in the first part of the twentieth century.

In 1928, Watson published what instantly became the most popular child-rearing book of its time, *Psychological Care of Infant and Child*. Watson insisted that "a happy child" is one who never cries unless actually stuck by a pin – who loses himself in work and play – who quickly learns to overcome the small difficulties in his environment without running to mother, father, nurse or other adult – who soon builds up a wealth of habits that tides him over dark and rainy days – who puts on such habits of politeness and neatness and cleanliness that adults are willing to be around him at least part of the day.[24]

That last line tells us everything about Watson's attitude towards children – and is no doubt one reason his parenting manual was so popular![25] But only one.

Watson's argument is classic Victorian self-control: don't mollycoddle a child if you want them to grow up strong and independent. If you must kiss your child, only do so once a year – say, on their birthday. Otherwise, "a good handshake is more than sufficient." How, one wonders, could such a chilling message have been so influential?

There were several factors involved. One was that this attitude was already prevalent. Another factor was the astronomically high infant mortality rate (nearing 100 per cent in institutions where children were put up for adoption).[26] A third factor was that Watson claimed that "science" showed that, if forced, children will develop the internal resources (viz., resilience) needed to deal with any adversity.[27] And the last factor was that, like determinism, Watson's method lifted the guilt from the shoulders of parents struggling with the burden of parenting or economic hardship.

Bowlby challenged and changed all this, despite – or because of – the fact that he was raised in just the sort of harsh, Victorian manner that Watson was defending.[28] He argued instead for the primacy of attachment. But contrary to the psychoanalytic thinking of the time, which saw breastfeeding as the root of attachment,[29] Bowlby insisted that the *primum mobile* of human evolution is "survival of the safest." Infant and mother have interlocking feedback mechanisms that serve as the substrate of attachment.

The dynamic is straightforward: baby gets scared, mommy comes running. The presence and proximity of mother tells the baby that they are safe. Attachment as such – that is, an emotional bond – grows out of this primal connection. The baby can then start to form a mental model of their world. Attachment thus serves not only to provide security but as a crucible for the child to learn about how people think and act.

This argument amounted to such a new way of thinking about child rearing because it asked an entirely new question. Not: How do you train a child to be compliant? Instead: How do you nurture curiosity in a child? Bowlby's answer: A baby will only explore if they feel safe. Harlow sought to show the same. Mary Ainsworth, who worked with Bowlby at the Tavistock Clinic in the early 1950s, developed the Strange Situation to expand on and test this idea.

The biggest complaint about Ainsworth's paradigm is that, at best, it gives us a narrow look at the relationship between baby and mother. Its big virtue, however circumscribed it might be, is that the protocol is replicable. The intention was to examine children's behaviour just after the *preattachment* phase, when the infant is starting to display stranger anxiety. Ainsworth's interest was in the point at which the primary caregiver has become a secure base: someone that a baby turns to when anxious, which typically occurs around eight to ten months.

The protocol consists of eight steps,[30] designed to see how the baby reacts when they see their primary caregiver in the final reunion. Ainsworth reported three primary types of attachment: secure, where baby is happy to see caregiver and wants to be held. Anxious/ambivalent, where baby is hesitant about coming to caregiver. And anxious/avoidant, where baby looks angry and avoids caregiver. Mary Mains then added a fourth D-type attachment style, in which baby goes into fight, flight, or freeze; has a meltdown; or becomes totally disorganized.

In Self-Reg terms, the baby who feels safe quickly restores Blue Brain/Red Brain balance. They return to exploring either because they have not exhausted their energy reserves during the experiment or because they have replenished the energy expended. Anxious/ambivalent and anxious/avoidant babies stay Red Brain, either because their limbic alarm has not been turned off or because they are having trouble restoring energy. D-type babies are dysregulated.

Robust and *Fragile* Secure Attachment

One of the most fascinating aspects of the Strange Situation is that it shows how early a child's acquired modes of self-regulation start to matter. A securely attached baby returns to (SEEKS) their caregiver to mitigate their stress. In an ambivalent baby, there are glimmers of this mode of self-regulation, but overridden when the child is overly stressed. The avoidant baby adopts a maladaptive mode of self-regulation, relying on catecholamines – especially epinephrine – to keep themselves safe. The D-type baby is in cacostasis.

Ainsworth came to a similar conclusion. She described the Strange Situation as a stress test and noted the signs of heightened stress in insecurely attached infants (e.g., how their shoulders would stay hunched). The test reveals how a child responds to a significant stress, but it can't tell us just how great that stress is for a particular child. Nor does it reveal anything about the child's Thayer state at the start of the study.

Not surprisingly, scientists found that attachment correlates strongly with vagal tone. Securely attached infants have high vagal tone; insecurely attached infants have low vagal tone.[31] In other words, the Strange Situation provides an insight into how much stress a child *has been under* and not just how much stress they *are under* during the encounter.

The standard interpretation of the test is that it provides an insight into how the child views their caregiver when threatened, based on how reliable a resource the caregiver has been in the past. It is important to bear in mind that secure attachment occurs roughly 50 to 60 per cent of the time. The point isn't that securely attached children are impervious to the stress of the encounter, but rather that they trust – i.e., that their limbic system "expects" – that the caregiver will return.

Ainsworth concluded that the source of this feeling of security is *sensitive caregiving*: that is, the caregiver is able to read and relieve the baby's distress. For the psychoanalytically minded, the securely attached child acquires an object representation of their mother that they resort to when alone and stressed. For the neurobiologically minded, the idea is that secure attachment leads to an HPA pathway that is primed to recover from stress. On all of these readings, the logic of the argument is reminiscent of Watson's view that it is a caregiver's behaviour that renders a child resilient.

In other words, in both the behaviourist and the standard attachment approach, there is a risk that we end up with what Kagan referred to as "infant determinism":[32] the idea that a child's experiences in the early years determine the contours of their development. But we observed an important phenomenon at MEHRI, which leads to the conclusion that we should be talking of *sensitive Interbraining* as opposed to *sensitive caregiving*. This distinction is important because *sensitive Interbraining is an ongoing phenomenon*.

All the children who came to MEHRI were highly challenging. In fact, this was very much the criterion for being admitted into the MEHRI treatment program. The therapists had to help the parents identify hidden stressors that they were not aware of *as stressors*, and then develop better strategies for keeping their child in homeostatic balance. The problem here is that something as easily overlooked as the scent of a soap can be dysregulating for a child with a heightened olfactory sensitivity. (Anyone who is intensely bothered by the scent of cigarette smoke will know exactly what this feels like.)

All our parents worked very hard at figuring out their child's sensory issues and tailoring their interactions accordingly. They all learned the signs of when a meltdown was imminent and how to avert this; or how to restore a state of calm once a meltdown had occurred. Their child was indeed securely attached, despite all the biological challenges. But here is the crucial point: some had been securely attached *before* they came to MEHRI. It was only when the child entered day care, preschool, or primary school that things fell apart and the child became insecurely attached, not because the parenting had changed but because the child had gone into allostatic overload.

What we learned from this phenomenon is that there are two species of secure attachment: *robust* and *fragile*. The child with robust secure attachment can withstand a sharp increase in stress load, such as a stranger entering a room where the child is quietly playing. A child with fragile secure attachment can stay organized only because their parent knows which stresses to reduce or avoid and can read the signs of mounting stress. Pretty much every one of the children that we saw at MEHRI had fragile secure attachment. For their parents to be told, even if nonconsciously, that their child's problems at school were due to a lack of sensitive caregiving was one of the greatest injustices that could be done to them, not to mention yet another huge stress imposed on already overstressed parents.

In many cases, the children's problems only became serious *after* they had transitioned out of the home to a new environment that increased their stress load significantly. Or when they were placed under the care of adults who lacked the parents' intimate knowledge of the child's hypersensitivities. Or when the caregivers had too many charges to give the child the kind of attention they had received at home. Or in the worst-case scenario, when the caregivers were adults who subscribed to Watson's way of thinking; that is, adults who thought that, *for their own good*, such children had to acquire self-control. These were the cases in which the child's limbic system registered no empathy because none was present.

A major challenge for all children is that they are exposed to a range of stressors in what are known as the *transition years* that go well beyond what they have previously experienced. It is why internalizing and externalizing problems escalate in kindergarten or Grades 1, 7, or 9, in the first year of university, or, for that matter, in retirement. Children for whom home was a refuge suddenly find themselves in an environment that feels anything but safe, an environment in which their alarms are constantly going off. But what was most disturbing was to see adults respond to the child's stress-behaviours as if they were misbehaviours.

These misperceptions are the result of the biases I mentioned at the outset, which lead people to see a child as *choosing* not to exercise self-control. Far from helping the child stay organized, they were having the opposite effect, sending the child into a full Red Brain state in which *choosing* is no longer viable and fight-or-flight is just a short step away.

The Interbrain operates throughout the lifespan. The narrow view of the Interbrain as being confined to the mother-infant Dyad was built into attachment theory from the start. Bowlby may have challenged the psychoanalytic view of the mechanism that binds infant to mother, but not the primacy that psychoanalysts assigned to the mother-infant relationship. The crux of the Interbrain thesis is that it is about limbic-to-limbic connections in general, not just mother-child or father-child, but relative-child, friend-child, teacher-child, coach-child, child-child, adult-adult, or, as in the case of Arturo, senior-baby.

We saw in the preceding sections just how significant the Interbrain is in the development of temperament. In the last section we will see how it has equally important implications for the crucial role that Interbrain(s) play in the development of personality.

Reframing Personality

In the climactic scene in the BBC adaptation of *Martin Chuzzlewit*, Pecksniff (played by Tom Wilkinson) has just been exposed by Martin Sr. (played by Paul Scofield) and lies cowering on the ground. But despite the most damning condemnation imaginable, Pecksniff's countenance does not change one iota, and his parting words remain as sanctimonious and hypocritical as ever. How disappointed we would be had it turned out otherwise: if Pecksniff, like Scrooge in *A Christmas Carol*, had demonstrated genuine contrition in this denouement. The whole force of Dickens's moralistic intention lies in Pecksniff staying true to his character and receiving his just deserts.

This way of thinking about *personality* has been with us for an awfully long time. Pecksniff's persisting look of innocence dates back to Theophrastus, Aristotle's successor at the Peripatetic school. In the most influential of his 227 books, *On Moral Characters*, Theophrastus describes the different masks (*prosopeion*) that represent different personalities. This symbolic use of masks was the custom that led to the famous remark, attributed to Cicero, that "the face is a picture of the mind." The masks that the actors wore in ancient Greek drama served as a visual display of their character. It was precisely because the mask does not come off – the "character" hidden beneath the mask remains constant – that a satisfying moral story could unfold.

This leitmotif was repeated over and over, through Plautus's comedies, the medieval morality plays, Shakespeare and Jonson, the Commedia dell'arte, nineteenth-century novels, and right up to the stock characters that populate modern sitcoms and super-hero films. And it keeps being repeated in modern-day research on personality. Here, it's not just the questions we keep asking but also the way that we think that has stayed the same since the ancient Greeks. But then, as we saw in the opening section, the two are intimately connected.

The research tells us that, beginning around the age of eight to ten years, a distinctive pattern emerges in how a child thinks, feels, and acts. It is at this age, we might say, that the child "dons the mask" that they are likely to wear for the rest of her life. These patterns are thought to persist over time in the same way as the ridge patterns on someone's fingertips, and hence have come to be known as "behavioural fingerprints."[33] But there is one big difference. In the case of a dactylogram, the lines and whorls uniquely identify an individual, and how we describe the pattern is irrelevant. But in the case of a "behavioural fingerprint," *how we describe the pattern* is what determines how we identify the individual.

Of all the predictions that can be made from a personality test, per-haps the most striking is that we can predict, from a ten-year-old's personality score, what their score will be when they are twenty. And indeed, at the end of their life. If a child is classified as intro-verted at the age of ten, odds are they'll be classified the same way at eighty. Given that this is what we expect, it isn't surprising that psychologists should find corroborating evidence.

But, as always, it is imperative that we clarify the nature of the correlation. In this case, the prediction is that we will use the same terms to describe an adult as were used when they were ten years old. The correlation here is as much linguistic as behavioural. That is, it is not just the behaviour that doesn't change but also the way we describe that behaviour.

What is surprising is how nuanced that vocabulary can be. No one was more surprised than Gordon Allport himself when, in 1936, he came up with eighteen thousand words for personality traits. Through factor analysis, psychologists whittled this down to the "Big Five": extraversion, agreeableness, neuroticism, openness, and conscientiousness.[34] The immediate reaction to this hypothesis was disbelief, yet study after study found that these five broad categories do indeed encompass all eighteen thousand of the terms in Allport's catalogue.

And there matters stood until Ashton and colleagues asked a very simple question: What if we were to use a non-Indo-European dictionary?[35] They found that, if the factor analysis is based on Turkish, you need six categories.[36] This finding unleashed all kinds of studies looking at different non-Indo-European dictionaries. We now have two Big Sixes, a Big Two, a Big Three, a Four, even a One.

All this is the result of looking not just at different dictionaries but at what Michael Agar referred to as different *languacultures*.[37] That is what a dictionary is, a catalogue of how a given culture carves up the world, how it categorizes *behaviour*. Although it may seem that the terms that personality theorists use are purely descriptive, the truth is that they are all what Geertz referred to as "thick concepts": they carry subtle overtones of a society's Weltanschauung.[38] We can trace the attitudes still lurking behind the words we use in their etymology.

The terms that Allport first came up with do not just stem from Indo-European (IE) but from a specific branch of IE: the Hellenic languages. Generally speaking, a direct line runs from a term in Allport's corpus to an ancient Greek root. Wittgenstein's point turns out to have even greater import than we might have thought. Ancient Greek attitudes have been transmitted to us through the very language that we speak, words that determine that we see and respond to a child in much the same way as did the Greeks.

Take *conscientiousness*. Its original meaning in the seventeenth century was "controlled by conscience, governed by the known rules of right and wrong." This meaning of the term derived from the Middle French *conscientieux*, which in turn derived from the Latin *conscientia*, which meant "sense of right, moral sense." And that, in turn, derived from the ancient Stoic concept of *syneidos*, meaning much the same.[39]

Look at the concepts grouped under *conscientiousness* in the Big Five: for example, careful, thorough, deliberate, self-disciplined, reliable, industrious, persistent, self-motivated. Each carries a faint echo of the original sense of "moral awareness and shame." What they all have in common is that they are based on intentionality and the exercise of self-control. The Big Five encapsulate the self-controllist paradigm, and self-control contains a hint of ancient Greek values.

The pattern that emerges by the age of ten is the product of a languaculture that shapes how a child is seen. In those first ten years of life, we unconsciously wire the child's "personality" into their limbic system. The limbic system absorbs the normative messages that we unconsciously send. The terms that we use to describe the child's behaviour are covert judgments, and like all judgments, they mark the end of asking Why.

Suppose that a ten-year-old child shies away from group activities and that their parents would like to change this behaviour. As soon as they tell themselves that their child is introverted, they have introduced a note of fatalism that stops them from asking Why. They are like the doctor in *The Imaginary Invalid* explaining why opium induces sleep (the "dormative principle"). The child is reclusive *because* of being introverted. End of story. This is how behavioural fingerprints get shaped and maintained: by the *mind-blind Interbraining* evoked by determinism.

The point of reframing *personality* is not to deny the existence of behavioural patterns that persist over time but rather to ask Why they are there. But to answer this question in a non-tautologous manner requires that we learn a new language. Not a cognate language, but one with a different ancestor. And that is precisely what the Triune metaphor provides: a non-Hellenic, non-value-laden way of talking about behaviour and asking the new questions that the languaculture of Blue Brain, Red Brain, Gray Brain affords.

What if the ten-year-old *self-regulates* by avoiding group activities? What if their behaviour is not intentional, not due to an inherited trait, and certainly not the result of poor self-control? What if it is rather a response to stress, in some circumstances adaptive, in others maladaptive? Such questions lead not just to a deeper level of understanding but to a new range of possibilities for enhancing that child's development.

In other words, Self-Reg asks questions that were never, and that could not have been, asked in the Greek languaculture that we inherited – a languaculture in which there was no concept of *stress-behaviour*, only *misbehaviour*. It is time for us to see just what other sorts of questions we can begin to ask once we free ourselves of latent Greek biases. How would freedom from these biases change our view of children and teens and of ourselves? How would it inform our understanding of human nature?

Chapter 4

The Age of Reason(s)

Descartes's Act of Apostasy

In 1975, I went to Oxford to read for a BA in philosophy, politics, and economics. My very first tutorial question was: "What were Descartes's reasons for doubting? Were they good reasons?" I was hooked immediately.

Does the Cogito – "I think therefore I am" – assume the very thing that Descartes had set out to prove: namely, that there is an "I" (as Pierre Gassendi was the first to object, in 1646)? How did he know that "thinking" was going on, let alone what *thinking* is? Is the Cogito a tautology? (What does "I am" signify, if not that "I am thinking"?) Had Descartes committed himself to solipsism? (How can I ever be sure that someone else is a thinking being and not just a cleverly designed automaton?)

Like all who had gone down these paths before me, I found this heady stuff. I dug deeply into the discussions of Descartes's attack on sense data, his question of how he could be certain that he wasn't dreaming, that he wasn't under the control of a deceiving demon (or AI, as in *The Matrix*), his cosmological proof for the existence of God. I was diligent about these assignments, and my tutor seemed satisfied enough with what I'd done. (Although it was hard to tell, as he sat throughout the sessions with his handkerchief over his face while I read my papers.) But one day I summoned up my courage and asked the question that had been bothering me all term.

At the beginning of the *Discourse*, Descartes reports that, some years back, he had been struck by "the large number of falsehoods that he had accepted as true in his childhood, and by the highly doubtful nature of the whole edifice that he had based on them." He returns to this theme repeatedly, telling us how he wanted to free himself from the "false opinions"[1] he had accepted unquestioningly. What I wanted to know from my tutor was: What were these "falsehoods" that Descartes was referring to? What "false opinions" had he blindly accepted?

The most obvious answer is that he was alluding to medieval Scholasticism (the attempt to reconcile Christian theology with Aristotelianism and Neoplatonism). In this respect, Descartes was among the first to engage in the great "Ancients versus Moderns" debate. But the issue was far more serious than we might gather from *A Tale of a Tub*, the amusing satire that Swift wrote at the beginning of the next century.[2] It was serious enough that it led Descartes to hold back the publication of *Le Monde*.

Consider what happened to the meeting planned by leading Erudite Sceptics in 1624 to show how modern scientific discoveries refute Aristotelian doctrine. The event was cancelled by the Paris Parlement, which issued a decree outlawing – under penalty of death – teaching any view contrary to the ancient-approved authors, and holding any public debates other than those approved by the Doctors of the Theology Faculty.[3] The sad fate of Bruno, Vanini, and, of course, Galileo tells us just how serious the issue was in Descartes's time.

Descartes makes it clear, however, that he was not simply thinking of Scholasticism. He also refers to the different customs and conventions he had observed during his travels. Tired of the cloistered world of the scholar, he had gone out to learn from the "great book of the world," only to realize, by observing how irrational some of the practices he witnessed appeared, how much of his own behaviour must appear equally irrational.

And finally, he seems to be making a veiled allusion to something from his past. Perhaps, as Cook explores in *The Young Descartes*, he was thinking back to his life in Paris as a young man. He was described at the time as "coiffed in curls, wearing crescent-pointed shoes, his hands covered with well-lined snow-white gloves," and with a valet always in tow. I found this last category of "*mensonge*" particularly intriguing.[4]

I didn't get an answer to my question from my tutor. Instead, I got a question in response to my question: "Why do you think it matters?" I had just been formally welcomed into the world of philosophy.

I couldn't shake the conviction that it does matter. For one thing, it is all too easy to divorce the argument from the man, simply because so little is known about the man.[5] Why was Descartes so constantly on the move? Why did he use a dropbox to receive his mail? Why would such a devoted Catholic spend the latter part of his life in a Protestant country?

It was in terms of the philosophical argument where I felt that the question mattered most. I worried about seeing the Cogito as little more than a logical conundrum, akin to asking: "Why is a raven like a writing desk?"[6] The whole way that Descartes sets up the argument suggests a far more serious intent than merely coming up with a brainteaser, or, worse still, a way to exhibit his cleverness.

Descartes doesn't say, "Finding myself with a few hours to spare, I thought it might be amusing to try doubting everything I could and see how far I got." Rather, he describes how he had "an intense desire to learn to distinguish the true from the false, in order to understand my own actions."[7] This is why he wanted a "method" to be certain when something he believed was a truth, and more than that, *to understand his own beliefs*!

To be sure, Descartes lived in an age where virtually all of the great thinkers were searching for some *grand method* (just think of Newton). But Descartes wasn't searching for a way to turn lead into gold (although he too was interested in discovering the key to longevity). He tells us repeatedly that the impetus for the "method" he had developed was moral.

It was his need to discover "what he truly believed" that led him to articulate what, for the times in which he was living, could easily have been construed as an act of apostasy:[8]

> Our will tends to pursue (or avoid) only what our intellect represents as good (or bad), so all we need in order to *act* well is to *judge* well; and

judging as well as we can is all we need to act as well as we can – that is to say, to acquire all the virtues and in general all the other attainable goods. With this certainty, one cannot fail to be happy.[9]

The first line reads as a direct response to Plato, if not established theological doctrine. Not only was Descartes challenging Plato's argument for the need to strengthen *thumos*, but even more profane, the orthodox dogma espoused by the Church Fathers. Descartes was insisting that it was not a *lack of faith* that was the cause of his being a petit-maître; or a *failure of will* that led him to suffer a serious depression at the age of eighteen.[10] His breakdown, if such it was, was due to a *failure of reason*.

In political terms, "will" was taken to mean unquestioning obeisance to the Word of God, as expounded by theological leaders.[11] Everything that Descartes was saying about "reason versus will" could be seen – and was seen by leading theologians – as a rejection of their authority.

Grayling makes the point how the 1620s "constituted a crucial moment in the process of the modern world's tearing itself away from the old world." It was during that decade that "one saw the last major effort of the old world to repress the new; and in it some of the most significant founding ideas of the new world – among the very foremost of them those of Descartes himself – were forged and first expressed."[12]

Descartes's role in all this went beyond defending the Copernican world view. His act of apostasy amounts to a remarkably bold reframing of the concept of *rationality*. Descartes's "method" is about more than just challenging theological authority in matters scientific; it is about challenging theological authority in matters moral as well.

Here is the reason why I felt it was so important to understand what the "falsehoods" were that Descartes was repudiating. Not because of any wish to become embroiled in the subtleties of Descartes scholarship, but because I feared that we might have missed the import of what he was saying about *rationality*. He was not simply talking about the "false beliefs" he harboured as a youth. He was asking: *How can we protect ourselves from false beliefs?* From the conviction that such-and-such *must* be the case, when subsequent experience proves that it was not?

To be *rational* is not to submit to God's Will, as formulated in Scripture and then interpreted by Church authorities. *To be rational is to employ*, assiduously, the *gift* that God has given each of us. The essence of this gift is *to question*, not to follow blindly.

Herein lies what I believe is the real upshot of the Cogito: *to be rational is not* to act *for a reason. To be rational is* to use *one's reason.* Whatever that means.

The "Method"

Descartes's claim that "our will tends to pursue (or avoid) only what our intellect represents as good (or bad)"[13] needs to be carefully unpacked. In contrast to the orthodox view of God's Will as *reason's pilot*, Descartes is stating that an individual's will can only follow where their own reason leads. He tells us that his earlier actions were motivated by "false" beliefs: *false in exactly the same way* that the belief that the Sun revolves around the Earth is false. He had trusted in his teachers – in the widest sense of the term – and not in his faculty of reason.

This leads Descartes to articulate his famous argument that we know that something is a truth when it is self-evident and hence cannot be doubted, as hard as we might try. By appealing to *self-evidence*, he was merely echoing what Aristotle had said about the laws of thought that "are common to all sciences."[14] Descartes can hardly be faulted for stumbling over a problem that has eluded some of the greatest philosophical minds of all time. According to Kant, the laws of thought are synthetic a priori truths; Poincaré insisted they are analytic a priori; Russell held that they are high-level synthetic a posteriori; and Wittgenstein showed that these thinkers were all wrong: that they are disguised rules of logical grammar.[15]

Descartes's own approach is a form of psychological realism. He argues that the "attentive mind" recognizes basic truths as such because of a sort of "pop-out" effect: that is, truths stand out from falsehoods in the mind's eye because they are "clear and distinct."[16] This argument has become intimately bound up with the standard take on *rationalism*: the idea that we *know*, directly and indubitably, what our beliefs are. But before we find Descartes guilty of "naive rationalism"[17] – that is, of putting too much faith in the powers of introspection – we need to consider the overriding emphasis that he places on his *method*.

The fact that we may have direct access to the contents of our minds (*Principles* 1.11) does not mean we can be certain that what we think is going on there is veridical. The problem is that judgments are always subject to error, including beliefs about our own beliefs. That is the whole point of Descartes's "reasons for doubting." When it comes to knowing the contents of our own mind, we are every bit as subject to *cognitive* as to visual illusions. We may feel certain that we know why we believed something, but we can be *mistaken* about our "reasons" *in exactly the same way* that we can be mistaken about the movements of the solar system.

Descartes's *method* is meant to guard against this inherent fallibility. The *method* applies every bit as much to discovering the secrets of our own mind as to discovering the secrets of nature. Indeed, the two issues are fused in his thinking: "I couldn't have limited my desires, or been happy, if I hadn't been following a path that I thought was sure to lead me to all the knowledge of which I was capable, and in this way to lead me to all the true goods that were within my power."[18]

The *method* is necessary not because reason is unreliable, *but because we fail to exercise it*. That is the real culprit here. This is what the "reasons for doubting" are all about: an attempt to demonstrate that we mustn't ever simply assume that we know why we think or behave in the ways that we think or behave. Whatever the beliefs were that had driven him as a young man, Descartes had embraced them willingly. Nowhere does he suggest that he was guilty of lust, gluttony, greed, wrath, envy, or even pride. The deadly sin that he was guilty of was *sloth*: mental sloth. The failure to use his gift of reason.

Reason is not to be confused with *intelligence*. Reason will indeed, as Aristotle argued, lead us to virtue; the same cannot be said for intelligence. ("Sheer quality of intellect doesn't make the difference between good and bad: the greatest souls are capable of the greatest vices as well as the greatest virtues.")[19] Descartes even tells us that he has "often had a sense of being less well-endowed than others: I have wished to be as quick-witted as some others, or to match their sharpness and clarity of imagination, or to have a memory that is as capacious (or as promptly serviceable) as theirs is."[20] The *Discourse* is about *the power of the method, not the power of the intellect.*

The *method* is a form of systematic doubt until we arrive at a feeling of certainty (which we now attribute to the "power" of statistical analysis). It is disappointing that Descartes should have concluded that the discovery of truth – psychological or empirical – rests on a subjective experience. Yet in his defence, one might argue that it is not the *feeling of certainty* that he was focused on but rather the relentless questioning that is required to get to that point.

Psychological insight may not come easily, but it can be experienced by all. He tells us that, despite his intellectual limitations, his *method* has enabled him to increase his "knowledge gradually, raising it a little at a time to the highest point allowed by the averageness of my mind and the brevity of my life." This point applies as much to penetrating the mysteries of one's own mind as to penetrating nature's mysteries.[21] Slowly and methodically, we can recognize that our judgment has been "influenced." And therein lies the key to Descartes's view of *rationality*.

We come back to the reframed view of *human nature* presented in chapter 2:

The human being is a rational, an irrational, and on some (many? most?) occasions, a non-rational animal.

The irrational part is clear enough: viz., you are acting illogically or unreasonably (i.e., against reason).

But what about *non-rational*? Here is a case where you don't *use* your faculty of reason but could have done so. This is fundamentally different from, e.g., LeDoux's view of nonconscious processes. *Non-rational convictions* are such that you could have asked why you believe something but failed to do so. Where you have "unshakeable certainty" in what you profess.

Reason, according to Descartes, is a property of the mind bestowed on us by God: the ability to ask Why. Rationality is the activity that is made possible by that gift. Rationality resides in the awareness that our judgment may be influenced by misguided assumptions, ignorance, bias, passions, or deceiving demons – human and not just evil spirits. Rationality lies in recognizing the possibility that our beliefs might be mistaken, and for that reason, adopting the prophylactic of rigorous self-questioning. The reason why we need to be sceptical about our own beliefs is because we are so easily misled, either by authorities or by our own senses.

Descartes is not attacking the possibility of rationality, but rather reframing the concept. You cannot define rationality as *acting for a reason* if those very reasons can be "mistaken." I may be convinced that I know why I am φ-ing (where "φ" is a variable to any action). But rationality warns me that I may have been influenced by some factor of which I am unaware. The crux of his reframing is that *I can become aware of these influences* by applying his *method of doubt*. That, according to Descartes, is what it means *to be rational*: to be constantly questioning. Rationality is an activity, not an endowment.

Descartes's reframing of *rationality* was and is enormously important, but there are two major problems with it. One is of great concern for philosophers: namely, his view of introspection as a form of (inner) perception. The other is of great concern for Self-Reg: namely, his view of non-rationality as due to *a failure of the will*.

His *method* is very much a self-control approach: it is effort and discipline that lead to self-knowledge, not a calm and reflective mind.

Laying an Epistemological Confusion to Rest

Descartes's *method* amounts to forcing ourselves to keep asking Why until we reach the bedrock of certainty. But then, that leaves us in a precarious position: How can we ever be certain that we have reached bottom? Maybe what we think is "clear and distinct" only appears that way to our bewitched mind? (It is amazing how often someone inebriated thinks they have discovered some amazing truth, only to sober up the next morning.) One big reason why the Cogito stirred up so much philosophical controversy is that, having breathed life into the spectre of scepticism, Descartes was unable to lay it once again to rest.

Wittgenstein acted as both coroner and undertaker on this issue. He identified the source of the problem in how Descartes construed "I *am certain* that I believe *p*." Descartes saw this statement as having the same epistemological status as "I am certain that it is raining outside": something that I can verify or falsify by looking inside my mind, just as I can be certain about the weather by looking out the window. I apply the *method* to arrive at a point where I can be certain that what I *see* is "that I believe *p*." When I reach this point, I can no more doubt that I believe *p* than I can doubt that it's raining when I go outside and get drenched.

Wittgenstein identified the source of Descartes's false bottom in logico-grammatical confusion. Third-person psychological statements are descriptions, which, like any empirical statement, can be true or false. But first-person psychological utterances are avowals that *exclude the possibility of doubt*. The statement "I'm not sure whether or not I believe *p*" is categorially different from a statement like "I'm not sure if it's raining outside." The latter can be verified, but the former is used to do things like register a lack of confidence in the evidence for *p*: not as a confession of myopic introspection.

The reason why avowals *can be neither true nor false* has nothing to do with the way the mind works; rather, it is the way language works. It is because of their unique logico-grammatical status that first-person psychological utterances can have implicatures, that is, can be used to convey conventionally understood messages.

For example, I might say "I think I believe *p*" to convey that I am reluctant to commit myself. Likewise, if I state that "I *know* that I believe *p*," I am not *reporting* the results of introspection but conveying the strength of my conviction, e.g., telling someone that nothing that they say or do is going to shake my conviction. To be sure, there are countless circumstances where it makes sense to ask someone "Are you sure that you believe *p*?" A psychoanalyst might ask this in order to prod someone to be more introspective. But that is not at all like the optometrist asking you to cover one eye and read the bottom line.

"A man with conviction is a hard man to change"

Descartes's intention was to distinguish between *rational conviction*, which is arrived at by the method of doubt; *irrational conviction*, such as the delusions of those who are mad; and *non-rational conviction*, which is due not to faulty reason but, rather, to the failure to use one's faculty of reason.

The sovereign signs of rationality are listening; probing; agonizing; looking for complexity or confounds; being hesitant; reflecting; learning from experience; being able to change our mind when there are good reasons to do so; indeed, being able to recognize when there are good reasons to consider a change of mind; asking why we have the beliefs that we do rather than repeating them more loudly.

The big difference between irrational and non-rational conviction is that, in the case of the former, reason is *excluded*, whereas in the latter, reason is *eschewed*. For whatever psychological or physical reason, the irrational individual, on Descartes's reading, *cannot* engage in any of the above rational acts. But the non-rational individual, according to Descartes, *chooses* not to do so.

There are many reasons why someone might succumb to non-rational conviction. They might be driven by fear; an inflated ego; a strongly conditioned sense of duty; a lack of independence; groupthink; sheer ignorance. Perhaps blind conviction is a way of quelling uncertainty. Perhaps they have been bewitched by the beguiling words of a false prophet. Or perhaps they are simply lazy.

What matters most as far as our ongoing *privileging of rationality* (chapter 2) is concerned is Descartes's insistence that non-rational conviction is as much an *act of will* as rational conviction. According to Descartes, *freedom of will* "consists in our ability to do or not do something." The proof that non-rational conviction is *voluntary* lies in the intransigence of those who *refuse* to listen to reason. (Does this not sound familiar?)

Accordingly, we must be careful to ascertain whether, when someone "gives a reason" for their action, we are hearing the voice of *reason* or *will*. That is, what makes an act rational is not that someone says why they did or believed such-and-such. The mere act of *justifying* an action or belief does not render that action or belief rational.

Justification may have more to do with rationalizing than being rational. Appealing to authority, custom, a higher order, and, of course, "good sense" (which, according to Descartes, has to be "the best shared-out thing in the world; for everyone thinks he has such a good supply of it that he doesn't want more")[22] are all signs of *will ruling over reason*.

If ever there was a case of a classical philosophical argument that bears on the problems that haunt us today, it is this conception of *wilfully blind conviction*. Four centuries later, Festinger, Riecken, and Schacter were still making the same point as Descartes. They begin their classic *When Prophecy Fails* in words that resonate far more strongly today than was the case in 1957:

> A man with a conviction is a hard man to change. Tell him you disagree and he turns away. Show him facts or figures and he questions your sources. Appeal to logic and he fails to see your point. We have all experienced the futility of trying to change a strong conviction, especially if the convinced person has some investment in his belief. We are familiar with the variety of ingenious defenses with which people protect their convictions, managing to keep them unscathed through the most devastating attacks.[23]

When will overrides reason,

> resourcefulness goes beyond simply protecting a belief. Suppose an individual believes something with his whole heart; suppose further that he has a commitment to this belief, that he has taken irrevocable actions because of it; finally, suppose that he is presented with evidence, unequivocal and undeniable evidence, that his belief is wrong: what

will happen? The individual will frequently emerge, not only unsha-ken, but even more convinced of the truth of his beliefs than ever before. Indeed, he may even show a new fervor about convincing and conver-ting other people to his view.[24]

We still think in these terms. Indeed, Festinger's research on cognitive dissonance was informed by, and made a significant contribution to, Descartes's argument. We are still seeking, vainly, to overcome *non-rational conviction* by appealing to reason. Still throwing up our hands in despair.

The Great Neo-Cartesian

The honour alluded to in the title of this section goes to Daniel Kahneman. In many ways his work exemplifies Descartes's *method*, namely, that we – with the aid of scientists – can become aware of how we're being influenced. His research goes much deeper than anything Descartes ever contemplated. But in the end, the argu-ment returns us to the idea that it is a *failure of will* that leads to the *failure of reason*.

Over the years, Kahneman and Tversky showed how we strug-gle with problems that would seem relatively easy to solve. We jump to conclusions when we should pause and deliberate. Our thinking is easily primed, that is, guided to go where someone wants us to go. And more often than we like to admit, our reasons are nothing more than excuses.[25] But most important of all is that we constantly seek to expend the least mental effort possible and hope for the best.

The crux of Kahneman's theory is that the human mind is gov-erned by two primary "modes of thinking": *System 1*, which is fast and automatic, and *System 2*, which is slow and methodical. System 1 relies on heuristics – inherited or acquired – to make its decisions, even though these are demonstrably far from reliable. System 2 has to compensate for System 1's recklessness. And that requires effort.

Figure 4.1 Müller-Lyer illusion

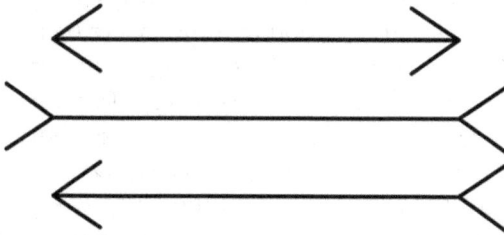

One of the "main characteristics" of System 1 is said to be its "laziness, a reluctance to invest more effort than is strictly necessary."[26] Hence the role of System 2 is said to be to "suppress or modify" System 1's "judgments." But ruling over System 1 is a demanding job, and we are all subject to fits of "mental laziness" in this regard.

Take a classic example like the ball-and-bat problem:

> If a baseball and bat cost $1.10 together, and the bat costs $1 more than the ball, how much does the ball cost?

System 1 jumps at the answer of 10¢. It's up to System 2 to rein in this impulse and think hard about the problem (and come up with the correct answer of 5¢). The fact that it's presented as a brainteaser is all the information needed to motivate careful thought, and those who answer 10¢ are said to be ardent followers of the law of least effort: "They find cognitive effort at least mildly unpleasant and avoid it as much as possible."[27]

The "ball-and-bat" problem is an example of a cognitive illusion. A whole branch of modern psychology is devoted to the study of this phenomenon, in much the same way that visual illusions are studied by psychologists of perception.[28] Take, for example, the famous Müller-Lyer illusion (Figure 4.1).

The point here is that it is a function of the way our visual system works that we see the lines as having different lengths.

It requires some careful checking to ascertain that in fact they are the same, and if someone declines to do this, it must either be because they hadn't understood that they were being prompted to do so ("Are these lines the same length?") or were simply too lazy to act on this cue. The same argument is applied to biases in the human information-processing system: for example, shortcuts that we apply unconsciously when we make decisions.

The pressing question here is not whether we resort to heuristics – although the question of *why* we resort to heuristics is important – but rather, whether "laziness" is the appropriate term to describe what's going on. If I am sick and can barely sit up, much less get out of bed, I am not being lazy: I am sick. There is a profound difference between *laziness* and *illness*. The latter *cancels out* the value judgments that apply to the former, not because of the way *the mind works*, but because of the way that *logical grammar* works.

There is a cluster of normative concepts connected to the concept of *laziness*: for example, *indolence, lack of motivation, negligence, carelessness*. All carry an undertone of vice. Sloth, after all, is one of the seven deadly sins. But these concepts do not apply to someone who is sick, because they all presuppose the capacity to act or choose differently, which is precisely what is absent when a person is ill. That's why someone with Epstein-Barr is not described as suffering from chronic indolence.

The law struggles with this point when it comes to assigning guilt. Here too, illness obviates responsibility precisely because the *capacity to govern one's actions* is judged to be reduced. In cases of non-criminal responsibility, the court rules that the individual was not fully capable of controlling their actions, not because of ego depletion but because of mental *illness*.

The point here is that the concept of *laziness* presupposes the *possibility of effort*. According to Kahneman, there are vital problem-solving or thinking tasks that only System 2 can perform because they require an act of self-control in which the intuitions and impulses of System 1 are overcome.[29] But what if there are instances of System 1 operations that clearly have nothing to do with effort or self-control?

That is not to say that there is no such thing as "mental laziness"! We all suffer from this failing; all wish it were never the case. But the attribution of laziness – mental or otherwise – must always involve the *possibility* of trying harder – for logical, not physiological, reasons. Yet the question of when or to what extent someone is actually capable of *trying harder* can be complicated, for neurophysiological and not logical reasons.

Lazy or Limbic?

To address this question of whether we are dealing with laziness or something very different, we have to get System 2 (if there is a "System 2") to look carefully at the distinction between System 1 and System 2 (which provides an ironic twist on the notion of mental laziness). There is something intuitively appealing about the idea that we need to constantly battle the lure of "cognitive ease." We can all think of occasions when we impulsively jumped to a conclusion, maybe to our subsequent regret. And few can read about "reasoning biases" without thinking of occasions where these apply to themselves.

But is *lack of effort* always the right concept to bring into this matter? The list of phenomena that Kahneman groups together as System 1 operations is significant: for example, not just biases and assumptions but also reflexes, instincts, associations, and automatized behaviours. What they have in common is, loosely speaking, that they are all caused and not actions done for a reason. Yet there is a categorial difference between, e.g., reflexes and associations, between subcortical processes studied by neurophysiologists and "mindless" behaviours where we are guided by biases and assumptions.[30]

Take one of Kahneman's more powerful examples: we automatically shrink at the picture of an angry face. There is now a considerable body of research telling us that this reaction is the result of an evolutionary memory,[31] a hardwired response in the amygdala to what was a threat signal in ancient times. The facial expression triggers our limbic alarm. We may learn a great deal about this mechanism, but that will not prevent us from having this reaction (although, as Paul Ekman showed, we can learn to mask it).

Now, suppose I react negatively to someone on the basis of their skin colour, how they talk, what they're wearing, where they're from, who they vote for, and treat them as a threat without making any attempt to know that individual: Am I being "mentally lazy"? Is prejudice or bias due to "an innate urge for cognitive ease"? Or is the problem here that other factors are at work, blocking rationality, which is why it is so difficult to overcome racism and partisan politics – or, for that matter, why it is so easy to convince so many that the 2020 election was stolen despite the mountain of evidence to the contrary?

The distinction between the two systems that Kahneman is drawing is not between *two modes of thinking* but rather, between *thinking* and *stimulus-response*, between *action and reflex*. The family of epistemic concepts that are tied to *action* cannot – logical *cannot* – be applied to *reflex*. The amygdaloid response to an angry scowl is not cognitive: not an intuitive "judgment." The amygdala does not believe (neuroconceive) that I am in danger. If I tap on the glass of an aquarium and the fish dart into their castle, it is not because they *think* that I pose a danger.

Reflexes exclude epistemic operators like being able to choose, act deliberately, pause and reflect, correct, give reasons. They are not beliefs that can be true or false; not decisions that can be well or poorly thought out; not actions that can be justified or explained. A neuromuscular, expressive, autonomic, behavioural, and experiential sequence triggered by a stimulus is not a decision that some prehistoric ancestor made for us![32]

But what of non-rational convictions? Are they in some sense akin to reflexes? Not a case of *will over reason* but rather, a case of *neither will nor reason*? Not a case of *choosing the path of least resistance* but rather, a case of *being unable to choose any path at all*?

To say that someone *refuses* to listen to reason is to say that they could have done so had they so *chosen*. But what if epistemic concepts are excluded in the non-rational domain as well? What if the ability to *recognize when there are good reasons to change one's mind* is impeded by ancient survival systems? Metaphorically speaking, what if the Blue Brain is in thrall to the Gray Brain? If that is the case, then when an individual is challenged to explain themselves, what they say is not an expression of what they *believe* but rather, as Festinger put it, an attempt to lessen the stress (dissonance) created by this Gray Brain dominance.

Ancient survival systems don't just *precede*, they can shape, constrain, and in the case of activated PECs, overcome (System 2) thinking. The frightening problem with racial bias is how rationality is completely absent when a subject is gripped by a conditioned fear, anxiety, or anger response.[33] What is involved here is not a clash between *two different modes of thinking*, one of them slow and reflective and the other rapid and prone to error – sometimes dangerous errors. It is the distinction between *thinking* and being in a neural state that subverts the ability to think rationally about, i.e., question, some false belief.

What is perhaps most disturbing about this phenomenon is how easy it is to put someone into a state where they are *parroting talking points* rather than *expressing beliefs*. We will return to this paramount issue in the final chapters, where it is the future of democracy that is at stake. But first we must address the discoveries made in the psychology of reasoning, which is the cornerstone of Kahneman's argument (chapter 5).

Nurturing Rationality

Psychologists, sociologists, and economists have all been busy tabulating the different cognitive biases – shortcuts if you will – that we use to simplify decision making. (We are up to 180 and still counting.) But the fact that we resort to biases and heuristics in the hurly-burly of everyday life does not overturn Descartes's view of *rationality*; if anything, it strengthens it.

Dan Ariely explains:

Descartes said, *Cogito ergo sum* – "I think, therefore I am." But suppose we are nothing more than the sum of our first, naïve, random behaviors. What then? These questions may be tough nuts to crack, but in terms of

our personal lives, we can actively improve on our [non-rational] behaviors. We can start by becoming aware of our vulnerabilities.[34]

On this reading, far from posing a challenge to Descartes's view
of rationality, the psychology of reasoning represents its crown-
ing achievement. Ariely's conclusion is remarkably close to what
Descartes had hoped for his *method*: to become aware of biases is
to subvert their influence. Or, unfortunately, to increase unscrupu-
lous actors' influence on the behaviour of others (see chapter 9).

How do we help children and teens develop the kind of self-
questioning that Ariely is describing: to avoid what, in his latest
book, Ariel describes as "misbelief"?[35] How do we help them recognize when they are being influenced, and more to the point,
become curious – if not outright annoyed – about these influences?
In short, how do we nurture their *rationality*?

It is a question that preoccupied Descartes himself. In *Rules for
the Direction of the Mind*, he set out to delineate his *method* in canon-
ical form. The first – and overarching – principle is that

> *The aim of our studies should be to direct the mind with a view to forming true
> and sound judgments about whatever comes before it.*

In other words, the aim is to think critically about anything and
everything. To blindly submit to an authority on personal as well
as scientific matters is to deny reason. This is the principle that
guided him at the outset and why he wrote the *Discourse* in French
and not Latin: so that not just academics but the general public,
"and even women" [*sic*], could learn to be rational.

This is also the reason Descartes did his best to see that *Rules*
would be taught in schools. His concern was that children were
being taught to be subservient rather than to think. If anything,
they were being trained to see submission to authority as the
supreme sign of rationality, when in fact it is its scourge.

Now more than ever we need to heed his concern: consider
whether – or how – we are helping children become rational
agents. Not rational in the sense that guides classical economic
theory – namely, choosing what is in their self-interest. Rather,

rational in the sense that Descartes intended. Namely, able to think for themselves. Indeed, able to think.

Interestingly, it was precisely this issue that motivated one of the most influential parenting authorities of our time, Diana Baumrind. Submissiveness was hardly her goal. If anything, it was the exact opposite.

Nurturing Democracy

Baumrind's groundbreaking research on parenting styles has come to inform much of how we think about this issue. Baumrind identified three distinctive patterns in her longitudinal research: what she called "permissive," "authoritarian," and "authoritative." She took these terms straight from political theory in order to make the point that how we parent a child has a profound impact on how – on whether! – we sustain democracy.[36]

The point here, as Hilary Putnam explained, is that democracy and rationality are *intrinsically connected*.[37] It was Descartes who laid the foundation for this argument, Lewin who applied it to politics, and Baumrind who came up with the terms that developmental researchers have employed ever since. And Self-Reg brings it all full-circle.

Baumrind's "permissive parents" (Lewin's term was "delegative leadership") are warm but overindulgent. They make few demands on their children and ignore failures to comply with these few demands. They avoid confrontation and seek to be their child's friend rather than their parent.

In today's world, these are the parents who allow their children to spend endless time on social media and leave it to others – that is, their teachers – to deal with the consequences. Children of permissive parents rank low in terms of happiness, and have poor impulse control and increased aggression.[38] These children are the fodder for books like *Glow Kids*.[39] They grow up to be politically disengaged and indifferent to democratic values.[40]

Authoritarian parents (a term she took from Lewin) are disciplinarians. The child is presented with strict rules and punished for failure to comply. In Baumrind's words, these parents are "obedience-oriented and expect their orders to be obeyed without explanation."[41] They make many demands on their children and use coercive measures to control behaviour. Far from encouraging a child's sense of autonomy, they make decisions for the child unilaterally.

Research shows that authoritarian parenting may indeed lead to children that are obedient, but many develop psychological problems later. They tend to have low self-esteem and rank lower in terms of happiness and social competence. They have increased internalizing and externalizing problems[42] and serious problems with aggression in adolescence.[43] They often develop the type of submissive personality that so concerned Descartes, and they struggle as parents themselves. Authoritarianism breeds both ends of the dominance/diffidence spectrum.

Authoritative parents (Lewin's term was "participative leadership") are warm, attentive, sensitive, and responsive to their child's needs. They set clear boundaries, but without imposing excessive limits. They resort to positive rather than punitive discipline and are consistent in how they enforce the demands that they make. They foster their children's sense of autonomy by encouraging them to express their own thoughts, feelings, and desires; and by engaging in joint decision making.[44] Baumrind's central thesis was that, if we want to sustain democracy, we need to strive to become this type of parent.

Reframed in Self-Reg terms, authoritarian parents discourage their children from asking Why. Their parenting mantra is "because I said so." Their parenting goal is compliance. A child will never learn to ask Why about their own behaviour if their parents have never asked Why in regard to their child's behaviour. In other words, authoritarian parenting leads to children whose capacity to choose has withered on the vine: children who actually find security in not choosing.

It might be tempting to think of permissive parents in Kahneman's terms as System-1-type parents. But it is not laziness that characterizes their behaviour but avoidance. The truth is, parenting is stressful at the best of times, and asking Why if one has no way of answering the question can be extremely stressful. Hence the permissive parent seeks to avoid the stress altogether, and the child does not go through the steps of learning how to form sound and true judgments. Instead of learning when to ask Why, the child's credo is: why not.

Authoritative parents teach their child to ask Why by constantly doing so themselves. Parents who become aware of their vulnerabilities – that is, their biases and assumptions – are not just reframing their child's behaviour. They are teaching their child implicitly – modelling – *when they need to ask Why*. Their priority is not to manage behaviour: it is to cultivate rationality.

It was inevitable that Baumrind's terms should be used to describe teaching styles. Permissive teachers make little effort to enforce discipline in their classroom and ignore misbehaviour for as long as possible. Far from trying to build trusting relationships, they tend to disregard and even distrust their students. They put minimum effort into their teaching, which they regard as more of a burden than a calling.

Not surprisingly, permissive teaching is associated with similar sorts of social and emotional problems as are seen in permissive parenting. Students tend to display heightened impulsivity, lack of motivation and persistence, chronic anxiety, and poor academic outcomes.[45] Schools that allow permissive teaching to go unchecked are at risk of becoming anarchic.

Authoritarian teachers are preoccupied with enforcing strict discipline in the classroom. They offer students little opportunity for discussion, which they see as undermining their authority. Authoritarian teachers are highly intolerant of rule infractions or failures to meet deadlines and use punishment and reward as the primary tools for managing classroom behaviour. Students who fail to abide by the rules are seen as refusing to make the necessary effort to control their impulses and having only themselves to blame should they fail.

Authoritarian teaching has been shown to have a long-term damaging effect on students' self-esteem, motivation, and self-efficacy. Few of the social/emotional benefits associated with a trusting student-teacher relationship and positive classroom climate are observed. Significantly, it also appears to be extremely taxing on the teachers themselves.[46] Yet schools struggling with rampant behavioural problems may feel that they have no choice but to adopt an authoritarian stance.

Authoritative teachers are responsive, supportive, and treat students as responsible individuals. They place limits on their students but also encourage their independence. They are careful to explain the reasons behind rules and have students take an active role in designing these rules. They tend to be much more tolerant if students disagree with what they are saying. They pay attention to discipline but administer consequences for violations of classroom rules in a fair and consistent manner.

Like authoritative parenting, authoritative teaching boosts students' development in all five of the Self-Reg domains. Research has shown that authoritative teaching produces students that are socially competent, responsible, and, in general, more mature. Authoritative teaching has also been shown to promote positive classroom and school environments.[47] I have yet to meet an educator who didn't embrace the concept of authoritative teaching, or one who found this easy to maintain.

From Descartes to Self-Reg

Influential as Baumrind's taxonomy has been, the terms she employed are not without their problems. "Permissive parenting" is used pejoratively, as a judgmental comment. But what we are really dealing with here is not so much a "parenting style" as a maladaptive mode of self-regulation.

Dealing with a child's implacable demands can be highly stressful, and some children are clearly far more challenging in this respect than others. But capitulating to these demands can lead to much greater stresses down the road, as the list of downstream negative traits associated with permissive parenting attests. Perhaps it would have been better to have described this category as "parental denial": a consequence, not just of the stress of raising a child, but of all the stresses of modern life layered on top.

"Authoritarian parenting" also represents a maladaptive mode of self-regulation. It is better described as "repressive parenting," with a touch of regression thrown in. But are authoritarian parents as prevalent today as was the case when Baumrind was writing? And if not, why not? Is it because the rise of smartphones has made permissive parents of us all?[48] We are clearly seeing a rise of authoritarian rhetoric in political circles, but this has done nothing to stem the tide of internalizing and externalizing problems. And it now appears, as Baumrind foretold, that widespread permissive parenting is weakening the foundations of democracy.

The biggest difficulty of all that I had teaching this material – common, I suspect, to what many have experienced – is that students found it hard to distinguish between *authoritarian* and *authoritative*. They saw these two terms as variants on the same theme, and perhaps for good reason. The term I suggested in chapter 3 was *sensitive Interbraining*, in no small part because this applies as much to educators as to parents. But it is important to note that Baumrind's choice of "authoritative" was both deliberate and significant: it reflects her core assumption that democracy rests on the ability of its citizens to exercise self-control, and that this trait is best cultivated by authoritative control.

According to this way of thinking, where authoritarian parents seek to impose self-control through command and coercion, authoritative parents seek to promote its development via influence and explanation. *But both are after the same thing*: delay of gratification, frustration tolerance, focused attention, emotion regulation, compliance. As for permissive parents, since they have no self-control themselves, they cannot possibly breed it in their offspring.

When Baumrind explains "responsiveness," she refers to "The extent to which parents intentionally foster individuality, self-regulation, and self-assertion by being attuned, supportive, and acquiescent to children's special needs and demands."[49] She is guided here by the self-control view of *self-regulation* that was common at the time. Authoritative parents are best at producing children that behave as we want, that is, that conform to social conventions and values.

Suppose instead that she had said that "responsiveness" refers to the extent to which parents and teachers foster self-awareness and doubt? Authoritative parents don't encourage children just to express their own thoughts, feelings, and desires, but to *think* about them. In joint decision making, they are exposing children to the complexity and consequences of decision making. They are teaching children not just that they need to have reasons for their choices, but that they need to think hard about why they have those reasons.

Instead of seeing the contrast between *authoritarian* and *authoritative* as being about which style of parenting and teaching best fosters self-control, Self-Reg sees this issue as being about which style best *nurtures rationality* – in the sense that we have been examining in this chapter. How do we help children and teens recognize influences on their thinking? How do we inspire in them the very desire to identify the influences on their thinking?

For all the talk about children's sense of wonder and awe at the world around them, this does not extend to their own behaviour. On the contrary, children and teens are highly resistant to examining why they want or believe something; if anything, they epitomize what is meant by *will over reason*. But where permissive parenting or teaching leads to an undisciplined mind, and the authoritarian style leads to a submissive mind, authoritative parenting and teaching leads to a reflective mind.

In other words, Self-Reg reframes Baumrind's theory so as to highlight two very different questions:

- How do parents and teachers instil self-control?
- How do parents and teachers nurture rationality?

Postscript

This chapter has gone through this exercise in the History of Ideas not just to show how important it is to distinguish *self-regulation* from *self-control*, or *misbehaviour* from *stress-behaviour*, but to recognize how important these distinctions are for the world in which children and teens are growing up today. It's a world in which *demonic demons* abound, e.g., in the form of products or pastimes that have been meticulously crafted to hijack dopamine, or even more sinister forms of dopamine hijacking.

We will be looking more closely at these modern demons in later chapters and how to help children and teens free themselves from their insidious influence – how to free ourselves! But our starting point for all that follows is the fundamental Cartesian principle: Rationality is not about *saying* why we make the choices that we make. Rationality is about *wondering* why we make the choices that we make.

Looking back at my early days in Oxford, I wonder if the reason I was so fascinated by the *Discourse on Method* was because I so strongly resonated with what Descartes was trying to achieve: a Just Society ruled by reason and not authority. And a *method* – in the case of Self-Reg, a five-step method – that sustains the covenant that binds us by leading us to ask Why: calmly, confidently, and constantly.

But this chapter has raised an important question, perhaps THE question of our times. How are we to deal with an epidemic of non-rationality if not by being untiringly rational ourselves? How can we get through to someone who stoutly refuses to listen to the voice of reason?

As we will see in the next chapter, the point of reframing isn't just to *see* behaviour through a completely different lens. It is to respond to that behaviour in a completely different manner. The first step is to distinguish between misbehaviour – *refusing* to listen – and stress-behaviour – being *unable* to listen. Self-Reg then provides us with a pathway to restoration: in this case, *the restoration of rationality*.

Chapter 5

Privileging Rationality

The Grasshopper and the Ant

In ancient Greek mythology, Aergia and Horme stand guard over Hypnos, the god of sleep. Aergia is the goddess of laziness; Horme, the goddess of effort. Aergia has all sorts of servants to do her bidding; Horme can only rely on herself to get things done. Whether or not we wake up ready to take charge of our lives depends on which of these two goddesses has the greater influence on us.

It is fascinating to see the ancient origins of the idea that whether one is lazy or industrious is determined by some supernatural (genetic?) source beyond our ken, let alone our control. Even more important is to see how the contrast is drawn between *indolence* and *effort*, which was a recurring leitmotif in Aesop's Fables.

Aergia was the personification of sloth, with the implication that she could have worked harder had she chosen. Horme was the personification of activity and eagerness. Here is another example of how our attitudes were shaped by the ancient Greek langua-culture we have inherited. Aergia and Horme were rival deities, even antagonists, and that opposition carries over into modern thinking. *Lazy* originally meant "averse to labour, action, or effort," whereas *hormones* – the secretions that set a body into motion – derived their name from Horme.

But what if, as I suggested in chapter 4, the salient contrast is between two entirely different terms, namely, between *lazy* and *limbic*, Blue Brain and Red Brain? That is not to deny the all too real possibility of laziness but, rather, to raise the question yet again of whether there are frequent occasions when a child's behaviour – or lack thereof! – is a function of stress and not of character; that is, *caused* and not *intentional*.

This was the central point in our discussion in chapter 4 of Kahneman's System 1 versus System 2 thinking. The contrast is reminiscent of Aesop's fable of the grasshopper and the ant. Flighty System 1 says the first thing that pops into its head, while System 2 soldiers away at the hard work of solving problems. But like another of Aesop's Fables, the fox and the grapes, our discussion left a critical question hanging: Why does Kahneman see *rationality* as a function of *will* (effort)? Far from emulating the fox, whose reappraisal is the source of the expression "sour grapes," the answer to this question brings us one of the richest aspects of Kahneman's research, and to a profound insight into human behaviour – rational and non-rational.

The Secret Is in the Eyes

The subjects who saw that there was something fishy about the ball-and-bat problem and tried but failed to solve it all reached a point where they suddenly just gave up. To be sure, there was considerable variability in how long it took different subjects to arrive at that point, but they all experienced a growing feeling of discomfort that reached an intolerable peak, following which they abruptly stopped.

What is even more fascinating is that Kahneman could be outside the room and yet predict exactly when that point had been reached, solely by tracking pupil dilation and heart rate. He reports that his eureka moment came when he realized that "the tasks we had chosen for study were exceptionally effortful."[1] Kahneman had already done extensive research on the issue of how the pupils are "sensitive indicators of *mental effort* [my emphasis]."[2] He had shown that you can correlate the difficulty of a task – and hence mental effort – with pupil dilation and increased heart rate. But what happens if you remove "mental" from this statement?

The answer lies in a recent study that demonstrated the same effect with physical effort. The authors showed that "pupil size signals the level of effort invested in a task, irrespective of whether it is physical or mental. It also helps refine the potential brain circuits involved since the results of the current study imply a convergence of mental and physical effort information at some level along this pathway."[3]

In other words, pupil dilation and elevated heart rate are indicators of arousal: full-stop.[4] Were we to look, we would undoubtedly find other indicators of physiological arousal; for example, a rise in blood pressure and respiration, decreased salivation, constriction in the throat and gut, electrodermal activity. We would also see indicators of cortical arousal: increases in frequency and decreases in amplitude of EEG patterns, along with the release of glutamate and orexin.

Kahneman's finding that he could predict when subjects would give up by monitoring their pupils and heart rate makes perfect sense. Trying to solve the ball-and-bat problem consumes large amounts of energy, more for some than others.[5] The reason is that, without our realizing it, our body tenses up when we work on the problem. We grit our teeth, clench our occipitofrontalis muscles, increase the tone of the striated muscles. We breathe more rapidly. There is increased activity of the sweat glands, and the gastrointestinal tract is inhibited.

In other words, we go into an *ergotropic state* that evolved to provide the energy needed for hunting and survival, and is put to use in modern life to commute in morning traffic and to solve challenging problems like figuring out how much an item costs or which pair of stockings is the best value.[6] The more a subject's energy reserves are depleted to begin with, or the subject is affected by hidden stresses while working on a problem, or finds the problem itself stressful (it exemplifies what is meant by *cognitive stress*: i.e., it taxes working memory), the more quickly the "intolerable peak" is reached. The ant keeps going; the grasshopper looks for a diversion because *to keep going* is aversive.

The point is that when physiologists describe concentration *as a whole-body phenomenon*, they mean this in a way that goes beyond subjective awareness. There is a cascade of metabolic changes that consume energy and, every bit as important, inhibit energy renewal. But what is particularly fascinating about Kahneman's research is the manner in which subjects would abruptly stop working on the problem.

He describes what he observed as an "inverted-V curve," with the apex the point at which problem solving comes to a standstill. But why not a long-tail curve? Why do we climb up a steep incline and then screech to a halt when we find a problem has become too hard, rather than gradually give up? The significance of this question drives us deep into the question of why we continue to *privilege rationality*, and how we should be thinking about thinking instead.

Interlocking Brakes

I mentioned in chapter 2 how the distinctive two brain states, Blue Brain and Red Brain, act as brakes on each other. This is a metaphorical way of saying that when a subject is in Blue Brain, they are able to exercise cognitive competencies, such as self-distraction, self-soothing, and most common of all, reappraising a stimulus, like the fox who decides the grapes are not yet ripe. These are all modes of self-regulation, that is, learned behaviours that reduce stress.

When a subject is in Red Brain, hyperarousal impedes their ability to access these learned modes of self-regulation. But there is a Red Brain counterpart, *limbic brakes*, which act as a breaker, where the mechanical overtone of the metaphor is entirely the point. We saw in chapter 1 how an action that drains energy and thus exacerbates homeostatic imbalance (a drop in blood glucose) triggers aversive sensations. For someone having trouble with the ball-and-bat problem, the activity becomes not just pointless, but unpleasant. The aversive sensations reach a point where the brakes are suddenly triggered, just as when we try to do as many sit-ups as we can: brakes that serve to *stop the aversive sensations*.

The inverted-V curve that Kahneman observed in the ball-and-bat problem is also seen when a subject is asked to squeeze a hand-grip for as long as they can. They grit their teeth, scrunch their eyes, persist as long as they are able, and then suddenly let go. Letting go stops the aversive sensations created by the physical stress. We see the same phenomenon in delay-of-gratification tasks: an inverted-V curve in which the child tries and tries to avoid eating the marshmallow.

To say that the limbic brakes kick in is not to say that we *must* come to a screeching halt. It is possible to keep ourselves going, press on with the ball-and-bat problem, force ourselves to keep squeezing, avoid eating the marshmallow, even though the trying/squeezing/waiting is aversive. This appears to be what Kahneman is thinking of when he refers to "mental laziness": the fact that we can bypass our limbic brakes so as to persevere on a task. But should we force ourselves – *or be forced by another* – to override our limbic brakes too hard or too often, we risk plunging into fight-or-flight.

When this happens, the stimulus turns into a threat: that is, the amygdala alarm is triggered at the mere sight of the stimulus. Try testing subjects on the "nine dots" puzzle right after they have just struggled with the ball-and-bat and the limbic brakes will kick in almost instantly. The same with the hand-grips test. Try having the subject do as many pull-ups as they can right after they have given up on the hand-grips and you'll be lucky to get more than one.

We will return to this issue in the following chapters. There are everyday versions of the ball-and-bat problem that are sending large numbers of children and teens into fight-or-flight. We need to know when this is happening, and why, so as to avoid sending them into fight-or-flight where the very possibility of learning is curtailed. A short break is often all that is needed to solve the ball-and-bat problem – and much else. But our question for this chapter is: can we see a parallel between the ball-and-bat problem and, say, arguing with your Aunt Betsy, who has the opposite political views from your own?

A Case of Non-Moral Blinders

Kahneman lumps together limbic brakes and fight-flight-freeze.[7] He argues that in "modern humans, System 1 takes over in emergencies and assigns total priority to self-protective actions."[8] Yet the logic problems that Kahneman and Tversky were studying can hardly be called emergencies. Solving a problem like the ball-and-bat may be taxing, but is it something that requires a "self-protective action"?

The answer to this last question is a qualified Yes, but not in the sense that applies to urgent situations. Rather, this is a mechanism that was designed to avoid going into, or exacerbating, homeostatic imbalance. In fact, we can observe inverted-V curves in any case where there is a build-up of stress/depletion of energy, including, as we will see below, arguing. We are dealing with a hierarchy of ancient survival systems, ranging from avoiding a predator or an enemy, to the need for food and water, to struggling for dominance with conspecifics.

Limbic braking *cannot be described epistemically*. That is, the hypothalamus does not *choose* to stop working on the ball-and-bat problem. It does not *judge* that the solution is beyond our reach, or *decide* that it is not worth the effort. Nor are we being *lazy* if the hypothalamus halts an activity. Rather, the hypothalamus operates as a thermostat that monitors glucose levels and inhibits energy-consuming activities when blood glucose drops below the optimal range: unless there are energizing neurohormones to keep us going (catecholamines).

In emergency situations, we keep ourselves going by tapping into backup energy reserves. In non-emergency situations, the limbic brakes are applied to protect those backup reserves. The hypothalamus acts like a thermostat that evolved to hunt for food when energy dips, but to stop chasing an animal that has got away. We don't keep running doggedly in the hopes that the animal will turn around: we stop and sit down, gathering our forces to try again.

As it happens, this is a highly pertinent issue when it comes to looking at the impact of the hook model on children and teens (see chapter 9). Here is a case where *dopamine hijacking* is employed to keep youth glued to a hunting activity past the point where the limbic brakes have kicked in. A game is designed in such a way that prey is easily caught in the beginning but becomes more elusive at each new level. But how does the game designer prevent the hunter from "stopping and sitting down," as it becomes harder to capture their prey? That is where all the techniques of dopamine hijacking come into play (the use of "play" here is deeply ironic).

Limbic braking performs an essential role in maintaining homeostasis. There is a serious risk that, if unchecked, dopamine hijacking – or hijacking our own dopamine – will exhaust energy reserves at the cellular level. Overriding the limbic brakes too hard and too often leads to just this consequence and can ultimately result in an internalizing disorder – even when the activity is "just a game." Far too many parents have seen this happen to their once blooming child.

So often, we confuse a child's limbic brakes with a refusal to keep going on a task, just as we confuse a person's *non-rational conviction* with a refusal to listen to reason. I once watched as a gym teacher shouted mercilessly at a student who was cowering on the floor, unable to climb a rope. He was overweight, had poor upper body strength, and most of all he was frightened and embarrassed. In high school he developed a serious anxiety disorder.

The gym teacher clearly thought he was doing the right thing and that this child was being oppositional and would benefit from being pushed. Looking back at it, there is no doubt in my mind that the boy was in freeze. I suspect he had proprioceptive problems which made gym class a torment. He was a sweet boy, kind and clever, and one of the many victims of the self-control mindset. All the other kids in the class could see this; why couldn't the gym teacher?

Stop!

Kahneman's and Tversky's research provides a fascinating application of Porges's idea that, at an early point in human evolution,
H. habilis adapted a sympathetic nervous system that evolved for
(from, with) hunting for the purpose of making tools.[9] The point is
that the limbic system reacts to effortful challenges, physical and
cognitive, with the same neurophysiological response.[10]

Kahneman and Tversky were, in fact, exposing subjects to multiple stresses: the same type of experimental design that we see
in the Marshmallow Task. The room that the subjects sat in was
isolated and barren. They had to cope with the emotional stress
of frustration and fear of failure; the social stress of knowing they
were being monitored; and the prosocial stress of feeling that their
intelligence was on the line. On top of all this, there was the cognitive stress of the task, which demands working memory. Little
wonder that the result was similar to what Mischel observed in the
Marshmallow Task.

In the case of the latter, many children eat the marshmallow,
not because they lack "ego strength" (whatever that means), but
in order to stop the stress/aversive sensations. These are widely
seen as children who "fail to delay gratification." But reframed,
they are children for whom the only way to manage their stress is
to get rid of the stressor. In other words, *they self-regulate by eating
the marshmallow*!

The same is true for those who answer 10¢ on the ball-and-bat
problem. This answer is the cognitive version of eating the marshmallow. To begin with, virtually all subjects sense that 10¢ is the
wrong answer. But they come to experience a sort of closure, not
just because saying 10¢ causes the stress to stop, but interestingly,
because 10¢ starts to *feel* like the right answer. They feel this way
because the aversive homeostatic-imbalance sensations cease,
regardless of whether or not we have arrived at the right answer.

Herein lies a major reason why we rely on cognitive biases in
ordinary problem solving: *they serve to reduce the aversive sensations
created by cognitive stress*. Even inane decisions can be stressful, as
Nisbett and Wilson demonstrated in "Telling More Than We Can

Know."[11] Asked to choose from four identical pairs of stockings, the majority of the subjects exhibited a "rightward bias." Not only were they unaware of this fact, but when asked about it, most denied that this caused their decision and, instead, supplied a convincing reason. But their confabulation was equally about stress reduction: the prosocial stress of seeing themselves as not having a reason for their actions and the social stress of feeling they were being judged.

The interest in reasoning biases traces back to the work that AI scientists did on problem-solving heuristics.[12] One of the early versions of the ball-and-bat problem was the Wason Selection Task:[13]

> You are shown a set of four cards placed on a table, each of which has a number on one side and a coloured patch on the other side. The visible faces of the cards show 3, 8, red, and brown. Which card(s) must you turn over in order to test the truth of the proposition that if a card shows an even number on one face, then its opposite face is red?

It turns out that few of us (less than 10 per cent) can come up with the correct answer (viz., that you need to turn over the 8 and brown cards). Yet most people can solve the problem if it's presented in familiar terms. Wason showed this by presenting the task in terms of buying postage stamps. Cosmides and Tooby showed that university students could easily solve the problem when it's presented to them in terms they can relate to, namely, if you are drinking alcohol then you must be over eighteen and the cards have an age on one side and beverage on the other, for example, 18, beer, 25, Coke. Few students had trouble selecting the correct cards.

Lack of effort is not the reason why we have so much trouble with the formal version of the task; it's that the aversive sensations produced by the cognitive stress trigger our limbic brakes. Trying to solve a problem in abstract terms taxes working memory and, in many, causes anxiety, which further depletes working memory. Rogoff wrote a fascinating book about how children struggle over problems presented in abstract terms that they can readily solve when presented in familiar terms.[14] Remove the stress of being asked to think in an abstract way and the child's performance is transformed. Relaxation and automatization dramatically reduce the demands on working memory and, as a result, lower whole-body tension and anxiety.

Limbic braking is indeed self-protective, which is the reason why problems arise when we fail to recognize that a child's limbic brakes have been tripped. In such a case, the child's growing resistance is not a form of misbehaviour. To describe a child in this way presupposes that they are *choosing* to be oppositional; capable of acting differently. But when the behaviour is *limbic* – that is, a stress-behaviour – the effect of pushing the child to override their limbic brakes is to send them into fight-or-flight. Here the pertinent distinction is between *oppositional behaviour* and *Angstbeisser*, where the former is misbehaviour, the latter a non-rational stress-behaviour.[15]

Ultimately, cognitive biases are essential modes of self-regulation and, by and large, adaptive, since they reduce the stress of a decision without incurring too great a cost. It is really only with the publication of Bernays's *Crystallizing Public Opinion* in 1923, and the truly awful Torches of Freedom march that he organized in 1929,[16] that these modes of self-regulation were rendered maladaptive by "demonic demons" who ever since have sought to discover and exploit, not our "innate laziness," but rather the impact of stress on how we process information (see chapter 10).

The Poverty of Puritan Ideas

In the previous chapter, I thought back to my first philosophy tutorial at Oxford; now I can't help but think back to my first politics tutorial. The question I had been set was: "Discuss R.H. Tawney's view that 'A good society is an equal society.'" I didn't just agree. It was the reason that I had come to Oxford in the first place: to learn what we can do to help bring about a Just Society. What better place to start than with Tawney's views on egalitarianism?

I spent the week in the Magdalen College library reading through Tawney's writings. I wrote my paper on his remark in

Religion and the Rise of Capitalism that the Puritan "sees in the poverty of those who fall by the way, not a misfortune to be pitied and relieved, but a moral failing to be condemned, and in riches ... the blessing which rewards the triumph of energy and will."[17] I had seen the same thinking all around me growing up, and I was starting to wonder if that wasn't a big source of the problem.

The moral debate that the Puritans bequeathed us has served as the perfect breeding ground for pursuing *will over reason*. At the time that I was writing my paper, the UK was mired in exactly the same polarized debate as had beset the Victorians. The Labour party sounded like classic Owenites, and the Conservatives, like Malthus and Pearson.[18] Both sides defended their positions on ethical grounds; both were completely deaf to the other side's arguments.

The question I raised in my paper, but could not yet begin to answer – remember that my other tutorial was in philosophy – was: "What if this is not a *moral* issue? What if it's because we see this as being about character that institutional poverty persists?" I concluded with a line that I loved: "Ideology rushes in where science has yet to tread." I still do, although my understanding of *ideology* has advanced a bit since then!

In this case, I knew that my don approved of what I'd done because he stopped puffing on his pipe and, waving it at me, gently asked, "What sort of policies do you think might work?" I had just been formally welcomed into the world of politics – or at least, what I was to study for the remainder of that term, namely, the various initiatives that have all ignominiously failed to win the war on poverty.

The question that troubled me then and has troubled me ever since was: "If not about *laziness*, then what?" Seeing endemic poverty as a character issue blocks the rationality that we looked at in the preceding chapter. Both sides in this polarized debate need to be asking Why. Reformers need to ask why there is multigenerational welfare dependency, without falling back on social Darwinism; why the gap in school achievement is so hard to close. The (post-)Puritan needs to ask why draconian social measures, such as the truly dreadful Poor Law of 1834, not only fail to provide the anticipated moral incentive but, in fact, make social problems considerably worse.

Once again, the self-control mindset gets in the way of reason. It takes for granted what should be the very first question that we ask: Do subjects all face the same challenge? Note that this is far more complex than the question of whether subjects all have an equal *ability* to meet the same challenge. It is also different from the point that a challenge may require greater effort from some (for biological, neurodevelopmental, epigenetic, social, or environmental reasons). The question that I'm raising is: are they, in fact, all dealing with the *same* challenge? To borrow a term from psychology, we assume that *challenge* is an independent variable and *effort* is the dependent. But what if both are dependent?

Suppose we wanted to test motivation in gym class, and to that end we divided our sample into two groups, both of whom had to climb a rope and ring a bell at the top. But for the one group the ceiling is low, the climb only three metres; for the other the ceiling is high, the climb thirty metres. And then we compare how many from each group (randomly selected of course) *try* to climb the rope. It's hard to imagine getting funding for such a study, yet this is exactly what we do every day when we rank students in their academic subjects. And we do so unwittingly.

The Impact of Stress on Perception

In the previous chapter, I touched on Descartes's attack on the reliability of our senses. You might have thought that by this point in time there is nothing interesting left to say about this topic, but we now know that stress influences raw perception without our being aware that this is happening. It turns out that Descartes was right to be wary about the reliability of our senses; what he hadn't appreciated was the impact of stress and not just refraction.

In a fascinating study, subjects observed a cloud of dots on a computer screen moving either to the left or to the right, rather like a murmuration of starlings. They had to pull a lever on the left or right to indicate which direction the swarm was moving.

The experimenters then surreptitiously added weight to one of the levers, with the effect that if the dots were moving to the left it was harder to raise the left-hand lever. What then happened was amazing. We might have expected that the subjects would simply give up trying to raise the left-hand lever (remember the inverted-V curve). But instead, the subjects *saw the dots as moving to the right* and raised the right-hand lever accordingly (and, of course, vice versa).

Hagura et al. concluded that "perceptual decisions are biased by the cost to act";[19] that the brain makes its "perceptual judgments" like a classical economist. We have seen how careful we have to be about employing epistemic terms to describe neural processes. What we are dealing with here is not a judgment made by the occipital lobe but rather a case of stress *causing* us to see x rather than y.[20] Stress causes us to *perceive* 10¢ as the correct answer, to *feel* the wait as interminable, to *see* the rope as longer than it is.

In this case, stress-altered perception precedes and causes what we mistakenly describe as "avoidance." The reason why I say "mistakenly" is because avoidance belongs to the category of misbehaviour: i.e., the subject could have broached the challenge and chose not to. Avoidance is categorially different from flight-or-fight, where the subject apprehends the stimulus as a threat and consequently flees.

Similarly, the subjects in the four-stockings experiment may not have been rationalizing their decision. They may have been reporting *exactly what they saw*. The paradigm itself was a stress in multiples senses, to which was added the stress of feeling threatened about their judgment. When this is the case, it makes no sense to describe their confabulation in effortful terms. That is not to say that we can rule out experience:[21] only that we can rule out laziness.

The lesson here is that we have to factor in a subject's stress-reactivity when considering what the subject perceives. We cannot assume that students are all dealing with the same challenge in gym class, simply because *challenge* is so subjective. We cannot assume that the students all *see* the same length rope. An overweight and clumsy student may *see* an impossibly long climb. They are not being "lazy" if their limbic brakes have kicked in.

The perceptual bias operating here, selected over eons of limbic development, was designed to avoid overtaxing an already over-taxed system by stopping an inverted-V curve before it can even start. Who knows why this happened in that student who resisted climbing the rope? Perhaps his hippocampus had registered an earlier mishap. Perhaps he was overstressed by the gym itself; or by a uniform that was too tight; or by having other students gawk-ing at and teasing him; or by a motor system that found it harrow-ing to sequence different muscles; or by a vestibular system that shunned leaving the ground. Whatever the cause(s), the point is that we need to be careful to distinguish between *laziness* and *lim-bic braking* – assuming that our goal is to help this child get healthy, or learn, or simply get along with other kids.

We saw this issue up close in the MEHRI study. At the begin-ning of treatment, we conducted a facial expression task that is a standard tool in autism research. Like others, we found that the children had difficulty distinguishing between happy, angry, and neutral faces.[22] We knew that the inability to understand facial expressions would be a huge social stress down the road. We also knew that their problem had nothing to do with effort, and were we to coax them to attend to the pictures we could have inadvertently sent them into fight-or-flight. We needed to consider whether a child's response was a mode of self-regulating (saying the first thing that popped into their head to stop the test) or the product of negative bias (seeing all three pictures as threatening in different ways), or whether the child literally did not *see* any differ-ence between the three photos.

Here too, neuroscientists have made an important discovery. In what is known as the "cold-pressor" paradigm, scientists have found that when subjects immerse one of their hands in ice water for up to three minutes (a physical stress), their ability to process facial information is significantly impaired.[23] Given the heightened stress load that so many children on the spectrum have to cope with all of the time, their difficulty on the facial recognition task may be the result of reduced perceptual discrimination caused by the impact of stress, and not a breakdown in an "innate face-detection system."

It certainly never occurred to us to force a child to attend to the pictures so as to learn how to differentiate facial expressions; to do so would have gone completely against the grain of the DIR-type treatment that we were providing. Indeed, like the attempt to curtail poverty by forcing welfare recipients to be "motivated," such intervention techniques often have the opposite effect from what is intended: they add to the child's stress and anxiety.[24] Rather, our therapists worked on identifying and reducing the stresses of social interaction so that the children would begin to enjoy and seek out social experiences and spontaneously look at their parents' faces, thereby naturally learning the meaning of different facial expressions.

Likewise, the one thing we can say with total certainty about poverty is that children born into these conditions are exposed to intolerably high levels of stress, of all kinds. Endemic poverty persists because excessive stress persists. There could not be a more impoverished view of poverty than the Puritan idea that some children are born "morally deficient," incapable of making the effort that success demands. Here is a case, all too common, where mindblindness meets cruelty.

But now we come to a very interesting question. Really, the most interesting question of all. Suppose we ask the overweight child why he wouldn't climb the rope, or the long-term welfare recipient why they wouldn't seek a job. And suppose we are exasperated by their excuses. So, we undertake to convince them to change their ways, and if they don't listen to us, we throw up our hands in despair. Which is pretty much where we landed in chapter 2. Where we are today.

We need to dig deeper.

The point of reframing a child's behaviour is not simply to enable us to recognize instances of limbic braking. It is to afford a different – a neuro-enlightened – way of helping a child with hypersensitive limbic brakes. We are not seeking to instil a sense of parental guilt; only to enable parents to hear a child's limbic utterances.

1. The first step is to reframe: to recognize when we are dealing with *limbic braking* and not *mental laziness*. There is a world of difference between *not being able to make an effort* and *not making an effort*.

2. The next step is to identify the aspects of the challenge that make it so stressful. How it's presented? Lack of experience? The child hasn't acquired preliminary skills or strengths? Peers seem to have no trouble at all with the challenge?

3. Reduce the stress. We need to consider all of the Self-Reg stress domains, but when it comes to education, especially the cognitive. Some of the most effective literacy and maths programs succeed because the child is supported and becomes comfortable with the type of reasoning involved; core skills are acquired and automatized; the demands on working memory are reduced.

4. Develop stress awareness. *We* need to be aware of the difference between *lack of motivation* and *limbic brakes*, which is yet another example of the distinction between *misbehaviour* and *stress-behaviour*. *Children* need to learn what it feels like to be overstressed, what it feels like to be approaching the peak of their inverted-V curve, and be aware themselves that this is a stress and not a character issue.

5. Recognize the importance of restorative breaks. If there is one hugely important lesson to be learned from Kahneman's research it is this: *Restore before the peak is reached*!

Recovery takes considerably longer once limbic brakes have been applied. I liken this to the way the water system in my house works. Because we rely on well-water, we installed a four-hundred-litre holding tank. If the water in the tank dips below seventy-five litres, it trips a shutoff valve and we are not able to recharge the pump until the tank has completely filled again, which takes all day. But if we need to do a load of wash and see that the level is getting close to the shutoff line, we only need to wait an hour before we have enough water to do the wash.

If we can restore before the brakes kick in, the child may only need a brief respite before they are ready to go at it again. But push them past that point and you are going to have to deal with what has been called *output failure*. When this happens – and it can happen with any child – what is most important is to maintain

Interbrain contact, for your relationship with the child is the first thing that ruptures when RAGE and FEAR are activated – and not just in the child! But all too often we do the exact opposite from what's needed, *precisely because we see the child as being lazy*.

We push the child when this is the last thing that will help that child to stay connected. We insist that they try harder when what they really need to do is stop trying entirely and, instead, recoup. While they are restoring, we can set about trying to figure out why they are finding this problem so challenging.[25] Above all, we need to listen to the child's limbic system, rather than smiting the child with harsh words.

The Myth of Laziness

When a child persistently and precipitately gives up on a task that we are fairly certain they are capable of mastering, this is often a sign of some underlying issue. If we suspect that this might be the case, we need to become stress detectives to figure out what that problem might be.[26] Is it sensory or sensorimotor? A processing deficit? Anxiety? A function of how the child sees the world? How the world sees the child?

A child experiencing *output failure* has to work much harder than others, and harder than we appreciate. (Think of the child with ADHD.) Harder in the whole-body sense. A child has a limited ability to try harder on a task when their limbic brakes are holding them back. They are more prone to slip into fight-flight-freeze. Just raising your voice or looking stern is enough to send them there.

That's not to say we can't override a child's limbic brakes, any more than we can't override our own Basic Rest-Activity Cycle. We do this all the time, relying on fear or anger as motivators (or at least, the adrenaline that they produce). Or perhaps in our own case, we resort to a stimulant or rapid energy source to help out. Anyone who has gone through the ordeal of final university exams knows only too well what this is like. In my own case, I relied on endless cups of coffee, much to the detriment of my physical health afterwards. But push a child or teen to override their limbic brakes, and do this on a constant basis, and you risk their developing an externalizing or internalizing disorder.

In other words, "challenging" behaviours result from driving a child past their peak when we don't recognize the cues that this is happening. We attempt to force them to persist for the very reason that we think they are not trying. Perhaps we feel this way because we have seen them succeed on similar tasks on past occasions; or because the kids around them have a much higher stress tolerance; or because that's what the experts tell us about building perseverance. Or maybe we think, "This child needs to learn the hard way about the blessing that rewards the triumph of energy and will and the long-term consequences of succumbing to a moral failing."

But go back to that overweight child who found it so hard to climb the rope. Not only do we have to think hard about why he balked at the challenge, we also need to think hard about describing him as "balking," especially if what he was doing was self-regulating, and not necessarily in a maladaptive way. And then we have to think very hard about why we wanted to subject him to this trial in the first place. This isn't like cutting off some of the roast before you cook it because great-grandma's roasting pan was too small. His teacher's goal was for him to become healthy. But was climbing a rope – let alone doing this in a socially stressful situation – the way to pursue this goal?

Let us say that, for whatever reason, we are committed to rope climbing (rather in the way that we insist students pass Grade 12 math to graduate from high school). Now the question becomes, how can we help this child *paulatinamente*, so that their limbic brakes don't kick in? We might start with assisted pull-ups using resistance bands, starting with one that almost completely offsets the child's body weight. Slowly, over time, we reduce the amount of resistance. But it is not just scaffolding involved here; even more important is the reframing.

Parents and educators have a tendency to perseverate on what they think is good for a child, especially if they had to do it themselves as a child. "If rope climbing was good for me, it must be good for him." But consult an occupational therapist and they might give you a completely different picture of *what would be good for the child*. The first step, and always the key step, is to be clear about your goal and only then to agonize about the means.

If what his teacher was after was shifting this boy from mal-adaptive modes of self-regulation (eating junk food, endless gaming) to realizing the benefits of exercise, then he had to figure out how he could make the latter enjoyable, in exactly the same way that the MEHRI therapists had to figure out how to make social interaction enjoyable for each of the children that they worked with. What making something "enjoyable" means here is, *reduce the stress so that endogenous opioids are released* – by exercise or social interaction.

We have a strong tendency to resort to force rather than reason when we see a child as being *oppositional*. That is precisely what the *poor character* argument is all about: blaming the child for their poor self-control, blaming the poor for being poor. This response is *non-rational* in the sense that we have been exploring: in this case, caused by biases that we have inherited from our own parents, or from those around us. Rather than searching for an answer, we have stipulated from the start what the answer must be. And we do so because, of all the stultifying influences on rational thought, the self-control bias must surely rank near the top.

Distinguishing between *laziness* and *limbic braking* will not in itself suffice to change a child's trajectory; we then have to figure out the stresses causing the stress-behaviour. In the gym class example, input from an occupational therapist would have been a game-changer. That could help us ascertain why the child's limbic brakes are kicking in. The same applies to the student who is struggling in some academic subject.

The limbic system not only acts as a brake on a PFC that refuses – or is not allowed – to quit, but also remembers when and in what context a prior shutdown occurred. This is the reason we see children and teens go into fight-or-flight before even attempting to climb the rope. Likewise, the child or teen who is drawn to maladaptive modes of self-regulation when overstressed does so because of an embodied memory of the previous experience. What this child most urgently needs is not to be lectured on the importance of willpower, but helped to restore.

For this to happen – for us to perform the regulating role afforded by the Interbrain – we need to recognize how the very term *lazy* primes the way we see a child. Seeing a child as lazy, stupid, obstinate is a classic example of how we label children because of historical influences on our thinking. This is a perfect example of what we mean when we say *see a child differently and you see a different child*. And this applies – especially applies – to the character judgments that we are so quick to make.

The Truth about Lying

Pinocchio saw the Carabineer from afar and tried his best to escape between the legs of the big fellow, but without success. The Carabineer grabbed him by the nose (it was an extremely long one and seemed made on purpose for that very thing) and returned him to Mastro Geppetto. The little old man wanted to pull Pinocchio's ears. Think how he felt when, upon searching for them, he discovered that he had forgotten to make them! All he could do was to seize Pinocchio by the back of the neck and take him home. As he was doing so, he shook him two or three times and said to him angrily: "We're going home now. When we get home, then we'll settle this matter!"

Pinocchio, on hearing this, threw himself on the ground and refused to take another step. One person after another gathered around the two. Some said one thing, some another. "Poor Marionette," called out a man. "I am not surprised he doesn't want to go home. Geppetto no doubt will beat him unmercifully[,] he is so mean and cruel!" "Geppetto looks like a good man," added another, "but with boys he's a real tyrant. If we leave that poor Marionette in his hands he may tear him to pieces!" They said so much that, finally, the Carabineer ended matters by setting Pinocchio at liberty and dragging Geppetto to prison. The poor old fellow did not know how to defend himself, but wept and wailed like a child. "Ungrateful

> boy! To think I tried so hard to make you a well-behaved
> Marionette! I deserve it, however! I should have given the
> matter more thought."
> – Carlo Collodi, *The Adventures of Pinocchio* (1883)

In Walt Disney's hands, the moral of Pinocchio is straightforward: tell the truth and you'll be rewarded in life. In Pinocchio's case, *with* life. But Collodi's intentions were considerably more complex.

Part political allegory and part pedagogical primer, *The Adventures of Pinocchio* reads more as a confessional autobiography than a fairy tale. Collodi, who was childless and irascible, is said to have been just like the Geppetto described above. Most important, the deeply vexing question that Collodi raises in the above passage gets completely lost in the Disney rendition: namely, to what extent is this a story about Pinocchio, and to what extent is it about Geppetto?

Collodi/Geppetto's conundrum is that faced by any parent: How do we raise a truthful child and not just a well-behaved marionette? The social covenant that I mentioned in chapter 2 is built on trust. This is the reason why truthfulness is so highly prized: at stake here is whether a child will become an accepted – let alone respected – member of society. But this raises a major challenge for most, if not all parents:

- How do we deter a child from lying to avoid getting in trouble ("antisocial lying"), while at the same time teaching them when and why it's appropriate to lie ("prosocial lying")?
- Why is it so hard for some children to outgrow antisocial lying and learn prosocial?
- How do we help a child acquire the desire to be truthful as opposed to being submissive?
- How do we avoid turning these encounters with children or students into a power struggle, a battle of wills?

This last question is especially important vis-à-vis the child who is seen as doggedly lying when confronted with a transgression they've committed. For self-control, you need to *break* this child's will, much as you break in a wild mustang. According to this way of thinking, the worst thing is to be permissive, assuming this wasn't the cause of the problem in the first place. But we need to tread very carefully. Corporal punishment fosters dishonesty.[27] Truthfulness cannot be engendered by fear. Not only does harsh punishment fail to promote "moral growth"; it impedes it.

Emphasizing the benefits of telling the truth is significantly more effective for promoting honesty than stressing the negative consequences of lying.[28] But for Self-Reg, there is a more pressing question here: Was the child "doggedly *lying*"? To answer this question, we need to distinguish between *misbehaviour* and *stress-behaviour*.

In the case of lying, the child acts intentionally and could have acted differently. The child was aware that they shouldn't have done something and were capable of exercising self-restraint (i.e., the behaviour was voluntary). The child acted out of selfishness, greed, or sheer devilment. We punish the child's misbehaviour because we're trying to mould their character, develop a sense of right and wrong (bearing in mind that punishment must *always* be positive).

The problem is that in the case of *stress-behaviour*, the child's behaviour is not *intentional*. They didn't act a certain way for the wrong reasons; *they didn't act for any reason at all*. Rather, their behaviour was triggered by subcortical systems that, when overstressed, overrule and may even curb the Blue Brain state needed, where one is able to think about what one is doing or refrain from acting on an impulse. Punish a child for a stress-behaviour, and you add immeasurably to the child's stress load – and your own.

Lying is the quintessential misbehaviour: an intentional falsehood uttered in self-interest. Our problem is that, although *lying* is a clear case of a misbehaviour, sometimes the child is not lying at all but rather is *confabulating*. The distinction between *lying* and *confabulation* is not just behavioural: it is logico-grammatical. Confabulation is a stress-behaviour, and as such, non-rational. Someone who confabulates isn't *trying* to deceive. Rather, to use Dan

Ariely's term, they *misbelieve* that what they are saying is true (see below).[29]

The big problem when we think a child is lying is that it triggers anger in us, especially in cases where the behaviour is habitual. But if anger governs what we say or do, we risk sending the child into fight-or-flight and subverting any opportunity for moral growth – our own as well as the child's. That, in essence, was Collodi's point and the reason why the deeper lesson here applies as much to Geppetto as it does to Pinocchio.

Confabulation was the name originally given to a curious phenomenon seen in patients with brain damage that impairs their memory or self-awareness.[30] When asked why they φ'd, they create a false but often plausible story. There is no intention to deceive. The false memory might have been triggered by a cue, or is perhaps the product of a basic human drive to see ourselves and have others see us as rational agents in control of our actions. This drive leads us to confabulate in ordinary situations and not just in aphasia.

Confabulation is a mode of self-regulation. A way of reducing the stress of not really knowing why you φ'd. The stress of being yelled at. The anticipation of what might follow. It only turns into a maladaptive mode of self-regulation if it becomes habitual, or if adults fail to recognize it for what it is: not an intentional misbehaviour, but something altogether different. We see it as fight; in fact, it is flight.

Children hide when they are overwhelmed or overstimulated. The same can be said about confabulation. The difference between these two behaviours is not nearly as great as you might think. If dogs could speak when they are being yelled at, they would confabulate.

The Slippery Slope from Lying to Confabulation

What we need to remember in this whole issue is that the goal is the child's *moral growth*; not for them to become submissive. Brute force is only going to deepen the denial or send them into freeze.

Yet the authoritarian approach to discipline insists that it's for *the child's own good* that they be compelled to admit the truth. The child's denials are seen as a sign of incorrigibility.

Once you feel this way, any opportunity to foster truthfulness has been lost. The child stays stuck in an early stage of social development, which is why this issue is so important. It takes a great amount of emotional development before a child is able to disclose – to themselves! – what really happened.

Lying is said to begin around the age of two or three. As children get older, they become more adept at this skill. They learn how to stick to the story, add convincing details, control their facial expressions, maintain eye gaze. Far from lacking inhibitory control, the child is growing in this regard by leaps and bounds. It's just that these executive function skills are being used to persist in what, at bottom, is an infantile response to acting on what is likely an infantile impulse. That is the whole point of *moral growth*: helping a child move past this immaturity stage that they regress to in times of excessive stress so as to develop positive ways of dealing with social and prosocial stress.

Lying is a stress in its own right, which is the secret to lie detectors: they are designed to pick up on a surge in the subject's sympathetic nervous system. But when the stress of being held to account becomes too great, a neural shift occurs. Yet another example of the inverted-V curve. *Misbehaviour turns into stress-behaviour*. Like eating the marshmallow or letting go of the hand-grips, the child suddenly stops *lying* and starts *confabulating*. With repeated exposure to similar situations, the shift occurs almost instantaneously.

Confabulations are non-rational, in the sense explored in chapter 2. The subject cannot listen to anything that might challenge their conviction; can't probe their beliefs; look for confounding information; hesitate, reflect, learn from experience. And they certainly are not able to change their mind. Instead, they search for further "evidence" to confirm their misbelief, getting swept up in what Ariely calls "the funnel of misinformation." Counter-evidence is dismissed out of hand. The misbelief is unfalsifiable (which, indeed, is the defining feature of *misbelief*).

Because of our tendency to *privilege rationality*, we don't ask what kind of speech act we are dealing with, *lying* or *confabulation*. We assume that the child or teen is lying, and thus can be compelled – forced by the weight of reason – to admit the truth. But as we'll see in the next section, confabulation is the product of a totally different kind of psychological state, one that is resistant to overturning, because the limbic brakes have kicked in.

The child who doggedly confabulates is consumed by an urge to escape. Limbic utterances like the "I don't care" that we looked at in the first chapter are "flight" behaviours, invariably taken at face value. This is the reason why adults find these utterances exasperating. They are seen as compounding the infraction, rather than as stress-behaviour. The adult's annoyance leads them to ratchet up the stress rather than do the one thing they should in order to help the child develop the capacity for truthfulness: *reduce the child's arousal*.

A child or teen can only learn about the importance of truthfulness if they are in homeostatic balance. But if anger governs our response and it's our Red Brain *rather* than Blue that dictates what we say or how we say it, we end up with activated RAGE + FEAR ourselves, shouting or shutting down emotionally. Social engagement collapses, and with it, any chance of fostering moral growth in the child.

That is not to say we should ignore transgressions; it is to say that we must help the child turn off their limbic alarm, which is why we must turn off ours. Any child can learn – however slowly and with however much support – that certain impulses need to be resisted; that honesty is highly valued; that accepting responsibility is ultimately less stressful than fleeing from it. All children and teens can learn these lessons because of their deep desire to meet adult and peer approval; but only when they are calm.

The most frustrating aspect of dealing with a child or teen who is stuck in a *confabulation loop* is that nothing we say or do seems to help. But that is NOT because the child or teen is beyond help: it is because they can neither absorb what we are saying nor question what they are saying. They have shifted to a Red Brain state driven by FEAR and PANIC/GRIEF. We don't see their verbal acts in their true light, as displays of confusion, discharge behaviours, desperate attempts to flee, anguished cries for help.

Collodi intuitively saw all this. There is only one episode in *The Adventures of Pinocchio* in which Pinocchio's nose grows longer, and this is triggered not by lying but by stress. In fact, Collodi deliberately blurs the boundary between *lying* and *confabulation*, and the big lesson to be learned from his fable is that Pinocchio and Geppetto find themselves caught in a mutual stress cycle: a state of shared anxiety in which Pinocchio is no closer to truthfulness because Geppetto is so convinced that he is doing the right thing.

It is that utter conviction that we need to understand. Just the sort of conviction that Descartes sought to dispel. But why does someone hold on to a misbelief so fiercely? To answer that question, we need to dig deeper into confabulation.

A Mind at Unease

Michael Gazzaniga tells the following story:

> I had a patient who, although she was being examined in my office at New York hospital, claimed we were in her home in Freeport, Maine. I started with the question "So, where are you?" She replied, "I am in Freeport, Maine. I know you don't believe it. Doctor Posner told me this morning when he came to see me that I was in Memorial Sloan-Kettering hospital and that when the residents came on rounds to say that to them. Well, that is fine, but I know I am in my house on Main Street in Freeport, Maine!" I asked, "Well, if you are in Freeport and in your house, how come there are elevators outside the door here?" She calmly responded, "Do you know how much it costs me to have those put in?"
> . *Who's in Charge?*, p. 49

At the end of the nineteenth century, the Russian psychiatrist Sergei Korsakoff identified confabulation as a pathological condition resulting from polyneuritis: a case of damage to the peripheral nerve system caused by toxins (typically, alcohol), disease, tumours, dementia, and stroke, leading to a cluster of physiological, emotional, and cognitive disturbances. "Confabulation is an extremely peculiar form of amnesia in which the subject has false memories, along with irritability, agitation, and confusion."[31] But he found that the patients' stories were not out of the blue. They related to "*unconscious memories*," things they had read or heard, or thoughts that had been planted in their mind. Unlike delusions or hallucinations, there is always a stimulus – internal or external – that triggers confabulation.

Armin Schnider identified four different kinds of confabulation in pathological conditions:[32]

- "False memories"
- Disorientation or confusion
- Fantastical confabulations seen in disorders like anosognosia
- Momentary confabulations when an amnesiac is pressed to answer a question

In each case, what is most striking is the subject's *utter conviction* in what they "remember."

Schnider tells the story of a retired psychiatrist, Mrs. B, who was convinced that she was still practising following an aneurysm, an association triggered by her daily physiotherapy sessions. "The confabulations themselves were not the problem. The real problem was the conviction behind the confabulations, the degree of truthfulness they attained in her thinking." "Her false ideas were not just false verbal statements: they betrayed a confusion of reality, which Mrs. B held with the same conviction as any healthy person. She acted according to her false ideas. Nothing and nobody could make her change her mind about where she was and what she had to do."[33]

We might expect this phenomenon to be confined to aphasics, but Nisbett and Wilson reported the same sort of behaviour in their four-stockings experiment. "When asked directly about a possible effect of the position of the article, virtually all subjects denied it, usually with a worried glance at the interviewer suggesting that they felt either that they had misunderstood the question or were dealing with a madman."

We (rightly) think of confabulation as an ego defence, but there is something deeper involved. The subject's sense of reality is altered. They *see* what their limbic system *commands*. Mrs. B constructs a reality in which she is still a practising psychiatrist; the hospital-bound patient is still in her bed at home. Their minds have blocked out what was incredibly stressful: not knowing where they were or why.

Herein lies the reason why it is nearly impossible to get someone to *admit the falsity of their confabulation*. Trying to do so causes far greater stress to a mind that has fastened on to some alternate reality caused by neuroinflammation. Among other things, neuroinflammation can be caused by sustained excessive stress. The result is someone who is neurobiologically and not just emotionally susceptible to confabulation. The trigger can be anything: a sight, sound, smell, a sudden thought or memory, a subversive conspiracy theory, or a prime that has been planted.

In some ways, the conviction that marks out confabulation is akin to delusion – which is the whole point of referring to these speech acts as confabulations. But confabulations are not like *false statements* that can be overturned by evidence. Nor are they straightforward avowals, which are neither true nor false, even though sincere. An avowal is a criterion for saying "S believes such-and-such." But confabulations have a slightly different logical grammar. They are criteria for saying, "S *misbelieves* such-and-such."

Confabulations are signs of stress overload. We don't argue with aphasics or with someone suffering from dementia, we soothe. You could not *convince* Mrs. B that she was no longer a practising psychiatrist, any more than you could convince the patient that she was not in her home. Nor should you try. Their confusion was a sign that they needed to be comforted.

The most notable aspect of any type of confabulation is that, once it sets in, the subject suffers distress if we attempt to dispel it. **The implications of this last point for our current political crisis are STUNNING.**

A Society in Red Brain

Argue with someone in the grip of blind conviction and you will produce, not a change of heart, but agitation. Their lack of hesitation, or their rapid flip-flopping, is a glaring sign that the subject's statements need to be reframed. These are not irrational; they are non-rational. Which raises two pressing questions: WHY? and HOW SHOULD WE RESPOND?

It is our immediate response to reason with someone who is, in fact, "deaf to reason" that is meant by *privileging rationality*. Viewed through the lens of confabulation, it is clear that the subject does not *believe* what they are saying. Rather, they *misbelieve* what they are saying.

In the case of *misbelief*, the subject can still think, argue, speak cogently. They just can't do any of these things rationally about the misbelief in question, in the sense spelled out in chapter 4. That is, *they are impervious to doubt*, held to their conviction by their limbic brakes. Counter-evidence is a threat that must be resisted. RAGE + FEAR are activated, and in certain circumstances, PANIC/GRIEF and what Panksepp dubbed PLAY but is better termed DOMI-NANCE (at least in the case of adults, and perhaps older children and teens as well).

Knowing When to Argue and When to Assuage

The key to confabulation is that it is ex post facto. A stress causes S to φ and then causes them to come up with an explanation as to why they had done so. Wearing a mask is a stress, so they tear it off (eat the marshmallow). Then they set their Blue Brain to work to find reasons to justify their behaviour. Confabulation is the caboose, not the engine.

FEAR is activated (e.g., the fear of global warming), and to turn it off the subject finds a reason (the HAARP conspiracy theory). Or rather, finds non-rational conviction. Confabulation follows where FEAR and stress lead. In this case, as in so many others, confabula-tion easily turns into maladaptive self-regulation.

The question we are grappling with is: What sends a subject from rational open-mindedness to non-rational conviction? The short answer is excessive stress, but how exactly? The answer lies in ancient survival systems. One or more PECs are activated – and it is usually more. FEAR + RAGE, but also DOMINANCE and

PANIC/GRIEF. The stress of being seen – of seeing oneself – on a low rung in the social hierarchy. The stress of being ostracized, someone who must live in their car. Dopamine drives the subject to join a cult as a way to stop the pain. Where else are they to obtain the oxytocin that all humans need?

We would not laugh at Mrs. B, or any similar case of confusion. Likewise, we should soothe in every case of non-rational conviction: clinical, non-clinical, the child who doggedly confabulates, the blind(ed) political supporter. Not for the sake of getting them to be "more open-minded." Rather, for the sake of helping them to experience calm.

The big lesson we learnt with our two neurodivergent teens is that they confabulated when they were in distress. Often, this was the result of their own actions, some of which were deeply worrying to their parents. But no amount of arguing could change their mind. Only when they turned to restorative activities could they begin to ask themselves Why, and chart a different course. Our part was to offer them what advice we could when we could, help them to restore, and listen in the deepest sense of the term.

Misbelief can never feed the subject's real need, which is to feel calm and hopeful. What those in the grip of non-rational conviction desperately need is a co-regulating Interbrain to help turn off their stress response.

This is the one lesson that humans seem incapable of learning: how to respond when a family member, relative, friend, stranger, or community, when our society or another, goes Red Brain. We consistently try to reason with them, which quickly turns into shouting. The cost of *privileging rationality* in this manner – to our future, our children's future, humanity's future – has never been higher. But in Red Brain, we can't think about the future, only about how to keep going in whichever direction our limbic system is leading. A limbic system primed by others.

But what can we do to help those in deep Red Brain who are most susceptible to being primed by others? This is the question we will grapple with in the last chapter. How does a Just Society address the psychobiological needs of those who see themselves as being on "the bottom rung of the social hierarchy"? And perhaps a far more pressing issue, how do we help those who have been swept up in a wave of non-rational conviction? How do we avoid magical thinking, hoping that "maybe the problem will just go away on its own"? Here is a case where we do need to override our limbic brakes; for a Society can only become Just if it confronts these issues.

The survival of our species rests on our capacity to be rational despite the crushing stress load that humans have always had and will always have to contend with. *H. sapiens* may be *capable* of rationality, but that is not our default state. History is the devastating record of what happens to civilizations that remain mired in Red Brain. They did not collapse because people refused to return to rationality; this happened because they couldn't.

Self-Reg teaches us that we are not dealing with a case of Hanlon's Razor: viz., "Never attribute to malice that which can be adequately explained by stupidity." It is neither – neither a case of limited intelligence nor wilful denial. Rather, limbic brakes have been triggered and stay locked because the excessive stress remains. The car careens towards a crash, the steering wheel no longer responsive to the touch.

This argument may answer one question, but it raises another. Rationality is one thing; intelligence is another. But what exactly do we mean by *intelligence*, and what role do the limbic brakes play there? That is our topic for the next chapter.

Chapter 6

Reframing IQ

Paradigm for Our Times

Back in 2009, I gave an interview on CBC Radio in which I suggested, "Where IQ was the major paradigm of the twentieth century, in the twenty-first it would be *self-regulation*." The reaction that this comment provoked took me by surprise, stirring up a firestorm that I had not expected. And, truth be told, that I was not sorry to see. Sometimes a raw nerve really does need to be hit.

My intention was not to provoke a controversy in an area that is already controversial enough; not to belittle the theoretical work that has gone into the study of IQ, nor the analyses of the correlational matrices. And I definitely was not suggesting that *self-regulation* would turn out to be a better predictor of long-term educational and social outcomes than IQ.

Rather, my thinking was that, whereas IQ becomes fairly stable around the age of ten, self-regulation is something that can always be altered and enhanced, with profound benefits at any age for any child, teen, adult, or senior. But the more I thought about *limbic braking*, the more I wondered whether the concept of *IQ* needs to be reframed, not in terms of what it doesn't tell us, but rather in terms of what it does.

As I stressed in chapter 2, one of the major benefits of *reframing* is that we often discover new riches in a resource that we might have thought was exhausted. The goal is certainly not to add to the chorus of environmental critics shouting that we should never have been mining there in the first place. Some of the most rewarding aspects of this exercise are to be found in the very questions that IQ researchers themselves have found deeply puzzling.

Why, for example, is there a significant correlation between a child's IQ score at age ten and that same person's IQ at age sixty? Why, for that matter, do we not see this correlation until age ten? Why did IQ scores steadily rise in the twentieth century and now appear to be drifting down again? Why are we often struck by the feeling that an IQ test is not providing us with anywhere close to a true measure of a child's intellectual potential? And more important, why do we so often feel the reverse: that the test confirms our darkest concerns about a child's intelligence? Why does personality appear to have so much more impact on success than IQ? And even more puzzling, how can we explain the many examples of individuals with extraordinarily high IQs whose life has been a stunning failure?

Then there are all the questions that Stephen Jay Gould raised in his *The Mismeasure of Man* (1981), which exposed the scientific methods used to buttress biological determinism to intense scrutiny.[1] Controversies aside,[2] his questions are all important. Why do we tend to think that IQ must be fixed, if not by the child's genes, then by the environment, or by the caregiving the child received in the early years? Why do we think that IQ is a population trait, when everything we know about biology tells us what a truly specious concept *race* is?[3] Why do we even think that IQ is important, and then fall back on a Malthusian bias if our efforts at enrichment meet with scant reward?

There is no shortage of "Whys" here. But these aren't like the endless queries of a three-year-old, for whom this serves as a way of soliciting attention. The hope here is that these Whys will lead to a deeper understanding of *intelligence* – or at least, some aspect of intelligence – and thence more effective strategies for potentiating a child's intellectual potential. These are Whys that will hopefully lead, not just to a paradigm revolution in education, but to a Just Society.

Why Is It So Important to Reframe IQ?

Ultimately, an IQ test clearly reveals something; but clarifying what that "something" is turns out to be anything but straightforward. Sometimes a test reveals that a child has an exceptional working memory and processing speed, or advanced reasoning skills in particular domains. And sometimes it does the opposite, telling us *that* but not *why* a child has difficulty with certain kinds of learning.

The whole point of looking at IQ tests through a Self-Reg lens is to delve more deeply into the latter questions. The premise of *reframing IQ* is not that the tests are inherently flawed but rather that we have yet to fully grasp what we stand to learn from them. What's more, Self-Reg provides a framework for probing the possible benefits – and, perhaps, the wisdom – of IQ testing.

No matter where you stand on the great IQ debate, the one thing that's clear is that, whatever its role as a "dynamic helping agent,"[4] IQ testing has led to some grave consequences. Parents agonize about how "smart" their child is and how to make them smarter. Poorly trained testers have set back large numbers of children, their self-esteem and educational aspirations harmed by how teachers, parents, and even peers treat them as the result of being labelled with a low IQ. These students' educational opportunities are narrowed before they have a chance to develop their native gifts.

IQ has made its way into college entrance exams and employment hiring practices, with dubious results. Lower-income sectors have suffered from public policies inspired by those who continue to see socio-economic status as a reflection of innate intellectual capacity. And, of course, IQ continues to be a breeding ground for racist dogma.

The biggest problem of all, however, is the way that IQ shapes *the way we see a child*, even in those who are most concerned about the hereditarian overtones that have always dogged the field of intelligence testing. Without our being aware that this is happening, a determinist bias colours our thinking. We unconsciously communicate these thoughts through what we say or how we say it, and, just as serious, what we don't say. These messages are internalized by the child, become part of their implicit view of their intelligence and a critical factor in what becomes that child's reality.

Everything we have looked at so far has brought us to the point where we can address this bias. The most basic Self-Reg tenet is: "There's no such thing as a bad, lazy, or stupid kid." The third element of this triumvirate is often what those new to Self-Reg thinking find most counter-intuitive. After all, doesn't an IQ test merely confirm what most of us secretly believe: that some children are simply born less intelligent than others and there's not much that we can do about that?

IQ is both a consequence of and a further cause of our most entrenched views about how a child's intellectual potential is at least partially constrained by genetic factors. In 1969, Arthur Jensen published a chilling paper in which he argued that, for all the effort devoted to Head Start programs, these had only managed to budge IQ scores by around five points: hardly a good return on investment.[5] But if Self-Reg teaches us anything, it is that it is next to impossible to be certain about a child's intellectual potential, even when it seems to be set in stone. Children are forever surprising us and, for that matter, themselves.

But then, what about the statistical analyses done on large populations? What about all those positive correlations that drive the IQ story; for example, between the different subtests on the WAIS, or between different kinds of test (e.g., between WISC and Raven's Matrices)? Or between IQ scores from one year to the next? Or between parents and offspring? Identical twins separated at birth? IQ at age ten and educational outcome, future income, social status, health (physical and mental), and even longevity? These correlations, though not as great as is sometimes suggested, are nonetheless real, and our primary objective in Self-Reg is not to *refute* or *resist* correlations that have been observed, but rather to *understand* them.

That means looking at IQ rationally, not non-rationally. That is, asking Why.

What Do the Tests Test?

What exactly do IQ tests test? One of the most famous – if not infamous – answers to this question is E.G. Boring's claim in 1923 that "intelligence is what the tests test."[6] It is customary to use this quotation to warn psychology students about the dangers of circular reasoning. Yet just before he says this, Boring explains how: "Intelligence *as a measurable capacity* [my emphasis] is what the tests test." Boring had no desire to get embroiled in a philosophical debate about the nature of *intelligence*; what he was after was simply a technical definition. But his way of operationalizing the construct rests on a couple of major assumptions.

The first is that IQ tests are *measuring differences*, however narrowly you define *intelligence*. This assumption has been present from the very first tests designed by Alfred Binet. Hence psychologists have spent so much time trying to identify cognitive processes that might account for these variations: for example, processing speed, perceptual reasoning, working memory, pattern recognition, verbal comprehension (or some sub-component).

In terms of the Triune metaphor, these are quintessential Blue Brain operations. And that is precisely why IQ needs to be reframed. That is, intelligence is not just a whole-body but a whole-brain phenomenon, for reasons we explore below.

The second big assumption is that we are measuring a relatively fixed capacity that varies from one child to the next. This assumption goes back to Galton's view that *intelligence* exhibits the same variation as is seen in other heritable traits (e.g., height).[7] Hence an IQ test establishes a child's place in a normal distribution (relative to what constitutes a representative sample for that child). Boring's basic question – which psychologists still struggle with – is: What exactly are we measuring?

His answer was that the tests are testing "work performed against time." That is, "measurable intelligence is like 'power' as the physicist uses the word: the amount of work that can be done in a given time." The association between *intelligence* and *power* dates back to the fourteenth century (with antecedents that trace back to Aristotle). Boring sought to translate this metaphor into modern mechanist terms by adapting the concept that James Watt had developed to sell his steam engines.

Watt calculated what he called an engine's "horsepower" by comparing its output to the amount of force exerted by a horse pulling an axle to grind corn, multiplied by the speed at which it did so. In similar fashion, Boring suggested that IQ tests establish how many different kinds of problems a child can solve ("output") in a fixed time. In other words, what the tests are measuring is "brainpower."[8]

At the same time that Boring was trying to operationalize intelligence, Spearman was arguing that if all the different scores in IQ subtests load on to a common factor, then that common factor – labelled g – must reflect an individual's overall mental capacity.[9] This basic capacity, "general intelligence," determines how you perform on the various intelligence subtests, in much the same way that "athletic ability" determines how well you'll do in the ten sports of the decathlon.

This theme continually crops up in IQ theory: the idea that there must be some underlying mental/neurobiological factor that determines a child's IQ. At various times this factor has been described as *mental energy, processing efficiency,* or *processing speed.* This idea hardly originated with Spearman; in fact, it finds its way all the way back to Socrates' argument in the *Theaetetus* that every mind contains a "block of wax" that determines how well the individual thinks and remembers.

Boring cautions that by no means is he suggesting that a child with "less brainpower" can't get to the same finish line as one with more (the racing metaphor is Boring's). It just takes that child longer to get up a hill in low gear. The problem is that children blessed with more brainpower get to the finish line faster and so are able to go on to another race if they so choose. In the endless slate of school competitions, they have the opportunity to pull ever further ahead. Not to mention enter the kinds of Formula One races like medical school that lie forever beyond the scope of a go-karter.

But there is a fundamental problem with Boring's metaphor. Unlike a horse mill, how fast you get to a finish line isn't solely a function of an engine's cc's; no less important are the brakes.

As the rally driver Jari-Matti Latvala once explained, the secret to winning Tours de Corse actually lies in the latter.[10] So to keep with the metaphor, the point that the Triune metaphor raises is that IQ tests aren't just measuring the capacity of a child's cylinders, but also, and no less significant, how smoothly the child brakes. That is, what the tests are measuring involves the whole brain: Red Brain as well as Blue Brain.

Anyone who has ever driven with sticky brakes that grab will grasp the importance of this point. What's more, anyone who has ever driven with the kind of engine brake known as a "governor" knows only too well that how much power is available to the driver involves more than just the size of the engine. Just as a governor controls the maximum speed of an engine, "acquired governors" control the speed at which a child processes information.

But the thing about governors is that they can always be changed. This isn't so much a case of *increasing* as *releasing* brain-power. And this is the reason Self-Reg insists that "There is no such thing as a stupid child." *Stupid* started to be used to signify "mentally slow" in the sixteenth century. The assumption was that a child is born that way and stays that way. But for Self-Reg the question is always, Why?

For five centuries, answers to this last question were shaped by a hereditarian bias. Only now can we begin to think about this issue in dynamic terms of Red together with Blue Brain processes.

Acquired Governors

The Red Brain remembers what the Blue Brain forgets – or represses, or flat out denies. I had an experience the other day that touches on this point.

I wanted to install a new program on my computer that, according to the developers, would only take a few minutes. After trying for well over an hour, I gave up in total exasperation. What I was feeling wasn't just frustration: it bordered on despair.

I asked a colleague to install it for me and left her to it while I went off to relax with a book for what I thought would be several hours. But a few minutes later she was back in the room and smilingly said, "All done." Overcoming the impulse to throttle her, I started thinking seriously, not about the program, but about intelligence testing, for the episode had raised a number of intriguing questions:

- Why did I find this easy task so hard?
- Why did I so abruptly quit?
- Why was I so drained afterwards?
- Why did I vow to never install another program?
- Why did this utterly trivial experience affect my mood so strongly?

Multiple stressors were involved: physical (e.g., the glare from the screen, the hum of the fan, the fact that I tried to do this when I was already in LE/HT after a day's work). But above all was the cognitive stress, which troubled me. After all, I have loved math problems for as long as I can remember, and I loved learning how to program when I was in high school (which involved transcribing a program you had written onto punch cards). What happened?

Like Kekulé dreaming about his snakes, I had a vivid dream that night about an experience that had lain buried in my unconscious. I had one of the first desktops when I was in graduate school: an Olivetti M24. We lived in the English countryside and one night a lightning bolt hit our house just as I was putting the finishing touches on my doctoral thesis. When the power came back on, I encountered something very odd. Back in those days, you opened your document from a file directory, and the same number of files were still there, but every one of them had exactly the same number of bits: the computer had taken my total amount of information and divided this evenly, and quite randomly, between forty files!

The moment when I realized what had happened was traumatic. Fortunately, I had kept a hard backup, so the next day I started the onerous task of re-entering everything from scratch. Little wonder I'd suppressed this memory. But while I may have seemed to have forgotten this crisis, my hippocampus had not. In more ways than one, my limbic system was thwarting my efforts to do something that should have been straightforward. If this happens while you are driving, you have to take your foot off the gas and let the car slowly coast to a stop; but when our limbic brakes kick in, problem solving seizes up.

I actually enjoy working on reasoning problems that require a large number of steps, but this doesn't apply to computer programming. Trying to unravel the reasons that I have this flaw (if that's what it is) feels a bit like reading one of Barbara Tuchman's masterful books. And that's the point: namely, that there's a complex history to why I find this kind of reasoning task hard and, indeed, a history to why I so abruptly gave up. The same point applies to IQ tests.

This was a lesson we learned early on in the MEHRI study. IQ was one of the baseline measures that we had to collect to satisfy the demands of experimental rigour, even though we were primarily interested in social-emotional and language gains. As is generally the case, our psychometrician saw significant gains in the children's IQ scores when she reduced their test anxiety. But despite these measures, there was always a point at which the children would refuse to answer any more questions, questions that the psychometrician felt sure they could, in fact, have answered.

The more I puzzled over why the children would adamantly refuse to go any further, the more I began to wonder whether we weren't confronted here with a much larger issue than just test fatigue. Here we were, trying to figure out how to reduce factors like anxiety that we worried were interfering with – giving a false read of – a child's IQ, when the tests were telling us that "effort" wasn't the issue. The problem was that a child's governors were kicking in when the tension became too great.

Limbic brakes cause the cognitive processes I mentioned above to slew, which is why acquired governors have such a profound impact on reasoning ability, interest, and motivation. Considerable research has been done on the biological governors that affect IQ (e.g., visual, hearing, and spatial deficits; specific language impairment), but little has been done on acquired governors, or, in dynamic systems theory terminology, the "attractors" that have formed in the child's mental landscape.

An attractor is a complex system in which the constituents are bound together in a web of mutually reinforcing co-actions. (Think of Chris Waddington's example of water flowing down a mountainside that turns into a stream and then a river.) We saw in chapter 3 how a child's personality is an attractor; that is, a pattern of predictable behavioural responses to social and emotional stress (a "behavioural fingerprint"). The same is true of how the child responds to cognitive stress.

Attractors are extremely stable and constrain future possibilities of change or growth. The fact that IQ stabilizes around the age of ten, that it is resistant to change thereafter, and that we can make long-range predictions based on the child's IQ at age ten indicates that we're dealing here with an attractor: the product of a complex nature/nurture synthesis that serves as a governor on the child's intellectual potential.[11] By age ten the pattern seems intractable and unalterable.

Like all attractors, IQ is a function of internal and external factors, biological and experiential. By no means have external factors been overlooked in IQ research; the problem is that only abuse, the effects of deprivation (e.g., lack of stimulation and poor nutrition), and environmental toxins have been seriously studied. Missing is any consideration of *the effect of inherited determinist biases on the things we say or don't say*, the messages we unconsciously communicate. This point applies not just to parents but to all of the Inter-brains that are involved in the formation of a child's "intelligence/attractor."

The crux of the Self-Reg reframing is not that IQ tests don't provide an insight into a child's intelligence; it is that *intelligence as measured by the tests is a function of both Blue Brain and Red Brain processes*. There is a dynamic interplay between prefrontal and limbic systems. Limbic brakes have a pronounced effect on both the development and the expression of the various mental abilities. Far from being tangential, the Self-Reg reframing of IQ situates the child's limbic brakes at the very heart of assessing a child's intelligence (Figure 6.1).

But this brings us to an even bigger question: our concern here is not just how the brakes impinge on the tests but also how the tests impinge on the brakes.

Figure 6.1 Limbic brake wheel

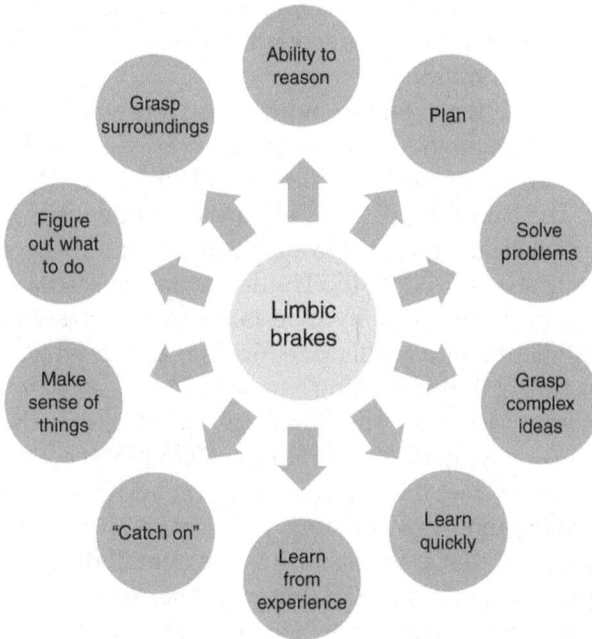

IQ Tests Are Stress Tests

Time after time we have seen how the experimental paradigms that have fuelled the resurgence of self-control thinking have turned out to be stress tests that were not recognized as such. That is not to say that the Still Face, Strange Situation, Marshmallow Task, temptation resistance paradigm, ball-and-bat problem, Wason Selection Task, etc. are without significance; it is to reframe what these tests are telling us about the child's response to different kinds of stress. The same point applies to IQ tests.

The first indication of this point – although it wasn't fully recognized as such – appeared in Liebert and Morris's classic studies on test anxiety back in the 1960s.[12] They broke test anxiety down into two components: "worry," and what they called "emotionality." By the latter, they were alluding to a child's autonomic reactions (such as perspiration and elevated heart rate). They concluded that when anxiety is high, the child's attention is divided between test material, mental intrusions, and somatic awareness. So, by reducing test anxiety, you raise test scores because you are reducing the splintering of attention.

Since the time that Liebert and Morris were writing, neuroscientists have developed a much more nuanced view of the connectivity between prefrontal and subcortical processes. It is on this basis that, in place of a "divided attention" model, Self-Reg looks at how subcortical processes impinge on attention. Accordingly, the basic question raised by the Triune metaphor is: to what extent do children underperform on IQ tests because they are distracted by internal mental and bodily phenomena, and to what extent do test scores reflect limbic braking?

Liebert and Morris's "emotionality" variables are the unmistakable signs of sympathetic nervous system (SNS) activation: the result of the very fact that concentrating on an IQ test is a whole-body phenomenon. It is not simply the fragmentation of "attentional resources" that is the issue: it is the overall drain on energy. Not "mental energy," whatever that might be, but *energy in general*. Test anxiety is both the result of being in a depleted state and a further depletion of dwindling resources, as has been so powerfully shown in the research on *scarcity mindset*. Our question is: Why does this happen in cases where "scarcity" as such is not a factor? Is it because biological challenges and/or cognitive deficits force some children to work harder than others? Is it the test situation? Past experiences? Something about the test itself?

The more pronounced a child's anxiety, the more likely that the answer is all of the above. But why is test anxiety such a serious issue for some children and not others? Some kids respond to an IQ test the same way as to Survey Monkey's "Fun Survey for Kids." Why don't they all?

The answer, of course, is precisely the fact that the latter is fun while the former is not. But an IQ test is not inadvertently stressful: the whole point of an IQ test is that it has been carefully designed to be increasingly stressful. Questions get steadily more difficult. Subtests probe areas that lie outside the child's comfort zone. Abstract reasoning tasks are meant to stretch the child's thinking.

There's the time element, which has been titrated to build the stress. The test situation itself is stressful, whether it's one-on-one with someone who can't control their leakage, or in a group setting that breeds social and prosocial stress. Or for that matter, the time of day the test is written and whether you're a morning or an evening person.[13]

Ultimately, we're testing how *this child* copes with the cognitive stress imposed compared to a group of other children (that are as similar as possible). It's largely because IQ tests are stress tests that we see the correlations that we do with downstream mental and physical health. That is why we see the same correlations here that we see with other stress tests, like the Marshmallow Task. Undoubtedly, an IQ test provides an insight into how the child responds to cognitive stress as opposed to a temptation (assuming that the marshmallow is, in fact, a temptation). But as with delay of gratification, the greater the child's stress load when the child comes into the test, the more stressful that child will find the test, and vice versa.

This is why we see the emotionality variables. These are, foremost, stress indicators: they manifest how hard a child is working to cope with this experience. And some children have to work much harder than others, not just because of processing challenges, or the fact that they are highly anxious to begin with, but because the cognitive stress overloads an attractor that has formed, in the way that a torrential rain causes the stream going down the mountain to overflow.

If you push a child too hard once their limbic brakes have kicked in, you risk sending that child into fight-or-flight. We saw this happen repeatedly with the kids in the MEHRI study. Convinced that their IQ was higher than the test was showing – and swept up in the idea that accurately assessing their IQ was somehow important – we ended up provoking a meltdown. It would have been easy to misconstrue this response as due to the child's "condition," rather than recognize that we had sent the child into fight-or-flight because we had failed to recognize the signs of limbic braking.

Indeed, the primary function of the limbic brakes is precisely to prevent this from happening; the cost of fight-or-flight in terms of energy expenditure is considerable and, in non-emergency situations, completely maladaptive. All too often, pushing a child to override their limbic brakes only results in the brake pads falling off. Asking Why isn't just about delving into a child's deficits, or the history of a child's response to cognitive stresses; it's equally about understanding the biases that lead to our blind spot in the first place.

"Ravels" versus "Khachaturians"

We might be tempted to conclude that the very fact that IQ tests are stress tests demonstrates conclusively why self-control is so important for academic and life success. If, for whatever reason, one child has to work harder than another on cognitive tasks, then either they make the necessary effort and, as a result, enjoy "the blessing which rewards the triumph of energy and will," or suffer the consequences of being or becoming "a pauper in blood and bones"[14] (see chapter 8). But it is science, not charity, that forces us to dig deeper.

A few years ago, Bronson and Merryman published an illuminating review of recent research on children's variable response to "competitive pressure."[15] In chapter 8 we will look at how this research bears on our understanding of *perseverance*.[16] But for the moment, we need to think about the neurobiological reasons why the stress of an IQ test brings out the best in some kids – in terms of their ability to reason, solve problems, and anticipate consequences – but causes others to freeze.

A key factor lies in dopamine, which triggers neuronal firing in the PFC. But in excess it has the opposite effect, creating an "overflow" condition that Adele Diamond likens to "flooding a car engine with too much gasoline."[17] Just as too much gas prevents the spark plugs from firing, too much dopamine causes what Diamond describes as a "meltdown" in the PFC. So excess dopamine has to be removed. But some children seem to be much more susceptible to dopamine build-up than others, leading once again to the question of Why. Part of the answer appears to be genetic.

Diamond's research suggests that how children respond to the stress of an IQ test is a function of the variant of the COMT gene that they have inherited.[18] There are two variants of the gene: a "slow-removal" version and a "fast-removal" one. Those with the former are said to perform best in situations where the stress slowly builds; those with the latter perform better in pitched conditions. Given the way an IQ test is designed, it comes as no surprise that those with the fast-removal variant have higher scores.[19]

One way to conceptualize the difference between slow- and fast-removal COMT genes is to think of two stunning but very different pieces of music: Ravel's *Boléro* and Khachaturian's *Sabre Dance*. In *Boléro*, the melody is of a slowly expanding musical tension over a steady-handed and strong percussion, while the *Sabre Dance* is marked by fast frenetic movement throughout. I would encourage you to listen to the two pieces as you consider how differently kids respond to cognitive stress.

It would seem that we are back to yet another version of Boring's racing metaphor: that is, that IQ tests pick out those Khachaturians who are going to finish first in today's highly competitive PFC-intensive races and so avoid the negative consequences that a Ravel-driver must endure. But concerns about reading too much into single-gene studies aside, the COMT research brings us back to the question of why some children have to stop so much earlier than others.

I mentioned above how the children in the MEHRI study would all reach a point at which they suddenly quit, even though we knew that many of them could have gone further, much as I did when I was trying to install the computer program. That's the whole point of an IQ test: to compare where a child stops vis-à-vis their peers. It's that point where the child *won't* – not *can't* – go any further that determines the child's IQ score. A reminder of Descartes's point of "will over reason." Kahneman's inverted-V curve.

The conventional line of thinking is that a child stops when they push up against the limits of their intelligence. But why would a child have such a "limit"? Simply because of their genes? To borrow another wonderful quotation from Russell: "The method of 'postulating' what we want [e.g., with a genetic determinist explanation] has many advantages; they are the same as the advantages of theft over honest toil." [20]

Self-Reg prompts us to consider whether a child has stopped because they find the test overly stressful. In other words, is the child self-regulating by stopping? To know why their stress is so great, we have to look at all five domains in the Self-Reg model. A vital element in the child's response is where they are in the Thayer matrix at the time of taking the test. No less important is the child's experience with this kind of material. And then, of course, there is the whole matter of whether the child has a processing deficit that requires them to work that much harder than their peers.

Rather than assuming that an IQ test has some sort of fixed "stress quotient," we need to bear in mind that *what is a negative stress for one child may be positive for another.* Cognitive stressors, like all stressors, are not the same for all children. Nor can we simply *assume* that the same problem produces the same amount of dopamine in all children and what distinguishes them is how quickly they can clear this so that their PFC stays within its optimal firing range. One of the things I've noticed about the person who works on my computer is that she doesn't feel anything like the kind of tension that I do installing a program; in fact, when I questioned her about this, she responded, "It's actually kind of relaxing!"

Similarly, some kids clearly are not distressed by an IQ test; on the contrary, they seem to enjoy working on the different problems. Whatever stress they are experiencing, it is positive; that is, it spurs them on. Moreover, we can predict on this basis that these kids (the top 10 per cent) are going to find similar cognitive challenges a positive stress. Processing factors can be a major reason that a particular problem is such a negative stress for a child.

Suppose, for example, a child finds it difficult to figure out word analogies. Recent research points to an underlying problem in working memory. But then, there might be any number of reasons why the child has a problem with working memory – at least in such-and-such a domain. It may be due to a constriction in the roots of cognition: for example, local and long-range connections between the senses, internal and external, that formed in the early years of life. The problem may relate to energy/tension; the more deeply a child goes into LE/HT, the more compromised their working memory becomes. Or the problem in working memory may have nothing to do with memory at all. Let me explain.

The fact that a child stops at a certain point does not signify that they could not have gone on. Scientists have shown that incentives such as money or sweets have a significant effect on test performance in lower-scoring children.[21] This may seem to confirm that motivation is the most important of the "nonintellective" traits that David Wechsler talked about in his seminal research in the 1930s.[22]

This idea has long been at the heart of IQ thinking. At the start of the twentieth century, Thorndike explained that "all our measurements assume that the individual in question tries as hard as he can to make as high a score as possible ... we rarely know the relation of any person's effort to his maximum possible effort."[23] So, on the classical self-control paradigm, the low-scoring child is simply not motivated to "try as hard" as the high-scoring child.

This line of thinking ties in with the still widespread view that "conative" personality traits – for example, poor self-control – result in social stratification.[24] But from a Self-Reg perspective, the effect of incentives on raising IQ in low-scoring children is not that this compensates for a personality defect but, rather, that we can push a child past the peak of an inverted-V curve. In fact, we do this to children all the time, not just through punishments and rewards but through all those nonverbal messages touched on above.

In some children, it is indeed possible to build stress tolerance; in others, the hippocampus remembers the experience of being pushed past a peak, especially if we have pushed a child too hard past their peak. When that happens, the child will balk at the very thought of repeating that experience, as we saw when we tried to get children who had quit early on their IQ test to try again on a subsequent occasion. The hippocampus keeps a very strict record of when going past the peak of an inverted-V curve resulted in fight or flight.

The lesson here is that *effort itself has a history*! This may be the most important of all the lessons that need to be learned regarding the question of why children stop where they do on an IQ test, why each of us has to emulate Barbara Tuchman if we are going to help a child.

Once a child is pushed past their peak, this lowers the threshold for limbic braking for the rest of the test. And recall the metaphor of the *Sabre Dance*: for some children, the test starts off with a bang and never lets up. A child who is jolted right out of the gate must write the rest of the test with their parking brake engaged. This may be a major reason why we see the correlations that we do between subtest scores; that is, the limbic brakes limit the expenditure of energy on each successive phase of the testing.

What's particularly significant is how, beginning around the age of ten, a child will continue to stop at relatively the same point vis-à-vis their peers. This phenomenon is eerily similar to the correlational model that Barry Pfitzner and Tracy Rishel developed to predict the order in which drivers would place in NASCAR races.[25] The kind of "objective, measurable variables" in their model is only too reminiscent of an IQ test. A child who places in the middle of the pack in Grade 3 is highly likely to finish in the same position in Grade 12. Or quit the race entirely the moment he gets the chance.

Why not let them quit? The answer, of course, lies in the extensive body of research showing the long-term benefits of education.[26] Really long term. While I was working on this chapter, research was published showing how the higher a person's level of education the better that person's cognitive functioning later in life.[27]

The problem is, we have tried forcing children and teens to stick with the race, without much success. Not only do draconian measures stifle the curiosity that is the lifeblood of education, but they also have a demoralizing effect on educators and students. What we need to figure out is how to release the limbic brakes that are holding back a student, and to do that we need to release the determinist brakes that impede our thinking about the difficulties a particular student is having.

We aren't trying to turn Ravels into Khachaturians. All students are capable of making beautiful music. The problem is when our own intellectual biases block them from developing their talent. What we really need to remind ourselves of here is the moral of yet another of Aesop's Fables: "The Tortoise and the Hare."

A Trophic Cascade in Education

The most pressing question that needs to be asked at the end of this chapter is: "Why bother to put so much effort into reframing IQ"? After all, you only reframe a theory or concept because a new and productive way of thinking emerges. If the issue here were simply that we need to be wary of IQ testing, that hardly calls for the kind of serious analysis involved in a reframing; just highlighting the potential dangers would be enough.

The whole point of reframing a theory or concept, as opposed to refuting or revising it, is that this leads us to think differently about something we have taken for granted. This isn't simply a philosophical diversion: what Russell referred to as an "idle tea-table amusement."[28] Philosophy can be fun, but it's also deadly serious.

Like it or not, the correlations mapped by IQ researchers are significant. One of the most arresting came out in 2013: Afia Ali and her colleagues found a significant relationship between IQ and happiness.[29] There are all sorts of confounds, and a large part of the paper's interest lies in how they sought to isolate as direct a correlation as possible. But for our purposes, there is no need to worry about "accounting for all the confounds": what matters is simply that, at the end of the day, IQ is related to long-term well-being.

The implication is that the more intelligent you are, the better your life is going to be. But then, this is the driving animus in all the work that we do with children: to give them as good a life as we possibly can. The last thing we want to hear is that a child's intellectual potential is going to limit their prospects of future happiness. Far from seeking to dismiss Ali's findings, our goal is to explore the basis for the correlation that she extracted from national IQ and mental health records.

Especially important is to grasp what IQ tests are telling us. Understand this and we'll be in a position to figure out what we need to do, not just to help a child do better in school or get a better job, but to have a better life. And reframing is so important because the determinist view of IQ is telling us that, in the end, there's very little that we can do. That was really the point of Jensen's article: to convince us to resign ourselves to the inevitable.

The truth is that Boring's way of thinking is never far beneath the surface in the IQ literature. The operative assumption, tacit or otherwise, is that the more brainpower you are born with, the more likely it is that you'll adopt a healthy lifestyle and make better choices. But Boring's view rests on the one-sided Blue Brain view of intelligence that we've been examining, which is precisely why he had virtually nothing to say on the remedial side of things.

What we saw above is that *intelligence* is a whole-brain phenomenon, as much a matter of brain resistance as brainpower. When we measure a child's intelligence, the score is a product of the interaction between Blue and Red Brain processes. The more entrenched an attractor, the greater the drag on reasoning – and, ultimately, on quality of life. But that's what attractors do: they affect the entire ecology.

An attractor, as we saw, acts as a governor: it constrains what kind of effort the child will make, which challenges the child will take on or shy away from. It is not just internal forces holding the attractor in place (e.g., neurobiological or psychological), but external as well; especially, how we respond to the child's limbic braking, whether we add to or reduce the child's stress load.

By definition, it is difficult to disrupt an attractor, but not impossible. The problem is that it requires less energy to maintain an attractor than to dislodge it. Think, for example, of the case of a child with specific language impairment. Because of the stress involved, the child avoids the very experiences that are needed to acquire functional language skills. It takes a great deal of work to overcome this attractor: on the part of a speech-language pathologist (SLP), the child's parents, the child. Yet through this combined effort, the connections between auditory, motor, and visual systems can be forged and the child acquires language skills.

The same point applies to IQ. The low-scoring child is often one whose brakes have kicked in early. Sticky brakes are a drag on a child's ability to learn: the child has to work much harder than those whose brakes are smooth. Not surprisingly, the child will avoid stresses that peers find stimulating. But the problem here is not that this child is unwilling to make the effort that we see others make; it is that they are already working too hard and the prospect of working even harder is what is beyond their capacity.

If we can release their brakes, we'll see a transformation in that child's ability to learn. But how do we do this? New technologies and programs are surfacing that target constrictions in the roots of cognition. Working memory exercises (e.g., visualization techniques) and executive function coaching are effective. But we need to do more. The parameters need to be broadened to encompass all five stress domains. Working memory, like thinking, is a whole-body phenomenon, and is similarly impacted by excessive stress. The child who scores low on an IQ test may be caught in a stress cycle, which is why we see all the correlations that we do.

The bell curve starts to look like a Yerkes-Dodson type of stress curve: in this case, strongly negative as you move left from the midline, increasingly positive as you move to the right. That is, what the normal distribution is telling us is that reasoning tasks are a negative stress – to varying degrees – for as many as two-thirds of all children, while around a quarter find them positive. The correlations drawn between IQ and academic testing tells us that the same will be true for schooling in general.

In that case, what an IQ test is really telling us is that we need to consider how we can make schooling a positive stress for all children. Far from inspiring a fatalistic view about a child's *intellectual potential*, a low IQ score should spur us on to reduce the child's overall stress load, not just in the cognitive domain, but in all five domains.

That's ultimately what reframing IQ is all about: turning what has hitherto been an irrelevant and possibly harmful tool for far too many children into something positive. Far from being an argument for streaming, IQ testing is one of the most powerful examples that we have for why it is so important for schools to become Self-Reg havens.[30]

But the ultimate reason why it's worth putting so much effort into reframing IQ isn't simply because it can help so many children – although that is reason enough. It's because helping these children will trigger the opposite of a "trophic cascade."

In "How Wolves Change Rivers," Sustainable Human describes how one of the most exciting scientific findings of the past half-century is the discovery of widespread trophic cascades. A trophic cascade is an ecological process which starts at the top of the food chain and tumbles all the way down to the bottom.[31] In the case of IQ, we are reversing the process and setting off a subterranean geyser at the bottom of the educational food chain that will flow all the way up to the top of societal well-being. Our ultimate goal here is not to win "the other arms race" (see chapter 7); it is to nurture in all students the rationality that democracy demands from each of its citizens. This could turn out to be one of the most exciting scientific findings of the next century.

But it all starts with us, with how we see a child, how we communicate our biases to the child, without realizing that we are doing so. But the child does. And before you know it, the child has internalized our biases.

Can IQ be changed? is the wrong question.[32] The right question is: Can we change? Can we see IQ, not as a measurement tool, but as one of the keys to unlocking a child's future?

Chapter 7

The Joy and Pain of Maths

Becoming a Philomath

When I was in Grade 10, I asked our basketball coach, who also happened to be our Latin teacher, why anyone would ever choose to study Latin in Grade 11. I loved basketball; Latin not so much. In those days, Latin was compulsory in Grade 10 but thereafter turned into an elective. His answer was not what I was expecting and was enough to make me stick with Latin until the end of high school. Latin, he said, is like basketball in so many ways. Where basketball improves your hand-eye coordination and stamina, Latin opens up a wonderful trove of classics, and inspires a deep love of learning languages. And he was right – more than he ever would have dreamt.

I've never had a hobby other than learning foreign languages. I love not just the challenge of learning a new language, but how it enables you to see the world in a completely new way. I find that I think differently in Spanish than in English (and not just because of the subjunctive!). I suppose that my love of reframing goes back to my experiences in high school Latin.

In fact, the love of learning a new language shaped all the work I have done ever since. For me, learning about neuroscience is learning a new language, with its own unique vocabulary and a distinctive way of thinking. I see psychology itself as not just a language, but akin to Indo-European, with all the different branches in psychology as the various romance languages that IE spawned. And then there is maths.

Maths, as Bethany a.k.a. "Math Geek Mama" put it, is "a foreign language: So treat it like one!"[1]

Maths is the first foreign language I learned. And I learned it not because I wanted to please my parents or my teacher, but because, like Tarzan learning how to read, I wanted to understand what all these squiggles meant. *Understand*, not *memorize*. I thought it was just another form of playing.

Hardly a day goes by when I don't encounter some article about how important maths is, and how badly our students are doing in it. Here, too, we need to be asking Why, not just why students are struggling – which I'll get to – but why we think maths is so important. And one big problem might be that maths is treated as a means to an end rather than an end in itself.

We are forever being told how essential maths is in today's highly mathematized world. First, there are the very practical benefits. How well an elementary student does in maths is a better predictor of subsequent academic achievement than reading.[2] You need maths to get a good job and advance in your career, balance your cheque book, figure out what time you need to leave the house to catch the bus, know how to split up a pizza evenly.

Then there are the more abstruse benefits. Maths reasoning generalizes to any sort of problem solving. Maths is good for physical, mental, and, indeed, brain health.[3] It is definitely good for neuroscience.[4] And ultimately, we come to the sublime: maths formulas have the same effect on the limbic system as an art masterpiece.[5] Maths gives us a glimpse of the transcendent.[6]

Maths is the ultimate example of the benefits of learning a foreign language. It is the foundation for learning any and every science. Maths, one might say, is the Proto-Indo-European of science. And my concern is that, for the reasons I will go into below, we have become so anxious about the importance of maths that we've ended up exacerbating the very problem that we're so desperate to overcome.

I suspect that, had Latin remained compulsory until the end of high school, or had the Programme for International Student Assessment (PISA) ranked Latin alongside science, technology, engineering, and mathematics (STEM) subjects, I would not have come to see learning a foreign language as one of the great pleasures that life affords. I wouldn't have jumped at the chance to read the *Aeneid* in Latin or *Don Quixote* in Castilian. And I suspect that, had I been forced to learn maths by rote, I would never have appreciated why the discovery of analytic geometry established Descartes as a leading thinker in the Age of Reason. I wouldn't have savoured Morris Kline's *Mathematical Thought from Ancient to Modern Times*. I would certainly not have delighted in the beauty of Gödel's second incompleteness theorem. Or the fun of seeing numbers as groups of rocks.[7]

Or struggled with the question of why we are turning so many students into monoglots.

"Stemming the Divide"

An initiative was launched in the United States in 2017, encouraging scientists to run for public office so as to bridge the divide between science and politics.[8] The goal is to ensure that government policy is based on current scientific knowledge, rather than on what politicians tend – or would like – to believe. As we saw in chapter 4, the enemy of rationality is non-rational certainty. But the attempt to quell anxiety about climate change by denying that the phenomenon exists amounts to the ultimate example of a maladaptive mode of self-regulation.

The MEHRIT Centre (TMC) could be said to be engaged in a similar mission as "STEM the Divide": in our case, the goal is to bridge the chasm between *what scientists are learning about learning* and *how we teach and parent*. But to stem any divide, we must first clarify why it exists. Is it simply due to a lack of knowledge, or is there a deeper factor at play: a clash between paradigms? Here, too, denial amounts to a maladaptive mode of self-regulation, and in this case, the data are telling us just how maladaptive.

There is an understandable fear that we are witnessing a revival in some government circles not just of avoidance but of outright hostility to science. But TMC's concern is not with the latest clash with Flat Earther mentality over environmental policy. Our legal brief vis-à-vis education concerns the divide between a teaching philosophy based on the *self-control* paradigm and an approach to teaching that is grounded in the science of *self-regulation*.

There have been major advances over the past decade in our understanding of the complex reasons why students find some subjects difficult to master and how to help them. It is rarely as simple as *lack of effort*. Time and again we find that the child who is having trouble at school is dealing with any number of biological or sensory issues, processing deficits, family issues, social challenges, problems in mood, or problems in peer relations. Quite often it is all of the above.

The point is, Self-Reg is forever asking *Why* a student is struggling. When we suspect that the problem is due to stress overload, we immediately set about to identify and reduce the various stressors at play. But those who believe that a child's problems are due to a lack of character will never go down this path, for they have already decided on the answer.

In practical terms, the divide we are concerned with is between those succeeding at school and those falling ever further behind. Educational stratification starts early. It is already evident by Grade 3, if not in junior kindergarten. And the question we need to address is: Why, for all the effort put into this matter, have we failed to close these achievement gaps? Without an answer to this question, anxiety and frustration only grow – at every level – for students, parents, teachers, administrators, and policymakers who must decide whether to turn to science or fall back on tradition to address the problem.

The perfect illustration of this point can be found in the current debate swirling around me as I write this chapter over the decline in Grade 3 maths scores on Ontario's Education Quality and Accountability Office test. Here we are confronted with a divide that is not just frustrating but, in many quarters, alarming; what we know about maths instruction is already considerable, and yet results not only continue to disappoint but are actually getting worse!

This slide has prompted the kneejerk reaction that students – and perhaps their parents and teachers – need to work much harder. Complacency and lack of commitment are seen as the heart of the problem. The unspoken conviction is that if students do not make the necessary effort, they must live with the consequences of that choice. But the result of this attitude has been a growing number of young students with High Math Anxiety (HMA).

The point of adopting a Self-Reg approach to this issue isn't to search for an "effortless" way to learn maths (as in trying to learn a foreign language in your sleep by playing a tape).[9] The point is rather to turn to the sciences looked at in chapter 1 to understand why a problem like HMA is so intransigent and how we can respond. The goal of Self-Reg is to *reduce* – but not *eliminate* – the effort of effortful control[10] by reducing the stresses triggering limbic braking. And what makes the debate over declining maths scores so interesting and important is that it illustrates what we might describe – in Urie Bronfenbrenner's terms – as an ecological system of stress.

The Hierarchy of High Math Anxiety

The influence of inherited biases tends to wax and wane depending on how much stress an individual or a society is under. The greater our anxiety, the more polarized and paralysed our thinking becomes. Traditional nostrums suddenly become compelling. Will rules over reason.

Back in 1986, when Britain was undergoing a disturbingly high level of societal unrest, Sir Keith Joseph published an introduction to a new edition of Samuel Smiles's *Self-Help*. It was this event that brought Smiles to my attention and, more important, the resurgence of the Victorian view of perseverance that we will look at in the next chapter. This attitude has surfaced again in the debate over the decline in maths scores. Success in maths, according to the perseverance mantra, depends on hard work, discipline, and self-reliance: not mollycoddling (another classic Victorian term, as we will see in chapter 8).

Yet with the resurgence of the perseverance outlook has come a corresponding increase in the number of students with HMA. HMA is used to designate a condition of acute emotional distress observed in a great many young students who are struggling with maths, but it also describes a societal condition. In fact, the two phenomena are more than just correlated, and the first step in a Self-Reg approach to HMA lies in unpacking the relationship between them.

The decline in Grade 3 maths scores has become a matter of great societal angst for many reasons. To begin with, research shows how important the early years are for downstream maths achievement and how hard it is to catch up. Research I touched on above also shows the importance of maths for dealing with the demands of modern life and, not surprisingly, the long-term impact of maths skills on socio-economic status. It has become clear that maths skills are a foundation not just for later academic success in STEM but for success in general. But the major source of "societal HMA" is what the *Economist* dubbed "The Other Arms Race": the international battle over maths standings.[11]

On 20 February 2014, English newspapers were filled with a story about how, in the case of maths, the children of cleaners and factory workers in China are two years ahead of the children of lawyers and doctors in Britain. Not long afterwards, the education minister in the United Kingdom was on a plane to Shanghai and Singapore with a delegation of headmasters and education experts to study what the papers were referring to as "the teaching practices and positive philosophy" that have led to these results. And yet, just a few months earlier (3 December 2013), the same papers were reporting a story about how over one-third of Chinese students are suffering from severe mood problems because of the excessive pressure they are under, and the deep concern of the Ministry of Education about this growing mental health crisis.

There is nothing new about the tension evident here. When William Forster introduced the Elementary Education Bill in 1870 – which marked the start of compulsory education for English children – he argued that the enfranchisement of society that occurred as a result of the 1867 Reform Act required an educated electorate. Only an educated citizenry would, as Jefferson had argued, be capable of sustaining democracy. Yet Forster went on to insist that "upon the speedy provision of elementary education depends our industrial prosperity."[12]

The strain between these two goals – an educated populace, united by its shared desire to sustain democracy, and a competitive spirit, in which every individual is motivated to excel – has been there from the start, as Michael Young so famously depicted.[13] But it has become particularly sharp in the past two decades as a consequence of globalism; children must now compete not just with their peers but with children from around the world.

Following his State of the Union address in 2013, President Obama told the students at the P-Tech school in Brooklyn:

> in previous generations, America's standing economically was so much higher than everybody else's that we didn't have a lot of competition. Now, you've got billions of people from Beijing to Bangalore to Moscow, all of whom are competing with you directly. And they're – those countries are working every day, to out-educate and outcompete us.[14]

In other words, families in the West have to compete with families in developing nations who, following the economic collapse that occurred after the Second World War, saw education as their only chance to escape from crippling poverty. Parents were willing to pay virtually any price to seize this opportunity. The fervour thus created has not abated.

In recent years, a number of important voices have warned about the perils of placing global competition in education ahead of children's well-being.[15] Maths has become the battlefront in this massive international war. For Western educators, it is bad enough that the same Far East nations keep dominating PISA; to make matters worse, replicating their teaching practices has not produced the same results.

Maths education has thus been caught up in a violent stress storm, with mounting pressures coming from above and below:

- The annual PISA death-knell
- Politicians and trustees inundated with reports about how far we are falling behind
- Alarmist media reports

- Parents worried about their children's future
- Teachers struggling to deal with the demands being placed on them
- Administrators buckling under the stresses coming from above and below
- Researchers struggling to understand why the "fixes" aren't fixing
- A constantly growing number of young students with HMA[16]

It is this last factor that is the most worrying of all, insofar as HMA fuels itself. HMA seriously impairs a student's comprehension and performance, leading to maladaptive modes of self-regulation that lead to further falling behind, and so on.[17] But what we are dealing with here is not a *lack of effort*; it is the *lack of understanding* as to when and why a student has HMA. To what extent is *societal HMA* a factor – possibly pivotal – in *student HMA*?

The Splintering of Attention

Scientists have been delving into the social and psychological causes of HMA: for example, negative maths experiences, poor self-esteem and self-confidence, gender and racial stereotypes. But the biggest problem of all is that anxiety breeds anxiety. The more anxious the student, the more they are drawn to maladaptive coping strategies (e.g., avoidance), which results in still greater anxiety down the road as the student falls ever further behind. The more anxious the adult trying to teach the child, the more anxious the child becomes, and vice versa. The greater the societal angst, the more all of the above are exacerbated.

In other words, *societal HMA* breeds *HMA students*. But even if we can remove the former from the mix, we are still going to see countless cases of the latter. There is something unusually stressful about maths, regardless of how we teach it. For that matter, there is something unique about HMA, which is why this phenomenon merits such close attention.

HMA is not an anxiety problem per se; it can occur in the absence of a generalized anxiety disorder (although its impact on general anxiety, and the reverse, is significant). Like other phobias, HMA involves a cluster of physical and psychological symptoms (tightness in the chest, faster heartbeat, nausea, headache, sweating). But what is most striking about HMA is that affected students may not experience anything comparable in other academic subjects.[18]

The crux of the issue is that *maths is a cognitive stress*: a paradigm example of what is meant by *cognitive stress*. The definition of *cognitive stress* is a problem demanding concentration with a consequent drain on energy. Educators have intuitively known this fact about maths for well over a thousand years, if not far longer. As far back as records go, there is evidence of educators developing techniques to ease the strain of learning maths.[19] But only recently have cognitive psychologists begun to unearth the reasons that maths should be uniquely stressful for so many students.

Maths makes unrivalled demands on working memory. The more working memory is overtaxed, the less we are able to stay focused on the task and the more anxious we become. But then, HMA can't simply be due to a problem with working memory. The same Grade 8 students who have trouble with word problems in maths may have no trouble memorizing the lyrics to dozens of songs. There has to be some further factor that accounts for the working memory problems seen in students with HMA.

The answer is that common among students with HMA are problems in *mathematical cognition*: for example, problems in number sense, counting, subitizing (recognizing the number of a small set of objects without counting them), or mentally comparing the magnitude of two numbers.[20] These deficits can have a severe impact on working memory.[21] Moreover, if a student struggles to acquire skills that come easily to peers, this can add immeasurably to a growing anxiety, which further taxes working memory. The result is a splintering of attention.

According to the *dual-task paradigm*, an HMA student's working memory is divided between maths problem and intrusive thoughts. The contents of working memory are said to be "tainted" by worries.[22] Excessive stress has been shown to heighten activity in the sensory-motor cortex and reduce activity in the dlPFC (one of the main systems subserving working memory).[23] Hence, mindfulness exercises can improve maths scores in older students with HMA because these practices reduce intrusive thoughts and thereby increase working memory capacity.

But none of this need bother those who believe that the student's difficulties with maths are due to lack of effort; on the contrary, self-controllers can argue that these findings only strengthen their case that what is different today is simply that students are unwilling to make the effort needed to overcome a handicap. After all, as just noted, we have known for a very long time that maths is unusually stressful, and nothing suggests that we are seeing a jump in the number of children born with problems in mathematical cognition. But what is different, according to those who emphasize the need for perseverance, is that children are "much less willing" to make the effort needed to overcome a handicap.

Any thoughts of the "joy of x" are fast disappearing. Maths looks like an endurance test in which the strong survive and the weak have only themselves to blame. In other words, we are back to where we started in the preceding chapter, with *maths success* turning into a character issue. And for educators, that should always raise a red flag.

Output Failure

To say that maths is a cognitive stress is simply to say that maths burns energy. A lot of it. And to say that maths is a greater *cognitive stress* for some children is to say that they expend more energy than their peers, which can lead to what has been described as *output failure*.[24]

Output failure is a sign that a child has been working too hard, not that they haven't been working hard enough. Kids with HMA – a group that encompasses far more than the 3 to 6 per cent of children with *developmental dyscalculia* – are a classic case of output failure. But what exactly does it mean to say that a child has been "working too hard"?

There is some evidence that "brain work" burns glucose,[25] but the findings here have been mixed.[26] While the brain consumes an inordinate amount of glucose relative to its size,[27] the amount of additional glucose consumed in a difficult mental task seems to be fairly negligible,[28] except when one especially pertinent factor is involved. That further factor is emotional stress.[29]

The more emotionally stressful a task, the more glucose is consumed.[30] The child with poor numerical processing finds maths highly stressful in the same way that a child with poor motor control finds physical education highly stressful. The clumsy child burns far more energy in gym class – and not just in gym class! – than the coordinated child. The former is at a heightened risk of metabolic syndrome, which is the reason the category of developmental coordination disorder (DCD) was first introduced.[31]

The fear at the time was that DCD was pathologizing the quite common experience of simply being awkward. But the reality, as John Cairney has explained, is that far too many parents and teachers see the problem as a character issue when it is actually neurobiological or motoric.[32] This bias leads adults to add to the child's stress load rather than reduce it. For these children, such a diagnosis can significantly improve their quality of life, "especially if they are given good advice about how to manage the problem."[33]

Exactly the same point applies to HMA: we need to understand the underlying factors, not just to avoid making the situation worse, but to manage it more effectively. The further implication of this point is that HMA is not simply a working memory problem – although, to be sure, the dual-task paradigm has had numerous cognitive load studies to back it up.[34] But HMA involves a physiological dimension in addition to the effect of intrusive thoughts and somatic awareness on working memory: the cost of hyperarousal.[35]

Engaging in a difficult cognitive task when not hyperaroused (for example, working on a thousand-piece jigsaw puzzle) does not affect blood glucose (at least, for those who enjoy it!). But add in (stress-caused) hyperarousal and – as has been shown to happen in writing the SATs – blood glucose can drop sharply, not because of added cognitive load, but because fear and anxiety elicit a powerful SNS response. We see a leap in tension, and thus, elevated heart rate and blood pressure, faster breathing, sweating, and higher levels of cortisol.[36]

This point is pivotal for understanding the factors that lead to HMA. A child with maths-specific cognitive deficits becomes hyperaroused when grappling with the basics of arithmetic. This may not occur when the child is asked how many objects are in a group of less than five items, but increase the group to ten and the child must shift from subitizing (namely, perception) to counting (working memory). But then, why would this cognitive shift cause hyperarousal? The reason is that other domains of stress are layered on top as the child sees themself lagging behind other children.[37]

The big reason that children with problems in mathematical cognition come to find maths "a source of huge anxiety is because they must exert tremendous effort to understand what is obvious to their classmates."[38] This point is critical. We tend to think of output failure as a purely mental phenomenon. But the fuel tank of the child at risk of HMA drops below the red line because they are fiercely clenching their occipital frontalis, temporalis, and deltoid, and also abdominal, gluteus, and leg muscles. And there is a reason why the latter large muscle groups are recruited.

The ergotropic shift – the mobilizing of the Sympathetic Nervous System (SNS) for the expenditure of energy – that supports the whole-body phenomenon of deep concentration is also triggered when we need to keep up with our group. And the typical classroom setting in which maths is taught manages to combine both, doubling the load on the child who is being held back by limbic brakes. In terms of the Thayer matrix, the hyperaroused student sinks deep into the bottom-right quadrant, while the calmly focused and alert student shifts between top right and top left.[39]

But this explanation still leaves us with a triad of Self-Reg questions:

- Why should hyperarousal *per se* lead to HMA?
- What can we do about hyperarousal before it reaches HMA proportions?
- What can we do about this problem after it has reached HMA proportions?

We are not simply dealing here with unpleasant negative emotions, which are both transient and fleeting. HMA is an exhausting mental state, which as such persists over time. HMA isn't just about disliking maths: it is about *dreading* maths. Even the thought of doing maths can set in train the SNS response outlined above. Why is it that a student – any student, and not just one with mathematical cognition deficits – should come to fear maths? What are we doing wrong? What do we need to do differently?

A Kindled Maths Alarm

A great deal of what we know about HMA is due to Mark Ashcraft's research on mathematical cognition. For the past two decades, he has been studying the processes involved in problems in addition, from simple problems to ones that require further operations (like carrying). But it is his research on the impact of anxiety on computation that has garnered the most attention.

He tells the story of an undergraduate in one of his studies who became so distraught while working on a simple problem in arithmetic that they burst into tears.[40] Why would elementary arithmetic cause any young adult, let alone one at university, such distress? More is involved here than just an unpleasant association: the mere thought of doing maths has been shown to cause the same neural response in HMA students as actual physical pain.[41]

Of all the discoveries that cognitive neuroscientists working in this area have made, the most remarkable is that HMA in children aged seven to nine is associated with hyperactivity in the right amygdala and anterior hippocampus and reduced activity in the frontoparietal systems associated with mathematical and numerical reasoning (intraparietal sulcus, or IPS, and dlPFC) and emotion regulation (vmPFC).[42] What this means is that these young students are about to go into, or are already in, fight-flight-freeze.[43]

But why would a young child see maths as a threat? Even more puzzling is when it is only maths among school subjects that the child sees as a threat. Why does having trouble learning the basics of arithmetic trigger a child's limbic alarm, poised to trip FEAR and possibly PANIC/GRIEF?

The Self-Reg answer to these questions lies in the consequence of *persistently overriding limbic brakes*. Ashcraft found that, on a test that becomes increasingly challenging (the basic IQ test design), university students with HMA often do well on the first part of the test, but as their anxiety mounts their accuracy begins to plummet, which further intensifies their anxiety. Then they reach a point where they suddenly stop. That is the peak of the inverted V-curve, the point where their limbic brakes have kicked in.

The same thing is happening to the young child with a numerical processing deficit. The child is under growing tension trying to keep up with the rest of the class. The limbic brakes kick in at the point when blood glucose drops below a certain threshold. And here is the critical point: *if that child is pressed to persevere – pushed past the peak of the inverted-V curve – the memory is registered.*

The hippocampus and amygdala keep meticulous records of experiences that exhausted energy reserves without a compensating (neurochemical) payoff (viz., endogenous opioids). The mere cues associated with that experience (e.g., pulling out the maths books) are enough to trigger a state of neuroceptive overdrive.

A child in neuroceptive overdrive starts looking for and seeing threats everywhere, which we misconstrue as heightened distractibility or poor attention. Startle reactions are misinterpreted as heightened impulsivity. The expectation of an aversive experience and the impact this has on concentration is misread as lack of effortful control. Problems in retention are misattributed to limited "mathematical intelligence." Limbic braking kicks in, which is misconstrued as oppositionality.

If a child's defensive behaviours are consistently misperceived, the result is that maths becomes a threat. But then,

1. Why are we pushing so many young children to override their limbic brakes – without realizing that we are doing so?
2. How can we avoid, or turn off, a "kindled maths alarm"?

The answer to the first question lies in the effect of *societal HMA* on our attitudes towards cases of output failure. Empathy turns off, old biases kick in. The answer to the second question starts by exposing and overcoming that bias.

Bridging the "Unbridgeable"

Output failure, like paradigm revolutions, does not happen out of the blue. The child shows us in all sorts of ways that a meltdown is looming; for example, in pupil dilation, changes in prosody, facial complexion, restlessness, heightened distractibility, avoidance. We misread resistance as lack of effort, we see anxiety as non-compliance. We persist in pushing or punishing when we should be pausing and probing: Why is this child, who is so active and interested in other school subjects, having so much trouble with maths?

The first step in helping such a student is to reframe. In place of misbehaviour, Self-Reg sees stress-behaviour, in all its subtle forms. The hard part is the second step: identifying the reasons maths is such an overpowering cognitive stress for that child. This is where we need to be constantly asking Why and reflecting on what we are learning about the student's processing challenges.

Instituting such measures as a classroom makeover, mindfulness, and exercise breaks or providing stress-relieving manipulatives may help (the third step of Self-Reg).[44] But in the case of HMA, this will likely not be enough. It is essential to reduce the cognitive stress, not just by working on problems in numerical processing or spatial sense but, in many cases, with exercises that address underlying sensorimotor deficits.

It is essential that the student become aware *that* and *why* they find maths so stressful (the fourth step of Self-Reg). They need to internalize that this is not a reflection of inadequacy but an example of the different kinds of processing deficits that modern science is learning to address. Bear in mind that there was a time, not so long ago, when myopia was seen as a weakness and wearing glasses a form of indulgence.

Finally, students need to develop pre/post strategies to maintain or restore Blue Brain/Red Brain balance (the fifth step of Self-Reg). They need to learn more constructive modes of self-regulation, not just in maths class, but in all aspect of their lives. The student with HMA who doesn't know what *calm* feels like will find it impossible to remain calm when faced with a sharp stress, such as they find with maths.

The better we can understand cognitive stress and how it inter-
acts with other stresses, the better we can alleviate how hard a student must work. Highly instructive in this regard is the work of
Christine Roman-Lantzy, director of the Vision Information and
Evaluation Clinic at West Penn Hospital in Pittsburgh. She has
developed a number of techniques to help students with cortical
visual impairment begin to read.

These are cases where the student's visual impairment is due
not to any damage to the retina or optic nerve but rather to how
the brain processes the visual information it receives.[45] To enhance
visual processing, Roman-Lantzy makes printed information more
salient by adjusting contrast, colour, and font; using coloured bor-
ders to highlight text; and eliminating peripheral "visual noise"
on the page (e.g., illustrations). By enhancing the salience of visual
information, she reduces the effort needed to process it and the
consequent build-up of tension. Just consider how tense you
become as you strain to absorb an important email that has been
sent in a much smaller font than you are accustomed to reading, or
trying to read the very small print on a pill bottle.

Psychologists are looking at similar ways to reduce the effort
required from HMA students; that is, figuring out ways in which
maths information can be made more salient while reducing external stresses (e.g., auditory and visual noise). Developing exercises
to promote kinesthetic, proprioceptive, and vestibular awareness;[46]
or that work on visualization.[47]

One of the big lessons here is that elementary maths skills need
to be taught in ways that young children find engaging.[48] Abstract
mathematical concepts need to be made both relevant and meaningful.[49] Executive function strategies have to be engaging (for
example, card and board games). And it is essential to address
social and prosocial stress (which, in the typical classroom environment, might be met with, for example, portable study carrels).[50]

By enhancing the salience of the information and reducing the
multi-domain stress load, we reduce the physical strain that the
HMA student is under. We soothe amygdalae. Only when a limbic
alarm is turned off and the student is calmly focused and alert can
we begin to increase the cognitive stress load: slowly, incrementally,

with as much support as is needed. But a deeper divide still needs to be bridged here: the idea that maths is completely different from working on social-emotional skills. The two areas are inextricably conjoined.

Imagine how empowering it must have been for Roman-Lantzy's students once they grasped the nature of their visual-processing deficits and how they could start to take control of their reading; for example, by adjusting the layout of text on a handheld reader or using a multimodal reading system to bootstrap. And, of course, by working on the last step of Self-Reg. When we talk about "restoring balance," we are referring to day-to-day activities that boost stress tolerance in all five domains, not just one where dysregulation problems stand out (e.g., emotion).

The anxiety that a child with HMA experiences may be subject specific, but the ramifications are not. The fact that maths plays such a big role in a child's academic life – short term as well as long – is all the reason that we need to take this issue seriously. But to overcome an ingrained threat response and the negative bias this evokes, the student must feel safe. Maths must cease to be seen as a threat.

A big problem with treating maths anxiety as a "weakness" is that this naturally fosters the view that fortitude is needed to overcome the problem. But an even greater problem is fatalism: the view that an achievement gap is fixed, either by character or by genes. Neither is true. But just as we will never know how fast a car can go when its motor is held in check by a governor, so too we will never know what a student's maths potential might be when that child is being held in check by limbic brakes.

If we are going to stem the ever-growing divide in early maths learners, we need to think hard about why students are developing HMA and how we can prevent avoidance from taking root. Where the self-control paradigm sees this problem as due to a lack of motivation, Self-Reg sees it as the result of maladaptive self-regulation – and an opportunity for us to learn more about learning and about ourselves!

Our ultimate goal here, however, is not to raise children's scores so that we can perform better in the "international arms race."

Our goal is simply and solely to provide students with an enriching experience. That is the greatest cost of all of the perseverance bias: namely, that we can so easily turn what should be a source of joyful learning into a penance. But as we saw in chapter 2, biases are more than just thinking habits. Biases are modes of self-regulation in their own right: a way of coping with something that we find stressful – such as not understanding why so many kids have HMA. And the fact that so many young students are developing HMA tells us that our own mode of self-regulating is maladaptive.

We come back to Descartes's attack on *non-rational conviction*: in this case, the misbelief that a child lagging behind peers for whom arithmetic comes more easily needs to be pushed to make a greater effort lest they fall behind right at the start. The greater the societal angst around maths, the more this attitude takes hold. And when that happens, we create the very problem that we are trying to avoid. It is the perfect example of how ideology rushes in where science needs to tread more firmly.

The Greater Lesson

In the late 1970s, Roger Porsolt developed the "swim test" that goes by his name, which is still used to study the effectiveness of anti-depressants.[51] A rodent is exposed to an aversive stress (cold water in an enclosed tube), and then timed to see how long it struggles before giving up. The effectiveness of a new medication is measured in terms of how long and hard the rodent struggles to escape. But the protocol has attracted even wider interest as a method for studying the physiological and biochemical effects of an aversive stimulus, where the stress response is measured in terms of the increase of glucocorticoids and the decline in blood glucose.[52] One wonders how our attitudes towards education might change were we to include such measures on students' report cards.

The Forced Swim Test reminds me of an experience I once had in Yellowknife. I had arrived late in October with the temperature hovering around 7°C. My taxi driver, whose name was Abdul, was so bundled up that you could barely see his eyes. He had a heavy toque pulled low down over his brow and a scarf wound several times around his face. Intrigued, I asked him where he was from and why he was in Yellowknife. He told me that he was from Galkayo, in Somalia, and had only just arrived in Canada. He had gone to Yellowknife in the hopes that it would be easier for him to find a job. He knew that winter was coming but, in a quavering voice, told me, "So far it's not so bad." What came through loud and clear, however, was how helpless he felt. He had no family or friends. He was sick all the time. He agonized about how he was going to cope with what he knew was coming. He asked me several times how bad I thought it would be, and I didn't have the heart to answer.

As it happens, I was back in Yellowknife a few months later, this time in the dead of winter, and I asked my driver if he knew anything about Abdul. It turns out that he had moved down to Edmonton, where there is a vibrant Somali community (the *ciyaal baraf*, or children of the snow). I'm not sure that Edmonton would be all that much warmer, but I am quite sure that, with a network of friends to support him, he would have been doing a good deal better.

I suspect that Abdul was suffering from cryophobia, which is not unusual in people who move from very hot to very cold climates. We also see it in individuals who are extremely sensitive to the cold, or in someone who has had a traumatic cold experience (e.g., cases of hypothermia). Yet it is a relatively rare condition in the Northwest Territories. If anything, residents seem to relish having frozen digits. But then, they are well versed on how to cope.

We tend to think of the cold as the same stress for all of us and that some are just hardier than others or more used to it. But the research done on acclimatization has provided for a more nuanced understanding. Inuit, for example, have a unique response to cold temperatures, which is measured by skin temperature in extremities and deep muscle tissue. In fact, they display a number of physiological differences – for example, in heart rate, blood pressure, blood oxygenation, and basal metabolic rate.[53]

It was recently discovered that Inuit have a gene similar to one found in the Denisovans, which causes a certain type of body fat to generate body heat.[54] But Inuit can cope so well in −40°C not simply because they inherited a gene from their ancestors who lived in Siberia. It is also due, if not more so, to their diet, clothing, shelter, and customs. In other words, the ability of Inuit to cope with intense cold isn't just genetic, but also the result of adaptive modes of self-regulation that have been passed down from one generation to the next; social practices that enable them to reduce the amount of energy they must expend to maintain an internal body temperature of 37°C.

The result is that, however many phobias we might see among Inuit, cryophobia isn't one of them (although thermophobia is becoming much more common as they struggle with the impact of global warming). They do not experience paralysing anxiety when the temperature drops precipitously, precisely because they know how to deal with it. But place Inuit in Galkayo in the middle of the summer, and they are likely to react much like Abdul; for equally, there are genetically determined mechanisms for extreme heat tolerance and adaptive modes of self-regulation that these societies have long practised.[55]

Our bodies can adjust to vastly different physical environments, albeit more slowly or less fully depending on biological factors, *provided we don't feel helpless*. The feeling that there is no escape from the cold can generalize to other stressors, which one simply endures without attempting to manage.[56] This can lead to *psychomotor retardation*, in which the ability to think, speak, feel, and even move are all seriously impaired. We are driven into maladaptive modes of self-regulation, caught in a seemingly inescapable stress cycle.

Looking at this issue through the lens of the Triune metaphor brings a further critical element into focus. Our first line of defence for dealing with stress is social engagement. This is not just a matter of feeling that we have control over a stress, but that we have support to deal with that stress, not to mention the oxytocin that others can trigger in us.

How different is this from the fear of being left behind in maths class? Is the classroom a version of the cylinder in the Porsolt Swim Test? Is maths the cold water? Does a student struggle until avoidance or more disruptive modes of escape set in? Does the teacher serve as a critical factor preventing escape, rather than as a vital means of providing security? Do we assume that the subject matter is the *same stress* for all students and that what varies from one to the next is how much effort they're prepared to make? Do we see HMA as a character weakness rather than, as Maier and Seligman argue in their revised look at "learned helplessness," a "default condition of the human brain" when it has been overstressed?

This last point is especially significant for Self-Reg. Maier and Seligman's original hypothesis, based on their experiments with dogs, was that if subjects feel powerless to escape from an aversive stimulus they simply give up trying, an example, they argued, of what behaviourists at the time referred to as "learned behaviour." But having studied this phenomenon for fifty years, they now conclude that it isn't *helplessness* but rather *optimism* that is learned.[57]

In Triune terms, a subject shifts into tonic immobility when fight-or-flight has proved ineffective. It is learning that we can manage an aversive stress before that point is reached that is pivotal to preventing tonic immobility from taking hold. And that, of course, is the whole point of Self-Reg.

Self-Reg isn't just a way of thinking about the stresses in our own or a child's life, but concrete steps to acquire restorative modes of self-regulation. For Self-Reg, this is not simply a case of learning how to manage an obviously aversive stress. In the classic stress test paradigms that were developed in the 1960s, the relevant stress was not just conspicuous – for example, the electric shocks that the dogs received – but indeed, had to be isolated in order to be manipulated and measured in the different *escape* and *yoked* groups. But in real life, it can take a great deal of work to identify the relevant stresses.

The importance of stress detection was one of the big lessons we learned at MEHRI. A child might come in listless and withdrawn; that is, displaying classic signs of "learned helplessness." But figuring out what the stressors were that had sent them into this state demanded extensive observation and thought. This is the reason why it is critical that we distinguish between stress-behaviour and misbehaviour, which, again in real-life conditions, may not be nearly as obvious as an animal struggling to escape.

This is the greater lesson to be learned from the study of HMA. We need to see when a child or teen is struggling to escape from something that they find highly aversive. We need to look for other stresses that might be involved, which lower the threshold for a stress response. We need to reflect on what role we might be playing in the onset of learned helplessness. And we need to consider whether the failure to notice signs of *struggling to escape* is due to inherited biases that resurface when we ourselves are overstressed.

What we have learned over the past fifty years is that the key for turning a stress from *threat* into *challenge* is to recognize that change is always possible.[58] Such a metamorphosis isn't simply a case of *managing* but of *transforming* a stress: shifting the emotion associated with it from negative to positive. It is hard enough for adults to "will" such a change, let alone expect it from an unaided child or teen. The latter need very strong Interbrain support to begin to think differently about something they have previously seen as a threat.

How we respond to their response to stress is the key to "raising children to love learning."[59] Even maths. Even the cold.

Chapter 8

No Child Left Behind

Hard Times

To prepare me for Oxford, Michael Laine gave me a copy of Cuthbert Bede's *The Adventures of Mr. Verdant Green, an Oxford Freshman.* This wonderful picaresque novel, published in 1853, provides a vivid portrait of what Oxford was like in the middle of the nineteenth century. And to my utter astonishment, I discovered that Oxford hadn't changed all that much.

Oxford would not join the twentieth century until I entered graduate school (marked by the purchase of a photocopier machine for the philosophy library). But in my undergraduate years studying Philosophy, Politics and Economics I was able to have a taste of Verdant Green's Oxford. Mine was the last cohort to wear gowns to all our lectures. We celebrated St. Frideswide's Day with a feast straight out of Harry Potter, and May Day with the choristers from my college singing *Hymnus Eucharisticus*, which had been composed by a Magdalen Fellow in the seventeenth century and sung in the Great Tower ever since. Christmas was an especially magical time, with the covered market transformed into a scene straight out of Dickens. The vendors all wore calico aprons or smocks, the women bonnets, and wild game and poultry were hanging everywhere you looked.

It was also during this time that Margaret Thatcher was elected leader of the Conservative Party. Now we began to hear that Britain desperately needed to rediscover its Victorian values. This wasn't just an appeal to nostalgia. In 1981 it became clear, when Sir Keith Joseph became the secretary of state for education and science, that the government was intent on bringing these "Victorian values" back into the school system. Britain's students were about to have a taste of what Sir Ken Robinson excoriates as the factory model of education.[1]

The first critique of the "factory model," and by far the most evocative, was published over a century and a half ago. Dickens had a front-row seat to the view that was shaping education and was profoundly disturbed by what he saw happening, especially in the north of England. *Hard Times* takes place in the hellish Coketown:

a town of red brick, or of brick that would have been red if the smoke and ashes had allowed it; but as matters stood, it was a town of unnatural red and black like the painted face of a savage. It was a town of machinery and tall chimneys, out of which interminable serpents of smoke trailed themselves for ever and ever, and never got uncoiled. It had a black canal in it, and a river that ran purple with ill-smelling dye, and vast piles of building full of windows where there was a rattling and a trembling all day long, and where the piston of the steam-engine worked monotonously up and down, like the head of an elephant in a state of melancholy madness. It contained several large streets all very like one another, and many small streets still more like one another, inhabited by people equally like one another, who all went in and out at the same hours, with the same sound upon the same pavements, to do the same work, and to whom every day was the same as yesterday and to-morrow, and every year the counterpart of the last and the next ... Fact, fact, fact, everywhere in the material aspect of the town; fact, fact, fact, everywhere in the immaterial. The M'Choakumchild school was all fact.[2]

The novel opens with a striking contrast between Sissy Jupe, who is being brutalized by the board superintendent,[3] and Blitzer, who is the school's star pupil. The opening scene satirizes Watt in the mechanical definition of "horse" that Blitzer mechanically recites. Blitzer goes on to become a spy at Bounderby's Bank, a man with no integrity, while Sissy ends up nursing Gradgrind when he is dying. That is the book's central message: compassion and empathy, not efficiency and uniformity, produce a healthy society.

A few years back, a Swedish freelance journalist wrote a fascinating account of the two years she spent at a Shanghai high school that could have come straight out of Dickens.[4] She recounts how students devote all of their time preparing for the Gaokao, China's version of the SATs, and then in their final year move to a different campus so that they won't be distracted by social life. The most riveting passage in her account describes how

> creativity and critical thinking are seen as objects of western frivolousness. Although Chinese students analyze literature, they never write essays and instead they simply memorize the texts. I have never memorized so much in my life as I did in Shanghai.

The fact that Shanghai dominates the PISA standing tells us that the rote approach to learning is producing the results that it seeks. The rationale for the heavy emphasis on memorization is that what matters is creating a strong foundation; creativity can come later. Whether that happens is another matter.[5] But my concern in this chapter is with Ringmar's point that the approach "is essentially elitist. Students that excel in school are rewarded with prizes and encouragement, but struggling students are abandoned."

In Dickens's romanticized vision, you cannot kill the fundamentally noble nature of a Sissy Jupe, a David Copperfield, or an Oliver Twist, no matter what you subject them to. But the reality of what happens to the child who gets left behind is rather different. And the Victorian view of his fate is far more chilling than anything that Dickens depicts. Hard times definitely lie ahead.

The Rise of a Secular Creed

According to the ideology that took grip in the latter half of the nineteenth century, the biggest mistake a society can make is to slow the pace of its front-runners to match that of its stragglers.

The central tenet of social Darwinism is that stratification represents a natural evolutionary dynamic, where the gifted rise to the top and the weak or unfit sink to the bottom.[6] And what distinguishes the weak or unfit individual is a disinclination to work. A strong society is one that will seek to counter the over-breeding of the indolent and under-breeding of the industrious. The notion of a Just Society is "airy-fairy": again, a term that we owe to the Victorians (in this case, Tennyson).

We cannot afford to ignore the element in Victorian thinking that led to this dark view of social engineering. We see the first signs shortly after William Pitt introduced income tax in order to pay for the Napoleonic wars. There was fierce opposition and the government was soon forced to retract. It wasn't until 1842 that income tax was reintroduced, and it was even more unpopular – at least among those whose annual income was greater than £150! This time the government was proposing to use taxes, not to pay for a war effort, but for social initiatives: improved sanitation, safe food and water, railways, housing, education, and libraries.

The thinking behind the Poor Law of 1834, as opposed to the "one-nation conservatism" that flourished under Disraeli, was that the state should not assume responsibility for those mired in poverty. The law stipulated that anyone who refused to enter a workhouse would be refused all means of social relief. But life inside the workhouse was so harsh that many chose instead to lead a life of destitution or thievery on the streets. (Think here of *Oliver Twist*.)

It might be tempting to dismiss the enactment of the Poor Law as simply the result of callous self-interest, but it is important to bear in mind how widespread was the fear of democracy.[7] The Whig government that passed the Poor Law genuinely felt that what they were doing was for the benefit of the poor (think *non-rational conviction*). Poverty was widely seen as the consequence of idleness and self-indulgence. It was a Victorian writer, Thackeray's oldest daughter, Anne Isabella, who came up with the proverb "Give a man a fish and you feed him for a day; teach him to fish and you feed him for a lifetime." The point of the Poor Law was to force the poor to learn how to fish. And everyone could become adept, if only the motivation were strong enough.

Towards the middle of the nineteenth century, a new type of proselytizing treatise started to appear that enshrined this way of thinking. Among the most influential was Samuel Smiles's *Self-Help*, which was published in the same year as *On the Origin of Species* (1859). Smiles's book was not the first self-help book ever published; that honour belongs to the Bible.[8] But it did represent a new, secular view of self-help, and it was wildly successful, selling over a quarter of a million copies.[9]

In his five-volume collection *Lives of the Engineers*, Smiles presented a series of biographical vignettes that were intended to convey the message that anyone can succeed in any endeavour "by dint of sheer industry and perseverance." The format was deliberately based on Butler's *Lives of the Saints*, the eighteenth-century English version of the great seventeenth-century *Acta Sanctorum*. It is fair to say that *Lives of the Engineers* played a similar role in an increasingly agnostic age, and indeed was dubbed "The Gospel of Self-Help" and the "Communion of Engineering Saints."[10] The scriptural attitude towards laziness was preserved, but now the "sin" was against society and not the Lord.

This secularized view played a subtle but significant role in the Victorian view of education. It is important to remember that the threat of exclusion is archetypal (Adam and Eve are banished from the Garden of Eden). The ancient Hebrews had a hierarchy of ostracism: being banned from society for a day (*Nezifah*), a week (*Niddui*), and permanently (*Herem*). Schools began to employ a similar "exclusion" hierarchy and continue to do so to this day, namely, detention, suspension, and expulsion.

The lesson that Smiles wanted children to learn is that "with WILL one can do anything."[11] But this was no rags to riches homily in aid of those seeking material success in a highly competitive free market. On the contrary, Smiles's harshest invective is directed against what he described as the "evils of mammonism," that is, the pursuit of money or success at the expense of others. Smiles's hagiography is devoted to individuals who overcame adversity to make some important contribution to the betterment of society. For this reason, Smiles's book was as much a political treatise as a practical guide for developing a "truly noble and manly character."[12]

The heart of Smiles's argument is that "national progress is the sum of individual industry, energy, and uprightness, as national decay is of individual idleness, selfishness, and vice."[13] It follows that "the highest patriotism and philanthropy" lies in "helping and stimulating men to elevate and improve themselves by their own free and independent individual action." But then, that entails providing them with the opportunity to "improve themselves," which is why bettering the living conditions of the poor was so important. Yet by no means was Smiles championing the values of the welfare state. On the contrary, he insists that "there cannot be more good than that of letting social progress go on unhindered; an immensity of mischief may be done in ... the artificial preservation of those least able to care for themselves." And the same point must apply, a fortiori, to education.

Unlike those opposed to universal public education on the grounds that this would be doing more harm than good (i.e., that the "lower orders" are not intelligent enough to be properly educated, and certainly not intelligent enough to have the right to vote), Smiles believed that everyone should be given an opportunity to rise above their station in life. That is the whole point behind universal education or making public libraries accessible to workers. But then, public education must be such that it strengthens and does not weaken the national fabric. That is, it must be based on the principle of motivating children to elevate and improve their lot in life.

It's hardly surprising, then, that Smiles looks at education through the same perseverance lens:

> The maxim that "Labour conquers all things" holds especially true in the case of the conquest of knowledge. The road into learning is alike free to all who will give the labour and the study requisite to gather it ... In study, as in business, *energy is the great thing* [my emphasis]. It is astonishing how much may be accomplished in self-culture by the energetic and the persevering, who are careful to avail themselves of opportunities, and use up the fragments of spare time which the idle permit to run to waste.[14]

The ultimate role of school "is to separate the wheat from the chaff," the resolute from the weak-willed.[15] Children must be taught right from the start that the only way to succeed in their studies is by effort. Energy is a function of willpower, not of glucose. An enlightened education system is one that doesn't just foster but forces competition. Children become *Les Enfants Perdus* (another nineteenth-century abomination, what the English military referred to as the Forlorn Hope): foot soldiers guaranteed promotion to officer rank should they survive the battle.

Self-Reg doesn't just represent a compassionate response to this draconian outlook: although it certainly is that! More fundamentally, Self-Reg seeks to move the debate out of the sphere of moral philosophy, where it serves as a classic *"is versus ought"* debate between *perseverationists* and social activists. Howsoever we view the proper role of government in education, Self-Reg is not prepared to abandon a child, any child. The question Self-Reg insists we ask is: "Why is THIS child being left behind?" Is it truly because the child is not willing to make the sort of effort that more successful peers are prepared to make? Or are there different factors holding the child back, factors that, once understood, can be addressed?

Victorian thinking gets in the way of probing this question. It has already decided on the answer: namely, it is due to a lack of character, whether acquired or innate. (It was Galton who coined the phrase "nature versus nurture.")[16] But Self-Reg seeks to understand why it's hard for a particular child to keep up. The principle governing Self-Reg is that you may never know the answer to this question, but you will never stop digging, no matter how convinced you might be that you have arrived at the answer.

One thing is clear: no child chooses to be left behind, and if it seems that way, you have not dug deeply enough. It was a point I first started thinking about while watching a group of apes.

No Hominoid Left Behind

The most interesting education experiment I have ever observed took place in the Language Research Center (LRC) at Georgia State University back in the 1990s, where Sue Savage-Rumbaugh was studying language acquisition in nonhuman primates. Once accustomed to my presence, the bonobos in the group pretty much ignored me. They spent their time grooming, eating, playing (the language sessions fell into that category), sleeping, or, in Kanzi's case, just chilling in a children's wading pool.[17]

The apes had to be in this state to learn the use of words or lexigram symbols. Not, I hasten to add, through any sort of formal instruction. They had to be calm to attend to how the LRC team were using words or symbols. The second they became anxious, all learning was off. They would feverishly start scanning for danger and remain on edge until the threat had passed. Tempers flared and the atmosphere became fraught with tension.

It is a shame that, in the great debate that took place over whether the communicative skills the apes acquired were properly described as "linguistic," we lost sight of the fundamental point that, however you describe it, *learning* was taking place.

What brought this experience back to me was Joseph LeDoux's recent remark that humans – *qua* primates – are "anxious animals."[18] He doesn't mean by this that anxiety is somehow our natural state and the exceptions are those moments when we feel calm. He is referring to how swiftly we can become anxious – on our own and as a group – and the effect this has on our capacity to absorb new information or learn new skills.

I saw the force of his point on countless occasions when I was with the bonobos. A sudden noise or the intrusion of a stranger would instantly trigger their alarms. For example, there was the day that Jerome Bruner visited the lab. His arrival caused piloerection and nervous glances in every member. (Is this what is happening with a supply teacher?) But Jerry being Jerry, he was attuned to what was going on and was able to put them at ease by, quite literally, playing with them. To this day my biggest regret about that visit is that no one made a video of Jerry swinging on a branch with one of the apes, but then, this was in pre-smartphone days.

Sue had an amazing ability to turn off the apes' alarms, which no doubt was one reason the research program was so successful. A soothing vocalization or touch, sometimes just her presence, was all it took. But it wasn't just Sue; I saw bonobos themselves do the same. An infant would be picked up and held the moment it became fretful. What was especially striking was to see the same behaviour when the apes travelled through the forest surrounding the LRC. Young bonobos were encouraged to travel on their own, whether on the ground or through the trees. But the moment they became anxious or started to lag, they were picked up and carried.

Significantly, there is mounting evidence in the fossil record that the same was true for our early human ancestors. The skull of a five- to eight-year-old *H. heidelbergensis* child who lived at least 530,000 years ago was discovered at Sima de los Huesos in Atapuerca in 1994. The child, who has been named Benjamina, was suffering from craniosynostosis, which would have left her severely disabled. Such a child would have needed a considerable amount of care.[19]

There are many reports of individuals who were likely to have been supported by their group. One of the more striking is that of a forty- to fifty-year-old Neanderthal male at Shanidar who suffered from health problems affecting vision, hearing, and mobility. Someone with challenges so severe could have survived only if cared for by the other members of the group.[20]

What we are looking at here poses a major problem for Herbert Spencer's take on "survival of the fittest."[21] Spencer was already arguing before the publication of *On the Origin of Species* that progress depends on struggle and competition. It is hardly surprising that he seized on the theory of natural selection to buttress his argument. But the view emerging among paleoanthropologists marks a return to Alfred Russell Wallace's counter-argument that it was not competition but prosocial values that provided humans with a selective advantage.[22] What we are witnessing amounts to nothing less than a reframing of *survival of the fittest*: the idea that the concept applies at the group level, not the individual, and is grounded in empathy and not aggression.[23]

The fittest group would have been the one that was most *cohesive*, and harmony was strengthened, not undermined, by caring for those in need.[24] In other words, it was the security afforded by the group that was the key to human survival, and succouring the disadvantaged would have been pursued purely for its own sake and not because an impaired individual possessed some special skill that was valued by the group. That is, the kind of care that Benjamina or the male at Shanidar received is not to be explained by the Machiavellian hypothesis[25] but rather by the deepest of hominid instincts.[26] Young or old, strong or infirm: *the group cared for each other because that's what held it together as a group.*

My concern here isn't with altruism, however, but with the fact that we don't all travel at the same pace. The picture of Alistair Brownlee helping his brother Jonny finish the race at the World Triathlon Series in Cozumel was seen and celebrated around the world. Parents do the same all the time. They are unfailingly solicitous when their child can't keep up (just look at how many parents slow their gait or carry their child on their shoulders at Disney World). And then one day at the LRC I had an epiphany – one of many I was to have there. This isn't just a story about travel or winning a race.

For the purposes of research, one of the apes, Tamuli, had been isolated from the language-learning sessions. She served as a control to demonstrate that the linguistic advances being documented were acquired solely on the basis of being exposed to a language-enculturated environment. But it had become clear that some of these skills were being transmitted, thereby undermining Tamuli's role. Sue initially worried that a staff member might have been inadvertently exposing her to language sessions, until one day she discovered that it was the apes themselves who were showing Tamuli how to use the lexigram board. They were doing so at night, after they had bedded down in their nests.

It must have been incredibly hard on Tamuli, not understanding the sounds or symbols that the others were using. As it happens, whenever there was any sort of commotion in the group, you could be certain that Tamuli was involved. Looking back on it, I suspect that she was chronically anxious. It bears noting that she died at a relatively young age from a heart problem – think here of the Whitehall study, which showed how the greater the stress that civil servants are under, the higher the likelihood that they suffer from mental or physical health problems.[27] One thing that was clear at the time was that it made the other apes anxious that Tamuli couldn't understand spoken English or the lexigram board.[28]

The lesson to be learned from Sue's extraordinary research program is that the group travels together, feeds together, is happy or sad together, and *learns together*. But we are witnessing a resurgence of the mid-nineteenth-century idea that it is "naively utopian" to think that no one should ever be left behind. Like the Victorians, educational reactionaries insist that *we* aren't leaving anyone behind; *they are choosing to be left behind*. They *deserve* to be left behind, since they aren't prepared to make the effort required to keep up with the rest of the group. They aren't *strong enough* or *self-disciplined enough* or simply *smart enough* to keep up. You only harm the group if you cater to the laggard.

There could be no more powerful example of the harm that results – both to the individual and to the group – when ideology is allowed to trump science.

"Energy Is the Great Thing"

Many of the major educational gains now being realized with students who in earlier times would have fallen by the wayside are the result of screening children for biological conditions like vision and hearing problems, or neurogenetic conditions like autism and ADHD. Nutrition, sleep, and exercise programs have had a profound impact. The importance of safe learning environments and fostering healthy teacher-student relationships is now widely recognized. Classroom activities to help children develop emotionally and socially are standard practice. The next big advance is going to come from being able to "see and not just infer" what is going on inside a child's "black box" (as Skinner put it),[29] why certain brains have trouble processing certain kinds of information.

This way of thinking represents a radical break from the Victorian view that, *if children fail, it is because they did not try hard enough.* As it happens, Smiles was not denying the significance of individual differences, that is, the fact that some children struggle with greater impediments than others. He dwells so much on case studies of highly successful individuals who started out with the odds stacked against them in order to belabour the point that the *only* way to overcome a personal liability – whatever it might be – is by trying harder.

The heart of Smiles's message is that the greater the liability, the greater the effort required. But there are no "difficulties so great that the student of resolute purpose may not surmount and overcome them."[30] To be sure, the obstacles that Smiles was thinking about were primarily social and physical. But it was not a stretch to apply this way of thinking to "neurocognitive liabilities" as well.

The most famous expression of the latter was Winston Churchill's account of his struggles as a student. In his autobiography, he recounts: "I was, on the whole, considerably discouraged by my school days. It was not pleasant to feel ... so completely outclassed and left behind."[31] It is fascinating that Churchill highlighted the fear of *being left behind*. But we now know that the idea, promulgated by Churchill himself, that he was able by sheer perseverance to overcome a serious learning disorder and catch up was, at the very least, exaggerated; in fact, he won several prizes at Harrow.[32] Far from being a conscious act of self-aggrandizement, the narrative that Churchill constructed about himself was grounded in his Victorian mindset.[33]

The crux of Churchill's Victorian way of thinking is that "continuous effort – not strength or intelligence – is the key to unlocking our potential."[34] But the lesson from our recent look at IQ and HMA is that, far more often than we ever realized, *releasing a child's limbic brakes* is a key to unlocking their potential. That is hardly to say that Smiles's many examples of remarkable perseverance – such as George Stephenson and Josiah Wedgewood – should not be seen as such. The problem is that the Victorian paean to zeal and hard work can easily produce the very consequence it is trying to avoid.

"Energy" is indeed, as Smiles puts it, "the great thing." So many factors can sap a child's energy; not just biological deficits, but in today's world, a surfeit of products designed to keep a child "hooked" well past the point of exhaustion (see chapters 9 and 10). But whatever the cause, by pushing a child past the point where limbic brakes have kicked in, you do the one thing guaranteed to sap energy on future occasions, and then misconstrue the resulting "lack of effort" as proof of the student's lack of character. Not to mention the effect that this has on caregivers and teachers.

The Victorian outlook ends up producing the very thing it feared most: a quasi-permanent "underclass," marked by a lack of motivation and maladaptive modes of self-regulating. It ends up enfeebling society by fuelling anxiety, which breeds failure and apathy, and systemic poverty. Like *The Picture of Dorian Gray* (another Victorian masterpiece), you end up becoming what you most fear. Or perhaps Tennyson's "The Lotos-Eaters" is a more appropriate allusion to what we are witnessing today.

The Dangers of Victorian Misattribution

Victorian misattribution refers to the automatic perception of a child's failure to perform or behave as we hope or expect as being due to a lack of character when there are deep neural, emotional, cognitive, social, or psychological causes. As we will see in the next three chapters, this failure is the result of unleashing "ten thousand demons"[35] that sap children's energy and will – not to mention that of their parents and teachers.

Of all the exposés on the dangers of Victorian misattribution, one of the most powerful is the demonstration in *The Myth of Laziness* of how "apparently lazy" students have, in fact, been working far too hard. Several different case studies are presented to illustrate this point. The first tells the story of Russell, an eleven-year-old boy, the only child of successful professional parents. He is a bright, imaginative, and talented child, but he's having a great deal of trouble at school, social as well as academic. And one day, at the supper table, he tells his parents in a monotone that he has been thinking about killing himself. He hates school, hates the kids, hates himself, but he loves his mom and dad.

His parents are shocked and seek immediate psychiatric help. At first blush the source of Russell's depression seems apparent: he is obese and has been teased about this by the other boys; he is terrible at sports and dreads physical education; he can never get his homework done. Report cards all tell the same story: Russell is not "living up to his potential." The verdict is that he won't make the effort needed to succeed. He is thought to have no self-control: not in eating, not in schoolwork, not in exercise. He is seen as "lazy," not just by his teachers, but even by his parents, and they let him know what a disappointment he is in all sorts of ways.

We need to delve deeper, focusing in particular on the boy's graphomotor dyspraxia. Writing, for Russell, is sheer torture, not because of a poor attitude, but because his brain has trouble integrating the various fine motor sequences. He works hard to compensate for the stress of trying to get his thoughts down on paper, which then affects his attention to what he's working on, and thence, his mood.

The Myth of Laziness outlines a complex analysis of the seven stages of the "motor chain" and the three sub-steps where Russell was having visuo-motor problems. From there it works back up to the psychological level of poor self-esteem and the importance for Russell to develop interests in areas where he can excel. An essential part of the treatment is what has been called "demystification," that is, explaining to Russell why he has so much trouble writing, and then instituting strategies to compensate (including typing). In Self-Reg terms, Russell is working here on self-awareness and how it can reduce stress.

The point is not that all of Russell's problems can ultimately be traced to his problems in writing. There is still the importance of body image (obesity), his poor gross motor coordination, and his lack of understanding of why he was having such trouble at school. But it is clear that *family dynamics and teacher attitudes* were a critical factor in the boy's mounting anxiety. The whole point of the case study is to show how much harm had been done to this child by treating his *output failure* as the result of *laziness*, how an inquisitive and creative mind can be derailed.

Who knows how much deeper we could go in further exploration of the problems Russell had with exercise or eating? The fact that he is obese indicates that he was caught in a stress cycle and the possibility that other sensory issues are exerting a heavy toll on his nervous system. But then, this case study is not meant to be an exhaustive analysis; rather, it is intended as an object lesson in the dangers of *Victorian misattribution*.

Caught in a Dysregulated Neuroceptive Cycle

A child may be working too hard for all sorts of reasons. The one thing they all have in common is that *no child chooses to be left behind*. To see a child's behaviour as caused by a character flaw greatly adds to the problem by compounding the child's anxiety.

It is a chicken-and-egg situation, in which anxiety "can affect your memory in school, and therefore, your test performance. If you have memory problems in school, this can make you chronically anxious and depressed. It's a two-way street and it keeps going back and forth. We're also trying to get people away from saying which one is it mainly? Well, which caused which? It ends up just being something that exposes your biases."[36]

It's not just working memory that's at stake. Anxiety has a powerful effect on the full suite of cognitive processes, such as attention, perception, and problem solving, and, of course, motivation and learning. Even more important, anxiety has a pronounced effect on *precognitive processes*: for example, kindled threat detection and the neuroceptive discrimination between threat and safety. Conversely, negatively biased precognitive processes can lead to heightened anxiety.

This last point is one of LeDoux's central claims in *Anxious*, which we applied in our discussion of HMA. That is, it may not be anxiety that causes the child to see maths as a threat, but rather, the other way around. It is seeing maths as a threat that leads to HMA. And the question that we looked at in that chapter was: Why would a student have this neuroceptive response to arithmetic, or any other subject, and how does this lead to chronic anxiety?

A deeper problem can arise in situations where the natural function of the Interbrain has been flipped: instead of providing security, the adult amplifies the child's anxiety. High anxiety in maths – or any subject – is due not to the subject matter itself, but to *the manner in which we respond to the child*. Just as Interbrains are essential for turning off an alarm (ventral vagus), Interbrains trigger an alarm (dorsal vagus).[37] They inadvertently send a child into fight, flight, or freeze, with Blue Brain processes significantly constrained.[38]

The chronically anxious child is caught in a *dysregulating neuroceptive cycle* (Figure 8.1). The harder we try to force a child to persevere, or punish the child – implicitly if not explicitly – for "lack of effort," the worse becomes their ability to master a challenge. Instead, we need to address the factors that are fuelling the neuroceptive cycle. This is not a case of backing off from making any demands on the child but, rather, trying to understand as best we can why the child finds a task so stressful. This is what we are doing when we identify the specific stages in Russell's motor-cycle that are impeding his performance.

We definitely aren't trying to force a student to *run faster*; we are trying to release the brakes that are slowing them down. Granted, some children are naturally better sprinters than others: they can run longer, faster, and harder. But then, even great runners are not immune to the debilitating effects of glucose depletion. Two other stories in 2017, virtually the same as the Brownlee brothers', both went viral: a picture of Matthew Rees stopping to help David Wyeth in the London Marathon, and one of Ariana Luterman helping Chandler Self at the Dallas Marathon. In both cases, the front-runner's legs had buckled after hitting the wall just metres from the finish line.

Significantly, "weak leg syndrome" is also a diagnostic sign of severe anxiety.[39] We can lose a race not because of the build-up of lactic acid, but because we are too anxious. In golf it's called the "yips"; in basketball "tossing a brick"; in English pubs it's known as "dartitis." Is it possible that the same phenomenon also applies to IQ and HMA? That is, could a version of the "jelly legs" apply to learning? I'm not just referring here to freezing on a test but raising the question of whether "slow processing" can be a sign of anxiety. There is a growing body of evidence to show that this is indeed a question well worth asking.

Hereditary Genius

Psychologists are reporting a dramatic increase in the number of children they are seeing with problems in processing speed.[40]

Figure 8.1 Top: Dysregulating neuroceptive cycle. Bottom: Dysregulating neuroceptive cycle with more concrete terms

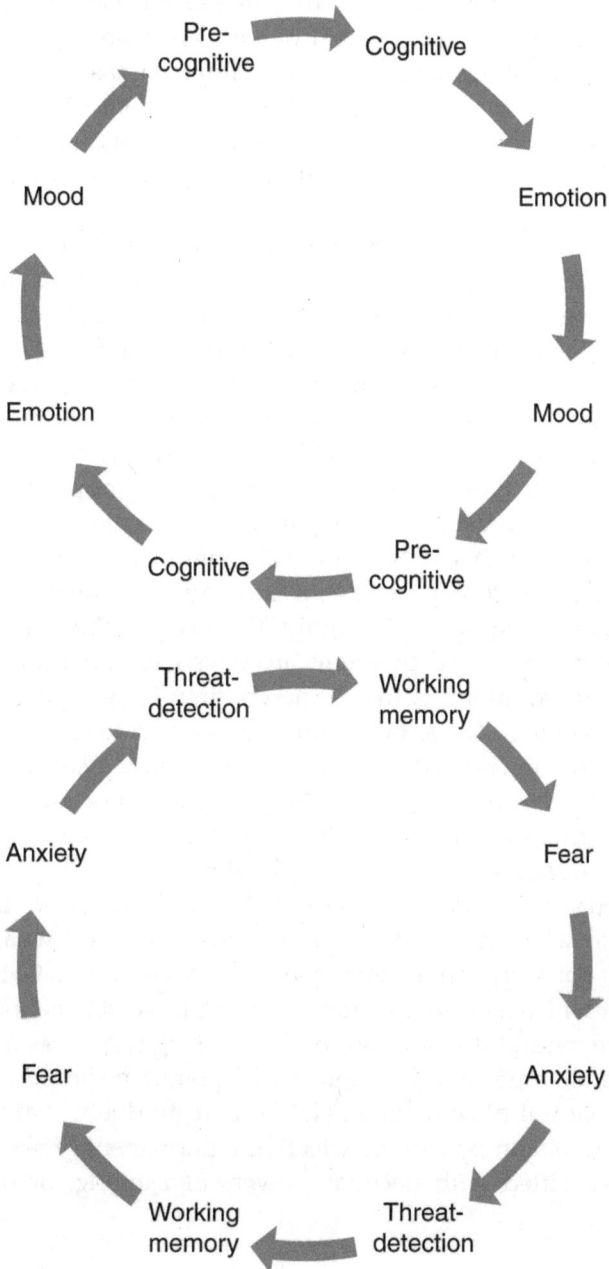

There could be any number of reasons for this puzzling trend. It might be because educators are trying to do too much too fast and those who could have dealt with a slower pace are having trouble keeping up. It might be that parents are more worried about their children falling behind. It might simply be that psychologists are more attuned to and looking for the problem. Or it might be because more children are anxious. Anxiety has a direct impact on how quickly a child can solve problems or absorb new kinds of information.

Whatever the reason, what all these explanations have in common is that they presuppose that it is *the child* who is having trouble keeping up. Experience clearly has a significant role to play here, as well as parenting and relevant natural gifts. The point is, *processing speed* applies to how the child performs on certain kinds of problems, just as *running speed* applies to how fast the child is and not to their legs. It is the *child* who learns quickly or slowly. But it is widely assumed that "processing speed" applies not to the child but to how fast their *brain* handles information.

According to this version of the "homunculus fallacy,"[41] if a child is having trouble in class, it is because his neurons process information more slowly. (Roughly 70 per cent of the children seen with processing speed problems are boys.) To adopt a computer analogy, the thinking is that some children have a much slower CPU than others. The assumption – dating back to Galton – is that *these children are born with a much slower CPU than others*. And more are having this problem today because the education system is increasingly geared to those with the faster CPU (as a result of the societal pressures we looked at in chapter 7).

Galton saw the difference between "quick" and "slow" thinking as due to what he called "synaptic efficiency" (and what a particularly apt Victorian metaphor that is!). According to Galton, the speed at which a brain operates is inherited. Hence there must be the same natural distribution for "processing speed" as exists for all heritable traits, and judicious social planning should be based on this natural phenomenon. Galton had no doubt that "as it is easy ... to obtain by careful selection a permanent breed of dogs or horses gifted with peculiar powers of running, or of doing anything else, so it would be quite practicable to produce a highly gifted race of men by judicious marriages during several consecutive generations."[42]

Galton's motivation, as he explains in the Preface to *Hereditary Genius*, was to challenge Smiles's way of thinking: "I have," he declares, "no patience with the hypothesis ... that babies are born pretty much alike, and that the sole agencies in creating differences between boy and boy, and man and man, are steady application and moral effort." Galton sought to show that, just as there is an innate difference between how fast individuals can run, so too there is one between how fast they can think. That is, not all brains are created equal, and it is contrary to the laws of nature to think otherwise. (Even Darwin was drawn to this way of thinking. He wrote to Galton that *Hereditary Genius* had "made a convert of an opponent" insofar as "I have always maintained that, excepting fools, men do not differ in intellect, only in zeal and hard work.")[43]

Galton's argument struck a resonant chord among those who saw the Chartist movement for social reform as inexorably leading to mob rule (bearing in mind how anxious Victorian society was about enfranchisement after the terrors of the French Revolution). The argument laid out in *Hereditary Genius* quickly came to define the twin pillars of the late Victorian conception of social stratification: the *either/or* view that (1) some sink to the bottom because they will not make the effort required to rise up out of their condition, or (2) some reside there because no amount of effort will make a difference insofar as genetic inheritance determines their place in society. Either way, it enfeebles the state if you deny an individual's limitations, a view that is every bit as potent today as it was 150 years ago.

Given his conviction that processing speed – and moral traits in general – are hereditary, and that social classes are a reflection of natural endowments, it is no surprise that Galton embraced – indeed, baptized – the field of *eugenics* (meaning "well-born"). Galton's thinking was that an enlightened society should encourage its "faster thinkers" to reproduce so as to counteract the polluting effects of the "slow thinkers" that sap its vitality. So strong was his belief that virtues are innate and that genetic "infirmities" cannot be overcome that he dismissed all contrary evidence (where the problem, he concluded, must have been with the test and not the theory). In this way does science turn into *non-rational ideology*. And in this way did "positive eugenics" breed the twentieth-century horrors of "negative eugenics."

The pressing question here is: What could have led so many late Victorian thinkers to venture down such a dark path? Far from being rhetorical, this question lies at the heart of any effort to create a Just Society. A number of streams converged that, together, motivated eugenicist thinking:

- The Industrial Revolution and the social displacement this produced
- Chartism and the political revolutions that swept through Europe in 1848
- Rise of a middle class
- Laissez-faire economics (Adam Smith)
- Utilitarianism (Bentham)
- Sociology (Spencer)
- Darwin
- Mendelian genetics
- Nationalism
- Imperialism (apogee of the British Empire)

The glue that held these diverse strands together was Spencer's idea that the theory of natural selection applies as much to societies as to species. Under the aegis of genetics, the way was being paved for government to play an active role in social engineering. But for Just Societers, no less ominous is the insidious way in which this outlook has shaped parents' and educators' views of a child.

To this day, the achievement gap is widely seen as due to a lack of effort or to a biological heritage that no amount of effort will overcome. Trying to close the achievement gap is thought to be like trying to flatten the Bell Curve: you are coming up either against nature or against human nature. The point of a paradigm revolution is not to take on one or the other of the horns of this dilemma, but to shift the discussion to an entirely new plane.

A Child's Greatest Fear

For the Victorians, stratification isn't a necessary evil: it is a social good. Stratification breeds vitality and societal strength; levelling leads to apathy and weakness. As Churchill put it: "The inherent vice of capitalism is the unequal sharing of blessings; the inherent virtue of socialism is the equal sharing of miseries."[44]

When Mr. M'Choakumchild in *Hard Times* asks whether a nation with "fifty millions" of money could be called prosperous, Sissy answers: "I thought I couldn't know whether it was a prosperous nation or not, and whether I was in a thriving state or not, unless I knew who had got the money, and whether any of it was mine."[45] But Smiles's response to Dickens was that a prosperous nation is one in which any individual can have a share of that wealth if they are prepared to work for it.

The factory model of education was based on precisely this principle: teaching children in a classroom setting wasn't simply a matter of efficiency. The only way to motivate children to push themselves is to have them learn as part of a competitive group, where to the victor go the spoils, while the losers get what they deserve.[46]

To shift this discussion to an entirely new plane is to abandon altogether the "survival of the fittest" mentality. The truth is, lagging behind the other kids in reading or in maths class is no different from trying to keep up with the faster kids on a cross-country run. Certain children are going to be stragglers, but they aren't choosing to dawdle: *They just can't keep up.* And now we are learning that, just as anyone can become a decent runner, provided they "start small, enjoy it, and build up,"[47] so too every student can do well in English or maths, provided processing deficits are addressed in the same sorts of ways that one prevents myopia or otitis media from interfering with learning.

Our primordial fear is said to have two aspects: being threatened and being forsaken.[48] *The greatest fear of any child is that of being left behind*, whatever the activity. The essence of attachment is the child's embodied sense that their caregiver will never abandon them. The same sense carries over to the child's feeling that their group and that group's leader will not abandon them.

Think of the child who can't keep up in something as seemingly trivial as mastering the rules of the latest playground game or mimicking the silly behaviour of peers. Children are endlessly inventive and notoriously intolerant of the child who can't follow or fit in. The child having trouble mastering the rules or behaviours may respond by avoidance, or become disruptive, angry, petulant, needy. All of which makes it considerably harder for that child to integrate with the group.

Childhood social problems predict a variety of negative outcomes, including delinquency, dropping out of school, substance abuse, academic difficulties, truancy, and psychological maladjustment. It turns out that *peer attitudes* are more predictive of a child's later psychological well-being than standard educational metrics, such as teacher ratings, grades, achievement scores, IQ, or absenteeism. It is extremely difficult for children to overcome peer rejection after this has occurred, and even harder to overcome Interbrain rejection. Little wonder that so many of them go on to have serious social and emotional, as well as educational, problems.

The key words here are "go on." The essence of Self-Reg is that this outcome is not baked in, neither in the child's genes nor in adverse early childhood experiences, socio-economic circumstances, or the constraints under which the system must operate. It's *how* we change the child's trajectory that is the major issue.

Suppose we were to institute a national hiking program: every child in the country has to cover x number of kilometres. And to make the program successful (we really do want a fit generation), we monitor how many children complete the course and institute a system of punishments and rewards that apply to the troop leaders, to motivate them to get as many children as possible to cross the finish line.

The question then is: How will these troop leaders respond to those children who can't keep up? Will they embrace the idealism inspiring the program and do everything they can to help? Will they harass the non-starters? Find ways to make their names "disappear" from the records so that the punishments aren't invoked? Concentrate on the ones that with a bit of coaxing can be pushed across the finish line and resign themselves to letting the others go? And then shift responsibility for their failure with the latter onto the kids themselves, onto their character or the possibility that they have lazy parents?

The problem is, without any understanding of *why a straggler is straggling*, let alone guidelines as to *how to help* such a child overcome personal hurdles, the program is destined to stratify its participants.

Old Paradigms Never Die

It is hard not to be struck by how many of the themes dominating political dialogue today have their roots in Victorian thinking. And this isn't a case of reading between the lines. In 1983, Margaret Thatcher gave a speech celebrating the Victorian values on which she had been raised by her grandmother: hard work, discipline, self-reliance, self-respect.[49] It was this message that had brought her to power in 1979 and kept her there.

I was living in England at the time. The country was in the throes of Red Brain, and Thatcher's appeal to "Victorian values" triggered the same sort of kneejerk reaction among voters that parents have when their child's behaviour sends them into Red Brain: "Spare the rod and spoil the society."

As far as education was concerned, the thinking was that these Victorian values had to be instilled in children early. The minister of state for education, Dr Rhodes Boyson, spoke about how much good the occasional caning at school had done him, and he was not alone. The central pillar of the Thatcherite view of education was that children have to be taught from the start that either they develop the character traits needed to overcome whatever adversity stands in their way or they fail and suffer the consequences on their own, without their parents or teachers there to catch them should they fall.[50]

As we look at the striking rise in internalizing and externalizing problems in students over the past generation, we cannot afford to overlook the role that the resurgence of this Victorian mindset may have played. In addition to the explosion of stressors children have to deal with, hidden and overt, we mustn't overlook what is happening at school. We need to consider the very real possibility that if educators don't understand when and why they are dealing with limbic braking, they can contribute not just to problems in mood and behaviour but even to a student's "slow thinking" and poor academic performance.

How should we respond to a child having trouble keeping up? Victorianism presents us with a stark alternative: either we push them to try harder or we *mollycoddle* them. By this point it pretty much goes without saying that the latter term is Victorian. In *Pendennis*, written by Thackeray senior, Warrington tells Pen: "A little necessity brings out your pluck if you have any, and nerves you to grapple with fortune ... [The problem is] you have been bred up as a mollycoddle, Pen, and spoilt by the women."[51]

We need to shift this debate to a new set of terms, which is the whole point of *reframing*. The problem with Victorian thinking is that it forces us to choose willy-nilly between these two alternatives: either we teach children to persevere or we allow them to malinger. When this sort of polarization occurs, *non-rational conviction* replaces doubt; denial is stronger than counter-evidence. But instead of swinging back and forth between authoritarian and permissive modes of self-regulating, Self-Reg asks: Why is this child so easily "distracted" and distracting? Why does this student have so much trouble organizing their thoughts? Why is it so hard for a student to master this material?

Outdated paradigms never die; they simply fade away and take up residence in the History of Ideas. Biases aside, would anyone continue to be Victorian in their thinking about a child if they knew that their trajectory, which is worrying, could in fact be changed? Knew that the child is not *choosing* to be left behind and certainly doesn't *deserve* to be left behind? Knew that the child is under a tremendous strain *trying* to keep up with the rest of the group, and, what is worst of all, more than smart enough and naturally curious enough to do so, if only we can release their limbic brakes?

This question is not some sort of naive denial of biology: it is a rational rejection of the non-rational "cannot." The crux of Self-Reg is that the better we can understand neurogenetic or developmental issues, the better we can *potentiate a child's potential* – and that of those around them. Just think of the impact on teachers, as well as fellow students, when the measures we are taking to help that child or teen are seen to be working, versus when we don't even try.

What effect does it have on the others to see one of their classmates being left behind? The apes were incredibly unsettled when a conspecific was anxious; there is no doubt that children are the same, *until the Victorian mindset takes hold*! It is so telling how the boys who answer Gradgrind at the beginning of *Hard Times* have turned into marionettes, not just oblivious of what Sissy may be feeling but totally indifferent.[52]

This is what the Victorian view of education is ultimately all about: conditioning children to think like Margaret Thatcher's Victorian grandmother. Training them to turn their backs on the classmate who can't keep up. To embrace social Darwinism when they enter the workforce, despite what is known about the effects of excessive stress and the reality of the stress gradient. To accept stratification as an inevitable fact of human existence, an unavoidable consequence of the natural distribution of human abilities. Not to mention using it as a way of applauding themselves for their achievement.

That is not to say that Victorian thinking is the cause of stratification, only that it is incapable of grappling with it, let alone nurturing the basic drive that made us human: namely, that no member of the group be left behind. That is one of the basic precepts driving Self-Reg, the fundamental principle that we can only create a Just Society when we set out to do so one child at a time.

Chapter 9

Becoming Free, Staying Free

Philosophy at Oxford

I first started thinking "rigorously" about *freedom* when I was still a (relatively) free spirit myself and an undergraduate at Oxford, back in the 1970s. Oxford was a paradox: you were free to go to lectures or not; free to work hard on your tutorials or spend your time at the Boar's Head. But every so often you had to check in with your moral tutor (yes, they were really called that), and, perhaps fearing how I might respond to so much liberty, Northrop Frye had arranged for Isaiah Berlin to be mine.

Initially, I thought that the idea of a "moral tutor" was just an antiquated way of describing an academic supervisor. But the intention was more serious than I realized, and more demanding. The role of the moral tutor, at least as far as Berlin was concerned, was to inspire a student to cherish intellectual freedom and rigour, *and to recognize that the two are joined at the hip*.

To this day I vividly remember the frisson I felt when given my first philosophy assignment: "What were Descartes's reasons for doubting? Were they good reasons?" The message here was clear: *First read, then think*. The thinking part, I quickly discovered, is hard work – and damned frustrating. Dons didn't regard the first-person utterance *I think* as an excuse for saying whatever popped into your head, or asserting your independence, or reciting what you had read. *I think* has consequences, beginning with being able to answer the question "Why do you think that?"

As I was also to discover when I studied political theory. Berlin had sent me to work under Alan Ryan at New College, and the first question he assigned was: "What is Berlin's argument for the distinction between positive and negative freedom in 'Two Concepts of Liberty'? Is it a good argument?"[1] The problem was, I wasn't sure it was a good argument; and to make matters worse, I knew that Ryan was seen by many as Berlin's protégé.

Paradoxically, I thought I understood what Berlin was saying about *positive freedom*, that is, freedom from internal constraints, like maddening impulses or the need for instant gratification. What I found hard was getting a grip on *negative freedom*: the freedom to act on our wishes and desires without external constraints, provided no one is harmed by our actions. Drawn as I was to Berlin's views about the "moral sovereignty" of the individual and having the opportunity to choose your own goals in life, I couldn't help but feel that there was a major problem lurking in his account of negative freedom. I just couldn't tell Ryan why I felt that way. At least, not in a way that he found satisfactory.

It would be easy to dismiss Berlin's *Two Concepts of Liberty* as a (dated) product of its time: an expression of Cold War anxieties, and, for that matter, the product of an Oxford that has since vanished. Berlin was devastated by the oppression he witnessed firsthand in Russia immediately after the war, and this comes through loud and clear in the text. A generation of intellectuals had been liquidated for the crime of championing freedom. But what matters today isn't so much the political dimension of *negative freedom* as a conceptual one; an issue every bit as pressing today as it was half a century ago. Maybe more so.

Berlin starts off: "Almost every moralist in human history has praised freedom." But sadly, not just the moralists. The agents of evil have done the same. The slogan of the Nazi party in the critical 1932 election was "Freedom and Bread." Clearly praising freedom is not enough.

I remember endless arguments with my peers about the rights and wrongs of the actions done in the name of freedom. Yet when I look back, it feels as if we were living in a bubble. The image that comes to mind is a day I spent punting on the Cherwell with friends, arguing about positive and negative freedom. The greatest threat that we faced was getting our pole stuck in the mud.

The idea that we would ever see a resurgence of authoritarianism in our own backyard would have been unfathomable. So, you can hardly fault us if we talked a little too glibly about how the last few strongmen who roamed the Earth would soon be vanquished by the democratic spirit, never dreaming that we ourselves would one day have to contend with a similar threat.

We may have relished freedom – ours, after all, was the Woodstock generation – but in many respects we took it for granted. We didn't appreciate how fragile freedom truly is. What it takes to experience freedom. What it takes to preserve it. Just maybe, we confused *natural right* with *natural endowment*, in much the same way as did Rousseau.

We aren't *born free*, we *become free*, and then we have to strive to *stay free*. Whether or not we succeed, or the extent to which we succeed, depends on neurobiological as much as political factors. Possibly more so. The authoritarian sets out to vanquish freedom. He does so by sending individuals into Red Brain. When that happens, you don't have to convince them to relinquish their freedom; they will do so voluntarily as they drink from the waters of Lethe.

Freedom Is Tied to Choice

To answer the question of why freedom is both so precious and so precarious presupposes that we understand what is meant by *freedom*. Berlin tells us that he is primarily interested in the "political sense of freedom or liberty," and that he will "use both words to mean the same." To be sure, this is common enough usage in the political context. But what about the psychological dimension? You might be living in a liberal democracy, but can you truly be free if your mind isn't free? And what exactly does it mean to talk about a "mind being free"?

That question may not receive a lot of attention in *Two Concepts* but it's there, and indeed, Berlin's answer underpins the distinction that he draws between positive and negative freedom. In the anti-determinist terms that Berlin embraced from his earliest writings, he explained that to be free means that I am "the instrument of my own will." That is, I am free "*to the extent that I am moved by reasons, not causes*": my actions are "*self-directed.*" He goes on: "*This is at least part of what I mean when I say that I am rational, and that it is my reason that distinguishes me as a human being ... I wish, above all, to be conscious of myself as a thinking, willing, active being, bearing responsibility for my choices and able to explain them by references to my own ideas and purposes.*"[2]

What Berlin is stating here – well, restating – is Descartes's view of rationality (chapter 4).[3] What was troubling me, although I didn't know so at the time, was that this argument was *privileging rationality*. The problem is, people in the throes of depression are not *free* in this sense, and certainly not able to "direct themselves" to cast aside their worries. The same can be said of someone who is subject to fits of rage, or who has severe social anxiety, or who is struggling with addiction. Or someone who votes for a would-be despot.

A free individual wouldn't just toss away their liberty. If they vote for a despot, this means that their mind was not free. It does not mean that their vote was involuntary; they weren't forced to cast their vote this way. Rather, they vote for the authoritarian who is poised to take away their liberty because they are caught in the vice of *non-rational conviction*.

For that matter, the *rationalist view of freedom* sits uncomfortably with everyday life. Think about trying to stick to a diet, to stop procrastinating at work, to prevent yourself from blurting out things you don't want to say, buying things you don't need, having that second (third ...) drink, or staying up all night playing online poker. Somehow the "instrument of our will" just doesn't seem up to the task of carrying out our everyday wishes.

Berlin's view of *freedom* will strike many – and not just closet authoritarians – as a philosopher's (pipe)dream: the musings of a cloistered All Souls don who, like everyone else at Oxford, was mesmerized by Wittgenstein, and who raises more problems than he solves. What exactly does it mean to describe myself as someone whose actions are "*moved* by my reasons"? How does a reason "bring about" an action? Is this even a binary matter: *either* my actions are moved by a reason *or* by a cause? Could they be neither, or both?

We all may share the same wish to see ourselves as rational agents; we certainly behave as if we do. But since the time that Berlin wrote this paper, there has been a relentless attack on the rationalist outlook as thus conceived (chapters 2 and 4). You may think you're the "instrument of your will," but social psychology shows us just how easy it is to lead you by the nose.[4] You may think that your PFC is in charge, but, according to Gazzaniga, neuroscience tells us that it is the subcortex that is really in charge.[5]

But then, Berlin's distinction between the two concepts of freedom is based on a *logical*, not an *empirical* proposition: viz., *to be free* means *to be able to choose*. This isn't simply a matter of not having a parent or a government dictate your actions. It's having a mind that is not under the thrall of an obsession or a compulsion, or that uncontrollably flits from one thought to another, or that is consumed by doubts and fears. We can choose well or badly, wisely or foolishly, carefully or impulsively, clear-headedly or blindly, but however we do it, *I choose*, like *I think*, has logical consequences.

I choose presupposes that I can be described as *conscious of what I'm choosing*; that I could have chosen differently; that I am able to explain why I chose as I did; that I take responsibility for my choices. I can be conflicted about the choices I've made, wish that I'd chosen differently, wonder what on earth I was thinking when I made that choice. But even though I can be manipulated to make certain choices (e.g., the "position effect"), it is still my choice, so, by definition, freely made.

But to say, as the Marxist does, that I am *imprisoned when I choose* – whether the chains are cultural or socioeconomic – is merely to say that *I don't choose*. We don't require neuroimaging or psychoanalysis to determine whether or not this last statement is true. It is a logical statement about the unbreakable relationship between the concepts of *freedom* and *choice*.

Hence the absence of the one cancels out the other. That is, one *cannot* – logically cannot – distinguish between "choosing freely" (a pleonasm, that is, redundant) and "choosing unfreely" (a contradiction in terms). The latter makes no sense. To describe people as "choosing unfreely" is merely to say that *they don't choose*, that their actions are caused.

This logical confusion is implicit in the Marxist doctrine of *false consciousness*, that is, the idea that the choices that our *phenomenal self* makes are such that our *rational self* would reject. What the argument is really stating is that we *misbelieve* that we are choosing when we are doing nothing of the sort. That is a different matter, and as we saw, not something that can be lightly dismissed. But then, I am pretty sure this subtle logical point wouldn't have troubled the ruthless tyrant who said: "Ideas are more powerful than guns. We would not let our enemies have guns. Why should we let them have ideas?"[6]

Berlin's defence of liberty comes down to the principle that individuals must be allowed to choose their goals, and in a democratic society, there will be fierce debate as to what those goals should be. But the authoritarian views this principle as hopelessly Romantic, belied by the long history of human irrationality. Since humans aren't capable of choosing rationally [*sic*], then they must have rationality thrust upon them – which is the crux of Berlin's remarks on positive freedom.

According to the determinist, Berlin's *"wish, above all, to be conscious of myself as a thinking, willing, active being"* is nothing more than that. Merely a wish, and a rather quaint one at that. But according to the determinist, even though "there's no such thing as free will," we may still be better off believing in it.[7] Far from being "self-directed," our "choices" [*sic*] are *always* "predictably irrational."[8]

"Forced to Be Free" Is a Dangerous Oxymoron

Throughout the rich and varied writings on the nature of freedom, one theme stands out as the *Urgedanke*, the core idea that "the mere impulse to appetite is slavery."[9] For every classical political theorist that you can think of – including both Berlin and Marx – "to be free" is to be "master of your appetites."

Marx's basic criticism of capitalism was that unfettered negative freedom enables a minority of "enslaved" individuals – in the sense defined above – to enthral the rest of society. That is, it gives them free rein to indulge their base instincts (greed) while denying benign ones (altruism). This laxity leads to the concentration of (economic) power that prevents the rest of society (the working proletariat) from enjoying their right to liberty. On the contrary, the more the masses can be induced to gratify their base appetites, the more secure the capitalist model.

For all the attention paid to Marx's view of religion as the "opiate of the masses," the origins of this moralistic argument go back to the Book of John (8:31–6), where the distinction between *positive* and *negative freedom* is laid out:

31 To the Jews who had believed him, Jesus said, "If you hold to my teaching, you are really my disciples. 32 Then you will know the truth, and the truth will set you free."
33 They answered him, "We are Abraham's descendants and have never been slaves of anyone. How can you say that we shall be set free?"
34 Jesus replied, "Very truly I tell you, everyone who sins is a slave to sin. 35 Now a slave has no permanent place in the family, but a son belongs to it forever. 36 So if the Son sets you free, you will be free indeed."

The point here is that the negative theorist confuses liberty with freedom: we are never free so long as we are enslaved by base appetites. Every individual has the capacity to be free; indeed, this freedom is the most precious gift that God bestowed on humanity. The story of the Fall was read as an allegory depicting how humanity came to be plagued by appetites precisely to have the opportunity to experience freedom. Freedom is not a natural endowment; it is the fruit of willpower.

But where the essence of the orthodox Christian view of *positive freedom* is that it is up to individuals to choose whether or not to be ruled by their appetites, the despot maintains – in terms that hark back to Rousseau's *Social Contract* – that individuals must be "forced to be free."[10] This idea is the antithesis of the Book of John, and perhaps, what Rousseau intended. What Rousseau meant is that in a free society, individuals must willingly obey laws they may not have voted for; that is, must see themselves as morally bound by the "general will." But for Stalin, this way of thinking took a satanic turn.

The seeds for The Great Terror[11] were laid in Engels's idea that, in capitalism, the ideology of the ruling class so permeates and perverts the thinking of the proletariat that the latter "choose to be enslaved"; that is, choose to support an economic system that alienates them from what they would have chosen had they been truly free. Stalin seized on "false consciousness" as a pretext to kill between twenty and twenty-five million people. He was not the first to espouse a doctrine of "false consciousness."

In *Paradise Lost*, Milton depicts the fallen angels who are bewitched by Satan's mesmerizing words. At the beginning of Book II, Satan tells the fallen angels, who have just been thrust out of heaven and are lying stunned on the floor of hell, that "the fixt Laws of Heav'n / Did first create your Leader, next free choice."[12] For Satan, "free will" means you are free because you can do as *I* please, namely, indulge your appetites.

The fallen angels then split up into groups, with some sitting

on a hill retired,

In thoughts more elevate, and reasoned high
Of Providence, Foreknowledge, Will, and Fate –
Fixed fate, free will, foreknowledge absolute –
And found no end, in wandering mazes lost.
Of good and evil much they argued then,
Of happiness and final misery,
Passion and apathy, and glory and shame:
Vain wisdom all, and false philosophy! –
Yet, with a pleasing sorcery, could charm
Pain for a while or anguish, and excite
Fallacious hope, or arm the obdured breast

With stubborn patience as with triple steel.

In modern terms, Milton is making the point that succumbing to your appetites may *charm pain or anguish* for a while, but the sedating effect of opioids wears off and leaves you in a far worse state. And presumably, the same can be said for philosophy: an opioid for unsettled minds!

Marx held a similar view of philosophy. Philosophers, he complained, "have only *interpreted* the world, in various ways. The point, however, is to *change* it."[13] In Stalin's hands, this maxim was to result in an orgy of killing. To be seen as an intellectual in Stalinist Russia was a death sentence. Sounding just like Beelzebub in *Paradise Lost*, Stalin reportedly said to Churchill at the Tehran Conference in 1943: "God is on your side? Is He a Conservative? The Devil's on my side, he's a good Communist."[14]

Berlin's defence of negative freedom comes straight out of Milton's *Aeropagitica*, which is without question the most influential liberal text ever written in the English language – and the forerunner of Berlin's "Two Concepts." Milton's basic principle is that

> the right and also the duty of every intelligent man as a rational being [is] to know the grounds and take responsibility for his beliefs and actions. Its corollary was a society and a state in which decisions are reached by open discussion, in which the sources of information are not contaminated by authority in the interest of party, and in which political unity is secured not by force but by a consensus that respects variety of opinion.[15]

Just the sort of thing to get fervid undergraduate minds all fired up. It's the question of how you actually get to this point that I found perplexing. Especially when it seemed that we were going in the wrong direction. What I saw around me in England at the end of the 1970s (let alone in the debate over Brexit) suggested a dearth of rational discourse. But how is a society supposed to enjoy political unity if non-rationality at the top is seeping down to the general populace?

Berlin was one of the great moralists of the twentieth century. He would have been horrified by the rising fascist currents that are swirling about us today. But the more I have thought about this issue, the better I begin to understand why I was so troubled in my undergraduate years by the manner in which Berlin treated the distinction between *positive* and *negative freedom*. As he framed the argument, both sides see self-control as the heart of the matter. But where one sees the ability to exercise self-control in a free market society as an impossibility, and so as a rationale for *imposing* freedom, the other sees the lack of self-control as a human frailty that needs to be contained by the rule of law.

To be sure, *self-controllism* is not the source of the problem; on the contrary, we all want our kids to acquire self-discipline. But the question I was grappling with was: Does the possibility of experiencing freedom rest on *the prior ability* to exercise self-control? Does the "slippery slope" that Berlin so worries about in "Two Concepts" – from *self-control* to *state control* – stem from precisely this premise? Or do we need to reframe the "freedom *if and only if* choice" logical proposition?

An Authoritarian Model of the Mind

The resurgence of authoritarianism throughout the West is thought to be due to the heightened level of societal stress, caused by the pace of technological and demographic change; unresolved historical and social tensions; environmental/geopolitical threats; the fear of immigrants, crime, or the "great replacement"; global interdependency and competition; and social media, used for malign purposes. All of these factors point to a surge in societal stress. But why should that lead to authoritarian rather than democratic thinking? Why are we seeing a disturbing spread of *non-rational conviction*?

The Freudian explanation is that we have a natural instinct to turn to an authority when highly anxious. In other words, the more dysregulated a society becomes, the more it regresses to an infantile state in which it turns to a parent figure for protection. Individuals don't so much have their autonomy stripped from them as willingly give it up. Is there a neurobiological explanation of this "instinct"?

Aeropagitica and *Two Concepts* sought to be a bulwark against this instinctive reaction to heightened stress, rousing individuals to stay resolute and rational. But the resurgence of fascism compels us to ask: Why are these two political masterpieces so quickly forgotten when stress becomes too great? That is not to deny the forcefulness of Milton's or Berlin's impassioned pleas for freedom and tolerance. But clearly passion, like praise, is not enough. Nor is logic. The problem is, logic tells us nothing about how one *becomes free*, only what it means *to be free*.

Far from serving as a roadmap to freedom – personal or political – Berlin's argument rests on a hidden tautology, which has been there from the start: namely, *one is free to choose only if one chooses to be free*. The implicit (self-control) assumption is that freedom rests on the inhibition of appetites. This is how we are able to be "self-directed," the author of our actions, rather than captive to compulsions.

This argument comes straight out of the Book of John. As Berlin himself remarks, "the logical distance between [positive and negative] freedom is not all that great."[16] The reason is that the proponents of both positive and negative freedom see choice as only possible when impulses are controlled. Both share the basic assumption, which dates back to the opening chapters of Genesis, that if you give in to your urges, you sacrifice your freedom: whether those urges come from the body, the mind, Satan, or the "modes of production."

Self-control, as Plato put it, results from a "courageous" determination to hold the reins firmly. The model for *courage* thus understood is Socrates (whom Plato casts as "the new Achilles"). Sounding just like Plato, Stalin insisted that "true courage consists in being strong enough to master and overcome oneself and subordinate one's will to the will of the collective."[17]

Berlin would, of course, have vehemently disagreed with the second part of this last sentence, but not with the first. Like every liberal thinker before him, Berlin was convinced that the long-term viability of democracy rests on the twin values of self-discipline and communal good. The problem is the very slippery slope that Berlin warned against; if not careful, we lapse back into the beckoning arms of authoritarianism.

The next step is to step back, to recognize that *Plato's very model of the mind is authoritarian*. According to Plato, reason must rule over appetites. But it can only do so when *thumos* comes to its aid. Without *thumos*, the mind descends into "civil war" (*stasis*). When *stasis* breaks out, the individual is incapable of acting for a purpose (RPK 352a). Hence, one of the chief tasks of education is to strengthen the child's *thumos* so that it can enforce reason's dictates. Freedom from "psychic anarchy" occurs only when, through self-control, the individual bludgeons their appetites into submission.

Demagoguery feeds on ancient survival systems – FEAR, RAGE, PANIC/GRIEF, SEEKING – then reassures the populace that only through strong government can its anxiety be relieved. The *charm* of such a message when one is prostrate and stunned by surging levels of stress involves more than just infantile regression. If an individual resonates with what a demagogue is saying, it is because they were already bred by the self-control paradigm to think in authoritarian terms. Wild horses need to be held in check, if not by a Strong Self then by a Strong Leader.

Plato saw internal conflict as the fundamental dynamic of the human mind and self-control as the only means to freedom. This paradigm has shaped Western thinking ever since. We must force our impulses into submission – and do the same to the liberal impulses of our political opponents. There is no freedom, however, if one side in a conflict vanquishes the other, but the causes of the conflict are left unresolved. *Only tyranny*. The idea that you can force someone – or yourself! – to be free is an oxymoron. And an incredibly dangerous one at that.

The Self-Reg Democratic Model of the Mind

In the fourth Book of *The Republic*, Socrates tells the story of how

> Leontius, the son of Aglaion, was coming up from the Piraeus under the north wall from outside and observed corpses beside the public executioner. At the same time he had an appetite to look and again felt disquiet and turned himself away. For a while he fought and covered

his face. But overcome by appetite, he stretched his eyes, ran towards the corpses and said, "See for yourselves, you wretches, replenish yourselves with the beautiful sight."[18]

This allegory was frequently cited in the Middle Ages and Renaissance. Like all allegories, it was used to reinforce a piece of conventional wisdom; in this case, that lack of self-control is a *weakness*, and a pathetic one at that. We might read the story of Leontius as an early version of the Marshmallow Task, although the very first version occurs at Genesis 2:16–17.

For Plato, this conflict between desires – morbid versus rational – is the essence of the human condition. It was because Leontius had not strengthened his *thumos* sufficiently that he lost the internal battle. For Self-Reg, the interesting question is not why he should have had the morbid desire, but why the stress of the situation sent him into quasi-dissociation.

It was not greater effort – supersized self-control – that Leontius needed in the moment, but self-soothing. Not stronger *thumos* to resist the urge to look at the dead bodies, but insight as to why he became dysregulated. Was it because of the Thayer state he was in, exhausted after a long journey? The stress of being weighed down by family matters? Prosocial stress stemming from a societal norm? ("We all have the same morbid desire, but only the weak are unable to resist it.")

Leontius behaves just like the children in the Marshmallow Task who can't delay gratification: he self-regulates by running to look at the corpses. Only in this way can he stop the stress. But it doesn't help; if anything, it makes things worse, precisely because of the cultural mindset that has turned this into a matter of self-control. The stress that self-controllism creates puts him in Red Brain, in which there is no choosing how he acts and clearly no freedom.

It is the nature of life to agonize over weighty matters, to balance immediate versus long-term goals, base versus benign desires, egoistic versus altruistic motives. The meaningful internal battles that we fight are not over marshmallows or morbid impulses. They are the moral issues that define our character, subserved by CARE and not by SEEKING. They restore social harmony, while selfish desires destroy it.

What we need if we are to grow from our emotional slugfests is not to bulk up our willpower but to recognize and reduce the stresses that are hindering rationality. We need time – maybe a lifetime – to resolve some of these inner conflicts; reframe impulses; recognize hidden as well as overt stresses in our lives and in our society; learn what *calmness* feels like and how to attain it; what consensus looks like and how to sustain it; how to be free in mind as well as body; how to restore ourselves biologically, psychologically, socially, emotionally, and spiritually. Without restoration we are susceptible to dysteroception, unaware of the internal signals that warn us of homeostatic imbalances that sabotage self-reflection, as opposed to self-control.

Where the authoritarian model of the mind seeks to shut down these internal debates through brute force (e.g., denial, avoidance, rationalization, justification, compartmentalization), Self-Reg seeks to learn from them. The former seeks submission, the latter, illumination. Where the former seeks to control unsettling impulses, Self-Reg sees them as an opportunity for emotional growth. Rather than shouting at his wayward eyes, Leontius might have reflected on the Why of his ghoulish impulse. (In modern terms, it might be the allegory of the rubber-necker.)

Accordingly, Self-Reg replaces Plato's authoritarian with a *democratic model of the mind*: one grounded in the checks and balances afforded by self-regulation. The democratic model of the mind is implicit in Berlin's argument. The crux of *negative freedom* is that the individual's actions are not dictated by an external force. Berlin is thinking about this in political terms, but the same point applies to the mind. A "free mind" is one that is not under the sway of suggestion, fixation, obsession, compulsion, mania, paranoia, neurosis, addiction, learned helplessness.

Someone whose mind is free is capable of choosing – carefully, if not wisely; capable of questioning and regretting their choices. It is not self-control that makes rationality possible: it is homeostatic balance. Just as a free society is one in which decisions are reached by consensus, a free mind is one in which decisions are the result of *deliberation* and not *compulsion*.

"To have a free mind" is to seek to understand, and as a result of this understanding, to modulate and reduce dysregulating stresses, as opposed to trying (vainly) to escape or subdue them. This is also the crux of the view of liberal democracy that Berlin espouses: a self-regulating comity that is able to withstand the stress of partisan politics for the sake of the common good. Otherwise, the two political factions are like rival fire departments standing in front of a conflagration and squabbling over who should be in charge of the rescue operation while the building burns to the ground.

What makes social harmony in the midst of discord possible is mindful self-regulation, at the leadership as well as the individual level. That is, social harmony is top down/bottom up. It can be inspired, but it cannot be imposed – not by the law, and not by a Fearless Leader. But equally, it is a calmly focused body politic that enables the "unity that is secured not by force but by a consensus that respects variety of opinion."[19]

Herein lies still a deeper aspect of the Self-Reg response to the major question raised above: the question of why authoritarianism feeds off of and in turn feeds heightened societal stress. Political theory cannot ignore the neurobiological and psychophysiological dimension of this issue: the multiplicity of stresses at the level of the individual that are building up steam in the communal pressure cooker.

At the political level, the secret of democracy's survival lies in its institutional self-regulating mechanisms: the executive, legislative assembly, and independent judiciary, and at a lower level, community organizations that nourish the spirit of self-governance. Next are the fourth and fifth estates: all those journalists, philosophers, artists, poets, musicians, and free-thinkers that Stalin sought to control and, where that proved difficult, exterminate. But it is at the individual level where the real secret of democracy's staying power lies: in healthy modes of self-regulation that promote and sustain homeostasis.

It's those who look at history through the same ancient self-control paradigm that cannot learn from it and, hence, are doomed to repeat it.

The Origin of Calmness

The corollary of *freedom* ↔ *choice* is *calmness* → *choice*. That is, the logical shift from *if and only if* to *if–then*. But calmness can be neither willed nor imposed; it is the result of "homeostasis: a physiological state of complete calmness or rest; markers include resting heart rate, blood pressure, and [breathing]."[20] The fact that *our ability to choose* is so dependent on *our being calm* may seem such an obvious point as to border on the banal, which has certainly not stopped philosophers from repeating it. It's one of those axioms that makes perfect sense, and maybe it's only because we hear it all the time that it seems banal.

The importance of calmness for *decision making* dates back to the classical principle of the "Golden Mean." This view is commonly attributed to Aristotle, but, in fact, it traces back to Plato, who said: "[We must know] how always to choose in such things the life that is seated in the mean and shun the excess in either direction" (RPK 10:619a). Even before Plato, we find a similar idea in the Confucian *Doctrine of the Mean* and the Cretan myth of Icarus.

Ever since antiquity, *calmness* has been tied to the notion of *choosing the middle path between extremes*. Again, we can glimpse a hidden tautology. Essentially the argument comes down to: *one chooses to be calm so that one can choose*. Hence the absurdity of telling a child in the midst of a meltdown to calm down, as if it were a matter of choice. But then, that is the core premise of Self-Control.

To be sure, we can do certain things to help ourselves calm down. We can go for a walk, take a bath, do some deep breathing. Self-help gurus have been offering this kind of advice for an astoundingly long time. (The very first self-help book was written around 2800 BC, the *Maxims of Ptahotep*, in which an elderly father counsels his son on the vital importance of exercising self-control.)

But note that each of these beneficial modes of self-regulation is grounded in the *solitary mind* approach. That is, *what I can do, on my own, to feel calm*. But there are times, especially when struggling with chronic anxiety, that nothing works. Deep breathing makes us feel worse. We are so agitated that we can't help but give in to morbid urges, which makes us even more agitated. But the brain harbours a deep embodied memory of what we would do in such situations.

We need to think here about the developmental origins of calmness. There are nociceptors scattered throughout the body: in the skin, muscle, joints, bones, and viscera. Their function is to alert us to injury, prevent or avoid further harm. But fortunately, we have opioid receptors as well that run throughout the brain, down the spinal cord, and widely throughout the body. Opioids bind to these receptors, blunting nociceptive signals travelling to the brain. In the brain, these opioids cause sedation and decrease pain sensation.

The very first thing that the "foetus-outside-the-womb" SEEKS is skin-to-skin contact and latching onto the breast. This has an instantly calming effect because of the oxytocin released. Oxytocin inhibits the release of corticotropin-releasing factor, stopping the stress response in its tracks while activating opioid receptors. The baby SEEKS social engagement because of the oxytocin and beta-endorphins this provides; and social engagement in turn shapes what the infant SEEKS. The caregiver shapes the rewards that the baby will SEEK because of the opioids this affords, beginning with herself.

Separation causes a drop in opioids *in both* mother and baby. This is both psychologically and physiologically aversive. Separation causes:

- A spike in cortical arousal
- A drop in human growth hormone
- A disruption of sleep patterns
- Heightened reactivity of the HPA pathway

Prolonged separation causes chronic opioid homeostatic imbalance. And not just in an infant/caregiver dyad. Reunion triggers oxytocin and beta-endorphins *in both*. Both feel warmer and both are calmer. Touch is especially effective, which is the reason why Michael Meaney's research was so important: viz., licking triggers oxytocin release in the pup, turning off nociceptors, just as touch and voice do in humans.

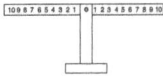

┬ : *Blue Brain/Red Brain Balance*

The humoralists had a simple solution for how to help an agitated mind, but MacLean's *fluid-dynamics* provides a rather more enlightened approach than bloodletting. There is a constant flux and flow between Blue Brain and Red Brain states. *Calmness* (homeostasis) occurs when the two "brains" are in balance.[21] Neuroimaging will show an even scattering of blue (prefrontal) and red (limbic) systems. The Red Brain is like a purring motor, keeping the Blue Brain ticking over.

Blue Brain/Red Brain cortical balance affords the physiological opportunity to deliberate. The Red Brain supplies the Blue Brain with the fuel and positive emotions it needs to solve problems. An equally important aspect of Blue Brain/Red Brain balance is that *the sense of time slows down while mental space expands*. This is a familiar phenomenon to anyone who plays tennis. When you're "in the zone" it seems as if you have forever to plan your next shot, and the service box seems twice as big as normal. But if pressed by your opponent, you start to rush your shots and, as Agassi remarked, the service box seems to shrink to the size of a napkin (see chapter 2).

The neural phenomenon operating here is known as *transient hypofrontality*.[22] According to this hypothesis, the sense of time slowing down and mental space expanding is more than just a figurative way of describing what it feels like to be in *flow*. Time is said to "dilate" as a result of a number of factors: as we become fully absorbed in what we're doing, we are oblivious to cues (internal and external) that we rely on for our sense of time, while the internal biological clock in the striatum speeds up. Limbic arousal abates, allowing for a dampening of prefrontal inhibitory systems, which in turn contributes to the feeling of time slowing down.

Meanwhile, mental space is expanding. This metaphor of *Gedankenraum* is fundamental to psychoanalysis: the idea that we need *mental space* to reflect, relate, and feel. Subcortical arousal diminishes at the same time as, or in part because, transient hypofrontality increases, which allows for more working memory because of the decrease in worries and intrusive thoughts. If we think of working memory in spatial terms, the idea here is that the less working memory is crowded by extraneous intruders, the more room we have for decision making.

In Blue Brain/Red Brain balance, cortical arousal is within an optimal neurobiological band involving the neurotransmitters glutamate and GABA. We might think of the "number balance" above as a flow chart, with a hyperaroused Blue Brain at the far left (a profusion of glutamate), a hypoaroused Red Brain at the far right (a profusion of GABA), and calmness in the middle (glutamate-GABA balance).

This latter state is referred to as the *window of tolerance*. Here the individual is best able to deal with stress; to receive and process information.[23] But the window of tolerance does not result from *forcefully inhibiting* impulses. The attempt to win such internal battles can leave us shattered and barely capable of a coherent thought. We can't *"will"* ourselves or *choose* to be in this state. Rather, self-regulation opens up this *time/space window* and, for that matter, keeps it propped open.

Herein lies, not just the manner in which Self-Reg helps us to achieve Blue Brain/Red Brain balance, but the principal reason why *calm* is so different from *quiet*. When we are calm, we have time to weigh different ideas without our limbic brakes kicking in. Time to *deliberate*, as opposed to *being compelled*. To be calm is to be in a balanced state across multiple domains:

- Physical: Low tension, slow heart rate, low blood pressure, slow breathing
- Cortical: Slow alpha waves, default mode is activated
- Emotional: A feeling of tranquillity, well-being
- Cognitive: Absence of intrusive thoughts or worries, creativity increases
- Social: Comforted by the presence of others
- Prosocial: Not overborne by demands that we make on ourselves

Where the *authoritarian model of the mind* conceives of freedom as the result of keeping a firm lid on subcortical pressures, the *democratic model* sees freedom as the result of balance across all of these domains. The result is precisely what eluded Leontius: the freedom to choose how one acts. The real message of the story of Leontius is that trying to assert self-control when one has gone deep into Red Brain is a sure road to dysregulation.

The Agony of Choice

Until I read Ben Hart's "Understanding Donkey Behaviour," I assumed that Buridan's ass would simply go for whichever it saw first, hay or water.[24] In fact, what Buridan saw as indecision may have been an expression of donkeys' natural stoicism. We used to think animals were incapable of reflecting before choosing, until Köhler destroyed that bit of human exceptionalism.[25] For that matter, we used to think the same about infants, until Alison Gopnik, Andy Meltzoff, and Patricia Kuhl set us straight on that as well.[26]

Such is the nature of the discipline – recall the lines from *Paradise Lost* quoted above – that philosophers have spent innumerable hours debating this paradox.[27] Buridan's point was that it is impossible to rely on willpower to choose between two alternatives when there is no reason for one or the other. He was thinking, of course, of moral dilemmas. His point was that the rational individual would wait until circumstances change and it becomes clear which is the right choice. But by that time the ass may be dead.

For Self-Reg, the point is that *choosing* – weighing up reasons – *is intrinsically stressful*; as we weigh, our body tenses, digestion is suppressed. Rather than serving as an illustration of the limitations of willpower, what is so interesting about the paradox is the insight it provides into how the mind seizes up when confronted with a choice that has become overly stressful – like elections!

It's not just moral choice; any kind of choosing is inherently stressful, and the more stressed we are, the more paralysed we become. Supermarkets capitalize on this fact by stressing us in all sorts of ways, such as keeping the temperature cold, having hard surfaces that bounce the noise being piped in, placing items we regularly buy at remote spots and making us walk through a maze to get to them, overwhelming us with choice. (It's because of these stressors – not to mention all the stressed-out adults – that children on the spectrum find supermarket shopping so challenging.) Having gotten us into this LE/HT state, the store places price reduction stickers on the items it most wants to sell, which relieves us from the stress of choosing.[28]

We don't practise Self-Reg *to be able* to choose (is anyone calm during grocery shopping?). We do Self-Reg *while* trying to choose. (Do several deep breaths and then ask yourself if you really want that jumbo-sized box of ultra-processed cookies.) This is another reason to ask Why, especially when stressed by a choice. By asking Why we insert a pause between the stimulus and our response. We are not doing this in order to reduce the intensity of an impulse. Were that the case, we'd simply be trying out another strategy to stay on a diet (gather internal resources to resist a temptation). This is not at all the intention.

Asking Why is a beneficial mode of self-regulation. It helps us acquire the non-judgmental stance critical to meditation, that of trying to *grasp* rather than *resist*. This is why it can be so helpful to take self-control off the table: trying to assert self-control can leave us more agitated, which gets in the way of insight. If after a moment's reflection you still want the treat, then go for it; that was never the issue. Among the things you're trying to understand when you first ask Why are: What happened during the day that led up to this craving? Am I avoiding some deeper issue that I need to confront? Is someone – or a group of someones – dysregulating me?

Wrestling with self-control only adds to our stress, which in turn has a marked effect on the window of tolerance. When we are overstressed, our perception of time speeds up; when relaxed, it slows down.[29] It is quite striking how, if you purposely slow yourself down, the same decisions aren't nearly so difficult. The problem here is that the sense of being rushed adds significantly to the stress. Quite often, the best choices are made when we stop thinking about them. In accounts of creativity, we are forever reading about how the solution to an intractable problem came "out of nowhere." Eureka moments occur because the stress of trying so hard to solve the problem has been removed.[30]

Stress has an equally marked impact on risk-reward decisions. The more stressed we are, the more we focus on the positives and pay little attention to the possible downside.[31] When the stress of trying to balance risk against reward gets too great, reward invariably wins out. Hence the *Extraordinary Popular Delusions and the Madness of Crowds*[32] – or the appeal of the authoritarian.

All too often, the effort to exert self-control triggers our limbic brakes. The tension that the self-control bias creates can paralyse our thinking. Had Leontius asked himself Why, he might have dwelt on the issues that philosophers have since raised when analysing this passage.[33] Was he secretly conflicted about what sort of society Athens should become? What attitude it should adopt towards justice? Seeing this as simply a matter of having the self-control to resist a morbid impulse oversimplifies and indeed trivializes the nature of his conflict.

This was precisely Berlin's point. His concern vis-à-vis the "agony of choice"[34] was with moral and political issues, not which spaghetti sauce to buy. "What do I think is *right*?" "What is just?" "What are the rights of an individual – and indeed, a child?" "Who will be harmed by this measure?" These are the questions that define character and that create a Just Society. They take time and mental space – a great deal of both – to resolve. But excessive stress can make it well-nigh impossible to weigh factors and remember past choices or future aspirations, to consider opposing arguments and reconcile conflicting goals.

"I choose" in the *moral realm* is not some sort of high-pitched shriek, akin to "I pick door number one." It is an expression of thought, doubt, and rarely certainty. Choosing in the moral realm is never easy. This was Buridan's point, and indeed, what Descartes is describing in his *Discourse on Method*: How the moral thinking he was engaged in was a demanding activity and not some sort of stream of consciousness. Difficult choices put us into an ergotropic state: a full-body experience that can be energizing or enervating. And the more momentous the issue, the more time and energy we need to think it through.

It is because choosing can be so stressful that we resort to potentially maladaptive modes of self-regulation: for example, reasoning biases, children's counting rhymes, tossing a coin, voting the way I've always done or the way those around me are doing, mimicking talking points rather than thinking through my beliefs. These are all ways to mitigate the stress of a decision. Quite often, they work by stopping thinking entirely. The contrary to *choosing* is not *rejecting*, it is *reacting*. It is when we are overstressed and mired in Red Brain that we are most susceptible to dopamine hijacking. And never is this truer than in adolescence.

Becoming Free

We must never lose sight of Nelson Mandela's warning that "to be free is not merely to cast off one's chains, but to live in a way that respects and enhances the freedom of others."[35] How could we have ignored this timeless wisdom when it came to our own children's well-being? To allow "Hook Modellers" to create a generation of teens that, like Eugene Henderson (the protagonist of Saul Bellow's great novel, *Henderson the Rain King*), are constantly chanting, "I want, I want, I want."

Granted, materialism has been around for a long time.[36] But there is something different about today's consumerism. Teens have long been an attractive demographic for advertisers. But what we're seeing is more than just a craving for luxury items, but utterly inane desires.[37] Henderson's desires turned out to be spiritual and not material; will the same be true for today's teens?

As in all such mass demonstrations, multiple themes swirled through the March for Our Lives in 2018. Teens around the world were proclaiming that if we won't address the harm being done to them, they will take matters into their own hands. Freedom persists because despite what we do to thwart it – knowingly or unwittingly – the drive to be free always eventually reasserts itself. And what is not in the least surprising is that the first stirrings of this natural instinct should emerge among life's "free spirits," who feel their spirit being quashed.

We tend to characterize adolescence as a time of mindless rebellion, but the adolescent drive for autonomy is "an excitatory state that is produced by a homeostatic disturbance."[38] A teen has a basic need to be free, and if this is stymied an unbearable tension results. In other words, the March wasn't just a political statement; it arose from a neurobiological, psychophysiological, and perhaps a spiritual need.

Becoming free is a lifelong quest, and adolescence stands out as a momentous and turbulent stage in this developmental process. Where the child is merely looking to be free from adult supervision, the teen is questioning adult norms and values. It is precisely this existential stage that is under threat today.

H.L. Mencken, the Sage of Baltimore, famously wrote: "We must be willing to pay a price for freedom." But at what price are you prepared to sell your freedom? If you're a teenager, the price may not be all that high. An Instagram influencer – a minor with hundreds of thousands of followers – revealed how he had been contacted by the Trump campaign to disseminate false claims about Joe Biden, $0.85 per conversion (people who click on the links), up to twenty-five thousand conversions. "There's a lot of money to be made. You just gotta know the right people." ("Trump Insiders Are Quietly Paying Teen Memers for Posts," *Huffington Post*, 9 September 2021).

Constant Craving

Experiments are all around us, if only we take the time to observe and reflect on them. We once had one with our sixteen-year-old son that would have been easy to dismiss as yet another inane teenager crisis. But this one clearly demanded some serious analysis.

He had come downstairs frantic about buying a pair of shoes that he'd seen online. He was in such a state of agitation that we agreed to buy them for him for Christmas, which was a month away. That set off another explosion: he had to have them now, that instant, shipped express. The whole thing was bizarre. But stranger still was his reaction when the shoes came. He was ecstatic while opening the box. He ran up to his room to send out photos he took on Snapchat. But within minutes he came back downstairs to tell us about the newest pair of shoes that he absolutely had to have. And he was every bit as agitated as he had been the first time.

A social psychologist couldn't have designed a better experiment to demonstrate the effects of "brain hacking," namely, triggering a surge of dopamine. Were it not for the consequences, one could not but admire how masterfully this overpowering desire had been created. First the company sent an email, complete with requisite associations (famous athletes and pop stars hawking the goods) and the promise of reward. Then they got him to invest just a little of his time by designing his own pair of shoes. To make sure they had him hooked, they played on his need for peer approval, added in a sense of urgency (only a limited time to obtain these gems), and created a sense of scarcity (to appeal to his hunting instinct) and value (these will instantly become collectors' items).

One has to marvel at the sheer artistry of the ads. They manage to capitalize on the creativity that has been unleashed by the gaming community, not for aesthetic purposes, but with the sole aim of ensnaring a vulnerable market segment. The problem is the cost, and here I am not simply referring to the expense of the shoes.

When he came downstairs our son was in full Red Brain. So overwhelming was his stress that it sent us into Red Brain, agreeing to something to which we would normally not agree (spending more than we had ever spent on trainers, letting him buy them without trying them on, giving in to an impulse), and then rationalizing our behaviour ("This will be his Christmas present"). But the worst part was seeing how when they arrived the shoes did not assuage his stress; if anything, they made it worse. Not just because they were a tad small, and not nearly as sensational as he had projected, but because that same day the company had launched its latest email assault.

What we are witnessing here goes far beyond creating a harmless desire. At the beginning of *Hooked*, Nir Eyal remarks how he had "embarked upon a journey to learn how products change our actions and, at times, create compulsions."[39] That was what we were experiencing: the full onslaught of *compulsion*, a non-rational state, in which a rush of dopamine creates an unbearable psychophysiological state.

The cost of compulsion is as much physical as it is mental. The effect of dopamine hijacking is an extraordinary amount of tension throughout the body and the recruitment of neurochemicals to meet the metabolic demand (catecholamines and stress hormones). This is where the tragedy of addiction starts: the need to find release from an aversive state so great that it overpowers any attempts at self-soothing, self-distraction, or reappraisal.[40]

The *stress of compulsion* does not simply refer to the emotional and physiological costs of being sent into Red Brain by dopamine hijacking. The "reward system" itself is placed under a huge strain. The individual goes into neuroceptive overdrive, with hyperactivity in the OFC, the connected paralimbic system (the anterior cingulate cortex), and the limbic system (the striatum and amygdala).

The child who has been well and truly *hooked* is caught by desires that *cannot be sated*; for it is the need for dopamine that drives the cycle and not any particular "reward." Such an outcome may be wonderful for a company's bottom line, but it is not so great for the child's well-being (not to mention that of parents). High levels of dopamine lead to all sorts of deleterious effects: anxiety and depression; agitation and aggression; poor concentration; poor motivation; excessive pleasure seeking; digestive problems and nausea; even delusions.

What is most disturbing about the new field of *behaviour design* is how many compulsions hook modellers are able to create or sustain. Especially worrying is when the driver becomes the very need for dopamine itself. When that happens, it is easy to induce kids (or adults!) to pursue "rewards" that, as Ian Bogost demonstrated with Cow Clicker, are utterly meaningless. In this particular game, you clicked on a silly picture of a cow and had to wait six hours before you could click on it again, collecting as many "cow clicks" as you could. And despite Bogost's satirical intentions, the game went viral.[41]

Of all the interesting comments on the Cow Clicker phenomenon, the most arresting was by an adult who was so hooked that he continued to visit the site long after the Cowpocalypse (when all the cows had disappeared forever – what Bogost called the "rapture"): "It is very interesting, clicking nothing. But then, we were clicking nothing the whole time. It just looked like we were clicking cows."

That is the great worry that arises here: not just that we are creating a generation that is being endlessly *hooked to the meaningless*, but the converse, a generation that is NOT being *hooked to the meaningful*. That is one of the goals of Self-Reg: to institute constructive and reflective habits that recruit the dopamine needed to form close relationships, be motivated to exercise, learn, and persevere in difficult tasks; to acquire skills that benefit others; to engage in activities that lead to satisfaction and peace of mind, and not, in the haunting lyrics of kd lang, constant craving.

Io and the Gadfly

At every talk I give, I am besieged by parents whose teens are consumed by anxiety. Once joyful spirits now battling depression. Desperate to change their lives or their looks or their bodies. Who have abandoned activities in which they excelled because of becoming hooked on gaming, social media, junk food, consumerism, exhibitionism, porn, sex, drugs, alcohol, performance enhancers. Teens who can in no sense of the word be described as "free."

Never once has it occurred to me to suggest to these distressed parents that they go read *Aeropagitica* or *Two Concepts*. What would I recommend they read? To start with, *Self-Reg*. Not because I harbour any feelings of grandiosity, but because parents need to understand that the above problems do not relate to poor self-control. These are all matters of dysregulation, and what teens themselves, and not just their parents, need to think about is how this has happened. They need to identify the hidden stresses in their lives, know when they are overstressed and what to do about it, know when and how they are being hooked.

Maybe the subtitle to *Self-Reg* should have been *A Guide to Becoming Free*. The freedom to choose is only possible when we are in the balanced state of calm in the sense described above. The problem is that teens are being subjected to engineered compulsions in virtually every aspect of their lives.[42]

Sadly, there is a great deal of research, some dating back more than a century, on how to insert a gadfly into someone's mind. As it turns out, it's not as hard as you might think. You need only play on the subjects' fears and hidden desires; vary the reward schedule and the size of the reward; gradually escalate the difficulty; reduce any feelings of losing (e.g., by looping into the next game before the sense of having lost can take hold); and figure out how to capture attention and how to turn prompted actions into habits. It turns out that dopamine is pivotal at every step of the way.[43]

The *hook model* capitalizes on vulnerabilities, it doesn't create them. Adolescence marks a strong surge in stresses across all five of the core stress domains. Exponents of the hook model seldom mention the amount of research that goes into identifying these stresses so that they can be exploited first neurobiologically, then commercially. But the real power of the hook model lies in capitalizing on a maturational phenomenon that occurs in the corticobasal ganglia-thalamo-cortical loop during adolescence, which results in heightened dopamine reactivity.

Dopamine sensitivity is instrumental for adolescent exploration and growth, personal as well as social. It is tied to increased risk taking, impulsivity, and, of course, utterly brainless acts.[44] Plus it exposes teenagers to maybe the biggest vulnerability of all: dopamine hijacking.

: Persistent Hypersubcorticality

Joe Paton's research on the effect of dopamine on the perception of time is both fascinating and, in light of the hook model, highly disturbing.[45] The release of dopamine in the midbrain slows down the internal clock in the striatum, which then speeds up our perception of time. Conversely, the inhibition of dopamine speeds up the striatal clock, which is what makes time drag at the end of a boring lecture.

Boredom – along with fear, anxiety, and pain – involves a decrease in dopamine, and thus, a slowing down in our perception of time, and a ramping up in the dysphoria of the experience. Conversely, "time flies when you're having fun," an adage that, as it turns out, should be taken literally. But it's not just pleasure and novelty that make time fly; hunting, of any sort, does the same. The increased dopamine keeps us doggedly chasing a quarry, oblivious to the passage of time and relishing the experience.

While dopamine is altering time perception, it activates the frontoparietal control network and deactivates the default network. The former system subserves our ability to focus, while the latter is the part of the brain that is active when the mind wanders. In other words, dopamine narrows our mental space, keeps the spotlight on a specific task while all else is tuned out.[46]

The evolutionary argument here is that dopamine teaches the brain which actions are likely to result in payoff. Time and space change hand-in-hand to accommodate this process. A sloweddown striatal clock keeps you in hot pursuit. When time drags, we disengage and look around for something more promising. Similarly, a narrowed working memory blocks out distractions. One and the same system drives adaptive behaviour, shapes our sense of time and mental space, and strengthens synaptic connections so that habits form.

What happens if this system is over-activated? The result is *persistent hypersubcorticality*. Where *transient hypofrontality* involves a cluster of neurotransmitters balancing off each other, persistent hypersubcorticality is all about dopamine. The exact opposite occurs in the latter from what happens in the former: the sense of time speeds up and mental space shrinks. A sense of urgency pervades, while the mind stays focused laserlike on a target. There is no *choosing* here; this is out-and-out *compulsion*.

The teen in persistent hypersubcorticality is constantly in a state of NEEDING THIS and NEEDING IT NOW.[47] (Our son and the sneakers.) By varying the size or nature of the reward, or providing cues associated with the reward, the hook modeller repeatedly activates a dopamine response, and before you know it, the teen is spending all their waking hours, and a large part of the hours that should have been spent in sleep, trying to seize an ever-elusive brass ring.

Working memory typically grows during adolescence, an experiential as well as maturational phenomenon. The ability to choose slowly improves as the teen starts to learn how to regulate energy and tension, modulate mood and affect, and co-regulate with peers. The pauses between stimulus and response grow longer, like the shadows at dusk, and choice starts to become more deliberate. But in persistent hypersubcorticality, this process is blocked; the teen stays locked in the mid-day glare of instant stimulus-response reactivity. There is literally – neurobiologically and cognitively – no time or mental space for choosing.

The contagion of persistent hypersubcorticality that we're seeing today is in no small part the result of being pushed into a dopamine-driven state of constant craving for everything from ultra-luxury goods to ultra-absurd distractions. The teen who has spent countless hours "learning the chilling truth about the undead Scourge in the mighty final battle of the Lich King" is not driven by curiosity or interest, but by the constant flow of dopamine. If they should finally discover that "chilling truth," this brings, not a sense of fulfilment or accomplishment, but a dysphoric feeling of a need that has not been met.

As a punishment for offending the gods, Tantalus was made to stand in a pool of water beneath a fruit tree with low-hanging branches. Every time he stooped to drink, the level of the water receded, and when he reached up for a fruit, the branches of the tree rose. Unlike the Percy Jackson version of this story (the comic figure of Daedalus), the myth was an allegory about the dysphoric state of constantly craving but never experiencing satisfaction.

> But where the ancient Greeks saw the moral of the story as that of *moderating one's desires so that they are satisfiable*, the hook model sees a lesson here about continually updating the trigger so as to jump-start the next dopamine cycle: the next WoW instalment as it were, or running the first few seconds of the next episode in a TV series before the credits of the last episode have finished (so-called post-play, which has become a big driver of binge watching).

The price paid by the teen who is well and truly hooked isn't just the litany of mental health problems listed above but an overall loss of freedom. The teen is literally at the mercy of those who take advantage of an overused and abused striatum. The faculty of choice withers on the vine.

This last point is particularly significant. Teens report that they game so much, or spend so much time on social media, because it's "interesting," "relaxing," "entertaining," "FUN!" These are precisely the descriptors one would attach to being in an intense dopaminergic state; whether they are accurate descriptors is another matter. But of all the comments by gamers that I've read, the most disturbing was that "the games make you free!": "You can perform amazing feats, get away with stuff that would never happen in real life, be somebody that you're not for a while."

Excessive gaming and social media addiction are maladaptive modes of self-regulating. They distract but do not restore, "charm pain or anguish for a while," but impair reality-based thinking. Not only do they not make you free, they have the exact opposite effect. They don't turn you into "somebody that you're not for a while"; they stop you from discovering who that somebody is that you want to become.

Worst of all is when the teen begins to crave the energizing sensation of dopamine *for its own sake*: that is, for the energizing and sedating effect it produces. Dopamine has become an end in itself and is no longer a means. In fact, the rewards, such as they are, may no longer produce any hedonic payoff at all; the need is simply to stay hyper-subcortical, to keep reality at bay, prevent time from hanging on your hands, avoid all the complexities and conflicts that are the driver of adolescent growth.

Panksepp described dopamine as the SEEKING neuromodulator, and if ever there was a qualifier to describe adolescence, "SEEKING" is it.[48] It is seeking that drives the extraordinary *personal* growth spurt that starts in adolescence. But then, of course, it all depends on what you're seeking. Meaning or escape?

Teens Need Purpose to Truly Experience Freedom

Berlin's lasting contribution to our understanding of *freedom* was that we need negative liberty to experiment and explore; to make mistakes, sometimes catastrophic, and then recover from them; to make life-defining choices. But liberty alone is not a sufficient condition for freedom to flourish; what's necessary is struggling with moral decisions.

This is the stuff of *teenage angst*: the first time in life when one starts to think seriously – and endlessly – about such matters. Teens struggle with how to act, who to associate with, their image, values, aspirations, gender, beliefs. I worry that we are a long way from *The Catcher in the Rye*; that we are seeing a generation that rarely ventures into such scary places. A generation whose beliefs and desires are determined by those who do not have their interests at heart, where "determined" really is the apposite word.

There is all the difference in the world between *angst* and *dopaminergic enervation*. Recall David Foster Wallace's line about how two young fish, when asked by an older fish swimming by, "How's the water?" ask themselves: "What the hell is water?[49] If all that a teen knows is compulsion, then asking them what it feels like to be free can only invite the response "What the hell is freedom?"

The hook model is designed to rob teens of the ability to ask this question, to make it harder for them to stop some dopaminergic activity than to keep going. Driven by a compulsive need for the next shot of dopamine, they lose the capacity to experiment and explore, the opportunity to make mistakes and learn from them, pursue personal and spiritual freedom, or just dawdle and dream.

To be sure, Berlin's argument is all about freedom from compulsion; but he only considers this issue from the political and not the psychophysiological perspective. Yet the resurgence of authoritarianism tells us that we can't understand one without the other; that is, you can't value political liberty if you don't know what it feels like to be mentally free, and you can't know what freedom feels like unless you have experienced calm.

Becoming free can be a messy affair at the best of times, and during adolescence, downright chaotic. My own *Sturm und Drang* was definitely chaotic (and I'm sure, dysregulating for my parents), but it was an essential rite of passage as I grappled with who I wanted to be and what I wanted to become. *But after the storm came the calm* as purpose came into focus. This kind of *calm* isn't a matter of being relaxed; it's the result of being in a balanced Blue Brain/Red Brain, both brain states working towards a common goal. It was during adolescence that I first experienced *flow*, and I found it intoxicating.

Trying to prevent a teenager from going into Red Brain is a bit like King Canute trying to hold back the tide. Nor should you even try. Going Red Brain provides teens with the strong emotions that fuel a passion, while keeping the ergotropic state going and the creativity flowing. Hook modellers didn't create the teen's predisposition to go into Red Brain: they capitalized on it, and, in so doing, created more than just a spate of internalizing disorders.

Becoming free is beyond the reach of someone gripped in persistent hypersubcorticality. You cannot find a *purpose* if you are in a constant state of urgency. And that too is a logical, not an empirical, proposition: a definition of "hypersubcorticality." In a way, it's what MacLean had in mind when he argued for an evolutionary reading of his Triune Brain hypothesis. But having goals isn't the result of being blessed with a new suite of executive functions sitting atop and ruling over the subcortex. It's being able to envisage the future and remember the past whilst experiencing the present. To be with and work with peers and not go it alone, which triggers PANIC/GRIEF.

How do we help teenagers in their quest to become free? In more serious cases of dopamine hijacking, more drastic measures may be called for, but all teens, and not just those "at risk," need to understand the ways in which they have been subjected to dopamine-induced compulsions. What they most need is to have their eyes opened to the malign forces that are robbing them of their birthright.

The instant that we read an article like "The Way the Brain Buys," the "science of persuading people to purchase things" loses its subliminal influence.[50] Limbic cues that play on fears and desires lose their bite. Blue Brain processes become active, not through an act of self-control, but as the result of insight: a self-regulation-produced "aha" moment.

The same point applies to teens seeking to become free today. Their striata clearly need a rest. We can't force them to avoid products designed to trigger a dopaminergic response, any more than we could force them not to smoke.[51] But we can explain how these products have been designed to fire up their striatum, in the well-founded belief that understanding the reason they have been shackled in dopaminergic chains will help to set them free, just as happened in the case of teen smoking.[52]

That is not to deny all the research that has been done in social psychology or the psychology of reasoning on the influence of hidden biases but rather to take advantage of this research. For *freedom* ↔ *choice* and *calmness* → *choice* are grounded in self-insight, which constantly deepens over the course of one's life. This is the reason why in Self-Reg we are forever asking Why. Our questions are continually changing and evolving, while our answers become ever more consequential.

Self-Reg is not about teaching teens how to choose sensibly. If it were, we would have succeeded in abolishing adolescence. Self-Reg is about helping teens to experience calm, where they will have the time and space to think and choose. Wisely and poorly, carefully and rashly, boldly and brazenly, and learning all the while.

In short, it is not self-control, but mindful self-regulation that enables teens, in Berlin's words, "to choose and explain their choices by reference to their ideas and purposes, precisely because they are forming ideas and having purposes." This is not only what it means to be free, but also to learn what *freedom* is and why moralists throughout human history have praised it.

Figure 9.1 Broken dopamine chain

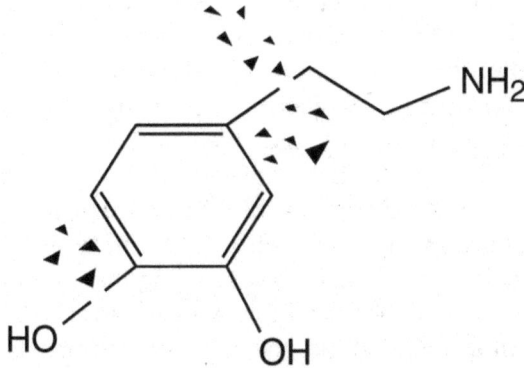

I'm still not clear about where to draw the line between positive and negative freedom; I'm not even sure that we're dealing with a dichotomy. Every individual, every generation, must struggle with this issue anew, and resist anyone or anything that would obstruct this precious and precarious dialogue: intrapersonal and interpersonal.

As I watched my teens battling through their own *Sturm und Drang*, I realized that both had embarked on their own march of their lives. It was impossible to say where this would and will lead them but glaringly obvious what they were seeking to leave behind. Each was struggling to escape from the feeling of being enslaved by dopaminergic chains that were not of their own choosing (Figure 9.1). Each was searching to understand who they are and what they want to be. Both had embarked on the struggle to become free, in both the positive and in the negative sense.

Not a disjunction but a conjunction. Free to AND free from.

Postscript

A note about the section headings. These were intentionally chosen to be the antithesis of the hook model. Instead of trying to play on or tweak associations, I've tried to raise questions in the reader's mind. I fully expect that every reader will form a different impression, just as every Self-Regger takes away a different insight from our Foundation's courses. An essential aspect of what we mean when we talk about Self-Reg as a *process* is that it is rooted in the individual's personal history and objectives.

We talk about *insight* as if it were some sort of passive and spontaneous event: the "bolt from the blue" that the ancient Greeks celebrated. But "insight" is also an effortful term. We have to work to experience insight, struggle with something that perhaps we don't fully understand, maybe form our own view that is different from what the author intended. So, the section headings are an invitation – or perhaps a warning – that work is about to begin.

Chapter 10

Reframing *Virtue*

The Demise of Virtue

The problem is easily enough stated: virtue is taking a beating. The very word has taken on the sort of quaint overtone that clings to terms like *chivalry* or *honour*. As David Bosworth puts it, we're witnessing not just the decline, but the impending "demise" of virtue.[1] As I write this, we are locked in a battle over the survival of democracy. Perhaps the real battle is over the survival of virtue.

I've yet to meet a parent or teacher who wasn't deeply concerned about the spread of bullying, materialism, greed, apathy, and feelings of entitlement in so many of our youth today. I don't think I've yet met a parent who was deeply concerned about the decline of virtue. Yet schools have become zones of what Durkheim referred to as *anomie*: the "malady of the infinite."[2] The condition in which "collective consciousness" is weakened and societal norms wither and die. What Durkheim really meant was a society that no longer cherishes virtue. Schools are the canary in the coal mine.

Educators have been given the unenviable task of cultivating character. Not surprisingly, given what is going on all around them, the character problems seen in schools are getting worse. And so, the hunt for who is responsible begins. The blame must lie with teachers, parents, politicians, religious leaders, athletes, artists, influencers, the media. Or the problems are due to the secularization of the West or wokeism or industries pandering to instant gratification and narcissism. Or a Zeitgeist that seeks to shield children from rather than prepare them for life's challenges.

Of course, it might be that this is nothing more than an anxiety that every generation feels about the moral state of its youth. A few years back, there was a lively debate as to whether Socrates had once complained:

> The children now love luxury; they have bad manners, contempt for authority; they show disrespect for elders and love chatter in place of exercise. Children are now tyrants, not the servants of their households. They no longer rise when elders enter the room. They contradict their parents, chatter before company, gobble up dainties at the table, cross their legs, and tyrannize their teachers.[3]

What was so interesting about the controversy surrounding this meme was not the question of whether Socrates had ever actually said this, but the assumption that our current anxiety can be traced back to the ancient Greeks. In fact, Self-Reg takes this point a step further and considers whether it is an anxiety that exists to some extent *because of the ancient Greeks*.

Wittgenstein once famously remarked:

> You always hear people say that philosophy makes no progress and that the same philosophical problems which were already preoccupying the Greeks are still troubling us today. But people who say that do not understand the reason why it has to be so. The reason is that our language has remained the same and always introduces us to the same questions ... I read: "philosophers are no nearer to the meaning of 'Reality' than Plato got ... " What a strange situation. How extraordinary that Plato could have got even as far as he did! Or that we could not get any further! Was it because Plato was so *extremely* clever?[4]

For present purposes, we might rephrase this to read: We are no nearer to propagating virtue than was Aristotle. How extraordinary that "The Philosopher" got as far as he did, or that we are still turning to *Nichomachean Ethics* in search of an answer to our problems.

The question that Wittgenstein would have us ask is: Has the lament stayed the same because the language – or rather, the languaculture[5] – has stayed the same? A way of speaking/thinking about *virtue* that has induced over a hundred generations of parents and educators to bemoan the perilous state of their youth and not know what to do about it! A languaculture that sees virtue as *a quality that needs to be imposed on a nature that is not naturally so inclined*. In the Great Chain of Being, humanity lies midway between the angels and the beasts. It is virtue that enables us to ascend the scale; its absence that causes us to descend.

If the youth of today – whenever "today" should be – are found wanting, it is not so much their fault as that of *those who are doing the imposing*. They have simply not imposed hard enough! Unless it is not a case of *imposing* at all, which is just a self-control way of looking at the issue.

What if prosocial emotions are triggered by impulses stemming from another of our ancient survival systems, CARE, which evolved to nurture our young and maintain group harmony? If that were the case, then we must ask whether there are other ancient systems – viz., RAGE, SEEKING, FEAR, DOMINANCE – that are blocking and perhaps even shutting down CARE? Our question shifts. Instead of asking, *How do we control these systems?* we need to ask: *How do we safeguard CARE?*

If nothing else, Self-Reg is relentless in its refusal to take for granted what has always been taken for granted. You might say this is a defining virtue of Self-Reg: boundless curiosity – if not humility! That and a deep-seated need to help create a Just Society.

Reason Comes Up Short

In my boxes of notes from graduate school days is a paper I started to write based on what I was learning from my moonlighting in virtue ethics. The paper starts off – and do bear in mind that I was a graduate student at the time – "A *virtuous person* is someone that enjoys *eudaimonia* (well-being) because they have *arête* (goodness). But *arête* is only possible if there is *sôphrosunê* (balance). The question is: What sort of *balance* and why should this lead to virtue?"

Like every other grad student, I struggled with the *problem of akrasia*: the question of why anyone would ever choose to act in a manner harmful to their well-being if they *knew* that this was the case. The Greek solution to this problem was to postulate a third faculty: *thumos* (*spirit*), which was later to evolve into our concept of *willpower*. What you *choose* is one thing; how you act on that choice is another.

For the classical Greek philosophers – and following in their footsteps, the Hellenistic and then early Christian philosophers – irrational acts occur because we are too weak to follow through on rational intentions. Reason tells us that greed is harmful to self as well as to society, but reason alone can't protect one from concupiscence. We need a further force to keep us true to the *logos* (Aristotle's middle way), and that force is *thumos*. In theory, *irrational* may have meant "without reason," but in practice it meant "with too little *thumos*."

The idea that *akrasia* is about the lack of willpower dates back to Plato's view that we must rely on *thumos* abetting reason in order to subjugate the "wild horses" – appetites and emotions – that test reason. According to Plato, *thumos* needs to be cultivated every bit as much as reason needs to be enlightened, taking into account an individual's temperament. Hence *education* writ large – i.e., moral as well as cognitive – is as much about the development of self-control as the acquisition of knowledge and thinking skills.

To keep *thumos* strong you need a strict regimen of diet, exercise, and sleep to restore and maintain humoral balance. In cases of severe character weakness, bloodletting and charms might be necessary. Above all, you need to study philosophy, which, as Pedro Lain Entralgo explained in one of the great books on this topic, *La Curación por la Palabra en la Antigüedad Clásica*, was seen as a form of psychotherapy.[6]

Philosophy, according to this outlook, constituted a "gymnasium for the mind."[7] This idea owed much to the Greek view of memory as akin to a muscle that can be strengthened through appropriate exercises.[8] The ability to recall long fragments of poetry was seen as the mental equivalent of lifting a heavy weight. An individual might be born with a naturally strong memory but, regardless of this biological inheritance, would still have to train hard to become an epic poet, just as the physically gifted had to train hard to become an Olympic champion.

The same for virtue. Aristotle believed that no child could acquire virtue until after puberty, simply because *thumos* training takes a long time. Until then, children are dependent on their parents to do the heavy lifting for them. For Plato, the Socrates of the *Apology* is the epitome of someone who, at the end of his life, possessed the kind of *thumos* that we should all aspire to possess. He was the "new Achilles," whose moral strength is not to be confused with Achilles' battle-frenzy (bearing in mind that Achilles was still just a teenager). In our own times, we see the same idea in Robert Bolt's depiction of Sir Thomas More, or for that matter, George Martin's Ned Stark – which, when you think about it, serves as a pretty interesting reflection on the persisting influence of the Greek view of virtue.

The underlying idea in these fictional treatments is that *virtue* is tied to the character strength displayed in unwavering moral constancy.[9] Virtue consists in reason assisted by willpower in ruling over (negative) emotions like fear or greed. Virtue is more important than life itself. Which means so is self-control.

A Guide for the Perplexed

When I turned thirteen, my Hebrew teacher decided it was time to throw a wrench into my moral education. I had been told from the moment that I started to talk that I had to grow up to be a *mensch*. (No doubt long before, but, you know, infantile amnesia blocks such memories.) For a child, this essentially involved a long series of "don'ts." But now my teacher told me that I had to learn the difference between *yetzer hara* (bad impulses) and *yetzer tov* (good impulses).

To be sure, this sounds like your standard self-control/virtue argument. Only the person who was teaching me my Bar Mitzvah portion was studying to be a rabbi, and his "topic of interest" was Maimonides' *A Guide for the Perplexed*. He would spend fifteen minutes working on my portion and then an hour telling me his ideas about the *Mitzvot*, which he saw as guides one must follow in order to become a *mensch*.

It was my first introduction to the idea that one becomes a mensch, not by restraining base emotions, but by having positive ones. Positive emotions prevent us from succumbing to *yetzer hara*: impulses that, without the balance afforded by positive emotions, are "perverted" and turn into negative emotions. Far from being the enemy, emotion – or at least, emotional equilibrium – is the source of human goodness.

Positive emotions, according to Maimonides, are the result of *experiencing inner calmness*, not *suppressing inner conflict*. There is a close connection between balance and goodness, one that is not just logical but also psychological. The same state of mind that produces the one produces the other. When calm, we are able to pause and reflect, feel empathy and humility. This is not because we lessen the intensity of *yetzer hara* to a point where they become "controllable." *Goodness is the result of what we do experience, not what we don't.*

To be sure, Aristotle and before him Plato had celebrated the importance of balance, but there is an important difference. Maimonides taught that balance comes not from self-control, but from personal growth. The result is that one experiences positive emotions that not only enable but also push us to be a mensch. We don't strive to be calm so as to subdue negative emotions; *we strive to be calm so as to have these positive emotions.*

For Maimonides, *yetzer hara* are not some innate aspect of human nature that, as Hobbes would later put it, must be subjugated for the good of the commonwealth. Rather, they *develop, just as yetzer tov develop. That is the point of the Mitzvot: rules that lead to osher, a deeper form of well-being. The yetzer tov develop from balance, the yetzer hara from imbalance – whatever "balance" means, which was the question I was struggling with in that unfinished paper.*

The Greeks thought that "negative impulses" are innate, which is why they linked *virtue* to *self-control*. It is hardly surprising that this way of thinking should have dominated at a time when Athens was undergoing what historians refer to as the "second period of Tyranny," that is, the rise of corrupt oligarchies that began around

400 BCE. The moral decline that this fomented was captured by Herodotus, who wrote extensively on the threat to freedom posed by tyranny of any kind (i.e., regardless of whether it should be enlightened or despotic).

It was witnessing the spread of egoistic desires throughout the populace that made the ancient philosophers so anxious about cultivating *thumos* as an antidote to the descent into hedonism. Here we are today in a similar situation, and not simply because of what is happening in the political sphere.[10] If anything, the influence is bi-directional. It is the widespread decline of virtue and the concomitant rise of vice that has created the conditions that brought us to where we are politically, with *yetzer hara* running rampant at the highest levels of governance.

From the moment that I read *Philosophical Investigations*, I was convinced that philosophy is essential for the well-being of the individual because of its commitment to creating a Just Society. Without such a moral imperative, philosophy is at risk, as Bertrand Russell warned, of becoming "an idle tea-table amusement."[11] But for Wittgenstein, philosophy was anything but. Philosophy demands rigour and resoluteness; it is uncompromising and unrelenting; it calls for honesty and objectivity. In short, it requires *intellectual virtue* in order to acquire moral virtue. But the former is not sufficient to acquire the latter.

Looking back on my childhood, I realize that I was introduced to what some might call a *virtue education* from a very young age. A Socratic-like instruction at the Friday night dinner table was sacrosanct and, for a young child, incredibly draining. I was forever being coaxed to become a mensch by being schooled in how to act morally and think rationally. But my desire to be a mensch was not the result of this early indoctrination. It was because I had menschen all around me and I wanted to be like them. Especially, like my dad.

No Such Thing as a Bad Kid

One of the questions I am most frequently asked at my lectures is whether, when I insist that "there is no such thing as a bad kid,"

I am implying that all kids are intrinsically good. The answer is that this dichotomy sets us off on the wrong track. Kids are born neither *bad* nor *good*; they are just little hominids, about to experience a burst of synaptogenesis followed by synaptic sculpting. Whether their brains are wired to anticipate a safe or a dangerous environment – which is critical for the capacity to experience calmness – is going to have a powerful impact on that capacity.

Both *bad* and *good* carry a heavy load of moral baggage. In English, *bad* originally meant "wicked, vicious, evil." At the start of the eighteenth century, it was used as the antithesis of *good*, which had long meant "righteous, pious, virtuous." The use of "virtuous" was tied from the start to "moral strength," conceived of as the willpower to "restrain base instincts": where *base* meant "sub- (i.e., below) human on the Great Chain of Being." Only by willpower can we crush the wicked instincts with which we are all born, including – and for some schools of thought, especially – children.

To this day there remains a strong association between *bad kid* and *lacking self-control*, and an equally strong association between *good kid* and *in possession of self-control*. These associations colour our thinking and reactions to children's behaviour or to tests like the Marshmallow Task. Unfortunately, these reactions most definitely impact the thinking and reactions of the child who is repeatedly called "bad." They come to see themself as morally weak, even if they have no clear sense of the meaning of the term.

My goal was to circumvent this long-standing influence on our thinking by looking at kids from an *acultural* – i.e., an evolutionary – standpoint. Like all hominid progeny, children arrive in the world with basic needs: safety, security, warmth, nourishment, play. But our particular genus of hominids comes with some unique traits and needs as a result of secondary altriciality.

In particular, children depend on co-regulation for a long time – *an awfully long time*. It's when that need is not met that stress-reactivity is heightened and an attractor that impedes the development of *yetzer tov* becomes entrenched. The basic principle here is that when their primal needs are met, children can be calm and able to develop positive impulses; if they are chronically threatened (by internal as well as external threats), they develop negative impulses.[12]

But what comes before *yetzer tov* and *yetzer hara*? *The answer is sensations.* We need to turn to neuroscience to understand the nature of these sensations. This is precisely where the Triune Brain hypothesis is so important (chapter 1). The ancient survival systems are pre-social and a fortiori pre-moral. The infant is assaulted by stresses, but CARE impels them into the arms of their caregiver where the stress response is, if not turned off, at least mitigated. PANIC/GRIEF impels them to shriek.

You would not describe the sensations activated by CARE as "good impulses," nor would you describe the sensations activated by FEAR, RAGE, PAIN, PANIC/GRIEF as "bad impulses." Rather, we describe them in hedonic terms: pleasant versus aversive. *Yetzer tov* and *yetzer hara* come later, or at least, what we describe as "good impulses" and "bad impulses" come later. The impulse to help or the impulse to harm.

The Little Boy Who Bit

As we saw in chapter 3, it is much more challenging to meet the needs of some infants and kids than others. But then, "challenging" is a moral universe away from "wicked, vicious, evil." Every single one of the children that we saw at MEHRI was challenging; in fact, this was the criterion for being admitted into the MEHRI treatment program. But not a single one of them was remotely close to being labelled a "bad" kid. And honestly, had anyone ever said such a thing to the therapists, they would have found themselves summarily kicked out of the clinic.

There are countless examples I could give of the challenges we encountered at MEHRI, but one stands out: a three-year-old who arrived the first day beet-red and shrieking while his mother had scratches and bruises on her face, arms, and neck. He had been assessed as nonverbal, but our SLPs were unwilling to confirm this diagnosis, since, in their view, he was too hyperaroused for them to know whether he was able to process speech, much less use words himself. Had anyone ever dared suggest that he needed to acquire self-control, their comment would have been met with either stunned silence or outright laughter.

Over the following months the therapists worked on identifying his stresses and developing strategies to soothe this little boy's nervous system and break his stress cycle. This could not by any stretch of the imagination be described as an easy or a straightforward process: there were endless setbacks and miscues. But over time you could see the team – which always included the primary caregivers – making significant progress.

By the end of the year, he had become a happy, verbal (very verbal!) little four-year-old who would dash down the hall when he arrived to "go play" (as I heard him shout to his father). But it is one of those occasions near the end of treatment that sticks out in my mind. The family was playing hide-and-seek, and mommy slipped and hurt her knee. Her son was instantly concerned and gently went up to her and said, "Mama want me kiss her boo-boo." I suddenly realized that, from the moment that the therapists had begun working with the family, mom had never again come to clinic with scratches or bruises.

Someone who knew nothing about the stresses that the kids in our study were dealing with might well have labelled them as bad kids. In fact, most of our parents had experienced exactly this reaction from strangers in public settings (like restaurants or grocery stores, both of which are extremely high-stress environments for all young children, but especially for children on the spectrum). On a few occasions, we even had parents who initially saw their own child this way, although one session with the therapists was always enough to correct such an atrocious misperception.

The "Failure to Socialize" Argument

One might read the preceding section and object: "But autism is a special case!" Around a third of neurotypical children display antisocial tendencies in infancy, but the majority are socialized by the age of four. According to the "bad kid" scenario, a small residue of "problem children" – 2 to 4 per cent – remain stubbornly resistant to "socialization." They seem to have come out of the womb aggressive, selfish, uncaring, even mean. They are kids who are said to have inherited *aggression genes* or to be the casualties of an attachment disorder.

Another problem with labels is that they stop us from asking Why, especially in those cases where it is critical to do so. I once watched a video of a three-year-old child mercilessly assaulting his baby brother. I was involved in a private meeting, and, like everyone else in the room, I recoiled at the scene. There was a collective groan, followed by muttering and head-shaking.

I was deeply upset by the video, barely able to think at all. It was only afterwards that, on a long walk by the sea, I was able to return to calm and begin asking myself Why. What exactly had I just seen? Why had CARE completely shut down in this child? What might have been going on prior to this event: that morning, the day before, the three years before? What sort of sensory or motor challenges might this child have? Caregiving problems? How could we help this child who so clearly needed help? How could we help this family who no doubt would have needed help?

There was no suggestion that this child was on the spectrum, but it was perfectly clear to me that what I had witnessed were striking stress-behaviours. The child's RAGE system had been triggered for no apparent reason, which is often a sign that a child is in chronic PAIN. (Just think how angry you can get when you are in pain and something relatively minor sends you off.) Remember what we saw in chapter 2: neuroception is activated by internal as well as external threats. In cases such as this, we recoil because we think the child is savagely reacting to no threat at all. To be sure, there was no external threat; but it was *internal threats* that we should have been thinking about.

This sort of unprovoked aggression can be a sign of an incipient bipolar disorder.[13] A child in allostatic overload can swing from acts of unprovoked aggression to complete shutdown; that is, the child is caught in fight (surge of epinephrine) or flight (surge of norepinephrine), and minor stressors can trigger one or the other response. The thought that seeing a trained counsellor or therapist could prevent a lifetime of suffering – and not just on the part of the child we had just watched – was enough to send me into prosocial freeze. I knew how unlikely it was that anyone would ever be asking such questions about this child or the countless others that are just like him.

Granted, it is possible that at least some children are predisposed to respond to social stress with epinephrine (fuelling anger) as opposed to norepinephrine (fuelling fear), and thus have a bias to the "fight" side of fight or flight when overloaded. But we need to back up a step: the immediate issue is *how we recognize the signs of impending overload* so that the child does not slip into heightened vigilance where even a defenceless sibling is seen as a threat. Despite how it might appear, explosive behaviours do not arrive out of nowhere; there is always a build-up of stresses, possibly going as far back as the womb.

Here is the perfect example of how labels are so pernicious. If we see a child's behaviour as "bad," we respond, automatically, in a way that reinforces – maybe even partly causes – a fight-or-flight reaction that takes the child's Blue Brain offline. When this happens, we short-circuit the very things we are so desperate to cultivate, compassion and empathy. But there is a much deeper point involved here than the shuttering effect of cultural blinders. It is the way in which we slip back into determinist biases when we are stressed by a child's behaviour.

You can appreciate how vexing it is for me to encounter the argument that, because of their genes or upbringing, some children are simply a lost cause. On this way of thinking, if a child is born with a certain variant of the MAOA or CDH13 genes or has been abused and/or severely neglected in the early years of life, that child will lack the neural connectivity or neurohormones that fuel virtue. In such a case, our only recourse is to drill obedience into the child, and if that fails, sequester them so as to protect other children. In the meantime, we should focus on the poor child-rearing that leads to this sorry state (coupled with genetic screening!).

The problem is that I had schoolmates who, to use the terminology of the literature, had been "securely attached" but had nonetheless completely lost their way; and I had seen schoolmates who I knew had come from troubled homes go on to become shining lights. Somehow, education was serving some and failing others. The question in both cases is: Why? Why did *yetzer hara* rear their ugly heads and disrupt the life of some while *yetzer tov* flourished in others?

The more fundamental question I was grappling with was: Is this really an issue about self-control or is it rather a matter of working on self-regulation? It is this question that leads us to reframe *virtue*. But the purpose of this exercise is not simply to clarify a complex concept: *it is to cultivate virtue*. According to Self-Reg, these two issues – theoretical and practical – cannot be separated. They are conjoined aspects of what is involved in *reframing virtue*, why *Blue Brain* and *Red Brain* are inextricably bound together in moral growth.

The Substrate of Virtue

In chapter 1, I touched on how the Interbrain is the substrate for the development of empathy. It is through back-and-forth interactions with their caregiver, in which the infant *feels* the pleasant sensations of being soothed, that they develop the desire to do the same for others: i.e., to feel the pleasant sensations that soothing another affords. The same can be said for the development of virtue.

One of the more intriguing questions in research on the development of virtue is whether "the substrate that makes virtue possible" is not reason, but regulation.[14] Whether the *substrate* on which virtue grows – the experiences that nurture virtue – traces back, not just to nonhuman primates, but to mammals, and indeed, proto-mammals.[15] A substrate that begins with the exaptation of oxytocin from vasotocin.

A growing number of primatologists, anthropologists, psychologists, and neuroscientists are exploring this idea. Darcia Narvaez, who spans pretty much all of these fields in her work, has a stunning line: "virtue is [not] an exclusively human affair."[16] A classic virtue ethicist might wonder what on earth she could be thinking of – even though Aristotle famously insisted that man is a social animal. "How," they might object, "can you divorce the concept of *virtue* from the concepts of *reason* and *self-control*?" But then, that is precisely the point.

Narvaez is looking at the significance of the human "evolved developmental niche" (EDN) for the development of virtue. i.e., the prototypical caregiver reactions triggered by limbic resonance (e.g., breastfeeding, touch, soothing vocalizations, softened gaze, comforting body posture and movements). The resulting secure attachment establishes the child on a species-typical trajectory that leads to *virtue* and *flourishing*, where these two terms are intertwined. The EDN creates an "'affective core' upon which a virtuous life is founded."

The development of virtue, as she puts it, *always* depends on "simple reciprocal interactions."[17] And not just in the early years. The interactions that occur in childhood and adolescence are every bit as essential for the development of virtue as what occurs in the early years. Possibly more so. These *reciprocal interactions* become more challenging as the child grows older. As social life becomes more complicated, emotions tend to become a little overwrought. Especially during the teenage years.

The development of virtue during adolescence hinges on the ability to deal with a mounting stress load that triggers ancient survival systems, PECs which, if hyperaroused, block CARE. To prevent this from happening, the teen needs ongoing Interbrain support, just as they did during childhood. But note that the key word here is "support." They need oxytocin from their peer-to-peer interactions, not more CRH.

Virtue grows from *yetzer tov*, which grow from the pleasant sensations produced by reciprocal interactions. Virtuous actions feel good. When a youth seeks to be virtuous, it is for that reason. Conversely, the absence of virtue is aversive.

Ordinarily, one might think that is enough of a factor to make virtue ubiquitous. But these aversive sensations can be blocked. Among other things, the individual who becomes corrupt – in whom homeostatic imbalance is an Attractor – suffers from chronic excessive stress, endless SEEKING without consummation, constant dopamine craving, and as a result, dysteroception.

This argument comes straight out of *A Guide for the Perplexed*, as does the conclusion that if a child receives *undercare*, they are at risk of heightened stress-reactivity, kindled FEAR, PAIN, RAGE, and PANIC/GRIEF.[18] Narvaez's lab has conducted multiple studies showing that a child who does not experience a nurturing EDN is at risk of not "absorbing" character strengths. Three further questions then naturally arise:

1. Does "undercare" [translate, underCARE] only apply to the first three years of life? Might a senior receiving underCARE display behaviours similar to those of an infant?
2. Can the effects of underCARE be countered? i.e., can CARE always be restored, and if so how?
3. Can the effects of nurturing Interbrains be undone, a moral trajectory skewed?

This last question is the most worrying of all. Lurking in the background is the disturbing possibility that virtue is being not accidentally but deliberately subverted these days.

The Assault on Virtue

Sometimes, asking Why can leave you wishing that you hadn't. If virtue is taking a beating, this is to a significant extent happening by design and not by chance. The problem is not simply that talking about virtue has become passé, but that virtue has been under sustained attack. Virtue is seen either as something to be exploited (e.g., our natural urge to reciprocate), or as something that needs to be squelched (e.g., guilty feelings about thrift).

One of the most unsettling books I have read on this topic is *Evil by Design*, which surveys fifty-seven tactics to "break down the barriers to rational thought."[19] These strategies capitalize on the seven deadly sins (pride, lust, greed, envy, anger, sloth, gluttony). But it is one thing to employ "persuasive technologies" and quite another to leave consumers happy – or at least, not unhappy – with the "decisions" they have made.

Simply put, customers won't keep coming back for more if they feel guilty about what they've done. So, you have to quell those pesky virtues that get in the way of repeat business – or what is even worse, prompt online critiques that deter other buyers. On this outlook, virtues are nothing more than cultural artefacts contrived to contain natural impulses. The astute business must quell these "habits" so as to tap into human frailties. To prevent customers from feeling guilty about buying something frivolous or extravagant, you need to help them rationalize their behaviour.

This point does not just apply to businesses. Politics is no different from any other enterprise involved in selling product. And if the product in question goes against voters' moral qualms, those inclinations have to be mollified, if not modified. If a society places a high premium on honesty, then you have to change that attitude.[20] Start talking about "alternative facts." Or as Goebbels put it, "If you tell a lie big enough and keep repeating it, people will eventually come to believe it." Or rather, *misbelieve* it.

The psychology of reasoning turns out to be an invaluable resource for the hook model. The first step is to identify relevant biases and then figure out how to exploit them. For example, if consumers are vulnerable to a *social proof bias*, provide them with endorsements from friends, celebrities, or even strangers that are seen as being "like me." As Stanley Ingram showed, it does not take many confederates placed strategically in a crowd to get attendees to think, "If others at the rally are chanting 'build the wall' then I should as well." Then turn consumers into endorsers (e.g., sell "I'm a Deplorable" T-shirts). Nothing aids rationalization like personal commitment, however slight this might be.

The problem is if the *virtue conditioning* we've been exposed to niggles at our conscience. ("Maybe a 'good person' doesn't condone separating children from their mother.") Yet here too the psychology of reasoning comes into play. For example, psychologists have found that anger intensifies the "biased assimilation of political information."[21] So if feelings of anger towards a faceless mom can be aroused, feelings of compassion for her are less likely to arise.

But now we have to start counting up the costs, and it turns out they are exactly what Aristotle warned against. He saw the *telos* of virtue as personal and communal well-being, where the two are inextricably bound together. And both are indeed suffering from the relentless assault on virtue. We would no doubt feel differently about the hook model were we not contending with an explosion of internalizing and externalizing disorders; health problems (especially the cluster of conditions connected to metabolic syndrome); the intensifying polarization and steepening of the gradient; the surge of populism and xenophobia; the resurgence of fascism. As things stand, we have to consider the possibility that, like the stock market or Big Business, the failure to regulate dopamine hijacking comes at a heavy cost.

How can we save virtue when so many cultural forces are now aligned against it?

Reframing the Link between Virtue and Reason

The answer to the question raised at the end of the preceding section seems deceptively simple: All we need to do to save virtue is ask Why. Why do I feel this way? React this way? Think this way? Feel this way? Want this? Why am I worrying about this? Why the sudden urge to check my email or the news or to surf the Internet or to have a drink? Why am I so angry with this co-worker or a driver on the road or someone who supports the opposite political side?

It turns out that asking Why can be devilishly hard, not for psychological but for neurobiological reasons. When SEEKING is activated, it operates like a heat-guided missile. It doesn't matter if it is SEEKING gold-embossed trainers or an orange-embossed authoritarian. The SEEKING drive is especially relentless when it's frustrated; then RAGE comes to its aid. Add in FEAR, PAIN, and PANIC/GRIEF and we are well on our way to *unshakeable misbelief*.

The secret to the hook model is that it sends us into Red Brain by creating a stress and then providing an escape valve. First make the marshmallow a stress and then plant the suggestion that saves you from that stress. That is how the hook model works. It capitalizes on emotions, images, biases, memes to create enough stress that *choice* is replaced with *compulsion*, and then convinces us that we are acting under our own free will. It is not self-control that we're lacking when this happens; it is reason itself: i.e., the ability to pause, reflect, choose.

The Greeks were not wrong to tie virtue to reason; the problem is that they brought in self-control as the intervening variable. Rather, it is (learned modes of) self-regulation that make virtue possible. Self-Reg is a case in point. We begin by reframing, which is a quasi-technical term for asking Why: a mode of countering the stress response by inserting a pause between stimulus and response. We then become stress detectives and reduce stresses and the stress response in order to return to calm. We are now positioned to restore reason. These, in essence, are the five steps of Self-Reg.

There is no point in the lifespan where these steps are ineffective. But there are some points in the lifespan when it is particularly hard to follow them. The teen years stand out.

The Power of Hope: The Teen Years

When teens are insecure, they have enormous difficulty asking Why. And sadly, hook modellers have discovered that nothing sells product like insecurity. Insecurity renders the teen much more reactive to social and emotional stress. If a negative bias sets in, there is a constant drain on energy. This is a big reason why so many teens suddenly begin to struggle with an internalizing or externalizing disorder. It is also a big reason why it is so hard for them to ask Why.

Narcissism, bullying, anger, apathy, anxiety, depression, feelings of entitlement (perhaps it's best I stop there) are none of them problems of *akrasia*. They are all the result of *unknowingly* acting in ways that are harmful to well-being. Or rather, the result of *being led* to act in ways that are harmful to well-being. Adopting habits that lead deeper and deeper into non-rationality.

There is only so long that dopamine can be hijacked before homeostatic imbalance becomes deep-seated. When a teen is stuck in bottom-right Thayer, what they most badly need is not self-control; it is soothing Interbrain support. Even – especially – when they reject that support. They need someone, not to lecture or chastise, but to guide them through the above five steps.

This point must not be confused with indulgence or permissiveness. A teen stuck in Red Brain who self-sedates or self-medicates rather than self-regulates may desperately need to have limits imposed. But these limits *must* be established with compassion when a teen is floundering. The transition from maladaptive to healthy self-regulation takes time, structure, repetition, and above all, self-awareness.

Self-awareness is essential for asking Why – and vice versa. This is not easy for a teen when denial and avoidance are core elements in their ego defences. But with patience and guidance, and counselling when appropriate, they can lower their guard and connect with insecurities, start to recognize when they are slipping into bottom-right Thayer and what they need to do to restore, and begin to have meaningful and rewarding goals.

To have this impact, we need to work equally diligently on our own self-awareness. It is only through the Interbrain that we will be able to help these teens – or fail them. It is the affects that we feel and can't help but transmit that determine which will be the case. And this is why it is so important to recognize when the egoistic or antisocial traits that we find so disturbing are stress-behaviours and not misbehaviours. Positive or negative emotions *in us* breed positive or negative emotions *in them*.

Teens ultimately have to learn all this for themselves. They have to be the ones that overcome the defence mechanisms they have constructed – albeit, with our help. This may take hard work, but not the kind that involves effortful control. It is the hard work of dealing with emotions or past experiences that they find frightening and seek to shut away. Ego defences are ultimately a mode of self-regulation, effective in their own way, but oftentimes maladaptive. They serve to deny and suppress rather than recognize and reduce, and in so doing can create even further stress.

It is incredibly hard for teens with strong ego defences to confront repressed fears, but it is possible – and only possible – if they feel safe. The key to our ability to provide them with a sense of security is to recognize that the behaviours that we find so worrying are not adamantine *yetzer hara*, but rather the result of being chronically overstressed and relying on maladaptive modes of self-regulation to get through the day.

The teen who succumbs to harmful behaviours – whether to self or to society – is not *making the wrong choices* or *lacking the character* to follow through on what they *know is right*. They are not *choosing* at all, and are only in the early stages of learning what is right. As long as we think their behaviour is intentional, we won't be able to help. On the contrary, we will make things worse. The teen *misbelieves* that they are in control of their actions and is oblivious of what they need for their own well-being.

Every teen can realize the qualities that define virtue, no matter what has gone on before or is going on now in their lives: courage, kindness, gratitude, duty, transcendence, wisdom. These are not quaint terms, and if it seems that way, it's only because of the anomie that has set in. But are these traits enough to achieve eudaimonia? Don't teens also need to have a sense of belonging?

Postscript: *Tsemisht* (Confused, Mixed Up, Troubled)

While I was working on my BPhil, I read a line in Norman Malcolm's *Memoir* about how the highest praise that Wittgenstein would bestow on someone was to describe them as a "decent human being."[22] I found this puzzling at first, until I realized that Wittgenstein must have said that so-and-so was *ein anständige mensch*, which Malcolm (or Wittgenstein himself) translated as "decent human being." But this doesn't come close to capturing the meaning of *mensch*.

A *mensch*, as Leo Rosten, the great authority on Yiddish, explained, is "someone to admire and emulate, someone of noble character. The key to being 'a real mensch' is nothing less than character, rectitude, dignity, a sense of what is right, responsible, decorous."[23] To be a *mensch* has nothing to do with wealth or status. In fact, there are countless examples of people with the latter who are manifestly *not* menschen – and maybe powerful and wealthy for precisely that reason!

I was forever being told, not just by my parents, but by my grandmother, that I needed to be a mensch. It is no exaggeration to say that a high point in my father's life was when a friend of his told him that I was a real mensch. I was fourteen at the time. The fact that I remember this incident so vividly tells you everything you need to know about the pleasure I experienced in the pleasure my father experienced. This motivated me like nothing I'd been exposed to at the dinner table to *want* to be a mensch: a very clear example of the power of positive emotions.

But then I started to wonder: what made me think that Wittgenstein was using *mensch* in the same way as my father? The Germans had their own concept of *menschlichkeit*, which dated back to the Enlightenment, which in turn dated back to Cicero's *humanitas*. In this context, the concept refers to the virtues possessed by great leaders and the reason they are great leaders. I found this puzzling, for, incredible as it may sound, I'm not sure I had ever heard the word "virtue" until I got to Oxford. The closest thing we had was the word *chayil*, which was used to describe Ruth in the Book of Ruth. (My father used this word to describe my new bride.) But *chayil* refers to strength of character and valour rather than being chaste and virtuous (although my wife is those as well!).

It seemed to me – it still seems to me – that while there is a more than significant overlap between *virtue* and *menschlichkeit*, they are not coterminous. I suggested above how the problem with the Greeks' model of virtue is that they tied it to self-control rather than self-regulation. But while self-regulation is necessary, it is not sufficient for *menschlichkeit*.

To be *virtuous* is to act in ways that are described as *righteous, moral, honest, humble, ethical, compassionate*, and most of all, *rational*. The argument presented in *Nichomachean Ethics* is that reason tells us that virtue is the only way to have a good life. Given that the *telos* of human existence is to be happy, it follows that if you are rational you will choose to be virtuous. The unvirtuous may *think* that they are enjoying the good life, but examine their mental or physical condition and you'll quickly see that they are anything but.

All of this sounded supremely important to me, yet in some way lacking. To be sure, *to be a mensch* is to be honest, moral, and compassionate, but *righteous*? There is a separate Yiddish word for that, *tzaddik*, and very few will ever be so described. More puzzling was the connection to reason. This would render *menschlichkeit* akin to the Prisoner's Dilemma. But *being a mensch* has nothing to do with calculating what is in your best interest; in fact, to be a mensch is not to think of yourself at all.

The concept of *menschlichkeit* does not go back to Cicero, it traces back to Exodus 24:7 and the foundational moment in the history of Judaism. The Israelites are gathered at the foot of Mount Sinai and have just listened to Moses read the Book of the Covenant, to which they respond:

> "We will do and we will hear [*na'ase ve-nishma*] everything the Lord as said."

This ringing declaration is the ultimate performative. The Israelites commit themselves to honour the Covenant that they make with each other in the presence of God, and the commitment they make to God. It is not reason that underpins *menschlichkeit*, it is trust (*emunah*): the trust that everyone will honour their moral commitment. Without trust, the polity cannot survive as a "holy nation."

Trust is the proper definition of *emunah* (as Buber explained in *Two Types of Faith*). Where faith is the ultimate example of non-rational conviction, trust is the ultimate example of how we bind ourselves. *Trust* is also one of those terms that has become quaint, to our great misfortune. In its place we now have *mis-trust*, which is the product of *misbelief*; that is, the *non-rational belief* in the sincerity of a false actor.

It was *hearing the voice of God* that led the Israelites to bind themselves to the Covenant. Hearing in the sense of striving to understand and internalizing. This theme is repeated throughout *Tanakh*. It is the crux of the most famous of all Jewish prayers, the *Shemah*, in which Jews urge themselves to listen.

Famously, when Elijah flees from Ahad and Jezebel and spends the night hiding in a cave on Mount Carmel, he hears the "still small voice" of the Lord. He wraps his face in his mantle and goes out and stands in the entrance of the cave. There he hears the voice again, asking, "What are you doing here, Elijah?" He responds: "The people of Israel have broken their covenant with you." But then, his trust in God renewed, Elijah leaves his hiding-place and sets out to restore the Israelites' moral commitment to the Covenant (1 Kings 19).

To hear the voice of God is to sense a higher truth, something above and beyond our narrow egoistic concerns. It is to feel the full weight of the Covenant for the well-being of our own and future generations. To feel morally bound to care for the well-being of every member of the community, including the stranger. To abhor the possibility that anyone should go hungry or homeless. To feel an awesome responsibility to teach the Covenant to your children. To "talk about it when you sit at home and when you walk along the road, when you lie down and when you get up" (Deuteronomy 6:7). Precisely what my grandmother and father did.

What happens to a society that no longer *hears the voice of God?* This is not the same as the question, What happens to a society that no longer *believes in God?* The difference between these two questions is the difference between *anomie* and *atheism.* This distinction could be the topic of another book (*Self-Reg for a Moral Society?*). But for the present, simply note the following.

To hear the voice of God is to feel wonder at the sight of nature. To hear the cries of all living creatures. To see yourself as a guardian of the earth rather than as someone who is entitled to despoil it. To see all humans as equal – that is, with the same rights to freedom and happiness, an equal say in matters spiritual and secular. To grasp that freedom is being able to choose, psychologically as well as politically, that which brings you purpose while harming no one else. To understand that one is only free if everyone is free. All this and so much more is what it means *to hear the voice of God.*

If ever there were a case of privileging rationality, it is the classical Greek view of virtue. It leads to *contract theory* which, as Daniel Elazar shows in his magisterial four-volume series on The Covenant Tradition in Politics, is fundamentally different from covenant. "A covenant is a morally informed agreement or pact based upon voluntary consent, established by mutual oaths or promises, involving or witnessed by some transcendent higher authority."[24] A *social contract* does not rest on this moral dimension. It is a secular arrangement that rests on a shared view of the need for government to uphold security (against both internal and external threats).

Herein lies the reason why the US revolution of 1776 was so monumental for the rest of the world. It was not simply because they overthrew tyranny and established a democracy. It was because they founded a covenantal society, not a secular compact, a society in which no particular religion was privileged. The constitution is so much more than a legal document that can be disregarded and even changed at will. It is a declaration that the foundation of eudaimonia is trust.

Chapter 11

Creating a Just Society

Wilting under Pressure

Reason alone will never lead to a Just Society.

The fact is, reason doesn't hold up very well in the face of sustained excessive stress. Before you know it, catecholamines are leading you by the nose, and you've shifted from giving reasons into rationalization and confabulation. Deeply held convictions are abandoned at the drop of a hat, to be replaced by their polar opposites.

What just a short while ago were regarded as abominable behaviours are now not just tolerated but even prized as evidence of character strength. Apparently pride, gluttony, wrath, envy, lust, greed, and sloth are not deadly sins if they get followers on a YouTube channel, let alone a stint as the head of government. Yet it is one thing to have a troubled individual project himself as a god and quite another to have a multitude embrace him as such; indeed, to devote considerable amounts of their time creating fantasy art depicting him as such.

Why are overstressed societies so susceptible to "moral convulsion," with rationality the first out the door and virtue fast on its heels?[1] The Greeks had a ready answer to this question: *we make the wrong choices* or *we are too weak to enforce the right ones*. But *strengthening thumos* doesn't seem to have served them – or us – very well. Especially when one considers the horrors perpetrated in the twentieth century under the name of willpower.[2] This is an issue that goes far beyond the reach of self-control, into the very heart of human nature.

I wrote the next paragraph five years ago. It reads as a warning of just how quickly non-rationalism can set in.

Like so many of my generation, I couldn't come to terms with the fact that so many seemingly decent Germans became Nazis, but mindful at the same time that so many did not. This is no longer a purely historical matter. As I write this, I am struggling to understand the meteoric rise of neo-fascist groups around the world. I am reading how the government in Italy is considering reinstating a census of the Roma. How the Polish government is subverting its independent judiciary – as, perhaps, would the current US administration if it could. How the government in Hungary is bent on instituting an Orwellian apparatus. I am monitoring with a growing sense of dread the brutal manner in which China and Russia are responding to their dissidents. Watching border fencing go up around the world. But most disturbing of all: seeing countless individuals that were raised to love freedom who are now prepared to countenance a return to authoritarianism, while political leaders drop any pretence to democratic sentiments and bask in the naked exercise of power.

Last night Rachel Maddow, someone whom I greatly admire, raised the following question:

This isn't just a case of a few misguided souls that have been swept up in a cult-like madness. We are talking about 50, 60, maybe even 70 million people whose rationality has been seriously compromised. How could this happen? What can we possibly do to help them return to reality-based thinking?

Journalists were asking the same question in the early 1930s. Dorothy Thompson was thrown out of Germany in 1934 for being a little too forthright in her description of

Hitler as "formless, almost faceless, a man whose countenance is a caricature, a man whose framework seems
cartilaginous, without bones. He is inconsequent and vol-
uble, ill poised and insecure. He is the very prototype of
the little man" (in her book *I Saw Hitler*).

This is a stunning example of just how wrong we can be
about authoritarians.

I never dreamt we would be dealing with a serious resurgence
of fascism in my lifetime. Not in our own backyard. But Self-Reg
teaches us that, before we react, we need to reflect, and resist the
mesmerizing allure of denial. As a start, it means we need to be
asking Why. Not as a lament, but as a matter of genuine puzzle-
ment and practical urgency. But the hardest part about asking Why
is that you can easily delude yourself into thinking you have come
up with an answer when you have merely described the problem
in different terms, or moved it down a level.

Aristotle spoke about the *painful path to virtue*.[3] It has become
downright tortuous. We are seeing the *problem of akrasia* on a
national scale comparable to what happened in Italy, Japan, and
Germany in the 1920s. But we have to think twice before describing
the growing numbers of "extremists" as "brainwashed members
of a cult."[4] Not simply because of concerns about the legitimacy of
these concepts, but further, because you are merely restating the
problem using emotionally charged terms – without explaining
anything.

I am hesitant to refer to non-rational movements in terms of
brainwashing or a *cult mentality*. The real problem with using terms
like *brainwashed* and *cult* is that they assume we are dealing with
an anomaly. But when an *aberration* becomes society-wide, we
need to consider whether we are witnessing a fundamental aspect
of human nature. Something that has been there from the start.
Indeed, something that the Old Testament warns against time after
time.

The most striking aspect of the upheavals we are seeing today is that individuals are abruptly abandoning what had previously been deeply held beliefs, and not even seeking to justify their reversal. Russia is evil. No, Russia is good. North Korea is evil. No, good. No, bad again, good again (I lost track of where we were on this one). It is the lability that is so unsettling, not to mention the paucity of reasons given to justify the about-face. **But most disturbing of all is the absence of uncertainty with each new turn in the conviction wheel**: the kind of hesitation and serious deliberation that is the hallmark of Descartes's view of rationality.

These violent ideological swings have long puzzled political scientists: How can the ethics of an individual, a group, or even an entire society change so quickly and dramatically? How can core convictions be dropped so readily and their polar opposites embraced? Is it merely the case that we will always be vulnerable to the emotive messaging of the demagogue or propaganda, or is this only a danger in certain conditions? And if that is the case, how can we guard against evil happening again – and again and again?

The intolerable stress created by moral instability impairs our ability to think rationally about these questions, blocks us from asking Why in a genuinely objective manner. Instead, we go into fight, flight, or freeze. But once we start asking Why, we see a number of stressors that are sending a group into full Red Brain, poised to slip into non-rationality, if they are not already there. Yet non-rationality is not ipso facto a negative state. It can, in fact, be the opposite. A group in Red Brain can perform extraordinary prosocial acts, like Satyagraha or the Civil Rights Movement.

We need to acknowledge that something that happens over and over throughout the course of human history can't be an anomaly. There has to be some dynamic at play: one that, in certain situations, boosts survival, and in others, leads to chaos. What is it about Red Brain that could lead the Israelites towards the Promised Land, but when they got tired and hungry, led them to long to return to slavery? What is it about Red Brain that, in some situations, leads the members of a society to work together, but in other situations, to be at each other's throats?

Figure 11.1 Disorganized and organized

What matters isn't that human beings are like herrings that swim together as an army. What matters is what that army is fighting for (Figure 11.1).

When Sharing Naturally Occurs

The dominant view for the past 2,500 years has been that if reason and virtue wilt in the face of powerful urges, this can only mean that reason's faithful servant – call it *thumos*, will, moral fibre, superego, the HPA pathway, Siri – wasn't up to the task. Self-Reg challenges both sides of this equation, both the assumption that social harmony is only made possible by the exercise of self-control, and the idea that the control in question is mind over "natural base impulses." If the same way of thinking keeps leading to the same sort of collapse, at some point we need to turn our attention onto the assumption itself.

Occasionally you come across an experiment that makes you do just that. Such was the case with a study by Christov-Moore and colleagues.[5] They used theta burst stimulation (short bursts of electrical stimulation) to disrupt the prefrontal systems that subserve executive functions and social cognition in subjects playing the Dictator Game (dlPFC and mPFC). The game (so-called) is designed to study the effect of social distance on sharing behaviour. The closer the recipient emotionally, the more likely the "dictator" will share a cash prize.

What Christov-Moore discovered is that players *share more* in the "knock-out" condition. To be more precise, what was *knocked out* were the dopamine receptors in the dlPFC. This allowed oxytocin receptors free rein over the subjects' sharing behaviour. That is, CARE triggered the release of oxytocin, which is the neurobiological substrate of what we call *trust*. We will return to this crucial point below.

But then, why would dopamine interfere with CARE? This doesn't happen in other species. Rats will share food with hungry conspecifics.[6] Food sharing is the norm in bonobos. The upshot of the research by Frans de Waal and Barbara King is that it was empathy, not competition, that enabled bonobos to survive for millions of years.[7] But then, it wasn't just dopamine that was inhibited. The game is designed to activate DOMINANCE, but the relevant prefrontal systems were then quelled (dlPFC and mPFC).

What is most striking about this study is that, sent into Red Brain, the subjects did not respond in the manner that the classical Greek model predicts. Greed and selfishness were not unleashed when self-control was inhibited. Rather, the subjects displayed a *human prepotent inclination* towards collaboration. Far from Plato's "wild horses" being let loose, it was when cognitive control was inhibited that CARE-driven sharing naturally occurred.

This point explains one of the reasons why humans enjoy social eating so much: CARE is activated, which releases positive hedonic sensations. Eating in a crowded food mall does not have this effect. The calmer we are, the more we share – and not just food. The more anxious we are, the more DOMINANCE is untethered. We stop sharing and start hoarding. We become like children, although it is not playground status but other forms of dominance that rear their ugly heads (e.g., over the rights of women or immigrants).

If a child violently reacts to a friend who merely wants to share the first child's toy, we need to understand why RAGE has been activated, blocking the positive hedonic sensations that sharing normally affords. The same point applies to adults. Interestingly, there was a dramatic increase in the incidence of Hoarding Disorder during COVID-19. The prevalence rate has not abated, although what overstressed individuals are hoarding these days has changed somewhat. Now it is political power that is being hoarded. The cause is not a drop in self-control over a *hoarding impulse*, but the effect of homeostatic imbalance on the oxytocin-opioid homeostatic system that circulates in the blood.

Speaking metaphorically, we might say that the Blue Brain needs the Red Brain to keep it on course, and vice versa. In Blue Brain/Red Brain balance, prefrontal and limbic systems temper and keep a check on each other. The Triune Brain is like a great sailing ship, navigating its way through calm and stormy waters, and all too often getting caught in the doldrums. Blue Brain without Red Brain is like a captain without a crew; Red Brain without Blue Brain is like a crew without a captain. When the latter mutinous state occurs, we expose ourselves to the danger of being hijacked by our own, or worse still, *by someone else's ancient survival systems*!

Group Red Brain

Hard as it may be to accept, the Trump phenomenon serves as an invaluable lesson for the creation of a Just Society. Talk about a grim reminder of Santayana's warning that "Those who cannot remember the past are condemned to repeat it."[8] Clearly, we are having trouble learning whatever it is that we're supposed to be learning; otherwise, we wouldn't be seeing yet another Cleon rise to power.

Or perhaps, a repeat of the Thirty Tyrants, the oligarchy that briefly ruled Athens after its fall in the Peloponnesian War. Today it is a shadowy group of billionaires who have found in Trump the perfect demagogue to serve their purposes, someone who can sway the *demos* into accepting measures that will protect, indeed increase their disproportionate wealth. What is it that we have (not) learned?

On the surface, it certainly looks as if the issue is about how strong emotions can overpower reason. The deeper question, however, is whether those strong emotions were cause or effect. That is, whether a heightened stress load, coupled with carefully scripted priming, is what led to the overpowering of reason.

Consider what happened at Trump rallies. Various techniques were employed to tamp up the stress. Excessive noise (visual and auditory), over-the-top warmups, pulsating rhythms, shills in the crowd, staged actors behind the speaker, ubiquitous shibboleths (hats, shirts, posters, mugs, sneakers), orchestrated chanting ("build the wall," "lock her up," "drain the swamp," "kill the infidels"), an orator who knew how to whip up negative emotions. All sorts of techniques to send the crowd into a flooded Red Brain state in which the most prominent shared emotions that took root were fear, anger, resentment, xenophobia, feelings of abandonment, belligerence, hate.

Why someone went to a rally in the first place is an intriguing and an important question. Common socialization leads individuals to seek out same-group experiences.[9] In some cases, the appeal might have been a matter of looking for entertainment; in others, an outlet for pent-up frustrations. But in all cases the common factor was that the individual was already dealing with high levels of stress, unconsciously looking for catecholamines, and inadvertently adding to their stress load. In a great many cases, what they were looking for was an altered state of mind.

What is particularly significant is how rugged individualists willingly, even enthusiastically, gave up their autonomy, not just in terms of *will*, but in their sense of *self*. As a group, they were primed to do whatever the leader decreed – even if this should run directly contrary to hitherto deeply held convictions – *without agonizing over the consequences*. That is the key.

Public institutions (Intelligence, the Police and FBI, and Justice), not to mention the media, are the enemies of the people. Immigration is bad, tariffs are good, even if industries and individuals should suffer. Being kind to families, children, the poor, the elderly, refugees, minorities, or even legal immigrants is a weakness, not a character strength. Morality has turned into wokeism, which is anathema. Universal education is a liberal pipedream, and a subversive one at that. Corruption and sexual assault are venial sins as long as the greater good is being served.[10] Incurring massive debt is no longer a worry, as long as it is up to future generations to pay it off. Exposing children to toxic pollutants is not disturbing as long as it's other people's children.

The list is longer than what I've mentioned – and more worrisome. But what matters aren't the specifics: it's that a short time ago many of these same individuals would have insisted on the opposite. The very fact that we see this sharp attitudinal swing – particularly in subjects that had hitherto self-identified as "conservative" – tells us to look for the ways in which such a shift was guided.

In retrospect it is clear that Trump's opponents – Republican and Democrat alike – got their strategy dead wrong. They thought they could *convince* Trump supporters that they were being duped. In so doing, they ended up providing the very thing needed to feed the "confirmation bias." But you cannot argue with *misbelief*, for the very reason that misbelief is non-rational.

This is not meant as a disparaging remark, solely descriptive. As we have seen throughout this book, being in Red Brain *excludes* the epistemic concepts internally tied to intentional behaviour. Scaring a pandemonium of parrots will set them to screaming, but not because they *believe* they are in danger. The same applies to the screaming that occurred at a Trump rally. The members of the crowd did not *believe* that Secretary Clinton was guilty of some heinous crime. They were not *choosing* to join in the chants. What we saw instead was an example of limbic behaviour that excludes epistemic operators like *believing, choosing, acting deliberately, listening, reflecting*.

Limbic behaviours are *caused*, not done for *reasons*, even if the subject should try to offer one afterwards (i.e., confabulate; see chapter 5). Limbic behaviours are not intentional, not the result of *decisions* that were well or poorly thought out. They cannot be *explained* or *defended*. They are the effects of hyperaroused SEEK-ING, RAGE, FEAR, PANIC/GRIEF, or DOMINANCE. When all of these PECs are vibrating together, CARE is thoroughly extinguished. We have entered the realm of catecholamine drivers, where rationality is an outrider.

The Escape from Monkey Brain

Why did the Israelites need a Moses to liberate them? Why couldn't they liberate themselves? Presumably they were strong enough in numbers to have done so; otherwise, Pharaoh would not have so feared their presence. But the slavery they suffered from was psychological. That is why, lost in the desert, they longed to return to the fleshpots of Egypt. That is why only their offspring would be able to enter the Promised Land: a generation born into and that cherished freedom.

Why would anyone choose to vote for someone who campaigns on the platform of being a "Dictator for a Day"? But then, is "choose" the right word? Is this not the preeminent example of the problem of *akrasia*, assuming that to give up one's freedom is the ultimate example of self-harm? Which, indeed, was precisely the question that Aristotle was raising.

We see a similar pattern in children who have been abused by a parent that turn into spouses that are abused by their partner. A common response is: "I must have done something wrong and deserve to be punished." The transgressor becomes the victim. And in the case of his supporters, it is indeed Trump who is the victim: of the "fake media," the "deep state," an "illegitimate investigation," a "Democrat conspiracy."

In other words, it might look as if we are grappling here not just with secure but in some sense with *ultra-secure* attachment (e.g., the supporter who declares, "Nothing that Trump does or has ever done could shake my faith in him"). But in fact, these behaviours are characteristic of *insecure attachment*. The greater the fear, the stronger is the tie to an Interbrain playing on that fear, especially when everyone around you is feeling the same.

This last phenomenon is not an aberration. When a group goes into full Red Brain, individual Blue Brain processes are suppressed so that messages and sensations pass instantly throughout all the gathered limbic systems. Social contagion theorists have shown how ideas, attitudes, beliefs, emotions, and impulses sweep through a population like an infectious disease. Indeed, the same thing occurs with physical symptoms like nausea, fainting, and vomiting.[11]

When a group is in full Red Brain, a signal from the leader (the alpha male or, as we saw in England in the 1980s, the alpha female) can send the troop scampering up the trees or scurrying under bushes. So too can a signal from the leader have everyone shouting the same refrain. A "pandemonium of humans" – and that certainly feels like the appropriate term to use here, even though, strictly speaking, there is no such thing as an "alpha bird" – will, like any herd, turn on a dime if its leader so directs.

Because of our tendency to privilege rationality, we assume that what draws an individual to join a group in Red Brain is shared beliefs. But the research done on cults shows the exact opposite: What motivates$_{NS}$ the individual (i.e., "motivates" in the neuroscience sense) is the flight from self-awareness. It is not security, but insecurity. The potent factor is the relief afforded by *fleeing from one's own agitated Blue Brain*.

Teri Buford O'Shea gave a fascinating insight into this point.[12] She recounts how joining the People's Temple provided her, not just with a strong sense of security, but with *a sense of peace that came from not having to think*. A troubled Blue Brain is the source of the problem. The search is for Lethe.

In Group Red Brain, the Blue Brain systems that subserve individual deliberation and self-awareness are inhibited. This creates a vacuum that is filled by a powerful leader, whether a paragon of virtue or a Jim Jones. One way or another, the leader takes on the role of those executive functions that have been lulled into sleep in individual members of the group.

The key is to look at *group Red Brain* in non-normative terms. In the conditions that prevailed in the Pleistocene, situations must have arisen in which it was beneficial to have a single person making the decisions for the entire group. The alternative would be chaos, with everyone running off in a different direction or shouting out different orders.

In modern humans, this impulse can lead the group into *yetzer tov* or *yetzer hara*. In the case of an ennobling leader, positive emotions surge. In the case of the demagogue, negative emotions sweep through the collective. The danger for a group swept up in primitive negative emotions is that, should the alpha lose control, the group turns into a mob (as happened in France in 1794). If the alpha holds on fiercely to power, there is a frightening shift into *tonic immobility*. O'Shea's memoir is riveting on this point.

Jones started threatening the members of the Temple and took away their means of escape (by moving them to Jonestown) and then resistance (by surrounding them with armed guards), while repeatedly exposing them to severe threats. This sent the group, first into freeze, and then into tonic immobility as they watched passively while innocents were being killed. The culmination was the act of mass suicide. It was for a similar reason that Leipzig banned *The Sorrows of Young Werther* in 1775[13] and one reason we see suicide epidemics in at-risk schools that are high-stress environments.

The issue in extreme self-harm contagions is not simply imitation, but the effect of intolerable stress on a highly stressed individual: the stress of hearing of suicide on top of a state of stress overloads an at-risk individual. Executive functions go offline and a longing for release becomes overwhelming. It is not just suicide that concerns us, but the self-harm that results from forsaking the capacity to choose how one acts. Hence the calamitous rise of internalizing and externalizing disorders: not the result of making *bad choices*, but the result of being in a state where *one cannot choose*.

Here is yet another instance where the continuity thesis bears directly on how we understand ourselves, on how we look at self-harm. And, perhaps, for how we look at animals. For they too, like humans, are at risk of subsiding into tonic immobility when emotional pain is too intense. We now have abundant evidence not only that animals feel intense grief but even that, as a result, they may kill themselves.[14]

The debate over whether animals can commit suicide dates back to Aristotle's story of the stallion that committed suicide because of shame, and much more important, Claudius Aelian's catalogue of twenty-one cases of animal suicide in *De natura animalium*. But do animals that are suffering intense grief ever *choose* to kill themselves to find release from their grief?

This last question has the greatest of implications for how we lay the foundation for a just society.

Driving on Autopilot

We have witnessed the rise of a culture in which there are multiple forces dedicated to creating compulsions and then turning these into habits: self-sedating habits that are very different from the sorts of self-discipline habits that earlier generations embraced. And what is most distressing is how this is being done, not just deliberately, but openly, and with full government blessing.

One of the most disturbing studies in this respect is Schüll's *Addiction by Design*.[15] She starts the book with an arresting interview with Mollie, a denizen of Las Vegas who is struggling with her addiction to gaming machines:

> "The more I gambled, the wiser I became about my chances. Wiser, but also weaker, less able to stop. Today when I win – and I do win, from time to time – I just put it back in the machines. The thing people never understand is that I'm not playing to win." Why, then, does she play? "To keep playing. To stay in that machine zone where nothing else matters."[16]

The subjects that Schüll interviewed for her book speak lucidly about their addiction. They are not in denial about their behaviour. But neither do they understand it. They explain, all using remarkably similar language, how they find the activity "calming," even though – or perhaps because – their lives are in utter shambles. They seek out in gaming a state of mind in which all they are aware of is the machine and not the day-to-day worries and cognitive stresses that they find intolerable (especially their gambling addiction).

Being in this zoned-out state is the reward they are after. This is not solely or simply an attempt to keep the dopamine taps open[17] – although the addiction started this way – but rather, to experience what Schüll describes as a "subjective shift." Or rather, a "subjective shutdown." Regardless of whether they win or lose, it's being in a *machine zone* that leads those unfortunates who become addicted to cash in their paycheques and go deep into debt.

Mollie draws a map of her world, which is essentially a loop consisting of the different sites with gaming machines that she frequents. She describes herself as constantly ending up at one of these locations with no conscious intention of doing so and no idea of how she got there. She is literally driving on autopilot, complete with detours and tricky U-turns. Marc Lewis describes the same phenomenon in the interviews that he conducted for *The Biology of Desire.*

What we are dealing with here is more than just the *detachment* that we looked at in chapter 2. In detachment, one is driven by a limbic prime with marginal awareness of self or others. But the stories that Schüll recounts of gamblers oblivious of the heart attack victim lying right beside them are instances, not of blunted empathy, but of complete *non-awareness*: *they literally do not register what is happening at their feet.*

What we are witnessing is reminiscent of what Huxley described in his dystopia *Brave New World.* Being in a hyper-dopaminergic state has a marked impact on the ability to weigh risk against reward,[18] a fact that game designers themselves fully realize and nonetheless ignore when they themselves turn to playing. An electronics technician involved in the design of the machines said to Schüll: "I am a reasonably intelligent person, I'm rational. But when it comes to gambling, reason just skippity-hops out the door." Another who had "designed the math on these games" described how "it doesn't matter; I do risky, irrational things when I play." Exactly.

The real *risk* is that of becoming addicted to *dissociation*. Without question, the Hobbesian view of human nature reflects one possible consequence of unleashing of primitive aggressive instincts. But recall our discussion in chapter 1 about how in the final stage of hypothermia a "primitive and burrowing-like behaviour" occurs. In this state, awareness as well as thinking is deadened. To the extent that the person feels anything, it is a longing for release.

The chilling message of *Addiction by Design* is that subjects are seeking out the *machine zone*, not *despite* but *because of* this numbing effect. They are sending themselves into this state in order to escape from rationality. It is not just the overstressed adult who is at risk of drinking from this poisoned chalice. Teens and now even children who are just at the cusp of becoming aware of themselves and the world around them are now at risk.

Take the case of smartphones. Kids carry around what Tristan Harris describes as the ultimate "slot machine in their pocket," a device based on the same strategies as gaming machines: for example, a variable reward schedule, a sound or vibration to alert us to a reward, anxiety that you don't miss the next "payoff." The pocket gaming machine can be even more addictive, since it builds on the need that is especially strong in teens for social approval and belongingness.[19] Try talking to someone who is glued to their slot machine; try talking to teens who are glued to their handheld bandits.

In these circumstances, reasoning with teens about the benefits of mindful self-regulation is not going to spark a Blue Brain renaissance. A big reason is because these same teens will insist that they turn to their phones (the Internet, social media, gaming, shopping, bingeing) *because* they find this so calming. If there is a lesson here to be learned from addiction research, it is that we need to think very carefully about what they understand by "calmness" – and then figure out how to help them experience the real thing.

(Re)Awakening Wakefulness

Rick Riordan has a wonderful depiction of Schüll's main theme in the Lotus Casino episode in *Percy Jackson and the Lightning Thief*.[20]

In one sense, casinos are operating exactly in the way that Riordan depicts with the "lotus flowers." The physical layout, atmosphere, and machines that "engineer experience" are all calibrated to lead customers on and render them oblivious to time and space, with a consequent increase in time on device.

Schüll cites a harrowing remark by the CEO of a prominent hotel-casino: "When we put 50 slot machines in, we always consider them 50 more mousetraps. You have to do something to catch a mouse. It's our duty to extract as much money as we can from customers."[21] Only, unlike what happens to Percy Jackson and his friends, it turns out that the "mice" are fully aware that this is happening to them and engage for precisely that reason. In what is the ultimate parody of Aristotle's definition of the *supreme good*, they seek this state *for its own sake*. Oblivion doesn't sneak up on them: they grasp at it!

Herein lies the key to understanding one of the major sources of this addiction: namely, the release afforded by taking the Blue Brain offline. The "reward" is *an escape from awareness*: a regression to a womblike state where people feel "safe" (another term commonly employed) in an enclosed environment (at least, it *feels* enclosed). But, of course, with the loss of awareness goes any sense of their tension, which goes up with each game. Hence by the end of a session they are plumbing the depths of bottom-right in the Thayer matrix, subject not just to worries and intrusive thoughts that they sought to keep at bay but, on top of that, to the dysphoria of guilt and self-loathing, and a limbic longing to return to a temporary state of "nothingness."

In other words, *they are self-regulating with the machines*, which has to be one of the most maladaptive ways to self-regulate ever invented. And this is why we are so concerned about children and teens being led into similar maladaptive modes of self-regulation. The point is not that smartphones or the Internet are inherently dangerous; on the contrary, both can have tremendous benefits. The problem is rather when the technology is being used, persistently, as *a way of retreating from self-awareness*.

The latter is the case where at-risk children and teens need to learn – *need to feel* – the difference between *calmness* and *dissociation*.

We have looked at so many critical conceptual distinctions in this book, but this may be one of the most important for today's youth. We spend so much time worrying about how to build their *stress tolerance*, when the deeper issue we need to address is how to build their *awareness*.

Percy Jackson escapes from the Lotus Casino, not by an extraordinary act of willpower, but because of Poseidon's intrusion. ("No, Percy, don't eat the flower. It dulls the senses. Keeps you prisoner here.") Percy's lurch back into reality enables him to do the same for his friends. If only kids were all demi-gods, or at least listened to their parents' warnings. But harping on the need for self-awareness will, if anything, send it even further out of their reach. The great irony in the movie is that it makes this point about self-awareness in such a way as to keep the viewer spellbound, through all the hook techniques that film studios have mastered.

The paradox in all this is that the stress created by conflicting desires – the *desire to be free* and the *desire to be free of anxiety* – can lead kids to deny that there is any conflict. To stick with Nodder's terms, denial is the evil twin of rationalization: both of them tried-and-true methods for managing stress.[22] If we try to force teens to recognize that hours spent on gaming or social media do not in fact leave them calm, we run the risk of increasing their stress and thus eliciting this defensive reaction.

They have to develop an *embodied*, not just a meta-cognitive understanding of the difference between *calmness* and *dissociation*. But in order for them to grasp that the way they are self-regulating is maladaptive, we are going to have to shatter some illusions, beginning with the illusion that they are *choosing freely* when this is not the case; or the illusion of *progress* in the mastery of a (quite meaningless) skill set.

The magician David Kwong is interesting in this regard. Kwong's basic thesis, based on Michotte and Mettelli's theory of amodal completion, is that the brain makes "inferences" about what it is seeing.[23] For example, in the famous spoon-bending trick, the brain "assumes" that the magician is holding one spoon. But it only takes a brief glimpse of reality to spoil the effect of the illusion, to alert us, in Kahneman's terms, to exercise System 2 thinking on System 1 judgments (see chapter 5).

Reframed, Kwong's and Kahneman's point is not that the brain is some sort of independent "homunculus" that makes its own judgments (as in R.L. Gregory's theory of perception)[24] but, rather, that we are biased to assume that a familiar pattern will persist. It is so rare an occurrence to see someone holding two pieces of spoon instead of one that it is natural to assume that we are looking at a normal spoon. It is not that our brains make judgments over which we have no control but, rather, that the spoon-bending magician capitalizes on our natural tendency to draw on past spoon experience.

> As soon as you know that the magician is actually holding two separate pieces – that the laugh track stops and starts on cue to make you feel as though you're part of a group that finds something amusing – the illusion is ruined. The same thing happens when you discover that a menu has been designed to limit and guide your selections – any kind of menu – that a pathway has been sculpted to lead you to a specific destination, that "near-wins" are more carefully calibrated than actual wins, that a webpage has been crafted to direct your line of sight, that text has been written to prey on your insecurities, and so on and on and on. You feel manipulated because, of course, you have been.

Having students read Tristan Harris's essays, Eyal's *Hooked*, Nodder's *Evil by Design*, and Ariely's *Predictably Irrational* might help them to recognize the *illusion of choice* on which the hook model depends. But insight alone – that is, rationality – will not suffice. Far from it. As an addiction counsellor explained to Schüll: "Even if we demystify the machines through education, [gambling addicts] will still play them. Because once you're hooked in something else kicks in to keep you there; all trains of thought are evacuated and only one dominates."[25]

The "something else" is a *dopaminergic association* that has firmly taken hold. This is what led to Mollie's unconscious U-turns: a cognitive stress (a worry or intrusive thought) that triggered the thought of dopamine relief. A similar stress/relief association was the critical factor in the Vietnam vets that Lee Robins studied who were able to kick their heroin addiction when they returned to the United States.[26] This happened, not simply because they were separated from the visible cues that triggered their shooting up, but because they were removed from the intolerable stress they had experienced in the war and when they were surrounded by oxytocin-affording friends and loved ones.[27]

The lesson here is that teaching the principles and perils of dopamine hijacking may be a start, but it is only that. It is essential that kids come to know what calmness feels like. What it feels like to be overstressed. They need to recognize their anxiety as the warning sign that it is. Be able to identify the stresses in their lives and have personalized strategies for managing these stresses. They need to recognize when their way of dealing with excessive stress is maladaptive.

But most of all, their need is the same as that of an infant. They need to have trust in the Interbrains in their lives: peers as well as adults. Only then will they be able to acquire trust in themselves, and thence, in their society.

Democracy is built on trust. There could be no more telling indicator that trust is in sharp decline than the sharp rise of authoritarianism.

The Sharp Rise of Mis-Trust

We have seen an epidemic of conspiracy theories in the last few years. In no small part this is due to the monetization of "engagement farming": the exploitation of extremist views as a way of generating advertising revenue. But there is a deeper current involved. "The epidemiological and social crises brought about by COVID-19 have magnified widely held social anxieties and trust issues."[28] I had to deal with this issue first-hand at MEHRI.

This was the time when parents had become incredibly anxious about the MMR vaccine because of the paper that Andrew Wakefield had published in the *Lancet* in 1998. Parents were devastated by the thought that they had caused their child's autism. Families with one child on the spectrum were begging us to help them find a way to split the vaccine into three doses for their next child, or eschewing vaccination altogether. It wasn't until 2011 that we became fully aware of the extent of Wakefield's fraud. But by then the damage had been done. It is still being done.

We need to look at the explosion of conspiracy theories around the COVID vaccine in light of the furor over the MMR vaccine, and following that, the HNHI vaccine and then the measles vaccine. But what has happened since the pandemic is startling. Vaccine conspiracy theories are just the tip of the iceberg.

A meta-analysis came out in 2023 that confirms that there has been a precipitous collapse of trust in what would hitherto have been highly trusted figures or institutions.[29] The study confirms what we have long suspected: the "conspiratorial mind" sees threats all around, values intuition over reason, feels that it and like-minded individuals are superior to those who are not part of the elect.

You only need to read Ariely's *Misbelief* and the flood of wild conspiracy theories to which he has been subjected to see how this is most definitely not a rational issue. That is not to say that conspiracy theories are *ipso facto* irrational (although some clearly are); rather, it is to suggest that conspiracy theories are *non-rational*, in the sense that we have been exploring. Not only are they immune to doubt, but they actually grow stronger when factually challenged.

The conspiracy theorist is caught in the web of *mis-trust*. It is not just that they mistrust what were once highly respected authorities and institutions. *Nothing* those authorities or institutions could say or do would restore their trust. And yet we persist in trying to do just that: to restore their trust with facts and data.

The reason why we are drawn to privileging rationality here is simply because trust itself is the most rational of constructs. You have *grounds* for relying on another person or institution, reason to trust that they will not harm you. Without a rational foundation, *trust* is simply a misleading term for *fanatical devotion*.

The origins of trust are developmental. The securely attached baby learns that they can trust their caregivers and depend on them for comfort. Bretherton's "4 S's" refers to four key factors that underpin secure attachment. Infants need to feel "seen, safe, soothed, and secure."[30] But we can take this a step further: the origins of the 4 S's are physiological, dating back to the distant evolutionary past.

Panksepp showed how separation produces intense aversive sensations in both caregiver and infant. These sensations are generated by a PANIC/GRIEF circuit that runs from the dorsal PAG to the ACC. This PEC evolved from an ancient pain circuit that dates back to squamates. Thus, the "psychic pain" of PANIC/GRIEF has strong links to the aversive sensations that accompany nociception and CRF. Reunion triggers the release of oxytocin and endogenous opioids that turn off these nociceptors and the stress response.

Where the securely attached infant "expects" relief from their caregiver, the insecurely infant does not. The former associates the caregiver with those positive sensations that characterize homeostasis. In cases of D-Type attachment, the infant has no such association, or worse still, anticipates even greater distress. The securely attached infant SEEKS oxytocin; the insecurely attached infant SEEKS catecholamines. The securely attached infant restores homeostasis; the insecurely attached infant is frequently dysregulated.

In order to understand the epidemic of conspiracy theories in the US, we need to start with the epidemic of insecurely attached children (approximately 38 per cent). Securely attached children go on to have high levels of trust in their romantic relationships; insecurely attached individuals have far lower levels of trust, not for psychological, but for psychophysiological reasons.

If we want to restore trust, we need to go to the source of the problem.

Virtue Academies

I mentioned at the outset how, from the beginning, I shared the belief that the secret to creating a Just Society lies in education.

Endless studies have made clear that investing in public education has the greatest of social benefits. It leads to a healthier population, a higher standard of living, a reduction in crime, greater life satisfaction. But what if the opposite were true? What if it were leading to a large number of teens with internalizing and externalizing disorders; a generation that had no interest in work of any kind, let alone hard work; an increase in bullying, and a sharp decrease in resilience. Would we still feel the same about "investing in education"?

Every teen movie ever made tells us that high schools have become a toxic environment. Of course, that might simply reflect the influence of John Hughes on the genre. But I suspect that, in this case, the gap between art and reality is not very great. In 2019, the Yale Child Center found that nearly 75 per cent of high school students have highly negative feelings about school. They self-reported feeling "tired," "stressed," and "bored" all the time. And that was before the pandemic hit.[31]

The biggest shift since the time when I wrote the first version of this section has been the sharp rise in discipline problems. Not surprisingly, this has led to the self-control response that schools need to become more draconian in their disciplinary practices. Some of the proposed measures, such as banning the use of smartphones in classroom hours, seem like common sense. Zero tolerance does not. For what the self-reports reveal is a generation mired in homeostatic imbalance. And you cannot force, let alone enforce, virtue.

Every school motto I have ever seen was about virtue. Every school administrator I have ever met saw this as one of their primary duties. But many have given up on this noble goal and are now anxiously waiting for retirement. Meanwhile, 30 per cent of new teachers are leaving the field within five years, and the rest are dispirited.

It's not as if administrators aren't doing their best to turn things around. A colleague of mine was the principal of a large secondary school. A man of deep principles, he desperately wanted to turn his school into a Virtue Academy. He put an inordinate amount of time and effort into talking about character and holding spirit events; attending leadership seminars and constantly reading up on the topic; coaching (and coaxing) his teachers to model virtuous behaviour; doing one-on-one counselling with troubled students; and holding endless parent meetings. But for all that, he watched impotently as externalizing and internalizing problems escalated every year, while staff morale plummeted ever downwards. He told me that he felt like King Canute, and I know that many – if not most – senior administrators feel the same way.

My colleague was frustrated not because he was doing the wrong things but because he was saying and trying to teach all the right things, yet the situation kept getting worse. But what Self-Reg teaches us is that a dysregulated student will not be able to process, much less benefit from, the moral guidance my colleague was striving to impart. The problem is that homeostasis comes before moral development, and a majority of students are a long way from homeostasis.

The last thing any administrator in this situation wants is yet another description of the problems they are facing. What they want are measures that will help them turn the tide. But if what you keep doing isn't having an impact, then at some point you are going to have to ask yourself Why. Especially when the issue has been approached in the same way for such a very long time.

The heart of the issue is what we looked at in the preceding chapter. We are so used to tying *virtue* to *self-control* that our kneejerk reaction to its decline is to double down on effort and look for a culprit: the kids, their parents, teachers, social media. *We need instead to reframe, not because we are failing but because we don't know why we are failing.*

Teachers will tell you, and not without justification, that they are educators and not therapists trying to deal with problems that are not of their making. Their argument is that children spend a small amount of their waking time (13.64 per cent) at school and the remaining time at home. The not-so-hidden implication is that if a child is having character problems this must be because of what is happening in the home environment. In other words, you can't expect teachers to undo what is being done when kids are not under their watchful eye. But then …

Students encounter stresses at school that they do not encounter at home, sometimes so great that it tips them into allostatic overload. What's more, the direction of negative influence is often the reverse: it is while they are at school that many students acquire a set of defence mechanisms that were never seen in the home and that disrupt the harmony that the family had previously enjoyed. I can honestly say that this happened to us with our two neurodivergent kids.

Still another important point is that the school-to-home ratio is not as tilted as it might appear when one calculates total waking hours against hours spent in school. During the academic year, children spend roughly nine hours a day at school and getting to and from it. The more realistic number is around 1,600 hours consumed by school over 180 days. Of that time, around four to five hours a day is spent at home – bearing in mind that the time in the morning before leaving for school is, as every parent knows, a non-factor. The rest of the child's time in the home is – or at least, should be! – spent in sleep. The 1,600 school hours are counterbalanced by around 900 home hours, less amount of time spent on homework and extracurricular activities, and, of course, the hours consumed online.

For half of the year, two-thirds of a student's waking time is centred on school. It is no wonder that the traits acquired there should dominate a child's developing personality, especially when we factor in the neurobiologically driven decline of parental and corresponding increase in peer influence. It is amid peers that teens must develop virtue. And like it or not, what happens at school does not stay at school. So, schools must respond to the prosocial demands being made upon them, however great these might be.

This is not a novel idea. Since the beginning of the eighteenth century, philosophers have been insisting that the primary objective of schooling is moral. The self-styled "French Swedenborg," Charles Bernard Renouvier, was appalled by "the weakening sense of duty, justice, equality, reciprocity, and respect" in French students of the time, and called on schools to amend this condition.[32] But he saw this decline in terms of self-control, which he firmly believed could only be fostered through harsh discipline. His reaction was regressive and aggressive, the result of his own stress (coupled with his reading of Swedenborg?).

This is where we started, with Socrates (or was it Gilgamesh?) bemoaning the "waywardness of today's youth." Ever since Plato, we have accepted that we must look to schooling to thwart the "demise of virtue." It's the *how* that generation after generation of educators have found so elusive. But what has yet to be considered is *how to approach the how*.

Self-Reg Schools

The role of the school leader, *qua* leader, is not to choose for students and then compel them to abide by those choices. Rather, it is to help students become capable of choosing for themselves, to learn how to question and test hypotheses, absorb the lessons of history, be exposed to moral thinking, explore their creative side. That is the whole point of public education and the reason why it has such unparalleled social benefits. It is because we are teaching kids how to think for themselves, to question their own beliefs so that they don't succumb to the lure of misbelief.

To be a leader, any sort of leader, is to promote the shared sense of safety, both emotional and physical, that makes homeostasis/rationality possible. The demagogue does the exact opposite. He constantly returns to threatening themes to keep feelings of security at bay. Where the former instils calm, the latter foments chaos. Where the former cultivates autonomy, the latter seeks submission.

The lesson here for leaders who want to turn their school into a Virtue Academy is that their greatest asset, and their greatest liability, is the Interbrain. Limbic resonance sets the stage to lead a group in Red Brain into homeostasis OR into cacostasis. Create a calm environment and virtue can grow; create a culture of fear and instances of fight-or-flight will multiply, as will freeze or dissociation. When that happens, you can no longer privilege reason. Students will be in no state to process character messages; staff will be in no state to transmit such messages.

A Virtue Academy is constantly working on promoting Blue Brain/Red Brain balance, not just at the macro but also at the micro level. We need to encourage students to participate in what in anthropology are referred to as acephalous groups, in which there is no titular head and decision making is distributed. Red Brain processes promote cohesion, Blue Brain processes, rationality. This is why study groups, student councils, after-school clubs, sports teams, and community action associations are so important; but these are only functional when the individuals in the group are in homeostatic balance.

Look at any charismatic leader and you'll see how each was surrounded by charismatic leaders in their own right. Lincoln had Seward, Stanton, Grant, and Mary Todd Lincoln. Ghandi had Nehru, Patel, Kriplani, and Rajiji. Mandela had Tutu, Tambo, Sisilu, and Ramaphosa. Martin Luther King Jr. had Jackson, Young, Lewis, and, of course, Coretta Scott King. And a school leader has fellow administrators, educators, other staff members, and, not to be ignored, student leaders. But all need to be in Blue Brain/Red Brain balance if they are to inspire the same in others. All need to be doing Self-Reg themselves, not just to lead by example, but to lead.

The most important lesson to be learned from all this is that virtue needs balance to flourish. Dysregulation is its great nemesis. Homeostasis is top-down/bottom-up. Just as prosocial stress that we are feeling can prevent us from seeing that students, or for that matter staff members, are chronically hyperaroused, the same prosocial stress can lead us to embrace punitive measures in a desperate attempt to stop the tide. But just as mindful self-regulation develops *paulatinamente,* so too does homeostatic balance. Indeed, the two phenomena are joined at the hip. And ours is a culture where both are being systematically undermined.

Over the years, I have seen schools that were once renowned as Virtue Academies but have now declined morally as well as academically. Stirring character messages from a bygone era still line the walls, but only to gather dust, unread by anyone. The dominant mood is that of discouragement, bordering on despair.

But I have also seen examples of the exact opposite: schools that were once down-trodden, spiritually as well as physically, but are now thriving. Schools full of students that have begun to dream big. To pursue a dream requires effort. But you can neither force nor entice students to make the commitment required; rather, we want to help them experience *flow* so that they will embrace rather than flee from a challenge.

The lesson here is that if the brain remains plastic, so too does virtue. But what enables the growth of virtue is not a renewed burst of synaptogenesis; it is the empathy that feeds on limbic resonance. The Interbrain can be the conduit for remarkable restorative powers, and nowhere more so than in a school that is on the pathway to becoming a Virtue Academy. But a school can only arrive at this destination if its students are not compliant but, rather, all share a sense of belongingness. The research is unequivocal on this point.[33] The stumbling block, as always, is the How, and will remain so as long as we continue to think of virtue in terms of values that have to be imposed rather than instincts that need to be cultivated.

In *Self-Reg Schools: A Handbook for Educators*, Susan Hopkins and I set out to address this pressing issue of the How by mapping out the four major pathways that we have observed in our work with schools. The Self-Reg strategies and tools that we explore are designed to help staff and students experience the homeostatic balance that promotes virtue at both the individual and the institutional level. But this is a book that is intended to be read *with* students; they must never be excluded from these discussions.

For virtue to flourish once again, students must be capable of choosing how they act and what they believe. But for that to happen in today's world, they have to understand the hook model and the price they are paying for being constantly subjected to dopamine hijacking in everything from what they eat and wear to what they watch and want. They, ultimately, must be the ones to challenge the "Evil-by-Designers" that society has allowed to proliferate; what businesses are allowed to do *to them*, rather than *for them*.[34]

As happened with the dismantling of the Berlin Wall, youth have to take an active part in demolishing the disconnect that is harming their lives. Only thus will they become menschen, which means recognizing the forces that are preventing this from happening. And for us to help them, we have to shift our thinking from *force-feeding* to *nurturing*.

At the end of the day – or rather, the start of a Brand New Day – a Self-Reg leader is someone who inspires rather than exhorts.

The Message on the Lintel

My motto for MEHRI was: "Park Your Ego at the Door." I suppose I had Plato's Academy in mind.[35] Certainly not Dante's Inferno.[36] My thinking at the time was simply that, to live up to the mission that Milt and Ethel Harris had tasked us with, we had to keep our minds focused on that mission, which was nothing less than doing our part, however small that might be, in the furtherance of a Just Society.

Foremost, I was addressing myself. And then, of course, my colleagues. Not just the scientists, therapists, support staff, and all the students and volunteers at MEHRI, but a discipline that, I worried, had a tendency to lose sight of children and their families; that had begun to see autism research as a battleground between opposing ideologies (the prospect of government funding tends to fuel such conflicts). A fiercely competitive arena in which researchers saw themselves as engaged in a fight with fellow academics, each with their own research agenda, all battling for scarce university resources and honours.

In the terms that David Brooks employs, I worried about the conflict between the *two Adams* depicted in the Book of Genesis: Adam 1, who strives only for success, and Adam 2, who above all seeks to serve.[37] I hoped for a research centre where each of us was focused on the needs of THIS CHILD and THIS FAMILY. But the reality of modern academics is such that, by the end of the MEHRI study, I was swept up in the issue of whether the outcome data were robust enough to be published in a top-tier journal. I more than anyone had lost sight of my motto.

That, I hope, is the last time this ever happens to me. But I'm fortunate that it did. It forced me to think hard about how ego defences are as great an obstacle to *service* as ego needs. To realize that insecurity and avoidance can be every bit as great a deterrent to service as narcissism and grandiosity. To strive for "an ego that shrinks to a point of no extension"[38] so as to inspire the same in others.

I shared all this with Susan Hopkins and found in her a kindred spirit: someone who was driven for TMC to succeed *to help children and families*. Someone who recognized that we needed to park our egos at the door to pursue this mission. And it was watching what happened as a result of this mindset that led me to start thinking about the very real possibility of turning all schools into Virtue Academies, all communities into safe havens, to bring joy to all families, nuclear, extended, and societal.

By no means am I suggesting that TMC is a Virtue Academy. But we are certainly striving to become one. It has been fascinating to see how this aspiration has spread like a virus through the Self-Reg community: the desire to learn and teach; to be part of the movement and spread the message to others, including parents, organizations, and professionals outside the educational purview of Self-Reg; to nurture creativity, whether it be in poems, blogs, videos, and artwork, or participating in Foundations courses; to hold Institutes where the boundary between science and play is blurred.

We never set out to nurture such desires. At least, not consciously. We were focused on having:

- A shared goal
- A GPS to guide us, one that is continually interrupting to say, "You have left the planned route. Would you like to return to it or update your route?"
- Maybe even a GPS with a POI app that would help us to figure out what our next destination should be
- And most important of all: a true community, in which Susan and I may be *Primi inter Pares*, but certainly nothing more.

This last point is critical. Neither Susan nor I suffered from the Moses Syndrome. Our goal from the start was to absorb and disseminate as best we could the advances taking place in the science of self-regulation. For TMC to serve the needs of the Self-Reg community, we needed to listen and learn and never pontificate. One of the big discoveries that we made at our summer Institutes was that the planned restorative activities alongside the lectures sent us into Group Red Brain where the boundary between self and other was blurred: egos are sublimated whether you want this to happen or not.

As we saw above, the emotional contagion that sweeps through a group in Red Brain can go in polar opposite directions: positive or negative; inclusive or exclusive; calm or agitated; liberated or oppressed. The question is, what is the role of leaders in influencing the direction in which others proceed? We have seen the answer in our growing cohort of Self-Reg leaders. They are the ones who are turning the dream into a reality. But only because they themselves are tried-and-true Self-Reggers.

If a leader is anxious, angry, uncertain, or afraid, those are the emotions that spread through a group. When leaders are calm, collected, and confident, so too will be the group. No leader can fake composure, which is why, like method actors, they have to be calm themselves before they can lead, knowing that what they are feeling will *leak out*. When a group is in Red Brain, that is the communication channel to which they are attuned. Attitudes and biases are transmitted, ego defences cannot be concealed, compassion can never be feigned, hubris is always on full display.

Calmness begets calmness as balance begets balance. Strictly speaking, this is redundant. The most important lesson we learnt at MEHRI was that parents needed to be calm in order to have a calming effect on their children. The therapists needed to be calm in order to help parents feel the same. Devin and I needed to be calm in order for the staff to be calm. (I can't say how fortunate I was to have Devin by my side.)

I noted above how a vacuum is created in Group Red Brain into which steps a leader, *qua* surrogate executive function. In that role, a leader can either up- or down-regulate others, just as caregivers do with an infant. This means that those who are intent on creating a Just Society must first work on their own self-regulation. Only in a balanced Blue Brain/Red Brain state will they be able to calm those who are anything but.

Hyperarousal creates the conditions for fight-or-flight in the way that hot and dry weather creates the conditions for a forest fire: it doesn't take much of a spark to set off a conflagration. In fight-or-flight the return to homeostasis is far removed. What is truly extraordinary, however, is how a calm leader can have a calming effect in even the most combustible of conditions.

Watch the speech that Robert Kennedy gave in Indianapolis when he delivered the news that Martin Luther King Jr. had just been assassinated.[39] Conflagrations were happening all over the US, and if ever there was a spark to set off another one this was it. But listen to the tones and the soothing manner in which RFK spoke to the crowd about kindness and compassion, and you can literally feel the calm spreading through the crowd. By the end of the speech, all were singing from the same prosocial hymnal.

How was this possible? There is a fascinating physiological explanation. A soothing voice is literally a form of touch, caressing the inner ear with gentle airwaves. The result is the release of oxytocin, which serves to inhibit the stress response, just as does gently stroking the skin.

This point is the foundation of Co-Reg. It is a case of not just emotional but physiological resonance. When our CARE is activated, it modulates our voice, touch, gaze. Without being aware of this happening, we trigger oxytocin and endogenous opioids in another. As we explain in our Gray Brain Lectures (forthcoming), care begets care because CARE activates CARE. RFK triggered a chain reaction, a wave or oxytocin surging through the crowd.

This phenomenon helps us to understand one of the most remarkable aspects of this quite extraordinary PEC. CARE applies not only to one-on-one but also to one-many interactions. Whether we are talking of families, communities, schools, or societies in general, it is CARE, not competition, that enables humans to live in harmony.

Which brings me to the last conceptual distinction, highlighted above; namely, between *force-feeding* and *nurturing*. A Just Society disdains compliance and embraces growth. It is a society that seeks not to control children's nature but to nourish it; that recognizes just how great an obstacle inherited biases can be to potentiating human potential; that embraces the core value that *there is no such thing as a bad, lazy, or stupid kid*. Our thinking that this is the case is what leads to it being the case.

If I were to choose a new inscription for the lintel of the doorway into TMC – for the lintel of every doorway, whether it be over a home, a school, or the Houses of Parliament – I would say that Dante was six-sevenths of the way there. It's just the imperative that he got wrong. What it should say is this:

Embrace Hope All Ye Who Enter Here

Conclusion

I set out to write a book presenting as cogently as I could the far-reaching implications of the paradigm revolution described in these pages, namely, the primacy of relationships not just at the interpersonal but at the inter-neural level. Indeed, the argument of the first chapter is that you cannot understand the dynamics of the former without a grasp of the latter, and vice versa.

The message of all the scientists canvassed in these pages is that robust interpersonal/inter-neural *relationships* are needed – essential – if we are to create a Just Society. The last word must go, however, not to the scientists who have done this groundbreaking research, but to the Self-Reggers who are doing such extraordinary work on a daily basis. If not for the inspiration that they provide, I doubt I would have had the stamina needed to do any sort of justice to this project.

These words should not be treated lightly. My own Red Brain, like everyone's, craves role models – not the sort that you might read about in hagiographies (or what is more common, in autobiographies), but the sort that you observe when reading the reflections of Self-Reggers as they relate what they are learning in their TMC Foundations courses to the real problems they are dealing with in their classrooms or schools, in their homes, with friends and family, in their own lives.

With inspiration comes a new level of understanding. What we have witnessed at TMC has led me to think hard about this point that C.P. Snow made:

> I now believe that if I had asked [humanists] an even simpler question – such as, What do you mean by *mass*, or *acceleration*, which is the scientific equivalent of saying, *Can you read?* – not more than one in ten of the highly educated would have felt that I was speaking the same language.[1]

The idea that scientists and humanists are "speaking a different language" is more than just a metaphor. Like natural languages, every branch of science has its own unique vocabulary and grammar. Learning how to "speak neuroscience" involves more than just mastering terms and experimental procedures: it amounts to *learning how to think neuroscience*. Neuroscience is a languaculture every bit as unique as English – although maybe not as difficult to master.

If you try to travel in a foreign country armed only with an essential phrase book, you will quickly find yourself relying on gestures to communicate. It is impossible to speak a language properly without some command of its core reflexive concepts, such as *meaning* and *reference*.[2] The same is true for any science.

It would never occur to a physics teacher to ask their students to explain *acceleration* before they'd mastered the concepts of *vector* and *velocity*. Introductory courses invariably begin by talking about the interaction between matter and energy, and then taking students through the basics of scientific notation, just as we teach children to ask, "What does w mean?" before we get to simple sentences. Eventually we'll get to Shakespeare.

My hope was that *Reframed: Self-Reg for a Just Society* might serve in a similar way as an elementary primer in the language of *Tri-unese*. My thinking has long been that, with the collapse of the scientist/practitioner languacultural barrier, there will likewise be a collapse of the *two cultures* mentality. In its stead will be psychologists and neuroscientists, parents and educators, working together to potentiate every child's potential.

Certainly, there will continue to be sub-dialects. I can well appreciate how parents and educators might not want to learn the fundamentals of power analysis or why the P300 is such an important event-related potential. And psychologists and neuroscientists may not know – or want to know – the first thing about colic or diaper rash. Yet as far as concerns the behaviour of infants, children, and youth, they are all asking the same questions, and how each group sets about to answer those questions will strongly influence the thinking of the other.

In other words, there needs to be a constant exchange of ideas; and for any sort of fluid interchange to exist, we need to be speaking a common language. The scientist needs this conduit every bit as much as the parent or the educator. For as we have seen, the meaning of an experiment shifts depending on how it is viewed. With new ways of speaking/thinking, the significance of an outcome can change dramatically.

Take the Marshmallow Task. Mischel designed this experiment to measure self-control, and he assumed that his results did indeed provide an insight into the downstream consequence of its early possession.[3] There was an established tradition leading up to this interpretation, beginning long before Freud's writings on the superego. In fact, impulsivity had become a leading issue in the 1950s.[4] But all these studies were shaped by an ancient, self-control paradigm that informed Mischel's thinking.

The unspoken assumption underlying his interpretation was that the child *wants* the extra reward; *tries to restrain themself* so as to obtain it; and if they fail, it is only because they were not *strong enough* to resist the temptation. But even if we should abandon this self-control way of thinking, Mischel's results nonetheless still stand. Important results: just waiting, according to the canons of Self-Reg, to be reframed.

Suddenly, our way of thinking about the significance of the task is transformed. Instead of looking at the Marshmallow Task as a measurement of self-control, we see it as providing a glimpse into *how* – not *whether* – a child self-regulates. Do they seek to simply get rid of the stressor, or try to direct attention away from it? As a result of seeing the study differently, we begin to explore different ways of responding to the needs of the child who struggles with the task: we look for ways to enhance their self-regulation, rather than trying to "strengthen their willpower." In short: Self-Reg versus the Spartan Solution.[5]

The new languaculture of Self-Reg does not – could not – render the standard interpretation of a scientific study unintelligible. Rather, it exposes a new – and possibly richer – meaning waiting to be gleaned. And unlike the image that Snow made famous, where scientists and humanists at a cocktail party unable to communicate, it has both "sides" joining together and melding into a harmonious group, united not just by a common goal but by the shared understanding that renders this possible.

The same thing has to happen at the societal level if we are ever to build a Just Society. To start with, political dialogue needs to be reframed in much the same way that we reframe a scientific experiment. Take, for example, the common refrain that current political debate has become intolerably polarized. But then, that is just a way of describing the absence of genuine dialogue. We have to be careful that we don't treat a descriptive term as if it were explanatory. The reality is, actors are speaking past, not to, each other, in part because the two sides are speaking different languages.

In other words, we are dealing not just with a clash between ideologies but with different languacultures. This was the point we looked at in chapter 9: the different interpretations of *freedom* (positive versus negative). The one side sees *freedom* as signifying *You are the master of your own destiny*; the other, that *freedom* means *Your destiny is not determined by masters*. The former insists that unfree individuals have only themselves to blame for their condition; the latter, that subjugated individuals never had any *choice* in the matter.

So too with the meaning of *justice*. The one side insists that those who choose to violate the moral code must suffer the consequences (Cicero). The other, that justice depends on correcting inequities (Aristotle). You cannot begin to build a Just Society until everyone understands the same thing by the term. Herein lies the reason why institutions and laws alone will not suffice for its realization.

A Just Society requires that everyone can distinguish between *justice* and *injustice*. But that will only happen when everyone has mastered Triunese. And when they speak this not just with each other, but with children. And not just with their own children, but with all children.

Kids learn the rudiments of Triunese very early, via limbic communication. Long before categorical perception sets in, an infant is learning to distinguish between *safe* and *unsafe*. That is, neuroception precedes categorical perception.[6] A child doesn't just hear words; they feel the emotions conveyed in those words.

How we respond to an infant's neuroception shapes more than the child's stress-reactivity: it shapes how the child sees their caregivers, how they see others, how they see themselves. Just as we can't expect students to grasp *acceleration* before they have understood *mass*, or to read *Hamlet* before they can read *Dick and Jane*, so too we can't expect children to ever understand *justice* and *injustice* if they haven't experienced *empathy* and *compassion*. What matters here are not just the Blue Brain words that we use, but the Red Brain messages that we send.

The limbic messages that a child hears will then shape the language that they use to speak to themselves. This internalized, self-directed dialogue – what Lev Vygotsky referred to as "inner speech" – will shape their emotions and attitudes throughout life. But will it be the language of self-recrimination or self-compassion? Self-certainty or self-reflection? Self-control or self-regulation?

A Just Society is created by a united army of Just Societers, all of them fluent in Triunese. Parents, relatives, siblings, friends, neighbours, doctors, educators, artists, musicians, philosophers, psychologists, neuroscientists, complete strangers, all familiar with the core concepts of Triunese: the "differences I have sought to teach" between *misbehaviour* and *stress-behaviour*; *oppositional defiance* and *Angstbeisser*; *compliance* and *freeze*; *lying* and *confabulation*; *laziness* and *limbic braking*; *inattentive* and *offline*; *impulsive* and *reactive*; *rational, irrational,* and *non-rational*.

But ultimately, a Just Society is created by those who don't just understand that there's no such thing as a bad, lazy, or stupid kid, but actually do something about it.

Where Do We Go from Here?

How times have changed since the time I penned these concluding remarks! Or perhaps, what has really changed is our awareness of the seriousness of the currents that were bubbling beneath the surface when I wrote the first edition of *Reframed*. What we are living through now calls for deeper reflection and more vigorous action.

I am writing this final section in April 2024. The results of the US election are seven months away. This election has become a defining moment in the fate of democracy, worldwide. I am optimistic that the democratic spirit will triumph. But assuming that it does, it is essential that we do not lose sight of how close we came to chaos. And if history teaches us anything, it is how easy it is to forget.

I find it a little hard to believe, given the searing impact that the Eichmann trial had on me when I was growing up, that two-thirds of Europeans between the ages of eighteen and forty-four have never even heard of Eichmann.[7] But then, this is exactly the pattern that John Gray described in his *Straw Dogs*: A great evil is committed, soon to be forgotten, only to occur again. "What has been will be again, what has been done will be done again; there is nothing new under the sun" (Ecclesiastes 1:9).

But that is not the note on which I wish to end. I can't help but see the Book of Ecclesiastes as the musings of a tired old man whose final message is a reflection of his feelings of failure. This is the Solomon who ignored the moral precepts spelled out in Deuteronomy and amassed both riches and foreign wives, the Solomon who "turned his heart after other gods and his heart was not fully devoted to the LORD his God, as the heart of David his father had been" (1 Kings 11:4). It was this moral collapse that led to the destruction of the Temple and the splitting of Israel into two nations.

Better to say nothing at all than tell those whom you might still influence that "wisdom is meaningless," simply because all must die. Rather than resigning ourselves to the inevitability of chaos, we must never cease trying to *explain the seemingly inexplicable*. That, you might say, is the battle cry of Self-Reg. Our eyes are fixed on future generations as well as on our own.

The more I've thought about this issue, the more I've come to feel that one of the big lessons here is that it is time to move beyond Santayana's famous maxim that "those who do not learn history are doomed to repeat it." In its place we might substitute: Those who do not *understand* history are doomed to repeat it. But to understand history demands more than the tools that have traditionally been available to historians.

Starting with Thucydides, history has been seen as an attempt to understand the past though the narratives of the period, sifting through stories and documents. Yet the historian, like all social scientists, must – as Peter Winch argued in his great *The Idea of a Social Science and Its Relation to Philosophy* – be careful to distinguish between reasons and causes. And now Self-Reg introduces a further distinction.

First, Self-Reg reframes *causality* in the realm of human action, viewing behaviour not just in terms of psychological or social causes but, closer to home, the result all too often of ancient survival systems. But then, we need to look at these systems as both personal and interpersonal, communicated instantaneously from one limbic system to the next through the medium of limbic resonance. As a result of reframing, Self-Reg highlights a third variable to stand alongside rationality and irrationality: non-rationality. How individuals construct – or rather, accept – explanations of behaviour that they would otherwise find puzzling, shameful, or self-destructive.

The Self-Reg historian sets out to explain:

(1) What caused a group, or an entire Society, to slip into non-rationality
(2) What influenced the manner in which individuals construed their own behaviour

Confabulations are both individual and socially distributed, each reinforcing the other, neither operating in splendid isolation. Accordingly, we need a different model to explain Group Red Brain behaviour: the crowds, for example, lining the streets in Nuremberg, cheering the arrival of Nazism. Instead of privileging rationality and looking at this behaviour in Blue Brain terms – e.g., shared beliefs – we must see this behaviour as non-rational, a contagion of *misbelief*. Viewed thus, what we see is similar to the dizzying flight pattern of a murmuration of starlings, with emotions swooping and diving and wheeling through a group in unison, confabulations soon to follow like contrails.

The fledgling science of bird behaviour [*sic*] has developed a 3D simulation of what Craig Reynolds called a "flock of 'boids.'"[8] A team of computer scientists, theoretical physicists, and behavioural biologists found that starlings respond to the movements of the six or seven birds nearest them. The reasons why the birds congregate in flocks are much as you would expect: safety in numbers, keeping warm together, sharing information about food sources. Some of the factors that cause the balletic patterns that we see are the appearance of a predator (e.g., a hawk or falcon), a change in weather or thermals, the sudden detection of a food source.

The goal here is to understand the adaptive pressures that created this remarkable animal behaviour. A similar approach needs to be undertaken in regard to a pandemonium of humans. With one big difference. Where humans really are unique is that we – and only we – set about to *rationalize* why we are swooping and diving and wheeling together. Even when – especially when – we haven't the slightest clue. Here we need a different team of scientists working alongside historians: neuroscientists, social psychologists, and of course, Self-Reggers.

The approach pursued in *Reframed: A Self-Reg Revolution* is one that seeks to understand the forces that underlay crowd behaviour such as occurred in Germany in 1933. And then, the very different crowd behaviour that proliferated in Germany in 1945, when the stories swung from "Aryan master-race" to "persecuted victims" – either of Nazi propaganda or international aggression. The Nuremberg Defence was born in this swing: more defence mechanism than moral defence.

There is a deep lesson to be learned from how the Allies responded to the needs of post-war Germany, with a massive educational as well as economic restructuring. Not at all the lesson to be drawn from the Book of Ecclesiastes. The biological fact

that our limbic brakes kick in under acute emotional and prosocial stress does not mean that we are powerless to resist the spell
of demagoguery. But to do so we must first recognize *that and why*
we feel powerless. The key to helping a child shift from maladaptive to growth-promoting modes of self-regulation is to help them
grasp what it feels like to be calm. A similar point applies in the
prosocial domain: what it feels like to choose.[9]

Biden, in his acceptance speech at the 2020 Democratic National
Convention, spoke of how

> We can choose the path of becoming angrier, less hopeful, and more
> divided, a path of shadow and suspicion. Or we can choose a different
> path and, together, take this chance to heal, to be reborn, to unite – a
> path of hope and light.

That has been the goal of this new edition of *Reframed*: not just
to want, but to be capable of *choosing*, a different path. If history
teaches us anything, it is that, however soaring it might be, rhetoric alone will not suffice. We desperately need to understand the
factors that kept us on the path we were on. We need to create the
conditions that render such a choice conceivable.

When it seems that our fate is sealed, we have to understand the
stresses that have led to this feeling of hopelessness and helplessness. Only then can we forge a different path. That is the crux of
the extraordinary message at the beginning of the Book of Begin-
nings that "God created man in His own image" (Genesis 1:27).
What makes human beings unique is that they have their "own
mind to choose between good and evil" (Genesis 3:22). But first
one must know the difference between good and evil. And that is
only possible in "a mind that understands or eyes that see or ears
that hear" (Deuteronomy 29:4).

The goals that drive and revive my spirit whenever it flags are
to have a mind that understands; to help others in whatever way I
can to see and to hear; to long for a Just Society as much as I have
always done; to confront the enormous challenges that lie ahead,
together.

Notes

Acknowledgments

1 T. Axworthy and P. Trudeau, *Towards a Just Society: The Trudeau Years* (Markham, ON: Viking, 1990).

Introduction

1 S. Shanker, *Calm, Alert, and Learning: Classroom Strategies for Self-Regulation* (Toronto: Pearson, 2012).

2 S. Shanker, *Self-Reg: How to Help Your Child (and You) Break the Stress Cycle and Successfully Engage with Life* (New York: Penguin, 2016).

3 "Self-Reg Foundations Certificate Program," The MEHRIT Centre, https://self-reg.ca/learn/online-courses-with-dr-shanker/level-1 -certification-self-reg-foundations/.

4 The website for Xaeli K'ogola (Marion Village) is at https://tlichohistory .ca/en/stories/xaeli-kogola-marion-village.

5 Quoted in R. Graham, ed., *The Essential Trudeau* (Toronto: McClelland and Stewart, 1999), 16.

6 For a detailed account of the method, see Shanker, *Self-Reg: How to Help.*

7 See B.T. Swimme, *Hidden Heart of the Cosmos: Humanity and the New Story* (Maryknoll, NY: Orbis Books, 1999).

1. The Science of Self-Reg

1 Thomas S. Kuhn, *The Structure of Scientific Revolutions* (Chicago: University of Chicago Press, 1962).

2 Swimme, *Hidden Heart of the Cosmos.*

3 See S. Shanker, *Wittgenstein's Remarks on the Foundations of AI* (London: Routledge, 1998).

4 Paul D. MacLean, *The Triune Brain in Evolution: Role in Paleocerebral Functions* (London: Springer, 1990).

5 M.D. Lewis and R.M. Todd, "The Self-Regulating Brain: Cortical-Subcortical Feedback and the Development of Intelligent Action," *Cognitive Development* 22 (2007): 406–30; D. Tucker, *Mind from Body: Experience from Neural Structure* (New York: Oxford University Press, 2007).

6 M.D. Lewis, "Bridging Emotion Theory and Neurobiology through Dynamic Systems Modeling," *Behavioral and Brain Sciences* 28, no. 2 (2005): 169–94, 195–245.

7 George F. Striedter, *Principles of Brain Evolution* (New York: Oxford University Press, 2005).

8 Joseph LeDoux, *Anxious: Using the Brain to Understand and Treat Fear and Anxiety* (New York: Viking, 2015).

9 As it happens, this is not a novel argument; a similar idea can be found in T.H. Huxley's famous 1874 paper, "On the Hypothesis That Animals Are Automata." See Shanker, "Descartes' Legacy: The Mechanist/Vitalist Debates," in *Philosophy of Science, Logic, and Mathematics in the 20th Century* (London: Routledge, 1996).

10 A. Portmann, "Die Tragzeiten der Primaten und die Dauer der Schwangerschaft beim Menschen: Ein Problem der vergleichenden Biologie," *Rev. Suisse. Zool.* 48 (1941): 511–18.

11 Sharon Buck, "The Evolutionary History of the Modern Birth Mechanism," *Totem* 19, no. 1 (2011): 1; Sillymickel Adzema, "Secondary Altriciality and the Origins of Culture," https://angelsinnature .wordpress.com/2014/06/10/out-of-eden-part-four-secondary -altriciality-and-the-origins-of-culture-why-we-cant-get-no-satisfaction -and-what-it-has-to-do-with-being-born-helpless/

12 Shanker, *Self-Reg.*

13 S. Pinker, *The Language Instinct* (New York: William Morrow and Co., 1994).

14 Shanker, *Self-Reg,* Chapter 3.

15 S. Greenspan and S. Shanker, *The First Idea: How Symbols, Language and Intelligence Evolved from Our Primate Ancestors to Humans* (Cambridge, MA: Da Capo Press, 2004).

16 Stephen Jay Gould suggested nine months. See "Human Babies as Embryos," *Natural History* 85, no. 2 (1976): 22–6, republished in Gould, *Ever Since Darwin* (New York: W.W. Norton, 1981), 70–8.

17 See D. Narvaez, *Neurobiology and the Development of Human Morality* (New York: W.W. Norton, 2014).

18 Digby Tantam, *The Interbrain: How Unconscious Connections Influence Human Behaviour and Relationships* (London: Jessica Kingsley Publishers, 2018). The idea has been around for a long time. For example, Dan Stern talks about it in *The Interpersonal World of the Infant* (London: Routledge, 1985); Daniel Goleman refers to it as "neural wifi" in *Social Intelligence* (New York: Bantam, 2006).

19 See, e.g., A.N. Meltzoff and P.K. Kuhl, "Exploring the Infant Social Brain: What's Going On in There," *Zero to Three Journal* 36, no. 3 (2016): 2–9; V. Leong, E. Byrne, K. Clackson, S. Georgieva, S. Lam, and S. Wass, "Speaker Gaze Increases Information Coupling between Infant and Adult Brains," *PNAS* 114, no. 50 (2017): 13290–5.

20 C.A. Sandman, E.P. Davis, C. Buss, and L.M. Glynn, "Exposure to Prenatal Psychobiological Stress Exerts Programming Influences on the Mother and Her Fetus," *Neuroendocrinology* 95, no. 1 (2012): 7–21.

21 Ingfen Chen, "The Social Brain," *Smithsonian Magazine*, June 2009.

22 See L. Winerman, "What We Know without Knowing How," *APA* 36, no. 3 (2005).

23 See S. Blakeslee and M. Blakeslee for a fascinating application of this idea to pornography: *The Body Has a Mind of Its Own* (New York: Random House, 2007).

24 This is one of the areas in which Allan Schore's work has been absolutely pivotal. All of his books need to be read, but I would suggest starting with *Affect Regulation and the Origin of Self* (New York: Psychology Press, 1994). For an overview of the neuroscience research that has been done in this area, see J.A.C.J. Bastiaansen, M. Thioux, and C. Keysers, 'Evidence for Mirror Systems in Emotions," *Philosophical Transactions of the Royal Society B: Biological Sciences* 364, no. 1528 (2009): 2391–404.

25 For example, the concept of *information*: see S. Shanker, *Wittgenstein and the Turning-Point in the Philosophy of Mathematics* (London: Croom Helm Publishers, 1987).

26 But for starters, see C. Trevarthen, "Communication and Cooperation in Early Infancy," in M. Bullowa, ed., *Before Speech: The Beginning of Human Communication* (Cambridge: Cambridge University Press, 1979); Stern, *The Interpersonal World of the Infant*; A. Fogel, *Developing through Relationships* (Chicago: University of Chicago Press, 1993); S. Greenspan, *The Growth of the Mind* (New York: HarperCollins, 1998); D. Siegal, *The Developing Mind* (New York: Guilford Press, 1999); B. Beebe and F. Lachman, *The Origins of Attachment* (London: Routledge, 2013).

27 G.A. DeGangi, J.A. DiPietro, S.I. Greenspan, and S.W. Porges, "Psychophysiological Characteristics of the Regulatory Disordered Infant," *Infant Behavior and Development* 14 (1991): 37–50.

28 Walter Hess introduced the terms "ergotropic" and "tropotrophic," based on his research on the effects of stimulating different parts of the hypothalamus, to distinguish between the energy that an organism expends when exposed to a threat (ergotropic) and the mechanisms that promote recovery and the restoration of energy (tropotrophic). See W.R. Hess, *The Functional Organization of the Diencephalon* (New York: Grune and Stratton, 1957).

29 Greenspan and Shanker, *The First Idea*.

30 S.W. Porges, "Social Engagement and Attachment: A Phylogenetic Perspective," *Annals of the New York Academy of Sciences* 1008 (2003): 31–47.

31 Greenspan and Shanker, *The First Idea*.

32 S.W. Porges, *The Polyvagal Theory: Neurophysiological Foundations of Emotions, Attachment, Communication, Self-Regulation* (New York: W.W. Norton, 2011).

33 As we will see throughout the book, the recent history of the field has been an endless series of variations on a stress theme.

34 Marc Lewis and Rebecca Todd, "The Self-Regulating Brain: Cortical Sub-Cortical Feedback and the Development of Intelligent Action," *Cognitive Development* 22, no. 4 (2007): 406–30.

35 M.A. Rothschild and V. Schneider, "'Terminal Burrowing Behaviour' – A Phenomenon of Lethal Hypothermia," *International Journal of Legal Medicine* 107, no. 5 (1995): 250–6.

36 W.B. Cannon, *The Wisdom of the Body* (London: Kegan Paul, Trench, Trubner and Co., 1932).

37 Not surprisingly, this has led to the idea of a "shivering-diet." See F. Villarroya, "Shivering Unlocks New Way of Fighting Fat," *The Conversation*, 5 February 2014, http://theconversation.com /shivering-unlocks-new-way-of-fighting-fat-22662.

38 J. Hubbard, *The Survival Doctor's Complete Handbook* (White Plains, NY: Reader's Digest, 2016).

39 J.T. Burman, C. Green, and S. Shanker, "On the Meanings of Self-Regulation: Digital Humanities in Service of Conceptual Clarity," *Child Development* 86, no. 5 (2015): 1507–21.

40 D. Kessler, *The End of Overeating* (New York: Rodale, 2009).

41 D. Tantam, *Can the World Afford Autism Spectrum Disorder?* (London: Jessica Kingsley Publishers, 2009).

42 D. Casenhiser, S. Shanker, and J. Stieben, "Learning through Interaction in Children with Autism: Preliminary Data from a Social-Communication-Based Intervention," *Autism* 17, no. 2 (2013): 1–22

43 W. Mischel, Y. Shoda, and M.I. Rodriguez, "Delay of Gratification in Children," *Science* 244, no. 4907 (1989): 933–8.

44 T.E. Moffitt, L. Arseneault, D. Belsky, N. Dickson, R.J. Hancox, H.L. Harrington, R. Houts, R. Poulton, B.W. Roberts, S. Ross, M.R. Sears, W.M. Thomson, and A. Caspi, "A Gradient of Childhood Self-Control Predicts Health, Wealth, and Public Safety," *PNAS* 108, no. 7 (2011): 2693–8.

45 M. Sayette and J. Cresswell "Self-Regulatory Failure and Addiction," in *Handbook of Self-Regulation*, ed. K.D. Vohs and R.F. Baumeister (New York: Guilford Press, 2016), 571–90.

46 S. Shanker, "Caught in a Stress Cycle: When Self-Help Tips Aren't Nearly Enough," *Psychology Today*, 12 August 2016, https://www.psychologytoday.com/ca/blog/self-reg/201608/caught-in-stress-cycle.

47 T.A. Hare, C.F. Camerer, and A. Rangel, "Self-Control in Decision-Making Involves Modulation of the vmPFC Valuation System," *Science* 324, no. 5927 (2009): 646–8.

48 J.P. Herman, "Stress Response: Neural and Feedback Regulation of the HPA Axis," *Encyclopedia of Neuroscience* (Cambridge, MA: Academic Press, 2009), 292–8.

49 S.T. von Sömmerring, *Vom Baue des menschlichen Körpers*, Vol. 1 (Frankfurt: Varrentrapp und Wenner, 1791).

50 R. Cribiore, *Gymnastics of the Mind* (Princeton: Princeton University Press, 2005); see E.T. Berkman "Self-Regulation Training," in *Handbook of Self-Regulation*, ed. K.D. Vohs and R.F. Baumeister (New York: Guilford Press, 2016); N. Steinbeis, "What's Control Got to Do with It?," *BOLD*, 11 January 2017, https://bold.expert/whats-self-control-got-to-do-with-it/.

51 Porges, *The Polyvagal Theory*.

2. Reframing Human Nature

1 See P. Thibodeau and L. Boroditsky, "Metaphors We Think With: The Role of Metaphor in Reasoning," *PLoS One* 6, no. 2 (2011): 1–11.

2 Casenhiser, Shanker, and Stieben, "Learning through Interaction."

3 C.L. Crumley, "Heterarchy and the Analysis of Complex Societies," *Archaeological Papers of the American Anthropological Association* 6, no. 1 (1995): 1–5.

4 A.O. Lovejoy, *The Great Chain of Being: A Study of the History of an Idea* (1936; repr., London: Routledge, 1964).

5 Lovejoy, *The Great Chain*.

6 S. Porges, "Neuroception: A Subconscious System for Detecting Threats and Safety," *Zero to Three* 24, no. 5 (2004): 19–24.

7 L.E. Shapiro and T.R. Insel, "Infant's Response to Social Separation Reflects Adult Differences in Affiliative Behavior: A Comparative Developmental Study in Prairie and Montane Voles," *Developmental Psychobiology* 23, no. 5 (1990): 375–93.

8 B.J. King, *How Animals Grieve* (Chicago: University of Chicago Press, 2013); B.J. King, *The Dynamic Dance* (Cambridge, MA: Harvard University Press, 2009).

9 D. Narvaez, *Neurobiology*, 7; see also J. Panksepp, *Affective Neuroscience* (New York: Oxford University Press, 1998), 168.

10 D.E. Okobi, Jr., A. Banerjee, A.M.M. Matheson, S.M. Phelps, and M.A. Long, "Motor Cortical Control of Vocal Interaction in Neotropical Singing Mice," *Science* 363, no. 6430 (2019): 983–8.

11 C. Crockford, R. Wittig, and K. Zuberbühler, "Vocalizing in Chimpanzees Is Influenced by Social-Cognitive Processes," *Science Advances* 3, no. 11 (2017): 1–12.

12 D.F. Armstrong, *Original Signs: Gestures, Signs and the Sources of Language* (Washington, DC: Gallaudet University Press, 2002).

13 J. Panksepp and L. Bivan, *The Archaeology of Mind: Neural Origins of Human Emotion* (New York: W.W. Norton, 2012), 181.

14 A. Schore, *Right Brain Psychotherapy* (New York: W.W. Norton, 2019); Greenspan and Shanker, *The First Idea*.

15 R. Brewer, R. Cook, and G. Bird, "Alexithymia: A General Deficit of Interoception," *Royal Society Open Science* 12, no. 3 (2016): 1–9, https://doi.org/10.1098/rsos.150664.

16 Panksepp, *Affective Neuroscience*, 53.

17 Panksepp and Bivan, *The Archaeology of Mind*, 103.

18 "Mouse Research Links Adolescent Stress and Severe Adult Mental Illness," Johns Hopkins Medicine, 17 January 2003, https://www.hopkinsmedicine.org/news/media/releases/mouse_research_links_adolescent_stress_and_severe_adult_mental_illness.

19 F. De Waal, *Mama's Last Hug: Animal and Human Emotions* (New York: W.W. Norton, 2019).

20 King, *How Animals Grieve*.

21 B. Hare and V. Woods, *The Genius of Dogs: How Dogs Are Smarter Than You Think* (New York: Plume, 2013).

22 A. Bandura, *Self-Efficacy: The Exercise of Control* (New York: Worth Publishers, 1997).

23 G.J. Mogenson, D.L. Jones, and C.Y. Yim, "From Motivation to Action: Functional Interface between the Limbic System and the Motor System," *Progress in Neurobiology* 14, no. 2–3 (1980): 69–97.

24 G.J. Mogenson, C.R. Yang, and C.Y. Yim, "Influence of Dopamine on Limbic Inputs to the Nucleus Accumbens," *Annals of the New York Academy of Sciences* 537, no. 1 (1988): 86–100.

25 L.H. Margolis, G. Canty, M. Halstead, and J.D. Lantos, "Should School Boards Discontinue Support for High School Football?," *Pediatrics* 139, no. 1 (2017): 2016–22.

26 As always, Malcolm Gladwell is worth reading: see "Offensive Play: How Different Are Dogfighting and Football?," *New Yorker*, 19 October 2009, https://www.newyorker.com/magazine/2009/10/19/offensive-play.

27 See Wolf Pack Athletics, "Grit: A Journey with Nevada Football, Episode 1," YouTube, 21 July 2017, https://www.youtube.com /watch?v =c0e36weVJeo.

28 See E.W. Ris, "Grit: A Short History of a Useful Concept," *Journal of Educational Controversy* 10, no. 1 (2015): 1–18.

29 M. Ford, "What Is Priming? A Psychological Look at Priming and Consumer Behaviour," *MotiveMetrics*, 1 July 2013, http://blog.motivemetrics.com/What-is-Priming-A-Psychological-Look-at-Priming-Consumer-Behavior.

30 N. Hermann, "What Is the Function of the Various Brainwaves?," *Scientific American*, 22 December 1997, https://www.scientificamerican.com/article/what-is-the-function-of-t-1997–12–22/.

31 H. Jiang, M.P. White, M.D. Greicius, L.C. Waelde, and D. Spiegel, "Brain Activity and Functional Connectivity Associated with Hypnosis," *Cerebral Cortex* 27, no. 8 (2016): 4083–93.

32 A. Agassi, *Open: An Autobiography* (New York: Vintage, 2010), 3.

33 Agassi, *Open*, 11.

34 Agassi, *Open*, 28.

35 Agassi, *Open*, 29.

36 Agassi, *Open*, 21.

37 L. Greenemeier, "What Causes Someone to Act on Violent Impulses and Commit Murder," *Scientific American*, 12 January 2012, https://www.scientificamerican.com/article/anger-management-self-control/.

38 A.H. Maslow, *Religions, Values, and Peak Experiences* (London: Penguin Books, 1964).

39 R. Feynman, *"Surely You're Joking, Mr. Feynman!": Adventures of a Curious Character* (New York: W.W. Norton, 1985).
40 Art historians have speculated that one of the *ignudi* in the painting is not, as has been assumed, supposed to depict imperfection but rather a congenital back problem.

3. Reframing Development

1   R.L. Goldstone, "Influences of Categorization on Perceptual Discrimination," *Journal of Experimental Psychology* 123 (1994): 178–200.
2   G.P. Baker and P.M.S. Hacker, *Wittgenstein: Understanding and Meaning* (Oxford: Blackwell, 1980).
3   E. Goffman, *Frame Analysis* (New York: Harper and Row, 1974).
4   Burman, Green, and Shanker, "On the Meanings."
5   See S.G. Shanker, "Wittgenstein's Remarks on the Significance of Gödel's Theorem," in *Gödel's Theorem in Focus* (London: Routledge, 1988).
6   H. Wang, *From Mathematics to Philosophy* (London: Routledge, 1974).
7   N. Arikha, *Passions and Tempers* (New York: HarperCollins, 2007).
8   Sir J. Elliott, *Outlines of Greek and Roman Medicine* (London: W. Wood, 1914).
9   See W. Thomas Boyce, *The Orchid and the Dandelion* (London: Allen Lane, 2019).
10 In his wonderful book *La Curación por la Palabra en la Antigüedad Clásica* (Barcelona: Anthropos, 1987). I wonder sometimes whether Wittgenstein's view of philosophy was all that different, a question that the psychotherapist John Heaton explored in his fascinating *Wittgenstein and Psychotherapy* (London: Palgrave Macmillan, 2014).
11 See R. Sorabji, *Emotion and Peace of Mind: From Stoic Agitation to Christian Temptation* (Oxford: Oxford University Press, 2002); M. Nussbaum, *The Therapy of Desire: Theory and Practice in Hellenistic Ethics* (Princeton: Princeton University Press, 1994).
12 S. Shanker and D. Casenhiser, "Reducing the Effort in Effortful Control," in *A Wittgensteinian Perspective on the Use of Conceptual Analysis in Psychology*, ed. T. Racine and K. Slaney (London: Palgrave Macmillan, 2013).
13 H. Karp, *The Happiest Baby on the Block* (New York: Bantam, 2015).
14 "One keeps hearing the remark that philosophy really makes no progress, that the same philosophical problems that had occupied the Greeks are still occupying us. But those who say that do not understand the reason it is so. The reason is that our language has remained the same

and seduces us into asking the same questions over and over again."
L. Wittgenstein, *Big Typescript* (Oxford: Blackwell, 2005), 15.

15 A. Caspi and P.A. Silva, "Temperamental Qualities at Age Three Predict Personality Traits in Young Adulthood," *Child Development* 66, no. 2 (1995): 486–98.

16 Le Bain de Sonia, "Thalasso Bain Bébé Jumeaux – Twin Baby Bath," YouTube, 8 November 2013, https://www.youtube.com/watch?v =qY-d46-gPMI. See H. Holvoet, "Interview with Sonia Rochel of Thalasso Baby Bath," Baby Sleep Advice, 24 September 2018, https:// www.baby-sleep-advice.com/sonia-rochel-thalasso-baby-bath.html.

17 S. Porges, J.A. Doussard-Roosevelt, A.L. Portales, and P.E. Suess, "Cardiac Vagal Tone: Stability and Relation to Difficultness in Infants and 3 Year Olds," *Developmental Psychobiology* 27, no. 5 (1994): 289–300.

18 S. Porges, "Vagal Tone: A Physiologic Marker of Stress Vulnerability," *Pediatrics* 90, no. 3 (1992): 498–504.

19 M. Rothbart, *Becoming Who We Are* (New York: Guilford Press, 2012).

20 A. Fogel, *Body Sense: The Science and Practice of Embodied Self-Awareness* (New York: W.W. Norton, 2013); B. van der Kolk, *The Body Keeps the Score: Brain, Mind and Body in the Healing of Trauma* (New York: Viking, 2014); P. Ogden and J. Fisher, *Sensorimotor Psychotherapy* (New York: W.W. Norton, 2015).

21 Beebe and Lachman, *The Origins of Attachment*.

22 A. Thomas and S. Chess, *Temperament and Development* (New York: Brunner/Mazel, 1977).

23 I am indebted to Inge Bretherton's "The Origins of Attachment Theory: John Bowlby and Mary Ainsworth," *Developmental Psychology* 28 (1992): 759–75, and Deborah Blum's *Love at Goon Park* (New York: Basic Books, 2011), for the material covered in the first part of this section.

24 J.B. Watson, *Psychological Care of Infant and Child* (New York: W.W. Norton, 1928), 10.

25 A. Romano-Lax, *Behave* (New York: Soho Press, 2017).

26 The Department of Health had concluded that children should be placed in a sterile environment for their own protection. They seized on Watson's writings in the hope that if parents stopped kissing their children, this might prevent the transmission of germs. In other words, much like medieval Europe, their attitude was fear-driven. If you want your children to survive, don't touch them. Isolate them as much as possible so that you don't pass on streptococcus. Watson's approach to child rearing aligned perfectly with the government's attempts to counter the "miasma."

27 Of course, what the science had shown is how to condition a fear response; the positive attributes that Watson promised in "Psychology As the Behaviorist Views It," *Psychological Review* 20 (1913): 158–77 remained more elusive than ever.

28 He was shipped off to boarding school when he was seven years old and later remarked that not even a dog should suffer the same.

29 Anna Freud and Melanie Klein both remained committed to the classical Freudian idea that a child is attached to the mother because she is a food source.

30 In the first episode mom, baby, and experimenter are together in a room filled with toys. Then the experimenter leaves and mom and baby are alone for three minutes. Then a stranger enters. Then mom leaves, leaving the baby alone with the stranger. Mom comes back and the stranger leaves. Mom leaves and the baby is left alone for three minutes. The stranger comes back in. In the final episode, mom comes back.

31 C. Stifter, N.A. Fox, and S. Porges, "Facial Expressivity and Vagal Tone in 5- and 10-Month-Old Infants," *Infant Behavior and Development* 12, no. 2 (1989): 127–37.

32 J. Kagan, *Three Seductive Ideas* (Cambridge, MA: Harvard University Press, 1998), 5.

33 And indeed, have been put to the same use by criminal investigators. The FBI were able to catch the Unabomber by putting together a personality profile from the bits of information that they gathered.

34 Lewis R. Goldberg, "An Alternative Description of Personality: The Big-Five Factor Structure," *Journal of Personality and Social Psychology* 59, no. 6 (1990): 1216–29.

35 M.C. Ashton, K. Lee, M. Perugini, and P. Szarota, "A Six-Factor Structure of Personality-Descriptive Adjectives: Solutions from Psycholexical Studies in Seven Languages," *Journal of Personality and Social Psychology* 86, no. 2 (2004): 356–66.

36 In ALTAIC languages (including Turkic, Mongolic, and Tungusic language families), terms related to *honesty* and *humility* cannot be absorbed into the big five.

37 M. Agar, *Language Shock* (New York: William Morrow Paperbacks, 1994).

38 S. Kirchin, *Thick Concepts* (Oxford: Oxford University Press, 2013).

39 D. Marietta, "Conscience in Greek Stoicism," *Numen* 17, no. 3 (1970): 176–87.

4. The Age of Reason(s)

1 R. Descartes, *Discourse on Method and Related Writings* (New York: Penguin, 2000), 13.

2 J. Swift, *The Battle of the Books* (1704; repr., Scotts Valley, CA: CreateSpace Independent Publishing Platform, 2017).

3 A.C. Grayling, *Descartes* (New York: Walker and Company, 2006).

4 H. Cook, *The Young Descartes: Nobility, Rumour and War* (Chicago: University of Chicago Press, 2018).

5 Some of the most interesting commentaries – for example, S. Gaukroger, *Descartes* (Oxford: Oxford University Press, 1996) and Grayling, *Descartes* – show just how much is to be gained by looking at the texts in their historical and biographical contexts.

6 The answer, Lewis Carroll tells us *Alice in Wonderland*, is "because it can produce a few notes, although they are very flat."

7 Descartes, *Discourse*, 15.

8 Far more serious than the actual act of apostasy he was later falsely charged with: marrying a Calvinist in a Protestant church.

9 Descartes, *Discourse*, 13.

10 Baillet tells us that Descartes was in a state of high anxiety and nervous exhaustion when he had his famous dreams the night of 10 November 1619. See Grayling, *Descartes*.

11 As we see in the pusillanimous letters that Descartes sent to Mersenne, he was agonizing about whether or not to publish *Le Monde*.

12 Grayling, *Descartes*, 100–1.

13 Descartes, *Discourse*, 13.

14 The law of identity ($p = p$), the law of non-contradiction ($\sim.p$ & $\sim p$), and the law of excluded middle ($p \wedge \sim p$).

15 See my very first book, S. Shanker, *Wittgenstein and the Turning-Point in the Philosophy of Mathematics*.

16 "I call a perception *claire* when it is present and accessible to the attentive mind … I call a perception *distincte* if, as well as being *claire*, it is so sharply separated from all other perceptions that every part of it is *claire*." R. Descartes, *Meditations on First Philosophy, Early Modern Texts*, trans. Jonathan Bennet, 9, https://www.earlymoderntexts.com/assets/pdfs/descartes1641.pdf.

17 As P.K. Feyerabend argues in "Rationalism, Relativism and Scientific Method," in *Knowledge, Science and Relativism*, Philosophical Papers 3 (Cambridge, MA: Harvard University Press, 1999), http://cqi.inf.usi.ch/qic/Feyerabend1981.pdf.

18 Descartes, *Discourse*, 13.

19 Descartes, *Discourse*, 1.

20 Descartes, *Discourse*, 1.

21 In the *Apology* (38a), Plato attributes to Socrates the stirring lines: "if again I say that to talk every day about virtue and the other things about

which you hear me talking and examining myself and others is the greatest good to man, and that the unexamined life is not worth living, you will believe me still less. This is as I say, gentlemen, but it is not easy to convince you."

22 Descartes, *Discourse*, 1.

23 L. Festinger, H.W. Riecken, and S. Schachter, *When Prophecy Fails* (Minneapolis: University of Minnesota Press, 1957), 5.

24 Festinger, Riecken, and Schachter, *When Prophecy Fails*, 5.

25 See the classic paper by R.E. Nisbett and T.D. Wilson, "Telling More Than We Can Know," *Psychological Review* 84, no. 3 (1977): 231–59.

26 D. Kahneman, *Thinking, Fast and Slow* (New York: Anchor, 2013), 31.

27 Kahneman, *Thinking, Fast and Slow*. Gervais and Norenzayan ran a study a few years back showing that "mentally lazy" thinkers are more likely to believe in religion; see R.D. Fields, "Religion and Reason," *Psychology Today*, 26 April 2012, https://www.psychologytoday.com/ca/blog/the-new-brain/201204/religion-and-reason. And, not surprisingly, the same results have been observed in voting behaviours. See C.Y. Olivola and A. Todorov, "Elected in 100 Milliseconds," *Journal of Nonverbal Behavior* 34 (2010): 83–110.

28 See D. Ariely, *Predictably Irrational: The Hidden Forces That Shape Our Decisions* (New York: Harper, 2009); J. Bargh, *Before You Know It* (New York: Atria Books, 2017).

29 Kahneman, *Thinking, Fast and Slow*.

30 E.J. Langer, *Mindfulness* (Reading, MA: Addison-Wesley, 1989); Panksepp, *Affective Neuroscience*; LeDoux, *Anxious*.

31 Panksepp and Biven, *The Archeaology of Mind*.

32 G. Johnson, "Theories of Emotion," *Internet Encyclopedia of Philosophy*, accessed 15 November 2019, https://www.iep.utm.edu/emotion/.

33 R.M. Peters, "The Relationship of Racism, Chronic Stress Emotions, and Blood Pressure," *Journal of Nursing Scholarship* 38, no. 3 (2006): 234–40, https://www.ncbi.nlm.nih.gov/pubmed/17044340.

34 Ariely, *Predictably Irrational*, 45–6.

35 D. Ariely, *Misbelief: What Makes Rational People Believe Irrational Things* (New York: Harper, 2023).

36 D. Baumrind, "Effects of Authoritative Parental Control on Child Behavior," *Child Development* 37, no. 4 (1966): 887–907; D. Baumrind, "Current Patterns of Parental Authority," *Developmental Psychology* 41, no. 1 (1971): 44–50.

37 See L. Alcoff, "Democracy and Rationality: A Dialogue with Hilary Putnam," in *Women, Culture, and Development: A Study of Human*

Capabilities, ed. M.C. Nussbaum and J. Glover (Oxford: Oxford University Press, 1995), chapter 9, http://www.oxfordscholarship.com/view/10.109 3/0198289642.001.0001/acprof-9780198289647-chapter-9.

38 M. Lewis, I. Granic, and C. Lamm, "Behavioral Differences in Aggressive Children Linked with Neural Mechanisms of Emotion Regulation," *Annals of the N.Y. Academy of Science* 1094 (2006): 164–77.

39 N. Kardaras, *Glow Kids* (New York: St. Martin's Press, 2016).

40 R.S. Foa and Y. Mounk, "The Democratic Disconnect," *Journal of Democracy* 27, no. 3 (2016): 5–17.

41 D. Baumrind, "The Influence of Parenting Style on Adolescent Competence and Substance Use," *Journal of Early Adolescence* 11, no. 1 (1991): 62.

42 C.C. Robinson, B. Mandleco, S.F. Olsen, and C.H. Hart, "Authoritative, Authoritarian, and Permissive Parenting Practices: Development of a New Measure," *Psychological Reports* 77, no. 3 (1995): 819–30; C.C. Robinson, B. Mandleco, S.F. Olsen, and C.H. Hart, "The Parenting Styles and Dimensions Questionnaire (PSDQ)," *Handbook of Family Measurement Techniques* 3 (2001): 319–21.

43 M. O'Keefe, "Teen Dating Violence," Vawnet, April 2005, https:// vawnet.org/material/teen-dating-violence-review-risk-factors -and-prevention-efforts.

44 Children of authoritative parents have the highest levels of social and emotional development: L. Steinberg, J.D. Elmen, and N.S. Mounts, "Authoritative Parenting, Psychosocial Maturity, and Academic Success among Adolescents," *Child Development* 60, no. 6 (1989): 1424–36.

45 N. Eisenberg, F.A. Fabes, and T.L. Spinrad, "Prosocial Development," in *Handbook of Child Psychology: Social, Emotional, and Personality Development*, ed. N. Eisenberg, W. Damon, and R.M. Lerner (Hoboken, NJ: John Wiley and Sons, 2006), 646–718. See also K.R. Ginsburg, D.R. Durbin, J.F. García-España, E.A. Kalicka, and F.K. Winston, "Associations between Parenting Styles and Teen Driving, Safety-Related Behaviors and Attitudes," *Pediatrics* 124, no. 4 (2009): 1040–51; R.D. Parke and R. Buriel, "Socializaton in the Family," in *Handbook of Child Psychology*; M.C. Paulussen-Hoogeboom, G.J. Stams, J.M. Hermanns, T.T. Peetsma, and G.L. van den Wittenboer, "Parenting Style as a Mediator between Children's Negative Emotionality and Problematic Behavior in Early Childhood," *Journal of Genetic Psychology* 169, no. 3 (2008): 209–26.

46 K.R. Wentzel, "Are Effective Teachers Like Good Parents?," *Child Development* 73, no. 1 (2002): 287–301; G. Mugny, A. Chatard, and A. Quiamzade, "The Social Transmission of Knowledge at the University,"

European Journal of Psychology of Education 21, no. 413 (2006): 209–22; L.A.
Pellerin, "Applying Baumrind's Typology to High Schools," *Social Science
Research* 34, no. 2 (2005): 283–303; A. Quiamzade, G. Mugny, and J.M.
Falomir-Pichastor, "Epistemic Constraint and Teaching Style," *European
Journal of Psychology of Education* 24, no. 2 (2009): 181–90.

47 Quiamzade, Mugny, and Falomir-Pichastor, "Epistemic Constraint."
48 A. Alter, *Irresistible: The Rise of Addictive Technology and the Business of
Keeping Us Hooked* (New York: Penguin, 2017).
49 Baumrind, "The Influence of Parenting Style."

5. Privileging Rationality

1 Kahneman, *Thinking, Fast and Slow*, 34.
2 Indeed, Kahneman was one of the pioneers in the field of "pupillometry"
research; see, for example, his *Attention and Effort* (Englewood Cliffs, NJ:
Prentice-Hall, 1973).
3 A. Zénon, M. Sidibé, and E. Olivier, "Disrupting the Supplementary
Motor Area Makes Physical Effort Appear Less Effortful," *Journal of
Neuroscience* 35, no. 23 (2014): 8738, https://www.jneurosci.org/content
/jneuro/35/23/8737.full.pdf.
4 M.S. Gilzenrat, S. Nieuwenhuis, M. Jepma, and J.D. Cohen showed a
similar effect for drug-induced changes in arousal: "Pupil Diameter
Tracks Changes in Control State Predicted by the Adaptive Gain
Theory of Locus Coeruleus Function," *Cognitive, Affective and Behavioral
Neuroscience* 10, no. 2 (2010): 252–69.
5 Porges, *The Polyvagal Theory*.
6 E. Gellhorn, "The Emotions and the Ergotropic and Trophotropic
Systems," *Psychologische Forschung* 34, no. 1 (1970): 67–94,
https://doi.org/10.1007/BF00422863.
7 As did I when I first started working on this issue.
8 Kahneman, *Thinking, Fast and Slow*, 34.
9 And not just humans! See, for example, C. Boesch and H. Boesch-
Achermann, *The Chimpanzees of the Taï Forest* (Oxford: Oxford University
Press, 2000).
10 For example, pupil dilation also correlates with social anxiety.
11 Nisbett and Wilson, "Telling More."
12 If not before, to *Denkpsychologie* in the early twentieth century.
13 P.C. Wason, "Reasoning about a Rule," *Quarterly Journal of Experimental
Psychology* 20, no. 3 (1968): 273–81.
14 B. Rogoff, *Apprenticeship in Thinking* (Oxford: Oxford University Press,
1991).

15 See S.G. Shanker, "The Self-Reg View of 'Diagnosing' Oppositional
    Defiant Disorder," The MEHRIT Centre, 5 June 2016, https://self-reg.ca
    /2016/06/05/self-reg-view-diagnosing-oppositional-defiant-disorder/.
16 L. Tye, *The Father of Spin* (New York: Picador, 2013).
17 R.H. Tawney, *Religion and the Rise of Capitalism* (London: Routledge, 2017), 230.
18 According to Pearson, "It is to be feared that the confirmed loafer and the
    habitual vagrant are seldom capable of being reformed. It is a mistake to
    suppose that the typical pauper is merely an ordinary person who has
    fallen into distress through adverse circumstances. As a rule he is not an
    ordinary person, but one who is constitutionally a pauper, a pauper in his
    blood and bones. He is made of inferior material, and therefore cannot
    be improved to the level of the ordinary person." Quoted in J.R. Hay,
    The Development of the British Welfare State, 1880–1975 (London: Edward
    Arnold, 1978), 62.
19 N. Hagura, P. Haggard, and J. Diedrichsen, "Perceptual Decisions Are
    Biased by the Cost to Act," *Elife* 6 (2017): e18422, https://doi.org/10.7554
    /eLife.18422.
20 It may not seem that watching a bunch of dots on a screen and matching
    this with a physical action is a stress, but anyone who has ever had to
    bribe students to participate in this kind of study can attest to the fact
    that it definitely is.
21 As Adam Alter pointed out regarding the Müller-Lyer illusion in *Drunk
    Tank Pink* (New York: Penguin, 2014).
22 N. Wong, D.C. Beidel, D.E. Sarver, and E. Sims, "Facial Emotion
    Recognition in Children with High Functioning Autism and Children
    with Social Phobia," *Child Psychiatry and Human Development* 43, no. 5
    (2012): 775–94.
23 S.J. Webb, E. Neuhaus, and S. Faja, "Face Perception and Learning in
    Autism Spectrum Disorders," *Quarterly Journal of Experimental Psychology*
    70, no. 5 (2017): 970–86.
24 Tantam, *Can the World Afford*.
25 Morehouse and Gross interviewed famous athletes and artists who
    recounted how their personal breakthroughs occurred when they *stopped
    trying*. See L.E. Morehouse and L. Gross, *Maximum Performance* (New
    York: Simon and Schuster, 1977).
26 M. Levine, *The Myth of Laziness* (New York: Simon and Schuster, 2004).
27 V. Talwar and K. Lee, "A Punitive Environment Fosters Children's
    Dishonesty," *Child Development* 82, no. 6 (2011): 1751–8.
28 V. Talwar, C. Arruda, and S. Yachison, "The Effects of Punishment and
    Appeals for Honesty on Children's Truth-Telling Behaviour," *Journal of
    Experimental Child Psychology* 130 (2015): 209–17.

29 Dan Ariely, *Misbelief: What Makes Rational People Believe Irrational Things* (New York: Harper Books, 2023).
30 W. Hirstein, *Brain Fiction: Self-Deception and the Riddle of Confabulation* (Cambridge, MA: MIT Press, 2006).
31 N.J. Arts, S.J. Walvoort, and R.P. Kessels, "Korsakoff's Syndrome: A Critical Review," *Neuropsychiatric Disease and Treatment* (2017): 2875–90.
32 Armin Schnider, *The Confabulating Mind: How the Brain Creates Reality* (Oxford: Oxford University Press, 2018).
33 Schnider, *The Confabulating Mind*.

6. Reframing IQ

1 S.J. Gould, *The Mismeasure of Man* (New York: W.W. Norton, 1993).
2 See, for example, J.E. Lewis, D. DeGusta, M.R. Meyer, J.M. Monge, A.E. Mann, and R.L. Holloway, "The Mismeasure of Science," *PLOS Biology* 9, no. 7 (2011): e1001071, https://doi.org/10.1371/journal.pbio.1001071.
3 K.A. Appiah, *The Lies That Bind* (New York: Liveright, 2018).
4 S.B. Kaufman, "Intelligent Testing," *Psychology Today*, 25 October 2009, https://www.psychologytoday.com/ca/blog/beautiful-minds/200910/intelligent-testing.
5 A.R. Jensen, "How Much Can We Boost I.Q. and Scholastic Achievement?" (Speech at the Annual Meeting of the California Advisory Council of Educational Research, San Diego, CA, October 1967), https://files.eric.ed.gov/fulltext/ED023722.pdf.
6 E.G. Boring, "Intelligence As the Tests Test It," Brock University, 2007, https://brocku.ca/MeadProject/sup/Boring_1923.html. Originally published as E.G. Boring, "Intelligence As the Tests Test It," *New Republic* 36 (1923): 35–7.
7 F. Galton, *Hereditary Genius* (London: Macmillan Publishers, 1869).
8 By no means did Boring invent the term, which appears to have been common at the time. In James Joyce's *Ulysses*, for example, the sight of a prostitute prompts this remark by Bloom to Stephen: "You are a good catholic, he observed, talking of body and soul, believe in the soul. Or do you mean the intelligence, the brainpower as such, as distinct from any outside object, the table, let us say, that cup. I believe in that myself because it has been explained by competent men as the convolutions of the grey matter."
9 E.G. Boring, "Intelligence As the Tests Test It"; C. Spearman, *The Intelligence of Man* (London: Macmillan Publishers, 1923).

10 G. Stuart, "The Art of Braking, with Jari-Matti Latvala," Red Bull, 26 September 2016, https://www.redbull.com/nz-en/jari-matti -latvala-art-of-braking.

11 D. Shenk, *The Genius in All of Us: New Insights into Genetics, Talent, and IQ* (New York: Anchor, 2010).

12 R.M. Liebert and L.W. Morris, "Cognitive and Emotional Components of Test Anxiety: A Distinction and Some Initial Data," *Psychological Reports* 20, no. 3 (June 1967): 975–8, https://doi.org/10.2466 /pr0.1967.20.3.975.

13 D. Goldstein, C.S. Hahn, L. Hasher, U.J.W.I. Przycha, and P.D. Zelazo, "Time of Day, Intellectual Performance, and Behavioral Problems in Morning versus Evening Type Adolescents: Is There a Synchrony Effect?," *Personality and Individual Differences* 42, no. 3 (2007): 431–40, https://doi.org/10.1016/j.paid.2006.07.008.

14 R.H. Tawney, *Religion and the Rise of Capitalism* (London: Pelican Books, 1926), 230.

15 P. Bronson and A. Merryman, "Why Can Some Kids Handle Pressure While Others Fall Apart?," *New York Times Magazine*, 6 February 2013, https://www.nytimes.com/2013/02/10/magazine/why-can-some-kids -handle-pressure-while-others-fall-apart.html.

16 P. Bronson and A. Merryman, *Top Dog: The Science of Winning and Losing* (New York: Twelve, 2013).

17 A. Diamond, "Dr. Adele Diamond: Child Development and the Brain – Insight to Help Every Child Thrive," filmed at the Garrison Institute, 2012, http://www.video-downloader-online.com/Dr-Adele-Diamond -Child-Development-and-the-Brain-Insight-to-Help-Every-Child-Thrive -id-2579351#.X.C.jmMqVM93I.email.

18 A. Diamond, L. Briand, J. Fossella, and L. Gehlbach, "Genetic and Neurochemical Modulation of Prefrontal Cognitive Functions in Children," *American Journal of Psychiatry* 161, no. 1 (2004): 125–32.

19 C.-Y. Chang, quoted in E. Callaway, "Gene for Memory and IQ Gives Students Low Grades," *NewScientist*, 23 September 2009, https:// www.newscientist.com/article/dn17837-gene-for-memory-and-iq -gives-students-low-grades/.

20 B. Russell, *Introduction to Mathematical Philosophy* (1919; repr. Andesite Press, 2015), 62.

21 E. Yong, "IQ Scores Reflect Motivation as Well as 'Intelligence,'" *Discover*, 26 April 2011, https://www.discovermagazine.com/mind/iq-scores -reflect-motivation-as-well-as-intelligence.

22 D. Wechsler, "Cognitive, Conative, and Non-intellective Intelligence," All-About-Psychology.com, accessed 12 November 2019, https://www.all-about-psychology.com/cognitive-conative-and-non-intellective-intelligence.html.

23 E.L. Thorndike, "Measurement of Intelligence," *Psychological Review* 31, no. 3 (1924): 228.

24 A. Kohn, "Susan Ohanian.org: The Downside of 'Grit,'" National Education Policy Center (blog), 10 April 2014, https://nepc.colorado.edu/blog/downside-grit-alfie-kohn.

25 C.B. Pfitzner and T.D. Rishel, "Do Reliable Predictors Exist for the Outcomes of NASCAR Races?," *Sport Journal* 21, 4 March 2008, http://thesportjournal.org/article/do-reliable-predictors-exist-for-the-outcomes-of-nascar-races/.

26 G. Vandenbroucke, "Lifetime Benefits of an Education Have Never Been So High," Federal Reserve Bank of St. Louis, 15 July 2015, https://www.stlouisfed.org/publications/regional-economist/july-2015/lifetime-benefits-of-an-education-have-never-been-so-high.

27 B. Guerra-Carrillo, K. Katovich, and S.A. Bunge, "Does Higher Education Hone Cognitive Functioning and Learning Efficacy? Findings from a Large and Diverse Sample," *PLOS One* 12, no. 8 (2017): e0182276, https://doi.org/10.1371/journal.pone.0182276.

28 In B. Russell, *My Philosophical Development* (London: Routledge, 1959), 217.

29 A. Ali et al., "The Relationship between Happiness and Intelligent Quotient: The Contribution of Socio-economic and Clinical Factors," *Psychological Medicine* 43, no. 6 (2013): 1303–12, https://wrap.warwick.ac.uk/56682/1/WRAP_Weich_Relationship_between_S0033291712002139a.pdf.

30 See S. Shanker and S. Hopkins, *Self-Reg Schools: A Handbook for Educators* (Toronto: Pearson, 2020).

31 Sustainable Human, "How Wolves Change Rivers," 2014, https://vimeo.com/86466357.

32 Although there is certainly evidence to support this possibility. See S. Ceci, *On Intelligence: A Biological Treatise on Intellectual Development* (Cambridge, MA: Harvard University Press, 1996).

7. The Joy and Pain of Maths

1 "Think about it. If you are trying to learn Spanish, how would you go about it? Would you simply memorize a list of vocabulary words? If you memorized every word in the Spanish language would you know how

to put them together correctly to form sentences? Would the grammar be correct? Chances are, you would have a lot of knowledge, but very little understanding. You would know a lot of words, but not how to use them. "The same is true with mathematics. You can try to learn it by memorizing, and you may get by (after all, you will have a great deal of knowledge), but you will not truly understand. You may not always be able to put all the pieces that you know *together* correctly because you don't understand how all the pieces fit together. You will have a lot of facts or procedures memorized, but you won't be able to see patterns or solve higher order problems." See Bethany, "Math Is a Foreign Language: So Treat It Like One," *Math Geek Mama* (blog), 3 August 2015, https://mathgeekmama.com/math-is-a-foreign-language-so-treat-it-like-one/.

2 G.J. Duncan, A. Claessens, A.C. Huston, L.S. Pagani, M. Engel, H. Sexton, C.J. Dowsett, K. Magnuson, P. Klebanov, L. Feinstein, J. Brooks-Gunn, and K. Duckworth, "School Readiness and Later Achievement," *Developmental Psychology* 43, no. 6 (2007): 1428–46; E. Romano, L. Babchishin, L.S. Pagani, and D. Kohen, "School Readiness and Later Achievement: Replication and Extension Using a Nationwide Canadian Survey," *Developmental Psychology* 46, no. 5 (2010): 995–1007.

3 S.L. Tennstedt and F.W. Unverzagt, "The ACTIVE Study: Study Overview and Major Findings," *Journal of Aging Health* 25, no. 80 (2013): 3S–20S.

4 G. Luksys, M. Fastenrath, D. Coynel, V. Freytag, L. Gschwind, A. Heck, F. Jessen, W. Maier, A. Milnik, S.G. Riedel-Heller, M. Scherer, K. Spalek, C. Vogler, M. Wagner, S. Wolfsgruber, A. Papassotiropoulos, and D.J.-F. de Quervain, "Computational Dissection of Human Episodic Memory Reveals Mental Process-Specific Genetic Profiles," *PNAS* 112, no. 35 (2015): E4939–E4948.

5 S. Zeki, J.P. Romaya, D.M.T. Benincasa, and M.F. Atiyah, "The Experience of Mathematical Beauty and Its Neuro Correlates," *Frontiers in Human Neuroscience* 8 (2014): 68, https://doi.org/10.3389/fnhum.2014.00068.

6 E. Saenz de Cabezon, "Math Is Forever," filmed October 2014, video, https://www.ted.com/talks/eduardo_saenz_de_cabezon_math_is_forever?language=enandutm_campaign=tedspreadandutm_medium=referralandutm_source=tedcomshare.

7 S. Strogatz, *The Joy of X* (Boston, MA: Mariner Books, 2013).

8 S. Kaplan "This Group Wants to Fight 'Anti-Science' Rhetoric by Getting Scientists to Run for Office," *Washington Post*, 17 January 2017, https://www.washingtonpost.com/news/speaking-of-science/wp/2017/01/17/this-group-wants-to-fight-anti-science-rhetoric-by-getting-scientists-to-run-for-office/.

9 This in no way applies to the wonderful ways that educators are learning how to make learning maths fun: for example, by embedding maths instruction in fairy tales, or gamification.

10 Shanker and Casenhiser, "Reducing the Effort."

11 "The Other Arms Race," *Economist*, 28 October 2013, https://www.economist.com/special-report/2013/10/28/the-other-arms-race.

12 W. Forster, *Hansard*, 17 February 1870, accessed 12 November 2019, https://api.parliament.uk/historic-hansard/commons/1870/feb/17/leave-first-reading.

13 M. Young, *The Rise of the Meritocracy* (London: Routledge, 1958).

14 Quoted in Nancy E. Bailey, *Losing America's Schools* (New York: Rowman and Littlefield, 2016), 66.

15 M.J. Seth, *Education Fever* (Honolulu: University of Hawaii Press, 2002); Y. Zhao, *Who's Afraid of the Big Bad Dragon?* (San Francisco: Jossey-Bass, 2014).

16 G. Ramirez, E.A. Gunderson, S.C. Levine, and S.L. Beilock, "Math Anxiety, Working Memory and Math Achievement in Early Elementary School," *Journal of Cognition and Development* 14, no. 2 (2013): 187–202; J. Boaler, *Mathematical Mindsets: Unleashing Students' Potential through Creative Math, Inspiring Messages and Innovative Teaching* (San Francisco: Jossey-Bass, 2015).

17 Alana Foley assembled an international team to study this issue. Their research confirms that there is a negative correlation between maths anxiety and maths performance. Even in the Asian countries that top the PISA rankings, where both performance and anxiety are higher, this negative correlation is observed (at both the societal and the individual level). A.E. Foley, J.B. Herts, F. Borgonovi, S. Guerriero, S.C. Levine, and S.L. Beilock, "The Math Anxiety-Performance Link: A Global Phenomenon," *Current Directions in Psychological Science* 26, no. 1 (2017): 52–8.

18 O. Rubenstein and R. Tannock, "Mathematics Anxiety in Children with Developmental Dyscalculia," *Behavioral and Brain Functions* 6, no. 46 (2010), https://doi.org/10.1186/1744-9081-6-46.

19 S. Friesen, "Math: Teaching It Better," *Education Canada* 46, no. 1 (2006), https://www.edcan.ca/wp-content/uploads/EdCan-2006-v46-n1-Friesen.pdf; see also D.W. Jardine, P. Clifford, and S. Friesen, *Curriculum in Abundance* (London: Routledge, 2006).

20 E.A. Maloney, D. Ansari, and J.A. Fugelsang, "The Effects of Math Anxiety on the Processing of Numerical Magnitude," *Quarterly Journal of Experimental Psychology* 64, no. 1 (2011): 10–16.

21 A.M. Moore, N.O. Rudig, and M.H. Ashcraft, "Affect, Motivation, Working Memory, and Mathematics," in *The Oxford Handbook of Numerical*

Cognition, ed. R. Cohen Kadosh and A. Dowker (Oxford: Oxford University Press, 2015).

22 D.M. Stout, A.J. Shackman, W.S. Pedersen, T.A. Miskovich, and C.L. Larson, "Neural Circuitry Governing Anxious Individuals' Misallocation of Working Memory to Threat," *Scientific Reports* 7, no. 1 (2017): 8742, https://doi.org/10.1038/s41598-017-08443-7.

23 S. Qin, E.J. Hermans, H.J. van Marle, and G. Fernández, "Acute Psychological Stress Reduces Working Memory-Related Activity in the Dorsolateral Prefrontal Cortex," *Biological Psychiatry* 66, no. 1 (2009): 25–32.

24 Levine, *The Myth of Laziness*.

25 A. Scholey, S. Harper, and D.O. Kennedy, "Cognitive Demand and Blood Glucose," *Physiology and Behavior* 73, no. 4 (2001): 585–92.

26 D. Kohn, "Sugar on the Brain," *New Yorker*, 6 May 2014.

27 N. Swaminathan, "Why Does the Brain Need So Much Power?," *Scientific American*, 29 April 2008.

28 C. Messier, "Glucose Improvement of Memory," *European Journal of Pharmacology* 490, no. 1–3 (2004): 33–57.

29 J.P. Chaput, V. Drapeau, P. Poirier, N. Teasdale, and A. Tremblay, "Glycemic Instability and Spontaneous Energy Intake: Association with Knowledge-Based Work," *Psychosomatic Medicine* 70, no. 7 (2008): 787–804.

30 R.F. Baumeister and J. Tierney, *Willpower* (New York: Penguin, 2011).

31 CanChild, "Developmental Coordination Disorder," accessed 12 November 2019, https://canchild.ca/en/diagnoses/developmental-coordination-disorder.

32 J. Cairney, J.A. Hay, S. Veldhuizen, C. Missiuna, and B.E. Faught, "Developmental Coordination Disorder, Sex, and Activity Deficit over Time: A Longitudinal Analysis of Participation Trajectories in Children with and without Coordination Difficulties," *Developmental Medicine and Child Neurology* 52, no. 3 (2010): e67–e72.

33 P. Klass, "The Clumsy Child," *New York Times* (blog), 16 May 2016, https://well.blogs.nytimes.com/2016/05/16/clumsiness-as-a-diagnosis/.

34 R. Brünken, S. Steinbacher, J.L. Plass, and D. Leutner, "Assessment of Cognitive Load in Multimedia Learning Using Dual-Task Methodology," *Experimental Psychology* 49, no. 2 (2002): 109–19.

35 M.H. Ashcraft and J.A. Krause, "Working Memory, Math Performance, and Math Anxiety," *Psychonomic Bulletin and Review* 14, no. 2 (2007): 243–8.

36 F. Jabr, "Does Thinking Really Hard Burn More Calories?," *Scientific American*, 18 July 2012.

37 Ramirez et al., "Math Anxiety."

38 Rubenstein and Tannock, "Mathematics Anxiety," 9.

39 R.E. Thayer, *The Origin of Everyday Moods: Managing Energy, Tension, and Stress* (New York: Oxford University Press, 1996).

40 M.H. Ashcraft, "Math Anxiety: Personal, Educational, and Cognitive Consequences," *Current Directions in Psychological Science* 11, no. 5 (2002), https://doi.org/10.1111/1467-8721.00196.

41 I.M. Lyons and S.L. Beilock, "When Math Hurts: Math Anxiety Predicts Pain Network Activation in Anticipation of Doing Math," *PLOS One* 7, no. 10 (2012), https://doi.org/10.1371/journal.pone.0048076.

42 C.B. Young, S.S. Wu, and V. Menon, "The Neurodevelopmental Basis of Math Anxiety," *Psychological Science* 23, no. 5 (2012): 492–501.

43 C.B. Young, S.S. Wu, and V. Menon, "The Neurodevelopmental Basis of Math Anxiety," *Psychological Science* 23, no. 5 (2012): 492–501.

44 S. Shanker, "Reframing High Math Anxiety: Avoiding the Perils of a Victorian Paradigm," *Reframed: The Journal of Self-Reg* 2, no. 1 (2012), https://selfregulationinstitute.org/journal/current_issue /volume-2-issue-1/#article4.

45 C. Roman-Lantzy, *Cortical Visual Impairment* (Louisville, KY: American Printing House for the Blind, 2018)

46 "Me Moves (Calm Connect)," accessed 12 November 2019, https:// prio-health.com/home/.

47 J.S. Tanton, "The Power of Mathematical Visualization," filmed 2016, *The Great Courses*, Course no. 1443, video, https://www.thegreatcoursesplus .com/math-free-lec.

48 R. Andersone, "Through Fairy Tales to Math in the Lessons," *Acta Didactica Napocensia* 2, no. 2 (2009): 112–18.

49 D. Sperber, F. Cara, and V. Girotto, "Relevance Theory Explains the Selection Task," *Cognition* 57, no. 1 (1995): 31–95.

50 R.A. Barkley, *Executive Functions: What They Are, How They Work, and Why They Evolved* (New York: Guilford Press, 2012).

51 R.D. Porsolt, A. Bertin, and M. Jalfre, "'Behavioural Despair' in Rats and Mice: Strain Differences and the Effects of Imipramine," *European Journal of Pharmacology* 51, no. 3 (1978): 291–4, https://www.ncbi.nlm.nih.gov /pubmed/596982.

52 J. Krishnan, "Effect of Forced Fresh Water and Cold Water Swimming Stress Induced Changes in Selected Physiological and Biochemical Parameters in *Wistar albino* Rats" (PhD diss., Kerala University of Health Sciences, 2016), https://www.apjhs.com/pdf/4-EFFECT-OF-FORCED -FRESH-WATER-AND.pdf.

53 G.M. Brown, "Cold Acclimatization in Eskimo," *Artic Institute of North America* 7 (1954).

54 F. Racimo, D. Marnetto, and E. Huerta-Sánchez, "Signatures of Archaic Adaptive Introgression in Present-Day Human Populations," *Molecular Biology and Evolution* 34, no. 2 (2017): 296–317.

55 N.A. Taylor, "Human Heat Adaptation," *Comprehensive Physiology* 4, no. 1 (2014): 325–65.

56 This, of course, is the phenomenon that Seligman made famous in the 1970s, which led to his breakthrough research in positive psychology. See S.F. Maier and M.E. Seligman, "Learned Helplessness: Theory and Evidence," *Journal of Experimental Psychology: General* 105, no. 1 (1976): 3–46; M.E. Seligman, "Generality of Learned Helplessness in Man," *Journal of Personality and Social Psychology* 31, no. 2 (1975): 311–27.

57 S.F. Maier and M.E. Seligman, "Learned Helplessness at Fifty: Insights from Neuroscience," *Psychology Review* 123, no. 4 (2016): 349–67. See also M. Seligman, *Learned Optimism: How to Change Your Mind and Your Life* (New York: Vintage, 2006).

58 R.A. Dienstbier, "Arousal and Physiological Toughness: Implications for Mental and Physical Health," *Psychological Review* 96 (1989): 1.

59 D. Stipek and K. Seal, *Motivated Minds: Raising Children to Love Learning* (New York: Holt Paperbacks, 2014).

8. No Child Left Behind

1 Sir K. Robinson, *Creative Schools: The Grassroots Revolution That's Transforming Education* (New York: Penguin, 2015).

2 C. Dickens, *Hard Times* (Peterborough, ON: Broadview Press, 1996), 61.

3 S. Mamdouh, "Hard Times – Charles Dickens," YouTube, 27 February 2012, https://www.youtube.com/watch?v=2Rs3IClbrC4.

4 S. Ringmar, "Here's the Truth about Shanghai Schools: They're Terrible," *Guardian*, 28 December 2013.

5 Zhao, *Who's Afraid?*

6 C. Burdett, "Emotions," in *The Oxford Handbook of Victorian Literary Culture*, ed. J. John (Oxford: Oxford University Press, 2014).

7 See George Eliot's *Felix Holt, The Radical*, and later in the century, Gissing's *Demos*.

8 M. McGee, *Self Help, Inc.* (New York: Oxford University Pres, 2005).

9 K. Hughes, "The Middle Classes: Etiquette and Upward Mobility," *Discovering Literature: Romantics and Victorians*, British Library, 2014,

https://www.bl.uk/romantics-and-victorians/articles/the
-middle-classes-etiquette-and-upward-mobility.

10 A. Jarvis, *Samuel Smiles and the Construction of Victorian Values* (Stroud, UK: Sutton Publishing, 1997).

11 S. Smiles, *Self-Help* (London: John Murray, 1859), 14–15.

12 Smiles, *Self-Help*, 13.

13 Smiles, *Self-Help*, 6.

14 Smiles, *Self-Help*, 588.

15 C.A. Farrington, *Failing at School* (New York: Teachers College Press, 2014).

16 Galton's *Hereditary Genius* is a book about the supposed genetic inheritance of intelligence. It was first published in 1869.

17 S. Savage-Rumbaugh, S. Shanker, and T. Taylor, *Apes, Language and the Human Mind* (Oxford: Oxford University Press, 1998).

18 LeDoux, *Anxious*.

19 A. Gracia, J.F. Martínez-Lage, J.L. Martínez, C. Lorenzo, and M.A. Pérez-Espejo, "The Earliest Evidence of True Lambdoid Craniosynostosis: The Case of 'Benjamina,' a *Homo heidelbergensis* Child," *Child's Nervous System* 26, no. 6 (2010): 723–7.

20 E. Trinkaus and S. Villotte, "External Auditory Exostoses and Hearing Loss in the Shanidar 1 Neanderthal," *PLOS One* 12, no. 10 (2017): e0186684.

21 H. Spencer, *The Principles of Biology, Volume 1 (of 2)* (New York: D. Appleton and Co., 1864), 53.

22 J. van Whye and K. Rookmaaker, *Alfred Russell Wallace* (Oxford: Oxford University Press, 2015).

23 F. De Waal, *The Age of Empathy* (New York: McClelland and Stewart, 2009).

24 Greenspan and Shanker, *The First Idea*.

25 R.W. Byrne and A. Whiten, "Machiavellian Intelligence: Social Expertise and the Evolution of Intellect in Monkeys, Apes, and Humans," *Behavior and Philosophy* 18, no. 1 (1990): 73–5.

26 King, *How Animals Grieve*.

27 Sir Michael Marmot, G. Rose, M. Shipley, and P.J. Hamilton, "Employment Grade and Coronary Heart Disease in British Civil Servants," *Journal of Epidemiology and Community Health* 32, no. 4 (1978): 244–9.

28 See, for example, the scene in *Kanzi: An Ape of Genius* in which Kanzi repeatedly tries to show Tamuli how to perform what Sue is asking: https://youtu.be/dBUHWoFnuB4.

29 B.F. Skinner, "Selection by Consequences," *Behavioral and Brain Sciences* 7 (1984): 477–510.

30 Smiles, *Self-Help*, 588.

31 Churchill, *My Early Life* (London: Butterworth, 1930).
32 J.S. Golland, *Not Winston, Just William?* (London: Herga Press, 1991). Golland makes the point that what Churchill had was a lisp, not dyslexia, and certainly not a learning disorder.
33 A. Roberts, *Churchill: Walking with Destiny* (London: Allen Lane, 2018); L. James, *Churchill and Empire* (London: Weidenfeld and Nicolson, 2013).
34 This quotation is commonly attributed to Churchill, but it might actually have been Liane Cordes who said it in *The Reflecting Pond: Meditations for Self-Discovery* (Center City, MN: Hazelden Publishing, 1981).
35 J. Laudati, *Ten Thousand Demons* (Joe Laudati, 2017).
36 M. Levine, "All Kinds of Learning," *Children of the Code*, accessed 12 November 2019, https://childrenofthecode.org/interviews/levine.htm.
37 Porges, *The Polyvagal Theory*.
38 A.F. Arnsten, "Stress Weakens Prefrontal Networks: Molecular Insults to Higher Cognition," *Nature Neuroscience* 18 (2015): 1376–85.
39 J. Jarrold, "How Anxiety Can Make Your Legs Feel like Jelly," *CalmClinic*, 24 October 2018, https://www.calmclinic.com/anxiety/signs/weak-jelly-legs.
40 E. Braaten, *Bright Kids Who Can't Keep Up* (New York: Guilford Press, 2014).
41 A. Kenny, "The Homunculus Fallacy," in *Interpretations of Life and Mind*, ed. M. Glicksman Grene and I. Prigogine (New York: Humanities Press, 1971).
42 Preface to Galton, *Hereditary Genius*.
43 C. Darwin, letter to Francis Galton, 23 December 1869, https://www.darwinproject.ac.uk/letter/DCP-LETT-7032.xml.
44 Speech that Churchill gave to the House of Commons on 22 October 1945, https://api.parliament.uk/historic-hansard/commons/1945/oct/22/demobilisation#S5CV0414P0_19451022_HOC_300.
45 Dickens, *Hard Times*, chapter 9.
46 Said by Senator William L. Mary during a congressional debate in 1832.
47 L. Campbell, "How to Get Results from Your Fitness Regime This Spring," *Huffpost*, 20 September 2016.
48 M. Renz, O. Reichmuth, D. Bueche, B. Treichel, M.S. Mao, T. Cerny, and F. Strasser, "Fear, Pain, Denial, and Spiritual Experiences in Dying Processes," *American Journal of Hospice and Palliative Medicine* 35, no. 3 (2018): 478–91.
49 R. Samuel, "Mrs. Thatcher's Return to Victorian Values," *Proceedings of the British Academy* 78 (1990): 9–29, https://www.thebritishacademy.ac.uk/sites/default/files/78p009.pdf.

50 Bloomberg, "Margaret Thatcher Dies: How She Ended 'Nanny State,'" YouTube, 8 April 2013, https://www.youtube.com/watch?v=Aw8hMKOXJ1I.

51 W.M. Thackeray, *The History of Pendennis: His Fortunes and Misfortunes, His Friends and His Greatest Enemy* (London: G. Saintsbury, 1849), 393.

52 H. Over and M. Carpenter, "Putting the Social into Social Learning: Explaining Both Selectivity and Fidelity in Children's Copying Behavior," *Journal of Comparative Psychology* 126, no. 2 (2012): 182–92.

9. Becoming Free, Staying Free

1 I. Berlin, "Two Concepts of Liberty," in *Four Essays on Liberty* (New York: Oxford University Press, 1958/69).

2 The subtle allusion to Descartes suggests that the Cogito operates as a statement about the internal relationship between the active mental processes subsumed under *thinking* and *being free* – that is, not the pawn of a deceiving demon, or for that matter, dopamine.

3 R. Descartes, *Principles of Philosophy*, 1.8–12.

4 J. Bargh, *Before You Know It: The Unconscious Reasons We Do What We Do* (New York: Atria, 2017).

5 M.S. Gazzaniga, *Who's in Charge?: Free Will and the Science of the Brain* (New York: HarperCollins, 2012).

6 Quoted in R. Toricelli, *Quotations for Public Speakers* (New Brunswick, NJ: Rutgers University Press, 2001), 121.

7 S. Cave, "There's No Such Thing as Free Will: But We're Better Off Believing in It Anyway," *Atlantic*, June 2016.

8 Ariely, *Predictably Irrational*.

9 J.J. Rousseau, *The Social Contract* (1762; repr., Chicago: Dover Publications, 2003), 12.

10 Rousseau, *The Social Contract*, 11.

11 R. Conquest, *The Great Terror* (London: Pimlico, 2008).

12 J. Milton, *Paradise Lost* (1667; repr., Indianapolis: Hackett Publishing, 2005), 45–6.

13 K. Marx and F. Engels, *Marx and Engels on Religion* (Moscow: Progress Publishers, 1957).

14 R. Cross, *Fallen Eagle: The Last Days of the Third Reich* (New York: John Wiley and Sons, 1995), 21.

15 G.H. Sabine, "Introduction," in John Milton, *Aeropagitica and of Education* (Chicago: Harlan Davidson, 1951).

16 I. Berlin, "Two Concepts of Liberty," *Four Essays on Liberty* (Oxford: Oxford University Press, 1969), 126.

17 I.V. Stalin, *Stalin's Speeches on the American Communist Party* (Moscow: Central Committee Communist Party, 1930).

18 Plato, "Republic," in *Plato: Complete Works*, ed. J.M. Cooper (Indianapolis: Hackett Publishing, 1997).

19 J. Milton, *Aeropagitica* (1644; repr., CreateSpace Independent Publishing Platform, 2018), ix.

20 B.L. Seaward, *Managing Stress* (Burlington, MA: Jones and Bartlett Learning, 2018), xviii.

21 See R.J. Davidson and A. Lutz, "Buddha's Brain: Neuroplasticity and Meditation," *Institute of Electrical and Electronics Engineers* 25, no. 1 (2008): 176–4. Meditation involves activation in the dlPFC visual cortex, superior frontal sulcus, supplementary motor and intraparietal sulcus.

22 K.F. Hays, "The Transient Hypofrontality Edge," *Psychology Today*, 13 March 2017, https://www.psychologytoday.com/us/blog/the-edge -peak-performance-psychology/201703/the-transient-hypofrontality -edge.

23 "Window of Tolerance," *GoodTherapy* (blog), 8 August 2016, https:// www.goodtherapy.org/blog/psychpedia/window-of-tolerance.

24 B. Hart "Understanding Donkey Behaviour," *Hart's Horsemanship*, accessed 12 November 2019, http://www.hartshorsemanship.com /index.cfm?fuseaction=controller.viewPageThoughtDetail&thoughtUuid =A7571312–4063-C7B3–5E9299F94C28EF86.

25 Shanker, *Wittgenstein's Remarks*.

26 A. Gopnik, A.N. Meltzoff, and P.K. Kuhl, *The Scientist in the Crib: Minds, Brains and How Children Learn* (New York: William Morrow, 2000); A. Gopnik, *The Philosophical Baby: What Children's Minds Tell Us about Truth, Love, and the Meaning of Life* (New York: FSG Adult, 2010).

27 In fact, it was Aristotle who first said that "a man, being just as hungry as thirsty, and placed in between food and drink, must necessarily remain where he is and starve to death" (*On the Heavens*).

28 B. Schwartz, *The Paradox of Choice* (New York: Harper Perennial, 2004).

29 B. Roberts Chavez, "The Effects of Stress on the Perception of Time" (PhD diss., Uniformed Services University of the Health Sciences, Bethesda, MD, 2003), https://apps.dtic.mil/dtic/tr/fulltext/u2/a421211.pdf.

30 Shanker, *Wittgenstein's Remarks*.

31 "Stress Changes How People Make Decisions," Association for Psychological Science, 27 February 2012, https://www .psychologicalscience.org/news/releases/stress-changes-how-people -make-decisions.html.

32 C. Mackay, *Extraordinary Popular Delusions and the Madness of Crowds* (1841; repr., CreateSpace Independent Publishing Platform, 2016).

33 R.S. Liebert, "Pity and Disgust in Plato's *Republic*: The Case of Leontius," *Classical Philology* 108, no. 3 (2013): 179–201, https://www.academia.edu /4049498/Pity_and_Disgust_in_Platos_Republic_The_Case_of_Leontius.

34 P. Nieuwenburg, "The Agony of Choice: Isaiah Berlin and the Phenomenology of Conflict," *Administration and Society* (2014), https:// doi.org/10.1177/0095399703256778.

35 N. Mandela, *Long Walk to Freedom* (New York: Back Bay Books, 1995).

36 *Henderson the Rain King* was published in 1959!

37 J. Tanz, "The Curse of *Cow Clicker*: How a Cheeky Satire Became a Videogame Hit," *Wired*, 20 December 2011, https://www.wired.com /2011/12/ff-cowclicker/.

38 J. Seward, "Drive, Incentive, and Reinforcement," *Psychological Review* 63, no. 3 (1956): 195–203.

39 N. Eyal, *Hooked: How to Build Habit-Forming Products* (New York: Portfolio, 2014), 2.

40 M. Lewis, *The Biology of Desire* (Toronto: Random House Canada, 2015).

41 Tanz, "The Curse of *Cow Clicker*."

42 M. Ienca and E. Vayena, "Cambridge Analytica and Online Manipulation," *Scientific American*, 30 March 2018, https://blogs .scientificamerican.com/observations/cambridge-analytica -and-online-manipulation/.

43 C.A. Seger and B.J. Spiering, "A Critical Review of Habit Learning and the Basal Ganglia," *Frontiers in Systems Neuroscience* 5 (2011): 66, https:// www.ncbi.nlm.nih.gov/pmc/articles/PMC3163829/.

44 D. Wahlstrom, P. Collins, T. White, and M. Luciana, "Developmental Changes in Dopamine Transcription in Adolescence," *Brain Cognition* 72, no. 1 (2010): 146. https://www.ncbi.nlm.nih.gov/pmc/articles /PMC2815132/.

45 J. Paton, "Why Is Time So Variable?," YouTube, 14 November 2017, https:// www.youtube.com/watch?v=PF042_eeH.C.Mandfeature=youtu.be.

46 T. Lewis, "How Dopamine Tunes Working Memory," *Scientist*, 3 June 2016, https://www.the-scientist.com/daily-news/how-dopamine -tunes-working-memory-33417.

47 Rick Riordan has a nice take on this in the land of the lotus eaters episode in *Percy Jackson and the Lightning Thief* (Disney-Hyperion, 2006).

48 Panksepp and Bivan, *The Archaeology of Mind*.

49 D.F. Wallace, *This Is Water: Some Thoughts, Delivered on a Significant Occasion, about Living a Compassionate Life* (London: Hachette UK, 2009).

50 "The Way the Brain Buys," *Economist*, 18 December 2008, https://www .economist.com/christmas-specials/2008/12/18/the-way-the-brain-buys.

51 Although if it has reached the point of addiction parents may have no other choice.

52 T. Rosenberg, *Join the Club: How Peer Pressure Can Transform the World* (New York: W.W. Norton, 2012).

10. Reframing *Virtue*

1 D. Bosworth, *The Demise of Virtue in Virtual America* (Eugene, OR: Wipf and Stock, 2014).

2 E. Durkheim, *Suicide* (1897; repr. London: Routledge, 1952).

3 K.J. Freeman, *Schools of Hellas: An Essay on the Practice and Theory of Ancient Greek Education from 600 to 300 B.C.* (London: Macmillan, 1922).

4 L. Wittgenstein, *Culture and Value* (Chicago: University of Chicago Press, 1984), 15.

5 M. Agar, *Language Shock* (New York: William Morrow, 1996).

6 Pedro Lain Entralgo, *La Curación por la Palabra en la Antigüedad Clásica* (Madrid: Editorial Anthropos, 2013).

7 Cribiore, *Gymnastics of the Mind*.

8 M. Carruthers, *The Book of Memory* (Cambridge: Cambridge University Press, 2008); F.A. Yates, *The Art of Memory* (London: Routledge, 2010).

9 The epitome of this way of thinking is when More says to Roper in *A Man for All Seasons*: "Will, I'd trust you with my life. But not your principles. You see, we speak of being anchored to our principles. But if the weather turns nasty you up with an anchor and let it down where there's less wind, and the fishing's better. And 'Look,' we say, 'look, I'm anchored! To my principles!'" R. Bolt, *A Man for All Seasons* (New York: Vintage, 1990).

10 D. Brooks, *The Road to Character* (New York: Random House, 2015).

11 In B. Russell, *My Philosophical Development* (London: Routledge, 1959), 217.

12 Panksepp and Biven, *The Archaeology of Mind*.

13 S. Greenspan and I. Glovinsky, *Children and Babies with Mood Swings* (ICDL, 2007).

14 Narvaez, *Neurobiology*.

15 M. Bekoff and J. Pierce, *Wild Justice: The Moral Lives of Animals* (Chicago: University of Chicago Press, 2009).

16 D. Narvaez, "Baselines for Virtue," in *Advances in Virtue Development: Integrating Perspectives*, ed. J. Annas, D. Narvaez, and N. Snow (New York: Oxford University Press, 2016), https://www3.nd.edu /~dnarvaez/documents/NarvaezinAnnasetalBaselinesforVirtue 2016formatted.pdf.

17 Narvaez, *Neurobiology*, 19.
18 Panksepp and Biven, *The Archaeology of Mind*.
19 C. Nodder, *Evil by Design: Interaction Design to Lead Us into Temptation* (New York: Wiley, 2013).
20 D. Hugh-Jones, "Honesty, Beliefs about Honesty, and Economic Growth in 15 Countries," *Journal of Economic Behavior and Organization* 127, no. C (2016): 99–114.
21 E. Suhay and C. Erisen, "The Role of Anger in the Biased Assimilation of Political Information," *Political Psychology* 39, no. 4 (2018): 793–810, https://onlinelibrary.wiley.com/doi/pdf/10.1111/pops.12455.
22 N. Malcolm, *Ludwig Wittgenstein: A Memoir* (Oxford: Clarendon, 2001).
23 L. Rosten, *The Joys of Yiddish* (New York: McGraw-Hill, 1968), 237.
24 Daniel J. Elazar, *Covenant and Polity in Biblical Israel* (London: Routledge, 1995), 22.

11. Creating a Just Society

1 David Brooks, "America Is Having a Moral Convulsion," *The Atlantic*, 5 October 2020.
2 "If freedom is short of weapons, we must compensate with willpower." Hitler, Speech in Landsberg, 5 November 1925.
3 H.J. Curzer, *Aristotle and the Virtues* (Oxford: Oxford University Press, 2012).
4 Steven Hassan, *The Cult of Trump* (Free Press, 2019). Hassan escaped from Sun Myung Moon's Unification Church. He argues that Trump followers are deluded zealots who have been brainwashed by a charismatic leader.
5 L. Christov-Moore, T. Sugiyama, K. Grigaityte, and M. Iacoboni, "Increasing Generosity by Disrupting Prefrontal Cortex," *Social Neuroscience* 12, no. 2 (2017): 174–81.
6 A particular chemical odour is released when a rat is hungry, triggering others to share food. See K. Schneeberger, G. Roder, and M. Taborsky, "The Smell of Hunger," *PLOS Biology* 18, no. 3 (2020).
7 King, *How Animals Grieve*; F. De Waal, *The Age of Empathy: Nature's Lessons for a Kinder Society* (New York: Broadway Books, 2010); M. Bekoff and J. Goodall, *The Emotional Lives of Animals: A Leading Scientist Explores Animal Joy, Sorrow, and Empathy – and Why They Matter* (Novato, CA: New World Library, 2008).
8 G. Santayana, *The Life of Reason: Introduction and Reason in Common Sense* (Cambridge, MA: MIT Press, 2011), 284. There have been many profoundly important books written on historical precedents. For me the

one that stands out is A. Applebaum, *Iron Curtain: The Crushing of Eastern Europe 1944–1956* (Toronto: McClelland and Stewart, 2012).

9 J.T. Cheng, J.L. Tracy, and J. Henrich, "Pride, Personality, and the Evolutionary Foundations of Human Social Status," *Evolution and Human Behavior* 31, no. 5 (2010): 334–47.

10 The so-called King Cyrus Republicans.

11 As occurred in the famous "June Bug" epidemic of 1962. See A.C. Kerchkhoff and W.B. Kerchkhoff, *The June Bug: A Study of Hysterical Contagion* (New York: Appleton-Century-Crofts, 1968); L.R. Murphy and M.J. Colligan, "Mass Psychogenic Illness in a Shoe Factory," *International Archives of Occupational and Environmental Health* 44, no. 3 (1982): 133–8.

12 J. Rothenberg Gritz, "Drinking the Kool-Aid: A Survivor Remembers Jim Jones," *The Atlantic*, 18 November 2011, https://www.theatlantic.com/national/archive/2011/11/drinking-the-kool-aid-a-survivor-remembers-jim-jones/248723/.

13 The "Werther-Effekt" was sending too many young readers into Gray Brain.

14 King, *How Animals Grieve*.

15 N.D. Schüll, *Addiction by Design: Machine Gambling in Las Vegas* (Princeton: Princeton University Press, 2012).

16 Schüll, *Addiction by Design*, 2.

17 R.A. Wise, "Dopamine and Reward: The Anhedonia Hypothesis 30 Years On," *Neurotoxicity Research* 14, no. 2–3 (2008): 169–83.

18 J.P.H. Verrharren, J.W. de Jong, T.J.M. Roelofs, C.F.M. Huffels, R.R. van Zessen, M.C.M. Luijendijk, R. Hamelink, I. Willuhn, H.E.M. den Ouden, F. van der Plasse, R.A.H. Adan, and L.J.M.J. Vanderrschuren, "A Neuronal Mechanism Underlying Decision-Making Deficits during Hyperdopaminergic States," *Nature Communications* 9, no. 731 (2018), https://doi.org/10.1038/s41467-018-03087-1.

19 T. Harris, "How Technology Is Hijacking Your Mind – From a Magician and Google Design Ethicist," *Medium*, 18 May 2016, https://medium.com/thrive-global/how-technology-hijacks-peoples-minds-from-a-magician-and-google-s-design-ethicist-56d62ef5edf3.

20 Riordan, *Percy Jackson*, 29.

21 Schüll, *Addiction by Design*, 29.

22 Nodder, *Evil by Design*.

23 D. Kwong, *Spellbound* (New York: Harper Business, 2017).

24 R.L. Gregory, *Eye and Brain* (London: Weidenfeld and Nicolson, 1990).

25 Schüll, *Addiction by Design*, 96.

26 W. Hall and M. Weier, "Lee Robins' Studies of Heroin Use among US Vietnam Veterans," *Addiction* 122, no. 1 (2017): 176–80.

27 The same point applies to Alter's discussion in *Irresistible* of Aryeh Routtenberg's experiments with the squirrel monkey Cleopatra, where, in the latter case, it was the intolerable stress of being locked once again in the cage that triggered the association.

28 E. Pertwee, C. Simas, and H.J. Larson, "An Epidemic of Uncertainty: Rumors, Conspiracy Theories and Vaccine Hesitancy," *Nature Medicine* 28 (2022): 456–9.

29 S.M. Bowes, T.H. Castello, and A. Tasimi, "The Conspiratorial Mind: A Meta-Analytical Review of Motivational and Personological Correlates," *Psychological Bulletin* 149, no. 5–6 (2023): 259–93.

30 I. Bretherton, "The Origins of Attachment Theory," *Developmental Psychology* 28, no. 5 (1992).

31 J. Moeller, M.A. Brackett, Z. Ivceic, and A.E. White, "High School Students' Feelings," *Learning & Instruction* 66 (2020).

32 P. Stock-Morton, *Moral Education for a Secular Society: The Development of Morale Laïque in Nineteenth Century France* (Albany: State University of New York Press, 1988), 35; W. Schmaus, *Liberty and the Pursuit of Knowledge: Charles Renouvier's Political Philosophy of Science* (Pittsburgh: University of Pittsburgh Press, 2018).

33 S. Shanker, *Broader Measures of Success: Social/Emotional Learning* (Toronto: People for Education, 2014), https://peopleforeducation.ca/wp-content/uploads/2017/06/MWM-Social-Emotional-Learning.pdf.

34 See Adam Alter's description of Steve Jobs in *Irresistible*.

35 The inscription over the doorway to Plato's Academy was "Let no one ignorant of geometry enter here."

36 The inscription over the gateway into hell is "Abandon hope all ye who enter here."

37 Brooks, *The Road to Character*.

38 L. Wittgenstein, *Tractatus Logico-Philosophicus* (Oxford: Oxford University Press, 2023), 5.64.

39 M. Azzam, *Robert F. Kennedy Announcing the Death of Martin Luther King – A Great Speech*, 4 January 2013, video, https://youtu.be/GoKzCff8Zbs.

Conclusion

1 C.P. Snow, *The Two Cultures: And a Second Look: An Expanded Version of The Two Cultures and the Scientific Revolution* (Cambridge: Cambridge University Press, 1963), 16.

2 See S. Shanker and T. Taylor, "The House That Bruner Built," in *Jerome Bruner: Language, Culture and Self*, ed. D. Bakhurt and S. Shanker (New York: Sage, 2001).

3 W. Mischel, Y. Shoda, and M.I. Rodriguez, "Delay of Gratification in Children," *Science* 244, no. 4907 (1989): 933–8.

4 See E. Arce and C. Santisteban, "Impulsivity: A Review," *Psicothema* 18, no. 2 (2006): 213–20; D.C. Funder and J. Block, "The Role of Ego-Control, Ego-Resiliency, and IQ in Delay of Gratification in Adolescence," *Journal of Personality and Social Psychology* 57, no. 6 (1989): 1041–50.

5 N. Goeke, "The Spartan Solution: A 4-Step System to Increase Willpower Every Day," 12 October 2015, https://niklasgoeke.com/increase -willpower/; compare N. Anderson, *Mentally Tough* (Independently published, 2019).

6 One of the many astounding discoveries in psycholinguistics is that chinchillas demonstrate a form of categorical perception; that is, categorical perception results from a general limbic capacity to draw similarities and differences. See P. Kuhl, "The Special-Mechanisms Debate in Speech Perception: Nonhuman Species and Nonspeech Signals," in *Categorical Perception: The Groundwork of Cognition*, ed. S. Harnad (Cambridge: Cambridge University Press, 1987).

7 According to a poll conducted by the European Jewish Congress in 2010.

8 See https://www.rte.ie/brainstorm/2019/0207/1028162-the-science -behind-starlings-spectacular-acrobatics/

9 Even if only how one responds to evil. See Victor Frankl, *Man's Search for Meaning* (Boston: Beacon Press, 2006).

Index